PRAISE FOR DILIP HIRO

IRAQ: IN THE EYE OF THE STORM (2002)

"Noam Chomsky, the outspoken Massachusetts Institute of Technology linguistics professor, peace activist and author in his own right, recommends the works of Dilip Hiro. A frequent contributor to *The Nation,* Hiro is the author of *Sharing the Promised Land: A Tale of Israelis and Palestinians; Neighbors, Not Friends: Iraq and Iran After the Gulf Wars; War Without End: The Rise of Islamist Terrorism and Global Response;* and Chomsky's specific recommendation, *Iraq: In the Eye of the Storm,* a compact contemporary history that delves into the strengths and failures of sanctions, life on the street in Iraq and the cult of personality surrounding Saddam. 'Accurate and very readable, like his others,' Chomsky told MSNBC.com."

—MSNBC.com

"This is hard. So soon after very nearly swooning over Colin Powell's report to the United Nations Security Council, I find myself thinking the once unthinkable: I don't believe him. . . . Whence my change of heart? For one thing, I've had time to digest that tour de force performance of earlier this month. For another, I've been listening and reading (particularly Dilip Hiro's book *Iraq: In the Eye of the Storm*)."

—William Raspberry, *The Washington Post*

"One of the clearest accounts of recent developments in Iraq. . . . Hiro is a staggeringly prolific writer who has been writing about Iraq and Islamic fundamentalism since long before they became the twin obsessions of US foreign policy. He knows more than most about the threat posed by Saddam."

—Martin Bright, *The Observer*

"Dilip Hiro has written many books about the Middle East, but none as timely as this. *Iraq: In the Eye of the Storm* comes out too late for the edification of White House hawks, but in time for the rest of us to take a cool look at 'victory' and why it is likely to be messily Pyrrhic for the seeming winners."

—*In These Times*

SECRETS AND LIES

OPERATION "IRAQI FREEDOM" AND AFTER

DILIP HIRO

NATION BOOKS
NEW YORK

SECRETS AND LIES:
Operation "Iraqi Freedom" and After

Copyright © 2004 Dilip Hiro

Published by
Nation Books
An Imprint of Avalon Publishing Group Incorporated
245 West 17th St., 11th Floor
New York, NY 10038

Cartoon on p. v © The Times/Peter Brookes 2003
Maps on pp. xi–xviii by Mike Morgenfeld

Nation Books is a co-publishing venture
of the Nation Institute
and Avalon Publishing Group Incorporated.

Library of Congress Cataloging-in-Publication Data
is available.

ISBN 1-56025-556-0

9 8 7 6 5 4 3 2 1

Book design by Simon M. Sullivan
Printed in the United States of America
Distributed by Publishers Group West

TOP SECRET:

"God told me to strike at Al Qaida and I struck them, and then He instructed me to strike at Saddam, which I did."

—U.S. President George W. Bush to Palestinian Prime Minister Mahmoud Abbas on June 4, 2003

TOP LIE:

"The larger point is, and the fundamental question is, Did Saddam Hussein have a weapons program? And the answer is, Absolutely. And we gave him a chance to allow the inspectors in, and he wouldn't let them in. And, therefore, after a reasonable request, we decided to remove him from power, along with other nations, so as to make sure he was not a threat to the United States and our friends and allies in the region."

—U.S. President George W. Bush on July 14, 2003

The Times (London), May 30, 2003

See Appendix II: Iraq's Weapons of Mass Destruction and Means of Delivery: Alleged and Found

CONTENTS

Main Characters

IYAD MUHAMMAD ALAWI, Leader of Iraqi National Accord, 1990–Present; member of the Interim Governing Council, 2003–Present.

MOHAMMED ELBARADEI, Director General of International Atomic Energy Agency, 1998–Present.

MUHAMMAD BAQIR AL HAKIM, leader of Supreme Council of Islamic Revolution in Iraq, 1982–2003.

MASOUD BARZANI, leader of Kurdistan Democratic Party, 1987–Present; member of the Interim Governing Council, 2003–Present.

TONY BLAIR, Prime Minister of Britain, 1997–Present.

HANS BLIX, Swedish executive chairman of Unmovic, 2000–03.

PAUL BREMER, U.S. proconsul to Iraq; Senior Administrator of the Coalition Provisional Authority, May 2003–Present.

GEORGE WALKER BUSH, U.S. President, 2001–Present.

AHMAD CHALABI, leader of Iraqi National Congress, 1992–Present; member of the Interim Governing Council, 2003–Present.

DICK CHENEY, U.S. Vice President, 2001–Present.

JACQUES CHIRAC, President of France, 1995–Present.

DOUGLAS FEITH, U.S. Under Secretary of Defense, 2001–Present.

GEN. TOMMY FRANKS, commander in chief of U.S. Central Command, 2000–03.

QUSAY SADDAM HUSSEIN, Younger son of Saddam, head of National Security Bureau, 1992–2003.

SADDAM HUSSEIN, President of Iraq, 1979–2003.

UDAY SADDAM HUSSEIN, elder son of Saddam, commander of Fedayeen Saddam, 1994–2003.

RICHARD PERLE, member of U.S. Defense Policy Board, 2001–Present; leading neoconservative.

COLIN POWELL, U.S. Secretary of State, 2001–Present.

CONDOLEEZZA RICE, U.S. National Security Advisor, 2001–Present.

KARL ROVE, chief political adviser to U.S. President George W. Bush, 2001–Present.

DONALD RUMSFELD, U.S. Secretary of Defense, 2001–Present.

MUQTADA AL-SADR, leader of Iraqi Shias, 2003.

MUHAMMAD SAID AL-SAHHAF, Information Minister of Iraq 2001–03; spokesman of President Saddam Hussein.

ALI HUSSEINI SISTANI, leader of Iraqi Shias, Grand Ayatollah, 1999–Present.

JALAL TALABANI, Leader of Patriotic Union of Kurdistan, 1976–Present; member of the Interim Governing Council, 2003.

GEORGE TENET, director of U.S. Central Intelligence Agency, 1997–Present.

SERGIO VIEIRA DE MELLO, UN special representative to Iraq, June–August 2003.

PAUL WOLFOWITZ, U.S. Deputy Secretary of Defense, 2001–Present.

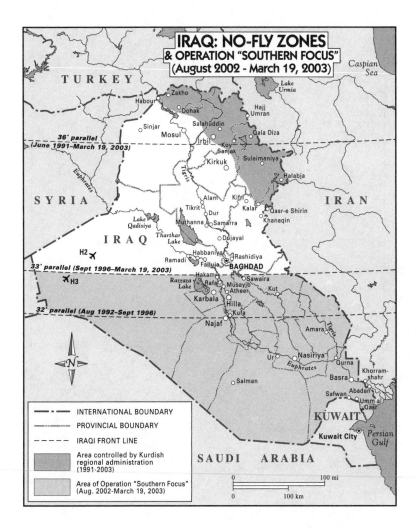

IRAQ: NO-FLY ZONES
& OPERATION "SOUTHERN FOCUS"
(August 2002 - March 19, 2003)

TURKEY

Caspian
Sea

Lake
Urmia

Habour
Zakho
Dohak
Hajj
Umran
Sinjar
Salahuddin
Mosul
Qala Diza
Irbil
Koy
Sanjak
Kirkuk
Suleimaniya

36° parallel
(June 1991–March 19, 2003)

Euphrates

Tigris

SYRIA

Halabja

Alam
Kifri
IRAN

Tikrit
Kalar
Lake
Qadisiya
Dur
Qasr-e Shirin
Muthanna
Samarra
Khanaqin
Tharthar
Lake
Dujayal

IRAQ

H2

Habbaniya
Ramadi
Falluja
Rashidiya
BAGHDAD

33° parallel (Sept 1996–March 19, 2003)

H3
Hakam
Razzaza
Lake
Rafa
Musayib
Sawaira
Atheer
Kut
Karbala
Hilla
Kufa

32° parallel (Aug 1992–Sept 1996)

Najaf

Amara

Tigris

Ur
Nasiriya
Euphrates
Qurna
Khorram-
shahr
Salman
Basra
Abadan
Safwan
Umm al
Qasr

KUWAIT

Kuwait City
Persian
Gulf

SAUDI ARABIA

N

INTERNATIONAL BOUNDARY
PROVINCIAL BOUNDARY
IRAQI FRONT LINE

Area controlled by Kurdish
regional administration
(1991-2003)

Area of Operation "Southern Focus"
(Aug. 2002-March 19, 2003)

0   100 mi

0   100 km

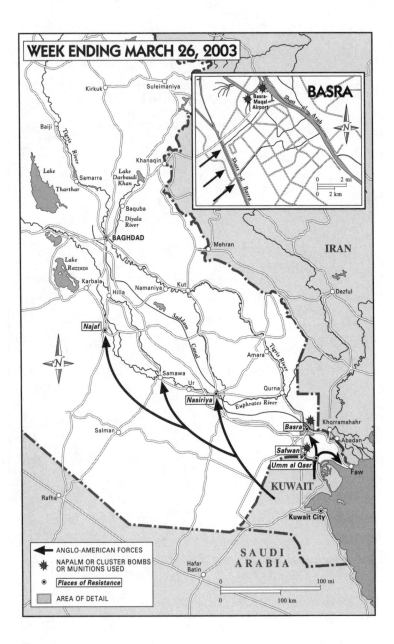

WEEK ENDING MARCH 26, 2003

BASRA

Basra-Maqal Airport

Shatt al Arab

Shatt al Basra

N

0   2 mi
0   2 km

Kirkuk

Suleimaniya

Baiji

Tigris River

Khanaqin

Samarra

Lake Tharthar

Lake Darbaudi Khan

Baquba

Diyala River

BAGHDAD

Mehran

IRAN

Lake Razzaza

Karbala

Hilla

Namaniya

Kut

Saddam Canal

Dezful

Najaf

Samawa

Ur

Amara

Tigris River

Nasiriya

Euphrates River

Qurna

Salman

Basra

Khorramshahr

Abadan

Safwan

Umm al Qasr

Faw

KUWAIT

Rafha

Kuwait City

SAUDI ARABIA

Hafar Batin

0   100 mi
0   100 km

ANGLO-AMERICAN FORCES

NAPALM OR CLUSTER BOMBS OR MUNITIONS USED

Places of Resistance

AREA OF DETAIL

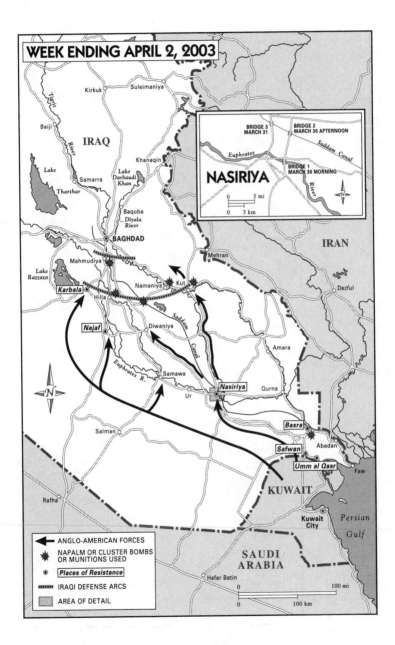

WEEK ENDING APRIL 2, 2003

IRAQ

Kirkuk Suleimaniya

Baiji

Tigris River

Samarra

Lake Tharthar

Lake Darbaudi Khan

Khanaqin

Baquba
Diyala River

BAGHDAD

Mahmudiya

Lake Razzaza

Karbala

Hilla

Namaniya Kut

Mehran

IRAN

Dezful

Najaf

Diwaniya

Saddam Canal

Euphrates R.

Samawa

Amara

Nasiriya

Ur

Qurna

Salman

Basra

Abadan

Safwan

Umm al Qasr

Faw

KUWAIT

Rafha

Kuwait City

Persian Gulf

SAUDI ARABIA

Hafar Batin

NASIRIYA (inset)

BRIDGE 3
MARCH 31

BRIDGE 2
MARCH 30 AFTERNOON

Euphrates

Saddam Canal

BRIDGE 1
MARCH 30 MORNING

River

0   3 mi
0   3 km

Legend

→ ANGLO-AMERICAN FORCES

✹ NAPALM OR CLUSTER BOMBS OR MUNITIONS USED

◉ *Places of Resistance*

•••• IRAQI DEFENSE ARCS

▨ AREA OF DETAIL

0   100 mi
0   100 km

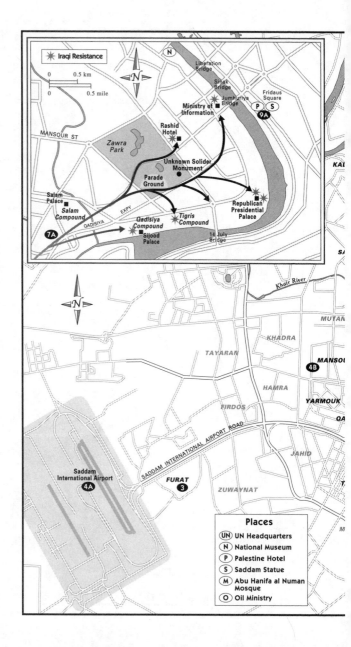

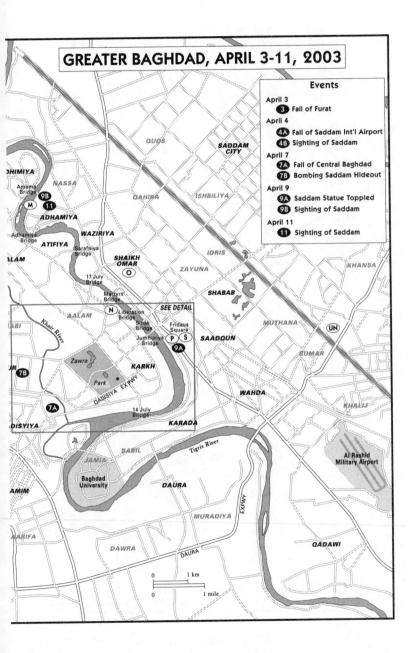

GREATER BAGHDAD, APRIL 3-11, 2003

Events

April 3
3 Fall of Furat

April 4
4A Fall of Saddam Int'l Airport
4B Sighting of Saddam

April 7
7A Fall of Central Baghdad
7B Bombing Saddam Hideout

April 9
9A Saddam Statue Toppled
9B Sighting of Saddam

April 11
11 Sighting of Saddam

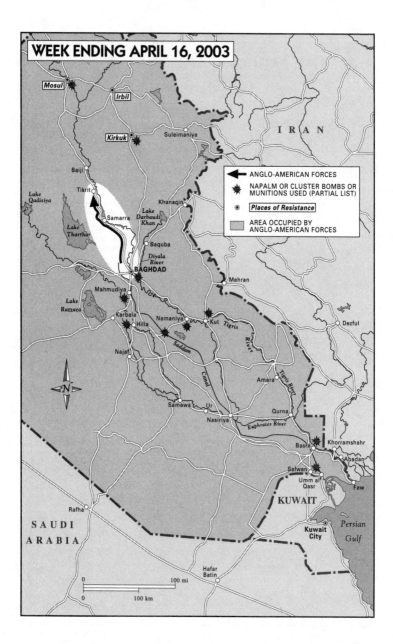

WEEK ENDING APRIL 16, 2003

ANGLO-AMERICAN FORCES

NAPALM OR CLUSTER BOMBS OR
MUNITIONS USED (PARTIAL LIST)

Places of Resistance

AREA OCCUPIED BY
ANGLO-AMERICAN FORCES

IRAN

Mosul

Irbil

Kirkuk   Suleimaniya

Baiji

Tikrit   Khanaqin

Lake
Qadisiya

Samarra   Lake
Darbaudi
Khan

Lake
Tharthar   Baquba

Diyala
River

BAGHDAD

Mehran

Mahmudiya

Lake
Razzaza

Karbala   Namaniya   Kut   Tigris
Hilla   River

Saddam   Dezful
Najaf   Canal

Amara

Tigris River

Samawa   Ur

Nasiriya   Euphrates River   Qurna

Basra   Khorramshahr

Safwan   Abadan

Umm al
Qasr   Faw

Rafha

KUWAIT

SAUDI
ARABIA

Kuwait
City   Persian
Gulf

0   100 mi

0   100 km

Hafar
Batin

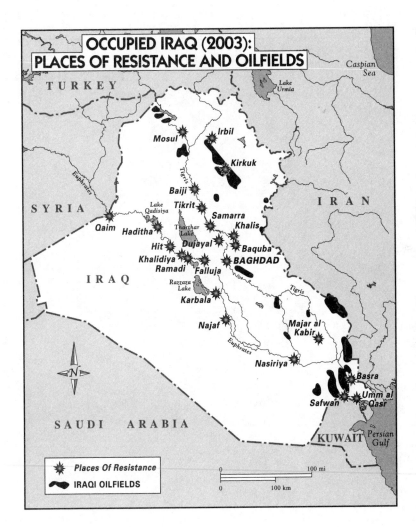

OCCUPIED IRAQ (2003): PLACES OF RESISTANCE AND OILFIELDS

Caspian Sea

TURKEY

Lake Urmia

Mosul

Irbil

Kirkuk

Tigris

Baiji

SYRIA

Euphrates

IRAN

Tikrit

Samarra

Khalis

Qaim

Haditha

Lake Qadisiya

Tharthar Lake

Dujayal

Baquba

Hit

BAGHDAD

Khalidiya

Ramadi

Falluja

IRAQ

Razzaza Lake

Tigris

Karbala

Najaf

Majar al Kabir

Euphrates

Nasiriya

Basra

SAUDI ARABIA

Safwan

Umm al Qasr

KUWAIT

Persian Gulf

N

0   100 mi

0   100 km

✹ Places Of Resistance

🛢 IRAQI OILFIELDS

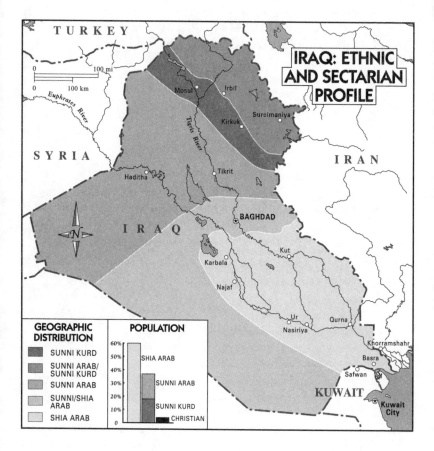

IRAQ: ETHNIC AND SECTARIAN PROFILE

TURKEY

SYRIA

IRAN

IRAQ

KUWAIT

0   100 mi
0   100 km

Euphrates River

Tigris River

Mosul   Irbil
Kirkuk   Sulelmaniya

Tikrit

Haditha

BAGHDAD

Kut

Karbala

Najaf

Ur   Qurna

Nasiriya

Khorramshahr

Basra

Safwan

Kuwait City

N

GEOGRAPHIC DISTRIBUTION

SUNNI KURD

SUNNI ARAB/ SUNNI KURD

SUNNI ARAB

SUNNI/SHIA ARAB

SHIA ARAB

POPULATION

60%
50%
40%
30%
20%
10%
0

SHIA ARAB

SUNNI ARAB

SUNNI KURD

CHRISTIAN

PREFACE

THIS BOOK IS a sequel to my *Iraq: In the Eye of the Storm* (2002), which is structured thematically. In contrast *Secrets and Lies* advances chronologically, a structure dictated by the subject: war.

I have known Iraq and its people since 1978, when I first visited the country in the course of researching my book *Inside the Middle East* (1982). Since then Iraq and its former president, Saddam Hussein, have figured prominently in several other works of mine, including *The Longest War: The Iran-Iraq Military Conflict* (1989), *Desert Shield to Desert Storm: The Second Gulf War* (1992), and *Neighbors, Not Friends: Iraq and Iran After the Gulf Wars* (2001). To this list I need to add *War Without End: The Rise of Islamist Terrorism and Global Response* (2002), which, written after 9/11, contains a description of the Afghanistan campaign.

The skills and experience gained in chronicling the above wars have helped me shape the narrative of this book. They have also led me to point out affinities between seemingly disconnected or dissimilar events in this and earlier armed conflicts, thus lending the text additional weight and depth, while leaving its pace intact.

After a prologue—where I draw a parallel between the fates of Majid Suleiman, an Iraqi civil servant who was my minder in 1978, and his hapless country ruled by Saddam Hussein—I start my main text with 9/11 and the efforts made by the neoconservatives inside and outside the

George W. Bush Administration to link Iraq to that atrocity committed by Islamist terrorists. The absence of credible evidence to establish such a connection did not deter the hawkish camp led by Vice President Dick Cheney. Indeed, following the counsel of his chief political adviser, Karl Rove, Bush set out to morph the elusive Osama bin Laden into the very visible Saddam Hussein. He succeeded. This manifested itself in the triumph of the Republican Party in the November 2002 midterm elections, which gave Bush the sort of self-confidence he lacked before. In these two chapters I sketch the profiles of Bush as well as the leading members of his administration.

Chapter 3 deals with the progress made by the United Nations in disarming Iraq of weapons of mass destruction (WMD), and the efforts of the Bush White House to foreclose the peaceful path to Iraq's disarmament, with Secretary of State Colin Powell making a determined but futile attempt in February 2003 to convince the members of the Security Council that Saddam possessed WMD. This failure did not stop Bush, backed by British Prime Minister Tony Blair, to rush to invade Iraq, which Bush had decided to do in August 2002—the subject of Chapter 4.

Several features of the Anglo-American invasion of Iraq make it unique among the conflicts of modern times. It was the first pre-emptive conventional war for nearly a century, the earlier example being the Austro-Hungarian emperor's invasion of Serbia in 1914. It was also the first war waged by America and Britain based purely on—to put it politely—intelligence assessments—or, to put it starkly, a compendium of deliberate misinterpretations, misinformation, disinformation, and outright lies. As a result, for the first time in history the popularity of the leaders of the victorious countries fell.

The Pentagon used the most advanced high-tech weaponry ever, more lethal than that deployed in the Afghanistan campaign, and implemented a strategy that combined the use of regular troops with the commandos of the Special Forces and the agents of the Central Intelligence Agency, carrying bundles of cash, on a much larger scale than in Afghanistan. Also, the use of cluster bombs against the Iraqi soldiers and civilians was more widespread than in the case of the Taliban. In addition, the U.S. Central Command (Centcom) dropped napalm bombs in Iraq.

What is more, while the invading countries conducted a seven-month-long air campaign under their Operation "Southern Focus" as a prelude to the ground attack in March 2003, the leader of the invaded country, Saddam Hussein, decided not to deploy any warplanes or combat helicopters, a unique phenomenon.

Another novel feature of this war was the "embedding" of some 700 journalists with the American and British troops, a procedure much publicized by Centcom, with no mention of the fact that an embedded reporter was required by contract to agree to obey the instructions of his government.

Given the advanced technology, television audiences felt they were watching the "real" fighting in real time—except that the gory images that are an inevitable part of any war were snipped out on the Anglo-American television channels.

Unlike in the 1991 Gulf War, when the BBC and CNN shared a duopoly in airing the images of the hostilities, this time the Arab TV channels—especially Al Jazeera—successfully broke the Anglo-American stranglehold over war reporting. Repeatedly Al Jazeera provided footage that contradicted claims made by Centcom. What incensed the Anglo-American alliance was the realization that the TV channels in Europe, Russia, the Far East, South Asia, and Latin America bought and aired Al Jazeera TV footage. Little wonder that Centcom made a point of rocketing the Al Jazeera bureau in Baghdad, killing one of its leading reporters.

The overall result of this healthy competition between the powerful, established Anglo-American television channels and the emergent Arab channels was that for the first time in history noncombatants, in most parts of the world, could see for themselves the horrors of real war as experienced by civilians and soldiers in real time.

Given this—the embedded and other journalists' reports; the diary kept by Thuraya al Kaissi, a young Iraqi student in Baghdad, for London's *Sunday Mirror;* the material put out on the Internet by Salam Pax, an Iraqi architect in the capital; and the interviews given later by former Iraqi military officers and former bodyguards of Saddam Hussein and Uday Hussein—I have produced a narrative of the war in Chapters 5–8 that runs simultaneously along several different levels, both descriptive and analytical.

Chapter 9 narrates and analyzes events since the invasion, and shows that the U.S. administration's problems emanate, in essence, from Bush's personal characteristics of impatience and "being a gut player" (in his own words). At present occupied Iraq is poised delicately between becoming a cradle of democracy in the region or an incubator for Islamist terrorism—and on a scale much larger than in Afghanistan, the subject of Chapter 10. Whatever happens in Iraq will profoundly shape the future of the rest of the Middle East in the coming decade, by the end of which America will have exhausted all its known domestic petroleum deposits and become irrevocably dependent on oil imports from that region.

In sum, as a result of the secrets Bush kept and the lies he told to launch a pre-emptive war against Iraq, which posed no imminent threat to the United States or to any of Iraq's neighbors—thus violating the UN Charter—in pursuit of a personal instruction from God and his own gut instincts (which came first remains a secret so far), he now finds that his re-election prospects have become hostage to the actions of Iraqi guerrillas.

To provide a historical perspective, I start the Chronology (Appendix I) with the coup by the Iraqi Baathist military officers in July 1968. The Chronology has a dual purpose. The reader can see when a particular event actually happened, even though knowledge of it may have become known much later. Secondly, the reader can follow a particular subject—the scandal of the outing of Joseph Wilson's wife, Valerie Plame, as an undercover CIA agent, or the British dossier of September 24, 2002—by scanning the text quickly instead of looking up the Index and shuffling through pages.

The notes are at the end of each chapter.

The Epilogue is not indexed.

Last but not least, my experience of working with Carl Bromley of Nation Books and Neil Ortenberg of Thunder's Mouth Press has convinced me that together they combine the best in editorial policy, relations with the author, and marketing strategy. It is a privilege to be associated with them.

DILIP HIRO
London
October 2003

PROLOGUE

WHAT HAPPENED TO Majid Suleiman, an Iraqi civil servant in Baghdad, between 1978, when he was a well-paid Ministry of Information minder, and 2000, when he was eking out a living as a freelance translator at the Ministry's Press Center, reflects the broad contours of recent Iraqi history: The promise of peace and prosperity, fueled by the enormous jump in petroleum prices in 1973–74, combined with the state policy of evenly distributing the oil wealth, soured irredeemably by the despotic rule of Saddam Hussein, who within a year of becoming president invaded Iran, triggering the longest conventional war of the twentieth century. This was followed by a vicious invasion and occupation of the small, weak Arab emirate of Kuwait a decade later, causing in its trail indescribable suffering for the Iraqi people.

In March 1978 the Ministry of Information, the first place to visit for any newly arrived foreign writer or journalist, was near Liberation Square in the city center. The ante-room where I waited, after filling out a form, was comfortable, even cozy, and amply furnished with glossy publications, announcing in image and word in English and in Arabic—a language I know—the endless virtues of the Republic of Iraq, ruled then by President General Ahmad Hassan Bakr and his thirty-one-year-old nephew, Vice President Saddam Hussein.

A thin, dark, balding man in a gray business suit entered. "I'm Majid Suleiman," he announced. I shook his steely and assured hand and introduced myself. "I'll be your guide and we'll have a chauffeur-driven car to ourselves." He pitchforked me out of my modest hotel to something posh on Saddoun Street, the Fifth Avenue of Baghdad. Then he hurried me to the duty-free shop meant for foreign travelers and diplomats. I had no need for cigarettes or whisky or perfume. But he did. And from the familiarity with which the shop assistants greeted him, it was clear that he was a frequent visitor. He deliberated over the brand names of the makeup and perfumes, which, he whispered to me, he would ardently present to his fiancée. Her name, I would later learn, was Salima.

Majid had a sense of proprietorship over Babylon. A special glow appeared on his skinny face with each assertion that it was his birthplace. One early morning, though, on our journey to Najaf and Karbala, the holy cities of Shias, Ibrahim, the chauffeur of my official car, startled Majid awake by banging on the shaky door of his parental home in a village that lay some distance away from Babylon. So Majid was not a true Babylonian after all, I inferred. But then who could resist the temptation of overlooking the few miles that stood between one's native village and a historic entity of Babylonian proportions? Certainly not me. Would anybody?

Najaf is holy, a place of prayer, contemplation, and burial, and it is 90 percent Shia. All Shias wish to be interred here. It is also a place where religion and commerce converge. The proof was before us. Traders ran shops stocked with rosaries, shrouds printed with appropriate verses from the Quran, and tablets made of Najaf's holy soil, to which the faithful would touch their foreheads when bowing in the course of the Islamic prayer. I stopped to marvel at the dazzling variety of worry beads, made of cornelian, plastic, olive wood, sandalwood, and mother of pearl. I picked up a rosary, each transparent bead a riot of kaleidoscopic colors. "Take it," Majid said. I demurred. "Take it," he repeated. "You'll need it," he added, enigmatically. He was armed with one. He was Sunni, the majority sect among Muslims worldwide, but not in Iraq, where three out of five Iraqis are Shia. Rooted in the early history of Islam, the Sunni-Shia divide bespeaks doctrinal, ritualistic, legal, theological, and organizational differences.[1]

As we neared Karbala, with the golden dome and minarets of the Imam Hussein shrine glistening in the afternoon sun, the environment changed. A canal of muddy water appeared: an unmistakable sign that we had finally abandoned the desert that surrounds Najaf, and were once again upon the alluvial soil of the Mesopotamian plain.

Karbala is a city of tragedy, of perpetual mourning. As I faced the shrine's gateway, which was crowned with a clock, Majid advised, "Take out your rosary." I did. A thin smile flickered on his severe face as he did the same. We crossed the threshold. The place was swarming with people—peasants, civil servants, artisans, soldiers, shopkeepers, housewives, teachers.

Gilded minarets stood like sentinels over the shrine of the Great Martyr, Imam Hussein, rising above the facade of arcaded columns with floral and geometric patterns in white, turquoise, and yellow. Majid and I climbed the platform in front of the shrine. A middle-aged priest of Islam in a camel-brown cloak, portly, trim of beard, and sporting a neat green turban around his red fez, greeted me. "*Al Hindi* (the Indian)?" he asked, smiling. "Yes," I replied, returning his smile: "*Al Hindi.*" Majid faltered, darted a narrow-eyed glance at me, then at the mullah, and moved on, thumbing his worry beads, visibly relieved.

Majid and I entered the shrine together, shoeless. Here was all gold, silver, light, glitter. I was dazzled by the silver-covered walls and ceilings reflecting the glow from the chandeliers and neon lights. I stood by the shrine, my fingers piously clicking the worry beads. I stood next to an aging, sunken-cheeked pilgrim with his eyes closed, clutching the silver bars that surrounded the sarcophagus, lost to the world in the suffocating midst of a swirling congregation. The sight hypnotized me. A sharp tug at my sleeve broke the trance. It was Majid, who had crept behind me. Time to move, he suggested with uncharacteristic discretion.

Outside, everything appeared pallid, the crowds lethargic. We walked slowly, indifferently, to the car, and eased ourselves into the back seats. "It's against the law for a non-Muslim to visit the inner sanctums of these shrines," Majid said quietly. I stared at him with disbelief and astonishment, then recalled his advice to carry the rosary in my hand as we approached the holy site. I recalled too the nervous look on his face when the turbaned mullah on the platform asked me if I was an Indian. "If somebody finds out that I took you inside, I'd . . . " Majid slashed his throat with his right hand, the tip of his index finger curving backward. I was shocked. "But," he said, taking my hand in a paralyzing grip, "you're my brother." I nodded. It was a while before he said, "I'll come to London." Moments passed. "And I'll take you around." I replied with as much enthusiasm as I could muster.

To his regret, Majid never made it to London. He did travel westward, though—but only as far as Athens, and at a time when Greek living standards were below those of Iraq. He worked there as the press officer at the Iraqi embassy. That was after he had taken a leave of absence, obtained a master's degree in English literature at the University of Baghdad, married Salima after showering her with many a bottle of French perfume, and sired two sons.

So he would tell me—twenty-two years later—at the Press Center on the ground floor of an eight-story building that now housed the Ministry of Information, near the Sinak Bridge over the Tigris River.

It was July 2000. For ten grueling years Baghdad and the rest of Iraq had been on the receiving end of the most punishing economic and trade sanctions imposed on any country in history. Before sanctions one Iraqi dinar was worth $3.21; now you needed 3,000 Iraqi dinars to buy a single U.S. dollar. This impoverishment manifested itself in several ways. Even though, as the capital city, Baghdad had top priority in public services, it looked shabby. The main roads were bearable, but the moment you turned into a side street, you saw an unpaved, potholed passage, criss-crossed by dark veins of sewage, and littered with uncollected garbage. Even in middle-class neighborhoods and in the administrative heart of the city, with the closely guarded Republican Presidential Palace at its center, the air was constantly permeated with the fetid smell of sewage. Ramshackle taxis with jammed half-open windows and shattered windshields plied the streets.

Had I not been assured by Narmeen, the ebullient Ministry of Information clerk dealing with foreign journalists, that she knew Majid Suleiman as well as his family, and that he was at the Press Center on the ground floor, I would not have recognized him. He had, it seemed, hopped from being a young man to an old one by skipping middle age. Gone was the infectious smile, the nervous enthusiasm of someone who wanted to please and was eager to be liked. Instead, there sat a bald man on a gray folding metal chair, thin, with an emaciated face with lusterless eyes, in the ante-room to the Press Center proper.

I thought he would rise and shake my hand with the steely grip that was his trademark as soon as I had introduced myself and jogged his memory a bit. After all, during his job as a government minder he had dealt with very few, if any, Indian writers or journalists, either from India or elsewhere.

But when I told him what was necessary about myself and my earlier visit to Iraq, he remained seated, motionless, without any expression on his face. Then he mumbled a brief update on his marriage and his posting to the embassy in Athens.

"How have you been since then?" I asked sprightly to counter his downbeat tone. "Bad." With hyperinflation raging after the 1991 Gulf War and civil servants' salaries almost frozen, poverty stared him in the face. "The first two years of sanctions were catastrophic as the value of our salaries plummeted sharply," he explained. "We just didn't know how to cope. Only in the third year did we begin to adjust to the new reality. There were tens of thousands of us—government employees. You know, one-third of the total work force was in the government or public-sector undertakings." It took a while to absorb the fact—to imagine 30 million Americans working for the local, state, and federal bureaucracies in the United States.

"Who are you with now, the Foreign Ministry or the Information?" I inquired solicitously. "Neither." Suleiman managed to smile wanly. "The only way to survive was to get into the dollar sector. So I left the ministry. Now I translate things for the Japanese news agency, Kyodo. I also translate local news for the visiting Japanese journalists. They pay in dollars." I knew. I was doing the same—except that in my case it was a gratuity that I gave: My minder was an employee of the Information Ministry.

"It would be nice to meet up again, Majid, and have a longer conversation, maybe have a kebab together," I said warmly, if only to beat off the gloom that filled the ante-room where he was sitting. "Give me your questions in writing," he said coldly. It was an automaton speaking, I thought.

Gone was the spontaneity that I had once associated with Majid Suleiman as well as the optimism. Life was now drudgery for him as well as millions of others. They all blamed America—pronounced "Amreeka"—for the sanctions that had brought them unending misery.

I related my encounter with Majid Suleiman to Abdul Razak, a U.S.-educated former military officer and professor introduced to me by his self-exiled brother in London. Abdul reflected for a while, his wrinkled dark brown face with a salt-and-pepper mustache tightening. "You see, we Iraqis are caught between internal pressure [read, Saddam Hussein] and external [read, America]. And there is no end in sight for our predicament."

NOTE

1. Worldwide, seven out of eight Muslims are Sunni. See further "Shia" and "Sunnis" in Dilip Hiro, *The Essential Middle East: A Comprehensive Guide,* Carroll and Graf, New York, 2003, pp. 585-86 and p. 502.)

PART I · TOWARD INVASION

Chapter 1

9/11 AND IRAQ: A PHANTOM LINK

"God told me to strike at Al Qaida and I struck them, and then He instructed me to strike at Saddam, which I did."
—George W. Bush to Palestinian Prime Minister Mahmoud Abbas[1]

ON SEPTEMBER 12, 2001, the mood was uncommonly grim on the second floor of the thirty-nine–story United Nations skyscraper—the home of the Security Council—along Manhattan's East River. It was the day after the Twin Towers of the World Trade Center—just four miles (6.5 kilometers) south of the UN headquarters—were attacked by Islamist hijackers who had used passenger aircraft as missiles and reduced the towers to ash, dust, and twisted metal. The outrage had killed more than three thousand people and covered lower Manhattan with smoke and ash. It was just before noon, the hour when the Security Council was scheduled to meet at the initiative of French president Jacques Chirac.

One by one the ambassadors of the fifteen members of the Security Council, looking grave, entered the debating chamber with its large horseshoe table—dominated by Norwegian artist Per Krogh's oil-canvas mural painted in the style of a tapestry, which depicts a phoenix rising from its ashes, a striking symbol of the world being reconstructed after World War II—their nostrils still recoiling from the smoke outside, which would take some months to dissipate. President of the council Jean-David Levitte—France's ambassador to the United Nations—formally opened the meeting. Each ambassador spoke for a couple of minutes, expressing shock at the atrocity and sympathy for the victims and the United States. At the end, they adopted Resolution 1368 unanimously with a show of hands, and left at 12:42 P.M., still weighed down by the gravity of what had happened a day earlier.

Resolution 1368 "unequivocally" condemned "the horrifying terrorist attacks," regarded "such acts, like any act of international terrorism, as a threat to international peace and security," and called on "all States to work together urgently to bring to justice the perpetrators, organizers and sponsors of the terrorist attacks," stressing that "those responsible for aiding, supporting or harboring the perpetrators, organizers and sponsors of these acts will be held accountable."

It was the first time in UN history that the Security Council had passed a resolution that applied not to a state or states but to individuals or groups. Resolution 1368 thus became a landmark document in international law. Yet it went largely unnoticed by the American media and commentators. And, in the coming days and weeks, Resolution 1368 would not be invoked, or even mentioned in passing, by high U.S. officials, including U.S. secretary of state Colin Powell, who was still regarded in those days as an internationalist.[2] Equally, at the North Atlantic Treaty Organization (NATO) headquarters in Brussels, Belgium, the members unanimously invoked Article 5—"an attack on one member should be considered an attack on all"—and for the first time they decided to help the United States by sending its AWACS (Airborne Warning and Control Systems) early warning system to the continental United States. By so doing, NATO agreed that Article 5 would now cover large terrorist attacks on a member state.

In contrast, the UN General Assembly failed to reach unanimity on the subject. Among its 189 members, there were three dissenters. China, Iraq, and Libya refused to fly their flags at half-mast at their missions in New York. Beijing was still recovering from its brush with the United States, whose air force had shot down its plane over the South China Sea in April; Libya had not forgiven the United States for bombing its capital in 1986 for its alleged role in a terrorist attack on American servicemen in Berlin.

And Iraq nursed a deep and lasting grievance against the United States, and declared that "America is reaping the thorns planted by its rulers." Iraqi president Saddam Hussein advised Washington against using retaliatory force, and cited the example of his country, where, in his view, such a strategy had failed. In an interview with a local magazine, Iraqi foreign minister Naji Sabri—a suave, bespectacled, middle-aged apparatchik always dressed in well-tailored suits, who was the director general at the Ministry of Information at the time of the 1991 Gulf War—recalled American "crimes against humanity." He invoked images of Hiroshima hit by an American atom bomb in 1945, killing 230,000 along with people, Vietnam, Central America, and Palestine—a bloody trail littered with millions of dead going back more than fifty years. "All Muslim and Arab people consider America the master of terrorism, the terrorist power number one."[3] Later, in his address to the UN General Assembly, Iraqi ambassador Muhammad al Douri, a balding, middle-aged man, would reveal that Iraq had sent messages of condolence to individuals in America, adding, "It would have been hypocritical to condemn the bombings, given the sanctions and bombings against Iraq."[4]

By the time the U.S. National Security Council (NSC) met at the White House on September 12 at 4 P.M.—based on reports by George Tenet, the Central Intelligence Agency (CIA) director, and Robert Mueller, Federal Bureau of Investigation (FBI) director—a consensus had grown that the culprits for the 9/11 attacks were the Al Qaida network and its leader, Osama bin Laden.

At this meeting, Secretary of Defense Donald H. Rumsfeld—a

tight-lipped, gloomy-looking intellectual with sad eyes—
reflecting the strongly held viewpoint of his deputy, Paul D. Wolfowitz, raised the prospect of including Iraq in the first list of the
countries to be attacked as part of the war on terror. He advocated
invading Iraq to topple Saddam, then extending the offensive
against the training camps operated by such non–Al Qaida factions
as Hizbollah in Lebanon and Syria. Powell disagreed. The time was
not opportune, he reasoned. "Any action [by us] needs public support," he said. "The American people want us to do something
about Al Qaida." Bush went along with Powell without disagreeing
with Rumsfeld and Wolfowitz, saying that they did not have to
resolve the Iraq issue there and then.[5]

All the same, Iraq cropped up again when the NSC met at
Camp David for a day-long deliberation on Saturday, September
15. During the morning session, Wolfowitz argued that "it is not
just simply a matter of capturing people and holding them
accountable, but removing the sanctuaries . . . ending states that
sponsor terrorism."[6] And among such states, Iraq was at the top of
his list. He warned that the Afghanistan war had the makings of a
quagmire. But he failed to convince the gathering. Yet Bush was
impressed enough to advise him, privately, to keep on pressing the
case against Baghdad, which he did. Both shared the view that the
United States should use its immense power to promote freedom
and overthrow tyrannical rulers. As a result Wolfowitz would
emerge as the Bush administration's most influential strategist on
national security, having already won for himself the sobriquet
"resident egghead."

A longtime proponent of hard-line policies in the Middle East,
Wolfowitz is a leading intellectual in the neoconservative (neocon,
for short) camp. The term neoconservative came into vogue in the
1970s as a counterpoint to the New Left, which had emerged in
the previous decade from the civil rights and anti–Vietnam War
movements and parted with the Old Left, which was committed
to the orthodoxy of class conflict.

The Vietnam conflict sharpened the division in the liberal camp between those who believed in peaceful coexistence with the Soviet bloc and those who, being staunchly anti-Communist in the mold of American Federation of Labor-Congress of Industrial Organizations (AFL-CIO) president George Meaney and Democrat senator Henry "Scoop" Jackson, wanted to see its collapse. It was the latter group that would be called neoconservative, a label it originally disliked. But, in the 1980s, as they gradually defected to the Republican Party during the presidency of Ronald Reagan (r. 1981–89), they came to accept it.

Like many neoconservative intellectuals, Wolfowitz's career revolved around public service and academia. Quite uniquely, though, he has the distinction of appearing as a character in the novel *Ravelstein*, Saul Bellow's homage to his late friend, the right-wing philosopher Allan Bloom, whose *The Closing of the American Mind* made an enormous impact on conservatives in the late 1980s. Abe Ravelstein, Bellow's eponymous hero and Bloom surrogate, takes enormous Socratic pride in the Washington policy makers he has mentored, one of whom is Philip Gorman, a member of President George Herbert Walker Bush's administration, and, of course, Bellow's Wolfowitz character. At one point Gorman laments to his mentor that, after the 1991 Gulf War, "his bosses leave the dictatorship [in Iraq] in place and steal away."

Born into a Polish-Jewish family in New York, Wolfowitz grew up in a strongly Zionist and pro-Israeli environment. After receiving a bachelor's degree in mathematics from Cornell University, he worked briefly as a management intern at the Bureau of the Budget in Washington, and enrolled as a graduate student in the political science department at the University of Chicago. As a doctoral student in the late 1960s, Wolfowitz came under the twin influences of Leo Strauss (d. 1973, a year after he awarded doctorates to both Wolfowitz and Abram Shulsky), who provided the philosophical underpinning, and of Albert Wohlstetter, a professor of mathematics and military strategist. A veteran of the Rand

Corporation think tank, Wohlstetter advanced the concept of limited, small-scale wars fought with precision-guided bombs—he was the guru of the Cold War hawks, who believed that détente with the Soviet Union and the accompanying disarmament verged on treason.[7] Wohlstetter believed he had a mission to enhance America's security at the cost of those who threatened it, and that was the only way to secure world peace. In other words, if you forecast an armed conflict with China two decades from now, you fight China now and remove that danger.

Student deferments kept Wolfowitz out of the military draft during the Vietnam War, which he now assesses with a certain scholarly detachment—a sharp contrast from the view of Colin Powell, who, having participated in it, considers Vietnam a paradigm of America's good intentions gone wrong—a story likely to be repeated in Iraq, which is in essence Wolfowitz's war.

Following a brief stint teaching at Yale University (1973), Wolfowitz joined the U.S. Arms Control and Disarmament Agency in the second Richard Nixon administration (1973–74), and stuck to the Wohlstetterian line on disarmament. During the Carter administration (1977–81), he became deputy assistant secretary of defense for regional programs (1977–80), where he helped create the force that would later become the U.S. Central Command (Centcom). Following another brief teaching stint at the Johns Hopkins University (1981), he served in the first Ronald Reagan administration as head of the State Department's policy planning staff (1981–82), where he helped shape Washington's hard-line stance toward the Soviet Union. Wolfowitz was then promoted to assistant secretary of state for East Asian and Pacific affairs. During Reagan's second administration (1985–89), he was appointed ambassador to Indonesia, whose military dictator, General Suharto, was firmly in the American camp during the Cold War. Though he spent three years in the world's most populous Muslim state, there is little evidence that Wolfowitz gained much understanding of the Muslim society there, or of Islam in general.

During the presidency of George Bush Sr., he was number three at the Pentagon under Dick Cheney (b. 1941). As undersecretary of defense for policy, he directed a seven-hundred-strong defense policy team that was responsible for strategy, plans, and policy.

In the 1991 Gulf War, he disagreed with Bush Sr. and his top advisers, who included Cheney and Powell, regarding their decision not to march on Baghdad, but apparently kept his own counsel as his superiors did not seek it.[8] He was well aware of the strength of the reasons—practical and ideological—that Cheney offered against advancing on Baghdad. While soliciting support for war from the Arab countries—including Syria—he had assured their leaders that the Pentagon would limit itself to expelling the Iraqis from Kuwait and weakening Iraq militarily. And, as a dyed-in-the-wool Republican from Wyoming, he was for limiting the activities of the federal government, not expanding it to occupy a country of the size and complexity of Iraq.

Following the collapse of the Soviet Union in December 1991, Cheney asked Wolfowitz to revise the Pentagon's *Defense Planning Guidance*. Working with Cheney's chief aide, I. Lewis Libby, Wolfowitz prepared a position paper that was endorsed by his boss. In March 1992 this draft was leaked to the *New York Times*. The paper asserted that it was not multilateral organizations like the United Nations that brought about stability, but a superpower like the United States: "The world order is ultimately backed by the U.S." The document proposed that the United States should prepare to disengage from its formal alliances and use its military might around the globe to prevent the emergence of any potential future rival, and to stop the spread of nuclear arms. It also stated that if Washington found itself having to consider using force to prevent the development or use of weapons of mass destruction (WMD) by another nation[9], its options should include "pre-emptive action." The draft also stated that Iraq and North Korea were among the countries at whom the new policy would be directed.

"Future alliances will be ad hoc assemblies, often not lasting beyond the crisis being confronted, and in many cases carrying only general agreement over the objectives to be accomplished," it said. "While the U.S. cannot become the world's policeman, we will have to retain the pre-eminent responsibility for addressing *selectively* those wrongs which threaten not only our interests but those of our allies or friends." The bellicose tone of Wolfowitz's document clashed with Bush Sr.'s attempt to co-opt the recently defeated Russia into the new international order. Bush Sr. also reckoned, rightly, that such an aggressive stance in foreign policy would provide ammunition to his Democratic rival in the upcoming presidential election. So he, his national security adviser, Brent Scowcroft, and Powell rejected the draft.[10]

Following Bush Sr.'s defeat in 1992, Wolfowitz returned to academia, briefly at the National War College, Washington, and then at the Johns Hopkins University as professor of international relations and dean of its School of Advanced International Studies (SAIS), until 2000. While at the SAIS, he read the manuscript of *The War Against America: Saddam Hussein and the World Trade Center Attacks: A Study of Revenge* (2000). Its author, Laurie Mylroie, an academic whose obsession with Saddam Hussein had led the Clinton administration to treat her as "a nut case," argued that Saddam was behind the 1993 bombing of the World Trade Center in New York, which killed six people (it is worth noting that Mylroie was once so friendly toward Saddam's regime that she wrote a letter to the *New York Times* in 1986 arguing that it was in the United States' interest to back Iraq against Iran and that Iraq's interests lay with "Arab moderates"[11]). Yet Wolfowitz, a hard-nosed Straussian, listened to Mylroie's ninety-minute presentation of her "evidence" and contributed a blurb, saying "[the book] argues powerfully that the mastermind of the 1993 World Trade Center bombing was actually an agent of Iraqi intelligence." Richard Perle, the leading light of the American Enterprise Institute (the publisher of Mylroie's book), and a cohort of Wolfowitz, enthused:

"Move over, Tom Clancy; Laurie Mylroie has written the year's best thriller. Based on a thorough examination of the evidence. . . ."[12]

In 1997 Wolfowitz became one of the founders of the Project for the New American Century (PNAC), a pressure group chaired by William Kristol, editor of the *Weekly Standard* (the leading mouthpiece of neoconservatives, which shared its office with the PNAC). PNAC's aim was "to explain what American world leadership entails; to rally support for a vigorous and principled policy of American international involvement; and to stimulate useful public debate on foreign and defense policy and America's role in the world." On the eve of the annual State of the Union address in January 1998, Wolfowitz became one of the many neoconservative signatories to an open letter to President Bill Clinton, which stated that containment of Saddam Hussein had failed and that his removal "from power . . . needs to become the aim of American foreign policy." Ever since the Iraqi National Congress (INC) was set up with CIA funding in June 1992, Wolfowitz had lent it support, forging close relations with the INC leader, Ahmad Chalabi, a bald, narrow-eyed, middle-aged Shia businessman based in London and holding a British passport, who was also close to Perle.[13]

It was not accidental that soon after 9/11 the INC became the source of stories that linked Baghdad with the September 11 attacks. On October 14, a former Iraqi army captain, Sabah Khodada, alleged in a joint interview with PBS's *Frontline* and the *New York Times* that Iraq had trained terrorists to hijack planes. In the same program another defector, identified merely as "a retired lieutenant general in the Iraqi intelligence," claimed to have seen foreign Arab students being taught how to hijack a Boeing 707 stationed at a training camp near Salman Pak, south of the capital.[14] Another story, published in *The Times* of London and relying on the translator provided by the INC, concluded that the interviewee, an Iraqi defector produced by the INC in London, had described how he had trained with Al Qaida terrorists at secret camps in Iraq in the deployment of chemical and biological arms.

But later, when a group of CIA agents interviewed the same defector, using their own interpreter, the interviewee said, "I worked at a Fedayeen [Saddam] camp, it wasn't Al Qaida," adding that there was no chemical or biological weapons training.[15] Such revelations would surface only in the spring of 2003.

In late 2000, the newly and controversially elected George W. (nicknamed Dubya) Bush entrusted Vice President Cheney with the presidential transition team. Cheney turned it into a reunion of the PNAC crowd under the roof of the Bush White House—Wolfowitz and Douglas Feith at the Pentagon, John Bolton as number three at the State Department, and Libby as his own chief of staff—thus effectively circumscribing the powers of Colin Powell, named earlier by Bush as secretary of state.

As number two at the Pentagon, Wolfowitz lobbied hard for financial and military aid to Iraqi opposition factions, and unquestioningly trusted the Iraqi oppositionists' claims that Saddam was attempting to develop, obtain, and finally use WMD. At the same time, given his Wohlstetterian convictions, he began highlighting China as the upcoming threat to U.S. supremacy.

Then came September 11, 2001. "9/11 brought home to all of us just what the stakes were in leaving threats like that untended," he told *Time*. These Islamist terrorist assaults gave Wolfowitz a second chance to sell the pre-emptive doctrine that Bush Sr. had rejected nine years earlier. What helped him was the esteem in which Bush Jr. had by then come to hold him. Even though he was only a deputy secretary, President Bush included him in the twelve-member war cabinet he formed in the aftermath of 9/11.

In Wolfowitz's view, 9/11 provided the United States with a rationale for attacking Saddam's regime. Yet, when questioned about the Iraqi leader's involvement in 9/11, he put the odds at 10 to 50 percent. Little wonder that those war cabinet members who remained unconvinced of the case against Saddam included not only Andrew Card, Gen. Henry Shelton, and Powell, but also

Cheney, who would publicly state on September 16 that there was no evidence of Iraq's involvement in the terrorist attacks.

At the NSC's September 15 Camp David meeting, Powell warned that the partners in America's antiterrorist coalition would defect if the Pentagon targeted Iraq. If we get "something pinning September 11 on Iraq," fine—let's publicize it now, and "kick them at the right time," he added. He proposed attacking the Taliban in Afghanistan for now; if that went well, the administration would have enhanced its ability to go after Iraq—provided it could show evidence of involvement. Bush agreed with Powell for pragmatic reasons. "If we could prove that we would be successful in the Afghan theater, then the rest of the task would be easier," he said, adding that trying to do "too many things . . . militarily" would lead to a lack of focus.[16] So the NSC's afternoon session discussed Afghanistan almost exclusively.

Yet Iraq was not totally out of the picture, as British prime minister Tony Blair, arriving in Washington the week after the U.S. war cabinet's Camp David meeting, discovered. In the words of Sir Christopher Meyer, then Britain's ambassador to the United States, Blair told Bush, "Whatever you're going to do about Iraq, you should [first] concentrate on the job at hand [to get the Taliban to surrender Osama bin Laden to Washington]." In reply, Bush promised to keep Iraq "for another day."[17]

Harried by Rumsfeld, General Tommy Franks, commander-in-chief of the Tampa-based U.S. Central Command (Centcom)—which covered twenty-five countries in northeast Africa, the Middle East, and Central Asia—prepared a task force in weeks to hit targets in Taliban-controlled Afghanistan. The Pentagon had decided on a code name for the forthcoming military campaign—Operation "Infinite Justice"—within a fortnight of 9/11.

By late September, Centcom was ready. Powell had stitched together an impressive international coalition, including Pakistan, which had helped create the Taliban. Within days Bush authorized the Pentagon to embark on Operation "Enduring Freedom" (the earlier title, "Infinite Justice," was dumped once Muslim scholars announced that only God could dispense infinite justice.) On October 7 the Arabic-language Al Jazeera satellite TV aired a long statement by bin Laden. "[W]hat America is tasting now is only a copy of what . . . our Islamic *umma* (nation) has been tasting for eighty years—humiliation and disgrace, its sons killed and their blood spilled, its sanctities desecrated," he said. "We hear no denunciation . . . from the hereditary [Muslim] rulers . . . Israeli tanks rampage across Palestine . . . and we do not hear anyone raising his voice or reacting. . . . The least that can be said about those hypocrites is that they are apostates. . . . Americans have been telling the world they are fighting terrorism. . . . A million children [killed] in Iraq, to them this is not a clear issue. . . . [18] Despite the great devastation inflicted on the Iraqi people by the Crusader-Zionist alliance . . . the Americans are once again trying to repeat the horrific massacres."

That same day Saddam Hussein issued a statement on the U.S.-led Afghan war. "The true believers cannot but condemn this act, not because it has been committed by America against a Muslim people but because it is an aggression committed outside the international law," he said. "These methods will bring only greater instability and disorder in the world. The American aggression could spread to other countries."[19] Little did Saddam realize that a year and a half later Iraq would head the list of "other countries."

Bin Laden's reference to Iraq was a gift to the hawks in Washington as evidence of Al Qaida's link with Saddam. But as early as February 1998, amid the deepening Baghdad–Washington crisis on the UN inspections, which resulted in the Pentagon assembling an armada in the Gulf, bin Laden and other Islamist leaders had issued an assessment that applied to the Middle East as a whole, rather than Iraq in particular. And it was in the aftermath of the Pentagon's Operation "Desert Fox" in December of that year that bin Laden called on Muslims worldwide to "confront, fight, and kill" Americans and Britons for "their support for their leaders' decision to attack Iraq."[20] But this did not prove any formal link between bin Laden and Saddam. After all, those who protested against the U.S.-backed UN sanctions against Iraq included many liberal and leftist politicians in Europe, North America, and elsewhere.

As Operation "Enduring Freedom" gathered momentum abroad, the anthrax-related illness of a journalist in Florida caused nationwide panic. U.S. hawks blamed Iraq. Almost simultaneously, the FBI issued a general warning on October 10, saying that "attacks may be carried out during the next week on U.S. targets at home or abroad." When anthrax reached the Senate offices on October 17, CIA director George Tenet said, "There is a state sponsor involved, the powder is too refined. It might be Iraq, Russia, might be a renegade scientist from Iraq or Russia."[21]

It was against this backdrop that, upon Wolfowitz's urging, Rumsfeld established the Office of Special Plans (OSP) under William Luti, a former aide to Cheney and a longtime advocate of an attack on Iraq, now serving as an undersecretary of defense. The OSP was set up so secretly that it was not until a year later that the *New York Times* revealed its existence. Assigned the task of producing proof of a Saddam–Al Qaida link and Iraq's possession of WMD was Abram Shulsky, the OSP's operational director, another disciple of Leo Strauss[22] who had served under Richard Perle at the Pentagon. The OSP analyzed not only information provided by the established intelligence apparatus, but also raw data from outside of it, indiscriminately accepting countless tips from the INC and other Iraqi opposition groups who, due to the unreliability of most of the information supplied by them in the past, had lost credibility with the CIA and the State Department.

Reliance on intelligence given by defectors and exiles has always been problematic. The administration of President John Kennedy burned its fingers by trusting defecting Cubans when its Bay of Pigs invasion of Cuba ended in a fiasco in 1961. Three decades later, in *Silent Warfare: Understanding the World of Intelligence*, Shulsky and his co-author, Gary James Schmitt, noted that "it is difficult to be certain that they [defectors] are genuine. . . . The conflicting information provided by several major Soviet defectors to the United States . . . bedeviled U.S. intelligence for a quarter of a century." They explained that such sources "may be greedy; they may also be somewhat unbalanced people who wish to bring some excitement into their lives; they may desire to avenge what they see as ill treatment by their government; or they may be subject to blackmail. There is a strong incentive to tell interviewers what they want to hear." Yet Shulsky and his neocon cohorts, as well as hard-bitten politicians like Rumsfeld and Cheney, would come to accept unquestioningly the tales of Iraqi defectors and exiles.

As if this were not enough, the OSP forged links with the ad hoc intelligence unit that Israeli prime minister Ariel Sharon had set up on his own outside of Mossad, the country's official foreign intelligence service. It offered more alarmist reports on Iraq than even Mossad was prepared to vouch for. The OSP managed to pass on a lot of its information to British prime minister Blair without the involvement of the U.K. Joint Intelligence Committee (JIC), which coordinated all intelligence. As a result, the OSP office, staffed initially by only ten people, was so overwhelmed with work that it hired temporary "consultants" who were often researchers from conservative think tanks and congressional staffers with little or no knowledge of intelligence. It circumvented the usual recruitment procedure by resorting to giving them personal service contracts, which allow a federal department to employ people without specifying a job description—a convenient device to pack the office with political friends and sympathizers, who now numbered one hundred.

The original intention behind using OSP was to place raw intelligence under the microscope to decode what the normal intelligence community couldn't see. In practice, though, the politically motivated OSP staff sucked in raw intelligence from highly tendentious sources, disinformation, and rumor, and transformed it into a series of polished reports secure in the knowledge that outside of the Pentagon they would be read at the very least by Cheney, Libby, and Stephen Hadley, deputy national security adviser.

Meanwhile, at the FBI headquarters in Washington, agents were feverishly trying to catch the anthrax culprit(s). The investigators would finally focus on Dr. Steven Hatfill, an American medical doctor and a bio-defense expert who had helped develop a mobile germ-warfare plant while working for Science Applications International Corporation, San Diego—a leading contractor for the CIA and the Pentagon's Defense Threat Reduction Bureau dealing with countering biological, chemical, and radiological weapons—until March 2002, when he was sacked. Seven months later this germ-warfare trailer would be set up at Fort Bragg, North Carolina, to help the U.S. Army's Delta Special Force learn what to look for in its search for biological weapons in Iraq. Many troops used the trailer in their training sessions. After intense interrogation by the FBI, Hatfill would not be charged with any offense.[23]

Fresh ammunition was provided to the hard-liners in Washington when Czech officials stated in late October 2001 that Muhammad Atta, one of the ringleaders of the 9/11 hijackers, had visited Prague six months earlier to meet Iraqi intelligence officer Ahmad Ani—posted as a diplomat—to plan an assault on Radio Free Europe's head office, which was beaming anti-Saddam programs to Iraq. However, the anti-Baghdad frenzy created by the American media did not lead to strikes against Iraq because the White House was focused on annihilating the Taliban and capturing or killing bin Laden.

The overnight flight of the Taliban government from Kabul on November 12–13, followed by the fall of Kandahar and the Taliban stronghold to the south, three weeks later, led to relief—combined with self-congratulation—among senior American officials. As the U.S. intelligence agencies and scientists had failed to establish Iraq as the source of the anthrax, most people in America and elsewhere considered the subject of Iraq's involvement closed. But this was not to be.

AFGHAN PRELUDE

Unknown to all but a few, in November 2001 a West African diplomat sold a bundle of documents to the Italian intelligence in Rome showing that Iraq had sought to purchase yellow cake—milled uranium oxide—from Niger. This was the seed that would in a year or more flower into a fully fledged scam of the highest order in both Britain and the United States. It all started in Rome, because that is where Wissam al Zahawi was posted as Iraq's ambassador to the Vatican. In February 1999 he traveled to four West African states, including Niger, to invite their presidents to visit Iraq. Though Niger's president, Ibrahim Barre Mainassara, accepted the invitation, he never made it to Baghdad: he was assassinated.[24] It was al Zahawi's signature that appeared on a letter dated July 6, 2000, regarding the purchase of uranium. Four years after his visit to Niger, al Zahawi would be questioned by the International Atomic Energy Agency (IAEA) about his visit to Niger's capital, Niamey, and asked to produce any signed letters he wrote while serving as ambassador in Rome. He did, and these would establish conclusively that the seventeen pages of correspondence in French bought by the Italian intelligence were forgeries. In any case, a quick Google search on the Internet by the Italians would have shown that the foreign minister, Allele El Hadj Habibou, whose signature appeared on some of the letters, had been removed from office in 1989, proving that the papers were forged. Yet their boss passed on this material to his counterpart in MI6.

In Washington the U.S. hawks obsessed with Iraq were in no mood to give up. Foremost among them were Wolfowitz, Douglas Feith, undersecretary for policy at the Pentagon, and Richard

Perle, chairman of the twenty-nine-member Defense Policy Advisory Committee Board—Defense Policy Board, for short—consisting of national security experts, which advises the Pentagon.[25] They were part of the neoconservative intelligentsia who had grown up as Cold Warriors, defining the world in dualistic terms—forces of absolute good confronting forces of absolute evil—and who were primarily interested in foreign policy, an area of marginal interest to the American public mainly because the popular electronic media, treating most news as entertainment, find foreign affairs too complicated to cover systematically or in depth.

By all accounts, Perle was the high priest of this clan, and, although not a full-fledged member of the Bush administration, he was also a strong defender of the Office of Special Plans, asserting that "lots of mistakes were made by the intelligence analysts," and that the OSP established "beyond any doubt connections that had gone unnoticed in previous analysis."[26] He was also the neocons' most visible face, being very much in demand for interviews on U.S. television, where his glib, provocative, right-wing sound bites played exceedingly well. Like his longtime friend Benjamin Netanyahu, former prime minister of Israel (1996–99), Perle was "made for television."

Since the early 1970s, he and Wolfowitz had complemented each other as Wohlstetterian acolytes, with Perle the day-to-day tactician and Wolfowitz the intellectual strategist. The nerve center of the antidisarmament network in the 1970s was the office of Henry "Scoop" Jackson, the Democratic senator from Washington, who was as militantly anti-Soviet as he was pro-Israel. Among Jackson's staff was Richard Perle.

Born into a Jewish home in New York, Perle graduated from the University of Southern California, Los Angeles, and obtained a master's degree in political science from Princeton. His closeness to Wohlstetter, well connected to Washington movers and shakers, firmly secured his political career. In 1969 Wohlstetter got him a job as executive director of the Committee to Maintain a Prudent Defense Policy, which lobbied hard against President Nixon's Anti-Ballistic Missile Treaty (1972) with the Soviet Union, but in vain. By then Perle had acquired a high profile as Jackson's top aide.

It was in Senator Jackson's office that Perle and Wolfowitz became cohorts in their battle against arms control. Perle fiercely attacked advocates of disarmament and of paring the Pentagon's budget on Capitol Hill—where, given his apocalyptic views and his dark looks and thick black hair, he became known as the "Prince of Darkness," a sobriquet that has stuck. Wolfowitz, meanwhile, served on a study group recruited mainly from the Committee on the Present Danger. Privy to classified CIA data, this committee once concluded that the Soviet military was about to overtake the Pentagon! It did so by using a blatantly politicized methodology—a tactic that Wolfowitz would use in the post-9/11 era to conclude that Saddam possessed WMD and that he had links with Al Qaida.

During the first Reagan administration (1981–85) Perle was appointed assistant secretary of defense for international security policy. In 1983, he was the subject of a *New York Times* investigation into an allegation that he recommended a weapons purchase from an Israeli company whose owners had paid him a $50,000 fee two years earlier. While acknowledging that he had received the fee, he denied any wrongdoing, explaining that the money was for work he had done before he took up the Pentagon job. He was not officially accused of any ethical violations in the matter. In the second Reagan administration (1986–90), he kept his old job. He was investigated for possible ties to the Israeli espionage case involving Jonathan Jay Pollard, a U.S. naval intelligence officer who was given a life sentence in March 1987. Perle was not accused of any wrongdoing. Nonetheless, he resigned and plunged into lobbying and business.

Perle became a leading figure at the Washington-based, pro-Israeli Jewish Institute of National Security Affairs (JINSA), which links conservative think tanks such as the American Enterprise Institute (AEI), the Heritage Foundation, and the Center for Strategic and International Studies (CSIS)—funded by old, established conservative foundations like Bradley and Olin—with the Israel lobby, led by American-Israeli Public Affairs Committee (AIPAC). Among other things, JINSA arranges trips to Israel by many non-Jewish defense and political experts, such as retired General Jay Garner, who would be appointed the first U.S. pro-consul of post-Saddam Iraq. Perle also became a member of the board of advisers of the Foundation for Defense of Democracy (FDD), a pro-Israeli organization that conducts research and education seminars on international terrorism. His colleagues on that board include Charles Krauthammer, a *Washington Post* columnist, and William Kristol, both well known for their staunchly pro-Israel viewpoints. Perle also became a director of Hollinger International, a newspaper publishing company owned by right-wing Canadian Conrad Black, whose titles include the *Daily Telegraph* (London), *Chicago Sun-Times*, and the *Jerusalem Post*.

In July 1996, Perle led the team that produced an advisory document for the newly elected Likud prime minister Benjamin Netanyahu of Israel, entitled *A Clean Break: A New Strategy for Securing the Realm*—the realm being Israel. The document advised Netanyahu to abrogate the Oslo Accords and "reassert Israel's claim to its land by rejecting 'land for peace' as the basis of peace"—meaning Israel should treat all of British-mandate Palestine as "its land"; strengthen Israel's defenses to better confront Syria and Iraq; and forge a new and stronger relationship with the United States based on self-reliance and mutual interest. In cooperation with Turkey and Jordan, Israel could weaken, contain, and even roll back Syria, the document claimed. "This effort can focus on removing Saddam Hussein from power in Iraq—an important Israeli strategic objective in its own right," recommended the report, commissioned by the Institute of Advanced Strategic and Political Studies in Washington. Overall, it called for "reestablishing the principle of preemption."[27]

Like Wolfowitz, Perle worked hard to see Congress pass the Iraq Liberation Act in October 1998. It authorized President Clinton to spend up to $97 million for military aid to train, equip, and finance an Iraqi opposition army, and authorized the Pentagon to train insurgents. The military strategy to destabilize Iraq was conceived by General Wayne Downing, a retired Special Forces officer, and Dewey Clarridge, a retired CIA officer who had worked with the anti-leftist Contras in Nicaragua in the 1980s. The plan involved the CIA, working in league with the Special Forces, training opposition military officers who would then train their men. Next, protected by U.S. air cover, they would start capturing lightly defended areas in southern and western Iraq as an opening gambit to attract defectors from the regular Iraqi army. As their guerrilla actions escalated, inducing an increasing deployment of Baghdad's air force, U.S. air power would intervene to protect the insurgents.[28] Those knowledgeable about the Iraqi military knew that this harebrained idea—which had the enthusiastic backing of Ahmad Chalabi, an ignoramus in military affairs—had no chance of succeeding, since the battle-hardened Iraqi commanders would make mincemeat of the insurgents, and that to save its prestige the United States would end up committing ground troops to end the massacre of the Iraqi rebels.

Yet Perle, schooled in the skeptical ways of Leo Strauss, argued in an article in the *Washington Post* that "it would be neither wise nor necessary for us to send ground forces into Iraq" because Iraqi exiles could do the job for themselves with U.S. weapons and air cover. Little wonder that Jude Wannaiski, who has known Perle since 1969, wrote: "When Albert [Wohlstetter] died, Richard [Perle] inherited his global network of political supporters. I have likened Richard to the Sorcerer's Apprentice, a Mickey Mouse who thinks he can do magic by using the Sorcerer's wand. If you scratch Perle, you will find a mediocre strategist, a checker player at best."[29]

The remaining member of the neocon defense trio was Douglas Feith, who got the same job under Rumsfeld that Wolfowitz had under Bush Sr.'s defense secretary, Cheney. As undersecretary for policy, Feith formulated defense planning guidance policy, the Pentagon's relations with foreign countries, and its role in U.S. interagency policies. In 1989, Feith established the lobbying firm International Advisors Inc., which recruited Perle as a paid consultant, a position he held for six years. Consequently, Perle lobbied, successfully, for Feith with Rumsfeld, who was initially unsure of what the boyish-looking Feith could accomplish. It was not the first time Perle had given a leg up to his protégé. In 1982 Feith's transfer to the Pentagon from the National Security Council, where he was a specialist on the Middle East, was arranged by Perle, then assistant secretary of defense. Feith would serve him as special counsel, given his magna cum laude from the Georgetown University Law Center and bachelor's degree (also magna cum laude) from Harvard.

Douglas Feith's Austrian-born father, Dalck Feith, joined Betar, the youth wing of the Revisionist Zionists in Poland, in the early 1930s. Betar advocated a Jewish state on both sides of the Jordan River,[30] and who would morph into the Likud bloc in Israel in 1973. After migrating to the United States during World War II, Dalck Feith joined the U.S. Merchant Marine and settled in Philadelphia. Thus Douglas grew up in an ultranationalist Zionist environment.

An active lobbyist for Israel, Feith wrote newspaper articles backing the policies of the Jewish settlers in the Palestinian Territories occupied by Israel since 1967. In 1977–78, he condemned the Jimmy Carter administration for its opposition to Israel's settlement policy since, in his view, this encouraged Arabs to believe they could win benefits from the United States by refusing to make concessions to Israel. After leaving the government, he kept up his criticism of any U.S. policy that differed from his hard-line Likud viewpoint, condemning Bush Sr. for denying Israel loan guarantees and pressuring the Israeli government to attend the Middle East peace conference in Madrid in October 1991. He is the most gung-ho member of the trio and closest to Israel, and the only one whose appointment was contested in

Senate hearings by the Arab-American Aniti-Discrimination Committee, specifically by its leader, James Zogby.

Feith was another of the authors of *A Clean Break: A New Strategy for Securing the Realm.* He went on to associate himself with a strategy document that suggested that the United States might lead a Kuwait-style invasion to "liberate" Lebanon from Syria. He emerged as one of the most vocal proponents of the 1998 Iraq Liberation Act. In the previous year, the Zionist Organization of America, which opposes peace between Israel and the Palestinians, gave Feith the prestigious Lewis J. Brandeis award at its centennial dinner, citing him as a "pro-Israel activist."[31]

In 2001, as undersecretary for policy at the Pentagon, Feith was directly involved in the strategic planning and implementation of military operations in the Afghanistan war. Hence, when the U.S.-led campaign resulted in the collapse of the Taliban in two months, with minimal U.S. casualties, Feith was not seen smiling effusively in public.

But it was Rumsfeld who, by virtue of his daily press conferences, established himself as the spookily confident face of the Bush administration, his rimless glasses shining in the arc lights used by television crews, his mouth spouting faintly incomprehensible, slightly menacing utterances in tortured syntax, which sometimes bordered on poetry—as the humorist Hart Seely discovered. In his October 12, 2001, briefing, for instance, he explained the absence of bombing in Afghanistan on the previous day, a Friday, the Muslim holy day, thus:

> Things will not be necessarily continuous.
> The fact that they are something other than
>   perfectly continuous
> Ought not to be characterized as a pause.
> There will be some things that people will see.
> There will be some things that people won't see.
> And life goes on.[32]

The refrain about seeing some things and not seeing others was part of the rhetoric that Bush had unleashed as part of his "war on terror" in the aftermath of 9/11, forgetting that such a statement applied as much to conventional wars as to unconventional ones.

What really counted was that it was at Rumsfeld's insistence that General Franks had put together an innovative battle plan that made extensive use of high-tech precision weapons as well as the Special Forces and the National Security Agency's (NSA) technicians, and equipped CIA operatives with bags of cash to win the loyalties of the Afghan tribal leaders. Centcom had its own Special Forces Regiment (SFR), which drew its personnel from five different forces belonging to the Army, Navy, Air Force, and Marines, totaling roughly forty thousand, with the actual line units being about a third of the total.[33] To wit, Centcom's SFR consisted of: 120 troops from the 160th Special Operations Aviation Regiment (SOAR, called Night Stalkers), based at Fort Campbell, Kentucky, and Hunter army field, Georgia, which flies helicopter night missions to provide air support to Special Forces operations, and is equipped with specially adapted Black Hawk long-range helicopters with night vision and all-weather navigation; about a third of the 2,500-strong Delta force, established in 1977 at Fort Bragg, North Carolina, specializing in close-quarter battle and reconnaissance and hostage rescue; a quarter of the 5,000-strong Green Berets, also based at Fort Bragg, acting as commandos specializing in explosives, communications, engineering, and linguistics, and deployed for search-and-destroy missions; a third of the 1,800-strong 75th Ranger regiment, the army's highly mobile, rapid deployment assault force, based at Fort Benning, Georgia; and a tenth of the 2,200-strong SEALs (Sea, Air and Land), the Navy counterpart to the Green Berets, specializing in snatch operations. Centcom's SFR was to work in conjunction with Britain's 14th Intelligence Company (total strength, 120 men); Pathfinders (40 troops); Royal Marines (6,000); Special Air Services (250); and Special Boat Squadron (100).[34] This template was to be used later—in March 2003—on a much larger scale to topple Saddam Hussein's regime in Iraq.

Responsibility for the day-to-day conduct of the war rested with General Franks. Twice daily he reported progress and proposed his next move to General Richard Myers and Rumsfeld. Working within the broad strategic decisions made earlier by the National Security Council, Myers and Rumsfeld provided Franks with guidance and direction.

With twenty-four years' experience in running large corporations, the freshly appointed Rumsfeld tried to transform the Pentagon's culture into that of a commercial business, sensitive to the needs of changing times. He wanted the Army to abandon its excessive reliance on the firepower of armored divisions, the Navy to give up its primary stress on aircraft carriers, and the Air Force to reconsider its maintenance of vast fleets of heavy bombers. But when he encountered resistance from the entrenched military hierarchy, he backed off—only to bounce back after 9/11 with a vengeance, to earn the nickname of "Bush's rottweiler." His barbed, acerbic style flowered. Otto Schilly, German interior minister, explained it by pointing out that Rumsfeld's ancestors came from a region of northern Germany noted for rough speech. At his gentlest, he dealt with questions from journalists in the manner of an aged ox swatting away flies with his tail.

Born into the family of a real estate executive in Chicago, Rumsfeld won a scholarship to Princeton, where he combined wrestling with his studies for an undergraduate degree in political science. After serving as a navy pilot, he worked for an investment bank in Chicago. At the age of thirty, he was elected to the House of Representatives from Illinois as a Republican. He was reelected three times and proved to be a tough and competitive congressman. He resigned from Congress to serve President Richard Nixon—first as director of the Office of Economic Opportunity, and then as director of the Economic Stabilization Program. In 1973, he was appointed ambassador to NATO in Brussels. On

Nixon's resignation in August 1974, he became the chief of staff of President Gerald Ford. When, the following year, he was promoted to secretary of defense—the youngest ever—Rumsfeld recommended Dick Cheney, his protégé in Congress, as his successor. Twenty-six years later, Vice President Cheney, by now close to Rumsfeld both personally and philosophically, would return the favor by putting him in charge of the Pentagon, thus conferring on him the distinction of being the oldest secretary of defense ever.

After Ford's defeat by Carter in 1976, Rumsfeld became a corporate executive in Chicago. In 1980 he tried to become vice president on the Reagan ticket, but lost to Bush Sr. In 1983–84, he served as President Reagan's special envoy to the Middle East. In the course of this job, he had a ninety-minute meeting with Saddam Hussein in Baghdad in December 1983, six weeks after Iraq had for the first time used chemical weapons against Iranian troops in its war with Iran, but he failed to raise the matter with the dictator. Instead he discussed the laying of an oil pipeline from Iraq to the Jordanian port of Aqaba, with the prospect of the contract going to Bechtel Corporation of San Francisco.[35] In 1988 Rumsfeld tried for a presidential nomination but lost once again to Bush Sr. Part of the reason was his reputation for aggressive language and behavior. In 1994 he was a non-executive director of European engineering giant ABB when it won a $200 million contract for two light water nuclear reactors to be supplied to North Korea by the United States, South Korea, and Japan in return for North Korea shutting down its heavy nuclear reactors.[36]

Though Rumsfeld became chairman of Senator Bob Dole's campaign for presidency in 1996, Dole did not adopt him as his running mate. The House of Representatives speaker, Republican Newt Gingrich, asked him to run a commission on the missile threat. In 1998 he actively promoted the passage of the Iraq Liberation Act, which made regime change in Baghdad official U.S. policy. By mid-2000, however, he had retired and gone to live on a large estate in Taos, New Mexico, with Joyce, his wife of forty-eight years. Rumsfeld's brief retirement ended in December with a phone call from Cheney. His performance at the Pentagon showed all the signs of an old man in a hurry. His pace quickened after 9/11.

The Pentagon's easy triumph over the Taliban in Afghanistan—a political entity that lacked a properly trained army and air force—secured with an innovative military strategy and deployment of fewer than ten thousand soldiers, emboldened the U.S. hawks to focus on Iraq. Rumsfeld felt confident employing a variation of the Afghan war template to overthrow Saddam's regime. They got a go-ahead in principle from President Bush.

"My hope is that all nations will . . . eliminate the terrorist parasites who threaten their countries and our own," Bush said in his State of the Union address to Congress on January 29, 2002. "Our second goal is to prevent regimes that sponsor terror from threatening America or our friends and allies with weapons of mass destruction. . . . North Korea is a regime arming with missiles and weapons of mass destruction, while starving its citizens. Iran aggressively pursues these weapons and exports terror. . . . Iraq continues to flaunt its hostility toward America and to support terror. . . . This is a regime that has something to hide from the civilized world. States like these, and their terrorist allies, constitute an axis of evil, arming to threaten the peace of the world." He also warned that "I will not wait on events."[37]

Bush's speech gave currency to the term "axis of evil," which soon turned into a Bush doctrine. Yet the origins of the term lay in the phrase "axis of hate," which David Frum, the president's junior speechwriter, had initially used—only to see "hate" changed to "evil" by Michael Gerson, a very religious Bush chief speechwriter.[38] So the Bush administration adopted the momentous doctrine of "axis of evil" almost by accident, and without any top-level debate.

In any case, since Iraq, Iran, and North Korea had not forged a pact against the United States, they did not constitute an axis in the way Nazi Germany, Fascist Italy, and militarist Japan, sharing a common authoritarian, expansionist ideology, did in World War II. As it was, the fifteen-member European Union was committed to pursuing a policy of constructive engagement with Iran, a country that had been hostile to the Taliban from its inception in 1994. Furthermore, since Iran and Iraq had not signed a peace treaty following their eight-year war in the 1980s, they were technically still at war.

None of this mattered to Rumsfeld, who had already asked General Franks to prepare a "conceptual" war plan on Iraq. The first draft envisioned a variation of the 1991 Gulf War, with four hundred thousand soldiers attacking Iraq from the south (Kuwait), north (Turkey), and west (Jordan). "Too troop-heavy," noted Rumsfeld, recommending an enhanced use of intelligence and Special Forces (as in Afghanistan), precision bombing, and blitzkrieg-style armored advances, with tanks and armored personnel carriers racing toward Baghdad at top speed instead of moderating their pace for the slower fuel truck to catch up. A realistic Rumsfeld also ignored the advice of Wolfowitz, who, relying on Chalabi, offered a conceptual war plan with seventy-five thousand troops hooking up with the rebellious Shias and Kurds, respectively, in the south and the north, and overthrowing Saddam's regime within days, a variant of the unrealistic Downing-Clarridge plan (see Epilogue). In the end, after several drafts over the next ten months, Rumsfeld would settle for 250,000 soldiers—with 150,000 in the theater and the rest on standby in Europe. Among the tasks assigned to the Special Forces would be searching for Iraq's WMD and missile launchers. Rumsfeld would also finally end up eschewing the ten-to fourteen-day air campaign before ground fighting by mounting—unannounced—Operation "Southern Focus" in August 2002.[39]

SADDAM AS BIN LADEN'S SURROGATE

When Bush and his senior advisers began discussing the second phase of the war on terror, with Iraq very much at the top of their list, they realized that they had to tackle the crucial question of establishing Iraq's complicity in 9/11. The Senate majority leader, Democrat Tom Daschle, knew that after a thorough investigation, U.S. intelligence agencies had concluded that Iraq was not involved in the September 11 terrorist attacks—a conclusion that would be confirmed in March 2002 in London by a report by John Scarlett, chairman of Britain's Joint Intelligence Committee (JIC).[40] In Prague, the authorities now conceded that they were no longer certain of the Saddam–Al Qaida connection. And after examining thousands of documents, FBI and CIA analysts found no evidence that Atta left or traveled to the United States in April 2001, when he was supposed to be in Prague. "We ran down literally hundreds of thousands of leads [and found nothing]," revealed FBI director Robert Mueller in April 2002.[41]

According to the longtime Saudi intelligence chief, Prince Turki, who possessed volumes of secret information on Iraq and bin Laden, "Iraq does not come very high in the estimations of bin Laden. He thinks of Saddam Hussein as an apostate, an infidel or someone who is not worthy of being a fellow Muslim."[42] Jamal al Fadl, a key Al Qaida defector, said there were individual Iraqis in Al Qaida but there was no specific Iraqi group that Al Qaida was backing. He repeatedly testified to the U.S. authorities that bin Laden criticized Saddam "sometimes for attacking Muslims and killing women and children, but most importantly for not believing in 'most of Islam,' " and for setting up his own political party, the Baath [Socialist Party]."[43] During his stay in Sudan from 1991 to 1996, bin Laden had denounced the leaders of the Yemen Socialist Party as apostates, and his partisans had resorted to assassinating them. The secular credentials of the Arab Baath Socialist Party were highlighted by the fact that Tariq Aziz (a.k.a. Mikhail Yahunna), Iraq's deputy prime minister and chief spokesman for the Western media, was Christian.[44] Until the mid-1990s the Iraqi government ran a brewery, producing beer and *arak* (liquor). Basra, a city of 1.37 million, had 150 liquor shops. Under the circumstances, the idea of a Saddam–Al Qaida alliance seemed bizarre.

Bin Laden and his colleagues were more concerned about the fate of the Iraqi people. On the eve of the formation of the World Islamic Front for Jihad against Crusaders and Jews—World Islamic Front (WIF) for short—on February 23, 1998, they referred to "the Americans' continuing aggression against the Iraqi people, using the Peninsula as the staging post. . . . Despite the great devastation inflicted on the Iraqi people by the Crusader–Zionist alliance, and despite the huge number of those killed, which has exceeded one million . . . the Americans are once again trying to repeat the horrific massacres as though they are not satisfied with the protracted blockade imposed after the ferocious war or the fragmentation and devastation [of Iraq]."[45]

Given this, it was not surprising that the documents found by Inigo Gilmore of the *Sunday Telegraph* in the bombed headquarters of the General Intelligence Department (*Mukhabarat*) in Baghdad in late April 2003 referred to the period after the formation of the World Islamic Front. These papers included a letter attached to a "Top Secret and Urgent" document that said that the envoy was a trusted aide of Osama bin Laden. "According to the above, we suggest permission to call the Khartoum station [of the Iraqi *Mukhabarat*] to facilitate the travel arrangements for the abovementioned person to Iraq, and that our body [should] carry all the travel and hotel costs inside Iraq to gain the knowledge of the message from bin Laden and convey to his envoy an oral message from us to bin Laden." The envoy stayed at Mansour Melia Hotel in Baghdad in March. The common starting point was hatred of the United States and Saudi Arabia. The talks continued for a week, the idea under discussion being a possible visit to Baghdad by bin Laden, then based in Afghanistan. Nothing came of it, even though the *Mukhabarat* representatives later visited the Afghan city of Kandahar.[46] Since bin Laden regarded Saddam as a *munafiq* (meaning a hypocrite, one who claims to be Muslim while leading an un-Islamic life), the ideological differences between the two proved insurmountable. Also, bin Laden was uninterested in any alliance with

Saddam, as he was not prepared to be beholden to him. Summing up, one well-placed British intelligence source told the *Guardian*, "We are aware of fleeting contacts [between Iraq and Al Qaida] in the past, but there were no long term official contacts."

Yet Bush and his predominantly hawkish senior advisers remained intransigent, buoyed by opinion polls that showed 88 percent support for military action against Iraq. "All the three countries I mentioned [Iraq, Iran, and North Korea] are now on notice that we intend to take their development of weapons of mass destruction very seriously," reiterated Bush.

U.S. officials argued that the administration had to have a plan to preclude the prospect of a terrorist group obtaining WMD from Iraq. Out of this eventuality arose the doctrine of a preemptive strike—early unilateral action against a foe suspected of posing a future threat to the United States, a radical departure from the traditional policy of a defensive war sanctified by international law as set out in the UN Charter's Article 51 and Article 2(4).[47]

The Bush team offered its scenario, based on *two* preconditions, as something novel. But it was not. The second Clinton administration had appointed a National Advisory Panel to Assess Domestic Response Capabilities for Terrorism to examine such an eventuality. In its December 1999 report, it concluded that the "rogue states" would hesitate to entrust such weapons to terrorists because of the likelihood that such a group's actions might be unpredictable even to the point of using the weapon against its sponsor—adding that the rogue states themselves would be unlikely to use such weapons due to the prospect of "significant reprisals."[48] Referring to the practicalities of WMD transfer from the Iraqi government to Islamist terrorists, Andrew Mack, director of the Human Security Center at the University of British Columbia, noted that the number of people involved in such an exercise would make concealment of Baghdad's role almost impossible over the long term, and that the mere revelation of such transfers would bring massive U.S. military retaliation against Saddam's regime.[49]

As it happens, the arrest of six North Africans in London on January 5, 2003, for possessing a small quantity of ricin—a chemical poison for which there is no known vaccine or treatment—undermined the very basis of the argument offered by the administrations of Bush and Blair. Since ricin is made from castor beans, there is no need for terrorists to approach any government: They can buy the raw material at a local store.

However, creating fearful scenarios was a major ploy in the scheme of the neocons, who—believing that civilized Western democracies were under constant threat from the unsavory, undemocratic parts of the non-Western world—were keen to restore the national-security state in the United States that had become de rigueur during the Cold War. The first step in that direction was an increased budget for the Pentagon. They succeeded. The $2.13 trillion federal budget for October 2002–September 2003 that Bush presented to Congress in early February showed a 13.7 percent rise in defense expenditure—taking it to $379 billion—compared to 2 percent for education.[50] Most of the extra cash for defense was earmarked for developing and producing advanced conventional and nuclear weapons. How such weapons would abet the fight against terrorists, engaged largely in guerrilla attacks or suicide bombings, remained unclear. Not that it mattered.

After conferring with Cheney in one of their frequent one-on-one meetings, Bush seemed to have decided in early March 2002 to oust Saddam by force. The initial, tentative plan was to invade Iraq with up to 250,000 troops in the following autumn—a date that would later be moved to early 2003 to allow the United States to build up its petroleum reserves to counter the expected oil price shock and to restock the high-tech weaponry that had been exhausted in the Afghanistan war. "F—k Saddam; we're taking him out," Bush reportedly announced, poking his head into the office of National Security Adviser Condoleezza Rice in March 2002.[51] Bush signed a new Intelligence Order on Iraq, allocating an extra $150 million to the CIA to increase intelligence-gathering in Iraq. And he apparently gave a go-ahead to Rumsfeld to build up the stocks of the high-tech weapons—an enterprise expected to take upward of eight months.

This was the backdrop against which Cheney—confident of the goodwill he had established in the Middle East as a highly trustworthy U.S. secretary of defense before and during the 1991 Gulf War—undertook a tour to engender a "new agenda" for the region: an anti-Baghdad coalition and an antiterrorism campaign to replace the "old agenda" of resolving the Israeli-Palestinian conflict, which had bedeviled Israeli-Arab relations since 1948, when Israel was founded.

He drew a blank. This became obvious in Bahrain, the headquarters of the U.S. Fifth Fleet. At a joint press conference with Cheney, when asked whether Bahrain would support military action against Iraq, Bahrain's foreign minister, Salman ibn Hamad al Khalifa, said: "In the Arab world the threat is perceived quite differently. The people who are dying today on the streets are not a result of any Iraqi action. The people are dying as a result of an Israeli action. And likewise people in Israel are dying as a result of action taken in response [by the Palestinians]."[52]

U.S. hawks got more bad news. The Arab League summit, held in Beirut in late March, resolved to reject "exploitation of war on terrorism to threaten any Arab country and use of force against Iraq," and went on to praise the eighteen-month-old Second Palestinian Intifada against the Israeli occupation. What further upset U.S. hard-liners was the sight of Saudi Crown Prince Abdullah embracing Izzat Ibrahim, vice president of Iraq's Revolutionary Command Council, dressed in traditional Arab garb, before television cameras—to enthusiastic clapping by the audience—thus signaling normalization of relations between Iraq and Saudi Arabia after twelve years. Next followed a handshake between Ibrahim and Kuwaiti foreign minister Sabah al Ahmad al Sabah, after the former had signed a document recognizing Kuwait's sovereignty and security.

Undeterred, Bush publicly announced in April a policy of

"regime change" in Baghdad. At the same time the administration's clandestine activities in the region were picking up pace. In early spring Centcom dispatched its Special Forces units to Iraqi Kurdistan, while the British government sent Special Air Services (SAS) units to the area, despite the professed ambivalence of the Kurdish opposition leaders, Masud Barzani and Jalal Talabani. During their clandestine meeting with American officials in Frankfurt, Germany, in April, they were asked to host two full-time CIA missions in their territories.

While the plans to "take out Saddam" were being devised in Washington, at the United Nations, Secretary-General Kofi Annan held a series of meetings with Iraqi foreign minister Naji Sabri to resolve the continuing differences between Baghdad and the United Nations. Annan wanted to discuss the readmission of UN inspectors to disarm Iraq, whereas Sabri wanted to talk about the lifting of UN sanctions and no-fly zones. The Annan-Sabri talks made little progress, while the discussion between the technical experts of both sides made some headway. These talks reconvened in early July in Vienna. Under U.S. pressure, Annan refused to open up the discussion beyond the modalities of the return of UN inspectors, and rejected Sabri's proposal that the United Nations acknowledge up front what had been achieved until December 1998 (when Chief Inspector Richard Butler withdrew his inspectors to enable the Clinton administration to bomb Iraq under its 100-hour-long Operation "Desert Fox"), and state that sanctions would be lifted fully if the inspectors found nothing objectionable. In reply Annan referred to the provisions in Security Council Resolution 1284 (December 1999): The inspectors would take sixty days to produce a work program *after* they had been let into Iraq. That resolution, however, remained to be accepted by Baghdad. Furthermore, Iraq tried to seek assurances from the Security Council that the United States would abandon its regime-change agenda if inspectors were allowed back. But they could not give such a guarantee, as they were not the ones to formulate Washington's foreign policy.

In early July, the *New York Times* published the outline of a five-inch-thick dossier on the "concept" of war on Iraq. It specified forces based on air, land, and sea to invade Iraq from the north, west, and south, with the use of combat aircraft from the bases in the six Gulf monarchies, Jordan, and Turkey.[53] The dossier contained precise details of the Iraqi military bases, surface-to-air missile sites, air-defense networks, and fiber-optic communications. The extraordinary list of targets led one military expert to describe it as "almost flagrant."

In the coming weeks there was a series of leaks about conflicting war plans, clearly designed to confuse the military planners in Baghdad. One of these involved mounting a proxy war against Iraq by using U.S. Special Forces, the CIA, Iraqi dissidents, and selective air strikes—a pet project of (Retired) General Wayne Downing of the Special Forces, now holding an important post at the National Security Council. Another leak described General Franks dismissing Downing's plan as insufficient to overthrow Saddam.

None of the leaks dealt with what Saddam would do as U.S. military buildup around Iraq got going. And regimes like Saddam's were not in the habit of leaking their war plans to the press, not even to confound the enemy.

The Bush team activated the Iraqi opposition groups, including the Iraqi National Congress and its leader, Ahmad Chalabi. Chalabi, already close to the pro-Israel lobby, the American-Israeli Public Affairs Committee, and the Jewish Institute of National Security Affairs, had forged ties with Rumsfeld, Feith, and Libby and had a high profile in the American media. Rumsfeld and Cheney embraced the INC and Chalabi. But, aware of their rejection by all of the Arab states and the European Union (except Britain), the State Department shunned them. When challenged by the Pentagon to find an alternative to the INC, the State Department approached numerous Iraqi exiles with military backgrounds not attached to the INC or the Iraqi National Accord

(INA) and urged them to come together. This led to the gathering of some sixty former Iraqi military officers in mid-July in London, the leading center of Iraqi exiles, to form the Iraqi Military Alliance (IMA).

The IMA declared itself ready to join "any effort to establish a new democratic federal regime, based on the rule of law and civil society," welcomed "any foreign help" to rid the country of Saddam, and urged all Iraqi soldiers inside and outside Iraq to work jointly to achieve this. It elected a military council of fifteen, including Najib al Salhi, a former Iraqi Republican Guard commander who participated in the Shia uprisings against Saddam after the 1991 Gulf War and was injured, and who would later emerge briefly as a rival to Chalabi.

From the U.S. hawks' viewpoint, the IMA, though sponsored by the State Department, served the objective of providing a military dimension to the predominantly civilian INC. All this was part of the psychological warfare against Saddam that they had unleashed, unannounced, while keeping alive the threat of a military option to overthrow his regime.

Much to their satisfaction, the debate on Iraq had by now come to revolve around "how" to oust Saddam, and no longer around "why." Only by offering strong reasons for the "why" aspect of the issue could President Bush expect to carry with him not only the skeptical Europeans and Arabs but also the U.S. public and Congress, argued Senator John Kerry, a veteran of the Vietnam War and a potential Democratic presidential nominee. The task was not simply toppling Saddam's regime with force, but also maintaining a large body of peacekeepers in Iraq for several years and investing in the country's reconstruction, he added. Among those who shared Kerry's views—albeit privately—was Powell, it would transpire later.[54] "If we are to achieve our strategic objectives in Iraq, a military campaign very likely would have to be followed by a large-scale, long-term military occupation," wrote Brent Scowcroft, the national security adviser to President Bush Sr., in an August 15, 2002, *Wall Street Journal* article.

At the Pentagon, while the debate was dominated by such civilian hawks as Wolfowitz and Feith, their military chiefs preferred the option of achieving regime change through Saddam's assassination or deteriorating health. The soldiers opposed the use of force. The policy of military and economic containment—naval enforcement of sanctions, no-flight zones, continuous presence of 26,500 U.S. troops in the region, rigorous UN administration of Iraqi oil sales, and continued UN supervision of Iraq's imports—had prevented Saddam from upgrading his armor and air force, two-thirds of which had become obsolete, and had severely reduced Baghdad's military threat, and should continue.[55] The military chiefs were, of course, unaware of the president's resolve to "take out" Saddam, which, it would later transpire, was God's instruction to Bush.

Bush's decision remained unaffected by the declaration of Dr. Hans Blix, the soft-spoken, chubby-faced, septuagenarian executive chairman of the United Nations Monitoring, Verification and Inspection Commission (Unmovic) on August 25, 2002, that there was "no clear-cut evidence" that Iraq possessed weapons of mass destruction.[56] Nobody was claiming an Iraqi breakthrough in the nuclear field in the near future, least of all the International Atomic Energy Agency (IAEA). Regarding biological-warfare agents—about which Unmovic's predecessor, United Nations Special Commission (Unscom), had described Iraqi disclosures as "incomplete, inadequate and technically flawed"—the major problem the possessor of these agents faced was maintaining them in a stable condition. The potency of any such agents, weaponized, at the latest, during the run-up to the 1991 Gulf War, would have by now expired—since five years is their average shelf life.

The White House made public the CIA's analysis that Baghdad owned 2,650 gallons of anthrax. Even if it did, however, Baghdad lacked the means of delivery. Of the 819 medium- and long-range missiles that it once possessed, all except two had been accounted for and destroyed by the UN inspectors. The Pentagon's worst-case analysis was that Iraq had about a dozen Al Hussein Scud-B missiles, with a 410-mile (650-km) range, but they were not assembled—and their components were not found after the Anglo-American invasion of Iraq in 2003.

Despite continuing lack of hard evidence to prove Iraq's possession of WMD, the Bush administration had succeeded in creating a wellspring of hatred of Iraq by repeating and reiterating its unproven charges. Its success on this front contrasted with its dismal failure to find the domestic source of the anthrax that killed five Americans and created nationwide alarm for weeks. In June 2002, Bush declared that he would launch preemptive attacks against countries "believed to be a serious threat to America," adding that Iraq posed "a continuing, unusual and extraordinary threat to the national security of the United States."

The debate on Iraq intensified during the next several weeks in the country at large and among Bush's close advisers. Cheney and Rumsfeld had frequent private meetings with the president, urging unilateral military action to topple Saddam; Powell, lacking the intimacy the Cheney–Rumsfeld duo enjoyed, sought to apprise Bush of the dangers of such action on the stability of the Middle East, the antiterrorist coalition, and a domestic economy burdened by the heavy cost of occupying Iraq. Powell finally got a chance to express his viewpoint at length on the eve of Bush's departure for a vacation at his 1,600-acre ranch at Crawford, Texas, on August 6. When Bush asked him to outline his alternative, Powell replied that means had to be found to co-opt allies, and one way to do so was to approach the UN Security Council to authorize the use of force against Iraq. Bush went along with the idea of cobbling together a coalition—something he had done in collaboration with Powell for the war in Afghanistan.[57] But, given his poor memory and his sheer inability to grasp details, Bush seems to have forgotten that, prodded by French president Chirac, the UN Security Council had given the United States carte blanche to punish those who had perpetrated the 9/11 outrages in the form of Resolution

1368. Nor, it seems, did Powell make this crucial point to him. But one thing Bush must have known: A president would be foolhardy to attack a sovereign nation without having his secretary of state on board. For that reason alone, Bush had to take Powell's advice seriously—or at least appear to do so.

In any case, the weighty subject needed to be discussed by the NSC. At the NSC meeting in Washington on August 16, Powell stated that a unilateral invasion of Iraq would damage NATO, enhance the image of the trigger-happy United States, and intensify anti-American feelings not only in the Arab and Muslim world but also in Europe. Therefore, he argued, the administration should approach other countries and invite them to join in, and added that taking the Iraq issue to the United Nations would help maintain international support without precluding other options. After Bush had asked each of the participants to comment, a consensus emerged to give the United Nations a try, with Cheney and Rumsfeld agreeing reluctantly.

For Powell, this had been an uphill battle. Though number three in the U.S. government, he lacked the access to the president that Rumsfeld and Rice—both junior to him in official status—had. It dawned on him slowly that there was something amiss: He lacked a rapport with Bush Jr., something he had had with Bush Sr. In May 2002, after sixteen months on the job, he requested private time with Bush to establish a rapport. They settled for weekly twenty- to thirty-minute sessions in the presence of Rice, who, as national security adviser, had her office at the White House.

Condoleezza Rice was personally close to both George and Laura Bush partly because, as a single woman without any siblings, husband, lover, children, or close friends, who often ate take-away food at her apartment, her personal life was uncommonly lonely. This drove her to immerse herself totally in her work at the White House. What she shared with George Walker Bush was her passion for American football, which she had acquired from her father, a high school teacher who also coached the sport. A dedicated athlete who works out daily, she briefly considered becoming a professional ice-skater.

As the only child of well-off African-American parents in Birmingham, Alabama, and a prodigy on piano, Condoleezza—named after the Italian musical term *con dolcezza*, "with sweetness"—became the center of parental love as well as the object of high hopes. She gave her parents much to be proud of. She enrolled at the University of Denver in 1970—at age fifteen—with the intention of majoring in music, but soon realized that she lacked the talent to become a concert pianist, her childhood ambition.[58] She got engaged to a football player in the Denver Broncos, but they did not make it to the altar. A chance attendance of a lecture on Soviet dictator Joseph Stalin by Professor Josef Korbel—a refugee from Czechoslovakia and father of Madeleine (who, as Madeleine Korbel Albright, would become U.S. secretary of state during Clinton's second presidency)—made Rice switch to political science and learn Russian, her third European language after French and Spanish. She pursued her interest in the Soviet Union further at the University of Notre Dame, where she secured a master's degree. Returning to her alma mater, she obtained a doctorate in Denver in 1981. A year earlier, disappointed by President Carter's handling of the Soviet military intervention in Afghanistan in 1979, she had abandoned her loyalty to the Democratic Party by voting for Republican Ronald Reagan. Since then she has been, in her words, "an all-over-the-map Republican."

In 1981 she became the first woman to be awarded a fellowship at the Center for International Security and Arms Control at the elite Stanford University, California. It was here in 1984 that she drew the attention of Brent Scowcroft, then head of the U.S. Commission on Strategic Forces, during the discussion that followed his lecture on Washington's strategic forces. He was impressed by the contribution this tense, skinny African-American scholar with a domed forehead made to the intellectual deliberation that day at Stanford. That year she published *Uncertain*

Allegiance: The Soviet Union and the Czechoslovak Army, followed by *The Gorbachev Era* (1986) with Alexander Dallin. When Scowcroft became national security adviser to President George Bush Sr. in 1989, he appointed Rice senior director of Soviet and East European affairs at the National Security Council, and special assistant to the president on national security affairs. While introducing her to the Soviet leader Mikhail Gorbachev (r. 1986–91), Bush Sr. described her as "the woman who tells me everything I know about the Soviet Union."

In March 1991, Rice returned to Stanford University. However, the two years at the White House had given her a sufficiently high public profile to win her a seat at the board of directors of Chevron (now ChevronTexaco) Corporation, to be followed later by Charles Schwab Corporation and the Hewlett Foundation—with Chevron naming a 136,000-deadweight-ton, double-hulled ship after her.[59] In 1993 she was promoted to provost, the number two administrator, of Stanford University, and became the first woman and the first African-American to hold that office. A conservative Republican, she voted against a resolution to make affirmative action a criterion in selecting professors, a step that made her unpopular with students, both black and white. In 1995 she published *Germany Unified and Europe Transformed*.

Her big political break came in 1998 when, during his vacation at the Bush family retreat in Kennebunkport, Maine, George Walker Bush, then governor of Texas, invited her to go fishing with him off the New England coast. They reportedly spent as much time discussing football as ballistic missile defense.

When Bush Jr. decided to run for the presidency, Rice became an adviser to his campaign. She began coaching him in foreign affairs. Since her specialization extended only to the former Soviet Union and Eastern Europe, she limited herself to that region, with Bush Jr. picking up some understanding of the Middle East and the Muslim world from such Likud Zionists as Richard Perle. As the winner of the two highest teaching awards at Stanford, the articulate, clear-thinking, and concise Rice proved to be a fine coach for the inarticulate Bush Jr., with his embarrassingly short attention span. Among the traits they shared was their faith in the Bible. While Bush turned to the Good Book at forty after he had been cured of alcoholism with the assistance of evangelist Billy Graham, Rice, the daughter of a Presbyterian minister, had grown up in a deeply religious environment. Given this, Rice and Bush developed an uncommon rapport, and their friendship became both personal and political.

By all accounts, Rice is more than an adviser to Bush. "It's a mind-meld," says James Lindsay of the Brookings Institution, quoting *Star Trek*. "There is in this relationship with the president the sense that before she tells the president something, she figures out where she thinks he's at." This dovetailed with Bob Woodward's assessment of Rice in his *Bush at War*: Her modus operandi is "not to commit herself unless the president pressed." Some attribute to Rice an uncanny ability to articulate Bush's famed "gut instincts," giving them texture and intellectual cohesion, thus rendering a unique service to Bush, noted for his simplistic thoughts expressed in simple sentences delivered "two or three words . . . at a time . . . speaking slowly . . ."—with his forehead furrowed and his deeply hooded eyes half-shut.

While Rice lacked the sort of standing that Cheney and Rumsfeld had built up over decades in the Republican Party, and was woefully bereft of gravitas, she contributed a good deal as an academic and intellectual to the conceptualization of the Bush administration's national security policy, covering not only foreign and defense affairs but also homeland security in the post-9/11 era. She would go on to prepare the first draft of *The National Security Strategy of the United States*, to be published on September 20, 2002, in which she emphasized America's "imperial" destiny, to the extent that even Bush found the document so overbearing or arrogant in parts that, according to White House sources, he edited it heavily.

Unlike the reedy Rice, the fleshy-faced, robustly built Colin
Luther Powell possessed gravitas as well as an illustrious career in
the military. He became a nationally recognized face during the
1991 Gulf War, when he was chairman of the Joint Chiefs of Staff
under President Bush Sr., a job he held from October 1989 to September 1993, well into the Clinton presidency. Because he was registered as an independent, and because he had served in both the
Republican and Democratic administrations, both parties tried to
woo him. His national standing was high in 1995, when his auto-
biography, *My American Journey*, became a number-one best-seller.

Born in the Harlem neighborhood of New York City to
Jamaican immigrants, and brought up in the South Bronx, Powell
had a remarkable story to tell. While studying geology at the City
College of New York, he joined the Reserve Officers Training
Corps (ROTC), graduated in 1958 at the top of his ROTC class,
and found his calling as a soldier. Powell was one of the sixteen thousand military advisers that President John F. Kennedy (r. 1961–63)
sent to South Vietnam to fight Vietnamese Communists in
1962. After being wounded while on patrol along the Viet-
namese-Laotian border the following year, he won the Purple
Heart and the Bronze Star, the first of the eleven decorations he
would receive in his thirty-five years in the military. A Democrat
in those days, he supported the campaign of Lyndon Johnson.
During his second assignment to Vietnam, in 1968–69, he was
injured in a helicopter crash. Back in the United States, he earned
an MBA at George Washington University in Washington, D.C.;
after being promoted to major, he won a White House fellowship.
He was assigned to the Office of Management and Budget (OMB)
during the administration of Richard Nixon, where he made a
lasting impression on Caspar Weinberger and Frank Carlucci, the
director and deputy director, respectively, of the OMB. He then
served as a battalion commander in South Korea and held a staff
job at the Pentagon. After finishing a course at the Army War
College, he was promoted to brigadier general and put in charge

of a brigade of the 101st Airborne Division. Following the arrival of Jimmy Carter in the White House, he worked as an assistant to the deputy secretary of defense, and then to the secretary of energy. After serving as assistant commander and deputy commander of infantry divisions in Colorado and Kansas, he returned to Washington to become senior military assistant to Secretary of Defense Weinberger, whom he assisted during the U.S. invasion of Grenada (1983) and the air raid on Libya (1986).

Powell was one of the five people in the Pentagon who knew about the illegal shipment of arms to Nicaragua's Contra rebels, which was masterminded by Colonel Oliver North of the National Security Council, and involved "rogue elements" in the Pentagon and the NSC. They sold weapons to Iran clandestinely and used that money to finance arms shipment to the Contras in 1986 in violation of the congressional law banning weapons supplies to the Contras. Powell was called to testify before a congressional committee, albeit on camera. He was not charged with any wrong-doing.

He was dispatched to Frankfurt, West Germany, to command the Fifth Corps, but he was soon recalled to Washington to serve as deputy to Frank Carlucci, after the latter became national security adviser in the wake of the Iran-Contra scandal. In December 1987, Carlucci was appointed secretary of defense and Powell, now a lieutenant general, succeeded Carlucci. He was the first African-American to rise to that position, as he has been in every office he has held since.

Soon after becoming chairman of the Joint Chiefs of Staff in October 1989, four-star General Powell assisted President Bush Sr. in his invasion of Panama. Following his retirement from the military in September 1993, he joined Jimmy Carter and Senator Sam Nunn on a successful peacemaking expedition to Haiti, which led to a peaceful transfer of power from the military to the elected civilian government—his first purely political move.

When he registered as a Republican in 1995, he did so not for any compelling ideological commitment but for pragmatic reasons: He owed his career advancement mostly to the top officials in the Republican governments. But he lacked a constituency in the Republican Party and had no track record of campaigning for public office at any level. In short, he was a top-notch bureaucrat with a military background who thought and acted pragmatically.

Powell's lack of personal rapport with Bush Jr. was his other major weakness. In his tussles on Iraq with Cheney and Rumsfeld, therefore, he was greatly handicapped. And, after his early equivocation— when he tried to conciliate the option of pursuing the UN path to disarming Iraq with the repeated White House refrain of "regime change in Baghdad"—he tried to fudge the issue. For instance, in his meeting with the *USA Today* editorial board in early October 2002, he said, "Should Iraq be disarmed, then, in effect, you have a different kind of regime, no matter who's in [charge in] Baghdad."[60] In retrospect, however, much of this was pure waffle. For the final and irrevocable decision to attack Iraq had been made by the Bush-Cheney-Rumsfeld trio by the end of August, with the signing of the necessary papers on August 29, 2002.[61]

While ostensibly on vacation at his ranch, Bush had working sessions with Cheney and Rumsfeld. After one such session, Rumsfeld secretly ordered the Pentagon to mount Operation "Southern Focus," unveiling an air campaign against Iraq in the south as an unannounced prelude to an invasion by its ground forces some six months later. It was easy to withhold this fact because, assisted by Britain, the Pentagon had maintained no-fly zones in the south of Iraq since August 1992 and in the north since October 1991 by conducting ongoing air patrols over the regions, whereby U.S.–U.K. warplanes targeted those Iraqi defense facilities that tried to hit them. Under Operation "Southern Focus," the Pentagon widened its targets to include Iraqi command and control centers and the fiber-optic links between Baghdad and Basra and between Baghdad and Nasiriya carrying military communications. As the cables were buried and impossible to locate, the Pentagon focused on locating aboveground cable-repeater stations used to boost the weakening signals after a certain distance by using spy satellites, U-2 photo reconnaissance planes and drones, and targeting them with precision-guided weapons (PGWs). As a result, during the next four months the U.S.–U.K. aircraft would strike Iraqi targets forty-eight times, an eightfold increase over the first four months of 2002.[62]

Overall, the only unsettled element in the war plan was the exact date of invasion. That in turn depended on two factors, one fixed—weather in the Iraqi desert, where temperatures reach one hundred degrees Fahrenheit in early April; and the other variable—the Pentagon's progress in procuring high-tech weapons.

CHENEY BLOWS THE WAR TRUMPET

Working closely with Bush, Cheney cleared to the last word his speech on Iraq to the Veterans of Foreign Wars national convention in Nashville, Tennessee, on August 26, 2002. Bush and Cheney reckoned that a belligerent speech would convince the UN Security Council that Washington would go solo, and thus facilitate securing the council's assent on taking military action against Iraq. It would also make the international community realize that UN inspections would be effective only if they were supported by a serious threat of force against Baghdad.[63] But, when asked at a press conference at his Crawford ranch whether a decision to attack Iraq had been made, Bush replied, "When I say I'm a patient man, I mean I'm a patient man, and that we will look at all options, and we will consider all technologies available to us, and diplomacy and intelligence."[64] This was an exercise in dissimulation.

"The Iraqi regime has in fact been very busy enhancing its capabilities in the field of chemical and biological agents," Cheney told his audience. "And they continue to pursue the nuclear program they began so many years ago." How did he know? "We've gotten this from the first-hand testimony of defectors," he grimly revealed, "including Saddam's own son-in-law [Hussein Kamil Hassan, who defected in August 1995]."[65] Cheney had "no doubt" that Saddam had chemical and biological warfare agents, and said, "Many of us are convinced that Saddam Hussein will acquire nuclear weapons fairly soon." (His statement contradicted the one made by Blix a day earlier on NBC-TV.) He added that "a return of inspectors would provide no assurance whatsoever of his compliance with UN resolutions. On the contrary, there is a great danger that it would provide false comfort that Saddam was somehow 'back in the box.' " On this premise he conjured up an apocalyptic scenario. Armed with nuclear, chemical, and biological weapons—and the power that came from possessing 10 percent of the world's oil reserves—he said that "Saddam could be expected to seek domination of the entire Middle East, take control of a great portion of the world's energy supplies, directly threaten America's friends throughout the region, and subject the United States or any other nation to nuclear blackmail." In short, in the hands of a "murderous dictator" like Saddam, these weapons of mass destruction were "as grave a threat as can be imagined" and therefore, "the risks of inaction are far greater than the risk of action." As such, war with Iraq was "inevitable," he concluded. What added weight to Cheney's fiery speech was the statement made by Rumsfeld to U.S. Marines at Camp Pendleton in California the next day: "I don't know how many countries will participate in the event the president does decide that the risks of not acting are greater than the risks of acting. Doing the right thing at the onset may seem lonesome [a code word for unilateralism]."[66]

Though unaware of the background to Cheney's speech, the world at large took it to be official U.S. policy, given the political intimacy he enjoyed with Bush, who had summed it up thus: "When you're talking to Dick Cheney, you're talking to me. When Dick Cheney's talking, it's me talking."[67] After all, it was Cheney who, as Bush's running mate in the presidential election, had lent the Republican ticket gravitas, weight, and administrative experience at the federal level, in which Dubya was singularly deficient. But his mortality came to the fore when he suffered his fourth heart attack, which required a quadruple bypass, soon after the presidential election in early November 2000.

After his election, Cheney assembled a staff of fourteen foreign policy experts for his office, but did not limit himself to international affairs. He wandered freely across the whole policy spectrum—from energy to national security, tax cuts to education, defense to social security, and foreign affairs to the CIA. He began frequenting CIA headquarters in Langley, Virginia, during the summer of 2002 for meetings with the analysts dealing with Islamist terrorism and the Middle East, leaning on them to find a link between Saddam Hussein and Osama bin Laden, and the Iraqi dictator's possession of WMD, under the rubric of producing a more "forward leaning" interpretation of the threat posed by Saddam. Such visits by Cheney and his Chief of Staff Libby were designed to pressure low-level specialists interpreting raw intelligence, but also put CIA analysts and their boss, George Tenet, on the defensive.[68] At policy meetings Cheney posed detailed questions (to which he knew the correct answers) with the aim of showing flaws in his antagonist's reasoning. In the internal debates he never showed his hand, saving his advice for private sessions with Bush, whom he saw daily.

Cheney comes across as a quiet but lethally effective, wily character, adept at playing his cards close to the vest—like "a gambler from Cheyenne," in the words of a critic. His admirers describe him as the affable, half-smiling Buddha in a corner of the Oval Office, a description at odds with his snake-cold eyes behind designer glasses. Given to mumbling from the corner of his mouth while speaking, he is a singularly uninspiring public speaker. Away from the media glare, he is a rough, tireless creature—a glutton for information—to whom President Bush has left much of the day-to-day administration. On September 11, 2001, it was Cheney who, along with his personal physicians, was whisked away by Secret Service agents to an "undisclosed location"—a bunker somewhere under the mountains of Pennsylvania—and kept there incommunicado for three weeks. This provided him with ample opportunity to read books, an activity no one has yet associated with Bush.

Like Powell—who described his former boss at the Pentagon as "incisive, smart, never showing any more surface than was necessary"—Cheney acquired a high public profile in the 1991 Gulf War when he was secretary of defense. Unknown to most people, his prime achievement was to get the initially reluctant Saudi king Fahd to invite American forces to his kingdom to protect it from a possible attack by Iraq. Aware of the popular opposition, expressed firmly by the religious establishment, to the presence of infidel troops on holy Saudi soil, Fahd was loath to appeal to Washington to dispatch its troops to his realm. But without land bases in Saudi Arabia, the Pentagon would have had to rely exclusively on aircraft carriers, and that would have dragged out the war against Iraq. Cheney succeeded in achieving his aim of getting Fahd to invite U.S. forces to his kingdom by scaring him with satellite pictorial evidence that Iraqi warplanes were being loaded with chemical bombs, that Iraq had positioned surface-to-surface missiles in occupied Kuwait aimed at Saudi targets, and that Iraqi ground troops were poised along the Saudi border. As it was, the satellite images shown to Fahd and his aides had been doctored—a fact that could not have been unknown to Cheney. Contrary to Cheney's briefing to Fahd, the scouts of the Saudi military would find no sign of the Iraqi soldiers anywhere near the Saudi frontier.[69]

Cheney's cabinet post in March 1989 came twenty years after his first job in government, at the Cost of Living Council in the Office of Economic Opportunity at the Nixon White House. When Gerald Ford succeeded Nixon in August 1974, Cheney served as deputy to Rumsfeld, the president's chief of staff. When

Rumsfeld moved to the Pentagon, Cheney became the youngest chief of staff of the president ever. His taciturnity earned him the code name "Backseat" from the Secret Service.

Following Ford's defeat in the presidential election, Cheney returned to Casper, a town of forty thousand and the oil and financial center of Wyoming, where he had grown up after the transfer of his father, a soil conservation officer of the Department of the Interior, from Lincoln, Nebraska. A scholarship took him to Yale, where he failed twice. On his return to Casper, he briefly worked as a lineman for an electric company. He then enrolled at the University of Wyoming, Laramie, and obtained a master's degree in political science when he was twenty-five. Between 1963 and 1966, he got four deferments for the draft, and that saved him from fighting in Vietnam. "I had other priorities in the 1960s than military service," he would later explain lamely.

He became assistant to Wyoming's sole congressman, a Republican, and joined those gathered around Donald Rumsfeld, then an up-and-coming brash congressman from Chicago. He won the state's sole House seat in 1977, and kept his seat in the next five elections. During that decade he survived three heart attacks. From 1981 to 1987 he served as chairman of the Republican Policy Committee, and the following year he became the House minority whip.

His voting record was so conservative that only eleven Republicans were farther to the right of him; the American Conservative Union gave him a 90 percent rating, and the liberal Americans for Democratic Action gave him a record 4 percent rating. He cast negative votes on imposing sanctions on apartheid South Africa, busing to desegregate schools, a holiday to commemorate Martin Luther King, a call to release Nelson Mandela, and the Safe Drinking Water bill. During the Iran-Contra scandal in 1986, he stood up for the "rogue" right-winger Colonel Oliver North, who was indicted on twenty-three counts of conspiracy to defraud the United States. He was distrustful of Soviet leader Mikhail Gorbachev and of détente. "I have never seen a weapons system I have not liked," he once declared. Little wonder that the arms industry was delighted when he became defense secretary in January 1989. Later in the year, he masterminded the invasion of Panama, followed by a "regime change" whereby President General Manuel Noriega was arrested, tried in a U.S. court, and convicted.

Following the defeat of Bush Sr. in 1993, Cheney returned to Casper. The next year he seriously considered running for the presidency but found the task of raising funds on what an American wit has called "the rubber chicken circuit" tiresome.

On a fishing trip with right-wing businessmen friends in 1995 he was offered the job of chief executive officer of Halliburton, an oil-services company based in Houston, Texas, with Kellogg, Brown & Root, a construction company, as its subsidiary. In 1998 he merged Halliburton with Dresser Industries, and this made Halliburton the world's largest oil-services company. Later that year, when oil prices collapsed, Cheney changed accounting practice to allow the company to book revenues it had not received, thus inflating the profits by $89 million.[70] Halliburton did not disclose the accounting change to investors for more than a year. It was only when the *New York Times* exposed the scandal that the Securities and Exchanges Commission instituted an investigation. In addition, with the asbestos-damages claims on Dresser rising more than fourfold, Halliburton's stock price dwindled from $54 a share to $9 during the period from August to December 2000. Little wonder that the American public remains evenly divided on whether or not to trust Cheney.

Bush Jr., of course, trusted him completely when he adopted him as his running mate in September 2000, and still does. The fact that Bush Jr. had also been part of the Texan oil scene, although much earlier than Cheney, gave them something in common. But the differences between their personalities remained stark. Despite his heart attacks, Cheney maintained an intellectually curious mind. After 9/11, he embarked upon a program in self-education in Islam and the Middle East, holding periodic meetings with Bernard Lewis, a retired Princeton historian of Islam and Judaism—and, like Cheney, an uncritical supporter of Israel—and Fouad Ajami, who, as director of the Middle East program at the Johns Hopkins University, was a former colleague of Wolfowitz. A Shia Lebanese-American, Ajami was in thrall to Israel and Zionism, and regarded the idea of a Palestinian state as a "phantom."

In his August 26 speech, Cheney approvingly cited Ajami's conviction that after the liberation of Iraq by U.S. forces, the streets of Baghdad and Basra would "erupt in joy in the same way as the throngs in Kabul greeted the Americans."[71] Cheney's failure to make any reference to the United Nations in his speech left Powell feeling betrayed. After all, at the last NSC meeting on August 16, chaired by Bush, they had agreed unanimously to give the United Nations a try. Now, noted Powell, the reaction to Cheney's speech was universally negative—from Canada to the Middle East via Europe, including Britain, where Blair, while agreeing with Bush on the ominous threat posed by Saddam, advised him in a telephone conversation not to bypass the UN Security Council. According to U.K. ambassador Sir Christopher Meyer, Blair said to Bush, "If you want to do this [attack Iraq] you can do it on your own; you have the military strength to go into Iraq and do it, but our advice to you is: 'Even the great superpower like the U.S. needs to do this with partners and allies.' "[72]

In France and Germany, the reaction to Cheney's speech was more robust. French president Jacques Chirac criticized "attempts to legitimize the deployment of unilateral and preemptive use of force"—not least because other nations would use this as a pretext to settle their own disputes. "This runs contrary to the vision of the collective security of France, a vision that is based on cooperation among states, respect of the law and the authority of the Security Council," he said. "We shall repeat these rules as often as needed, and notably over Iraq."[73] His stance did *not* constitute an endorsement of Saddam's government, Chirac stressed in an interview with the *New York Times.* "I condemn the regime in Iraq for all the reasons we know, for all the dangers it puts on the region and the tragedy it constitutes for the Iraqi people who are held hostage by it," he said. "I do wish for it [deposition of Saddam]."

Blair's Social Democrat counterpart in Germany—the most populous nation in the European Union, and ranking third in the world's economies—Chancellor Gerhard Schroeder, facing an upcoming election, asked why there was suddenly this urgency about Iraq when there was no new evidence of its acquiring WMD. He ruled out Germany's participation in any U.S.-led invasion of Iraq, even with UN and EU mandates. With two-thirds of Germans opposed to war, Schroeder's unambiguous stance on the subject would win him the closely contested election.

Electoral considerations were at work in the United States as well.

NOTES

1. *Ha'aretz* (Tel Aviv), June 24, 2003.
2. One side effect of Security Council Resolution 1368 was that Washington promptly paid its long-standing arrears of more than $1 billion to the UN.
3. *International Herald Tribune,* September 17, 2001; *Daily Telegraph,* September 23, 2001.
4. *New York Times,* October 10, 2001.
5. Bob Woodward, *Bush at War,* Simon and Schuster, New York and London, p. 49.
6. Cited in *Financial Times,* September 17, 2001.
7. Albert Wohlstetter's best-known work is *Between an Unfree World and None: Increasing Our Choices* (1985).
8. In a 1998 congressional hearing, he said, "Perhaps if we had delayed the cease-fire for a few more days, we might have got rid of Saddam." *Time,* March 31, 2003, p. 175.
9. The Nuclear Non-Proliferation Treaty (NNPT) went into effect in 1970; the Biological and Toxic Weapons Convention in 1975, and the Chemical Weapons Convention in 1997.
10. *Sunday Times Magazine,* July 6, 2003, pp. 47–48.
11. *New York Times* September 9, 1986.
12. The fact that, while the Bush Jr. administration, led by Paul Wolfowitz and his fellow hawks, sucked up even the slightest proof of Saddam's involvement in

international terrorism as supplied by the CIA-founded Iraqi National Congress, it paid scant attention to the forensic investigation by Laurie Mylroie, said much about her "evidence."

13. For the Iraqi National Congress and Ahmad Chalabi, see further Dilip Hiro, *The Essential Middle East: A Comprehensive Guide*, Carroll and Graf, New York, 2003, p. 219 and pp. 104–5, respectively.

14. A later inquiry by the investigative journalist Seymour Hersh would establish that these camps had been set up by the British Secret Intelligence service, MI6, to assist with Iraqi counterterrorism training after its civilian aircraft had been hijacked by pro-Tehran extremists in 1986 during the Iran–Iraq War. *New Yorker*, May 12, 2003.

15. Fedayeen Saddam—lit., Self-Sacrificers for Saddam—was an Iraqi militia under the command of Saddam Hussein's son Uday.

16. Bob Woodward, op. cit., p. 84.

17. *Guardian*, April 4, 2003, citing the PBS documentary *Blair's War,* shown a day earlier.

18. The estimates given by the World Health Organization in March 1996 were, "500,000 dead during 1990–94," and by Unicef in July 2000, "500,000 dead during 1991–98." *Guardian*, October 10, 2001.

19. Reuters, October 8, 2001; *The Times* (London), October 8, 2001.

20. See further Dilip Hiro, *The Essential Middle East*, pp. 95–98.

21. Bob Woodward, op. cit., p. 248.

22. Among other acolytes of Leo Strauss was Stephen Cambone, the undersecretary of defense for intelligence, who was especially close to Donald Rumsfeld.

23. The Pentagon had germ-warfare factories at Fort Detrick, Maryland (closed in 1969), and in Arkansas. In case these got destroyed, the Pentagon wanted mobile units. In 1997 Dr. Steven Hatfill took up a job at Fort Detrick, where he studied protection against deadly viruses like Ebola. In late 1998 he joined Science Applications International Corp., San Diego, and worked at its branch office in the Washington Metro area. In February 1999, he helped commission a paper by William Patrick, former head of product development at Fort Detrick, to assess the risk of anthrax spores sent through the mail. In it, the authors compared amateurishly produced anthrax with the weapons-grade variety. Based on information from a defecting Iraqi chemical engineer in late 1999, the United States concluded that Iraq was making mobile units to produce biological warfare agents. By early 2000 the Pentagon had set up a unit to build a mobile unit in the Washington Metro area—with a fermenter, centrifuge, and mill for grinding clumps of anthrax into small sizes to penetrate human lungs—to be taken to Fort Bragg, North Carolina, to train the Army's Delta Special Force to recognize it and make it harmless, or destroy it. *New York Times,* July 2, 2003.

24. *Independent on Sunday*, August 10, 2003.

25. The Defense Policy Board was established in 1985 during the Reagan presidency. Its predominantly Republican membership includes Dan Quayle, former vice president; Henry Kissinger, former secretary of state; James Schlesinger and Harold Brown, both former defense secretaries; Newt Gingrich, former speaker of the House of Representatives; and James Woolsey, former CIA director. Perle resigned as chairman in March 2003 due to a conflict-of-interest scandal, but was asked by Rumsfeld to stay on as a member. Its members have access to classified documents.

26. *Independent*, June 6, 2003. For a mere member of the quasi-official Defense Policy Board, he seemed to know quite a lot to make this claim.

27. For a full text of the report, visit <www.israeleconomy.org/strat1.htm>.

28. See further Dilip Hiro, *Neighbors, Not Friends: Iraq and Iran After the Gulf Wars*, Routledge, New York and London, 2001, p. 154.

29. See the website of Jude Wannaiski.

30. For "Revisionist Zionists," see Dilip Hiro, *The Essential Middle East*, pp. 446–47.

31. It was not surprising that when the members of the special intelligence unit set up by Israeli prime minister Ariel Sharon visited the Pentagon to confer with the Office of Special Plans, they were waved in on Douglas Feith's authority without having to fill out the usual clearance forms. *Guardian*, July 17, 2003.

32. Cited in *Guardian*, April 8, 2003.

33. *New York Times*, January 27, 2002.

34. See further Dilip Hiro, *War Without End: The Rise of Islamist Terrorism and Global Response*, Routledge, New York and London, 2002, p. 321.

35. Nothing came of this. Saddam wanted an assurance that Israel would not bomb the pipeline, and such a promise failed to materialize.

36. *Observer*, May 11, 2003.

37. See http://www.whitehouse.gov/news/2002/01/20020129–11.html.

38. That did not stop David Frum's wife from sending out e-mails to friends telling them that it was her husband who had coined the catchy phrase "axis of evil"— a step that would lead to the forced resignation of Frum.

39. *Time*, January 27, 2003, p. 20. See Map 1.

40. *Sunday Times*, March 10, 2002.

41. *Washington Post*, May 2, 2002.

42. *International Herald Tribune*, November 22, 2001.

43. *Washington Post*, September 30, 2001. It was the defection of Jamal al Fadl that gave the CIA its big break in its pursuit of Osama bin Laden. See further Dilip Hiro, *War Without End*, p. 247.

44. For Tariq Aziz's biography, see Dilip Hiro, *The Essential Middle East*, pp. 64–65.

45. See further Dilip Hiro, *The Essential Middle East*, pp. 572–73.

46. *Sunday Telegraph*, April 27, 2003; *Independent*, April 28, 2003.

47. The UN Charter's Article 2(4) reads, "All Members shall refrain in their international relations from the threat or use of force against the territorial

integrity or political independence of any state." Article 51 reads, "Nothing in the present Charter shall impair the inherent right of individual or collective self-defense if an armed attack occurs against a Member of the United Nations, until the Security Council has taken measures necessary to maintain international peace and security."

48. *Washington Post,* February 21, 2001. For the text of this report, "Assessing the Threat of Terrorism to the U.S.," visit http://www.rand.org/nsrd/terrpanel/. The subsequent reports, released annually, dealt with countering the threat, and listed forty-seven recommendations in five major areas: state and local government; health and medical capabilities; immigration and border controls; security against cyber attacks; and military roles and missions.

49. *International Herald Tribune,* October 10, 2002.

50. Ibid., February 2–3, 5, and 6, 2002.

51. *Time,* March 31, 2003, p. 172. Rice was conferring with three U.S. senators on how to deal with Iraq. "Bush waved his hand dismissively, recalls a participant, and neatly summed up his Iraq policy in that short phrase . . . [and then] left the room." Op. cit.

52. *International Herald Tribune,* March 18, 2002.

53. Subsequently, all eight countries would publicly oppose an invasion of Iraq. In practice, though, only Turkey, Oman, and the United Arab Emirates would stay out of the conflict completely.

54. Bob Woodward, op. cit., pp. 331–32.

55. Rehabilitating Iraq's military infrastructure with conventional arms would cost Baghdad an estimated $22 billion.

56. Interview on NBC-TV.

57. Bob Woodward, op. cit., pp. 332–34.

58. However, she did play the piano in a concert with cellist Yo-Yo Ma in Washington, D.C., in 2002, when she was forty-eight.

59. After Condoleezza Rice's appointment as national security adviser in 2001, Chevron changed the name to Altair Voyager.

60. *USA Today,* October 2, 2002. On the other hand, the hawkish John Bolton, number three at the State Department, said in mid-October, "All those fundamentally part of the Saddam regime will have to go. There will be no stability in the region until Saddam Hussein is gone."

61. *Washington Times,* September 3, 2003.

62. *Washington Post,* December 22, 2002, and July 20, 2003.

63. *Time,* March 31, 2003, p. 183.

64. Cited in *New York Times,* August 7, 2003.

65. The full record of Hussein Kamil Hassan's interview with the inspectors reveals that he also said that Iraq's stockpile of chemical and biological warheads, which were manufactured before the 1991 Gulf War, were destroyed—in many cases

in response to ongoing inspections. The interview, on August 22, 1995, was conducted by Rolf Ekeus, the head of Unscom, and two of his senior associates—Nikita Smidovich and Maurizio Zifferaro. "You have an important role in Iraq," Kamil Hassan said, according to the record prepared from Smidovich's notes. "You are very effective in Iraq." When Smidovich pointed out that the UN teams had not found "any traces of destruction," Kamil Hassan replied, "Yes, it was done before you came in [May 1991]." He also said that Iraq had destroyed its arsenal of warheads. "We gave instructions not to produce chemical weapons," Kamil Hasan revealed later in the debriefing. "All chemical weapons were destroyed. I ordered destruction of all chemical weapons. All weapons—biological, chemical, missile, nuclear—were destroyed." This was corroborated by Scott Ritter, Unscom chief inspector from May 1991 to August 1998, who had read the CIA and British MI6 scripts of their interviews with Hussein Kamil Hassan. *Independent on Sunday*, April 20, 2003.

66. Bob Woodward, op. cit., pp. 344–45.

67. *Sunday Times Magazine*, July 6, 2003, p. 44.

68. Another frequent visitor at CIA headquarters was Newt Gingrich, former House speaker, who re-emerged as a member of the Defense Advisory Board after 9/11 and often arrived at the agency as a personal emissary of the Office of Special Plans to urge the analysts to harden their assessments.

69. See further, Dilip Hiro, *Desert Shield to Desert Storm: The Second Gulf War*, Routledge, New York/HarperCollins, London, 1992, p. 116; pp. 121–22.

70. The new accounting practice was approved by the company's accountants, Arthur Andersen, with whom Cheney's relationship was so close that he appeared in an Andersen promotional video.

71. *Time*, March 31, 2003, p. 180. Dick Cheney conveniently forgot that the troops that were greeted in Kabul in November 2001 belonged to the Northern Alliance of Afghanistan and not the Pentagon, and that they arrived in a part of Kabul inhabited by ethnic Tajiks and not Pashtuns, the main backers of the Taliban.

72. *Guardian*, April 4, 2003, citing the PBS documentary *Blair's War*, shown on April 3, 2003. Tony Blair was reflecting domestic public opinion, with 52 percent opposed to British troops getting involved if the United States went into Iraq and 34 percent in favor. *Washington Post*, August 7, 2002.

73. *New York Times*, August 30, 2002.

CHAPTER 2

BIN LADEN MORPHED INTO SADDAM

"This administration has had a faith-based attitude. . . . 'We know the answers—give us the intelligence to support those answers.' "
—Gregory Thielmann, director of the State Department's Bureau of Intelligence and Research until September 2002[1]

ONCE THE LABOR DAY HOLIDAY, on September 2, was past, and Bush was back at the White House, he orchestrated a high-profile campaign geared primarily toward enhancing the Republicans' electoral performance at the November midterm congressional elections. Since Bush had lost the popular vote in the presidential election in November 2000 by half a million votes, he was desperate to have the Republicans regain control of the Senate and maintain their majority in the House.

The signs were unpromising. Bush's popularity rating had fallen to 63 percent, the lowest since 9/11, with approval for his foreign-policy handling down to 54 percent, a loss of fourteen points in a month. Equally disturbing was a *Los Angeles Times* poll that showed that while 28 percent regarded the economy and jobs as the most important issue facing the country, only 11 percent considered homeland security and terrorism their top priority.[2] At the same time, according to three-fifths of Americans, their government could not claim victory in its war against terrorism until and unless it had captured or killed Osama bin Laden. To counter this,

Karl Rove—an affable, outgoing man with a foghorn voice and thinning blond hair, affectionately called "the Man with the Plan" by Bush—recommended that the elusive bin Laden be metamorphosed into the very visible Saddam Hussein as the figure of burgeoning menace against whose regular forces the United States ought to stage a conventional war. This would prove to be a masterstroke that would enable Bush to turn Saddam into the most urgent issue on the planet on the eve of the midterm U.S. elections.

As the country prepared on September 11, 2002, to remember the 3,066 people who perished in the tragedy of 9/11, the Bush administration staged a well-crafted media campaign to sublimate bin Laden's atrocities and direct attention to Saddam. The idea was to channel the nation's grief and defiance, expressed at emotionally charged 9/11 anniversary ceremonies, into a national resolve to take the war on terrorism farther—to Iraq. By having Rumsfeld stand beside him as the band played "The Star Spangled Banner," Bush emphasized the military nature of the counterterrorism campaign as he visited the three sites where the Al Qaida hijackers had crashed their planes a year earlier.

Born in Utah to a geologist father, Rove attended the University of Utah–Salt Lake City, the University of Texas–Austin, and George Mason University in Virginia, but never graduated, since he was too busy pursuing his career as the rising star of the College Republicans, who would elect him national chairperson in 1973 in an election that was challenged, unsuccessfully, by his rival. He was by then well versed in playing dirty tricks. He once spoiled the opening of a local Democratic Party office by stealing their stationery, printing one thousand forged invitations, promising "free beer and food, girls, and a good time for all," and distributing them to people at a soup kitchen and a rock concert. Later, in his career as an adviser to professional politicians, he would resort to relying on planting bugging devices and disseminating malicious rumors about the personal lives of opposition candidates—all the while claiming to be a devout Episcopalian. After having his College

Republicans' elected office validated, he worked with George Herbert Walker Bush, then chairman of the Republican National Committee (RNC), in Washington. After this, Rove became a virtual fixture of the Bush clan.

In 1977, Rove moved to Houston to become the second employee of the quixotic Fund for Limited Government, a political-action committee dedicated to making Bush Sr. president. Rove's immediate assistance to George Walker Bush, then thirty-one, to become a U.S. congressman, failed: Texas was at that time a loyal Democratic state. His next move, though, succeeded. In 1978 he joined the gubernatorial campaign of Bill Clements, an oilman who became Texas's first Republican governor since Reconstruction. Clements appointed Rove his deputy chief of staff. Three years later, Rove left the governor's office to start a direct-mail business in Austin, specializing in public affairs. He worked for political candidates, nonpartisan causes, and nonprofit groups. His business prospered, and this enabled him to work for any Republican candidate he liked. He chose to campaign for George W. Bush when the latter ran for Texas governor in 1982. Bush Jr. lost again. Rove combined his public affairs business with forays into teaching at the LBJ School of Public Affairs and the Journalism Department of the University of Texas–Austin. Over time he honed his skills, learning, for instance, how to fill a thirty-second television commercial with the maximum number of "political messages" for a large audience marginally interested in politics.

Rove became adept at categorizing voters as "base" (or solid) and "swing" (or undecided), and spinning the candidate's slogans in such a way as to keep the base while extending it to include most of the swing voters. This is the strategy he employed while working as George W. Bush's chief strategist for his second bid for governor of Texas in 1994. It worked, barely—Bush won by a narrow margin. Four years later, Rove took charge of Bush's reelection strategy, which also succeeded. It was from this springboard that Rove helped Bush win the presidency. It was Rove who, during the election campaign in 2000, coined the term "compassionate conservatism," which the moderate, swing voters interpreted as "not rabidly conservative" and the committed right-wingers viewed as "conservatism combined with Christian values"—meaning opposing abortion and gun control and favoring small government, tax cuts, and a strong military. While Condoleezza Rice proved adept at articulating Bush's famed "gut instincts," it was Rove who implanted simple ideas into Bush's mind. As Rove's biographers, James Moore and Wayne Slater, put it in their book *Bush's Brain: How Karl Rove Made George W. Bush* (2003): "Karl Rove thinks it . . . George W. Bush does it. Bush is the product, Rove is the marketer. One cannot succeed without the other."[3]

By the time Bush occupied the White House in January 2001, Rove had acquired an extraordinary talent for giving a moral spin to what was electorally beneficial, but his Christian morality did not deter him from remarking cynically that "everything is measured by results, and the victor is always right." Even his detractors conceded that Rove was a formidable political operator who combined breadth of vision with an uncanny feel for public opinion. Like the previous occupant of the White House, Bill Clinton, Rove got into the habit of processing every aspect of a policy under discussion through the political filter, quantifying the implications of various voting groups. He had a remarkable facility with numbers. "Remember, in 1996, if education's your No. 1 issue, you vote for Clinton-Gore over Dole-Kemp by 76-16," he told Nicholas Lemann of the *New Yorker* in May 2003. "By 2000, you vote for Gore-Lieberman over Bush-Cheney by 52-44." He had come to visualize the American electors as a jumble of assorted toy magnets of varying electoral weight—some active (white evangelicals), others quiescent (African-Americans in the South); some mutually exclusive (Hollywood liberals and the oil lobby), and others mutually attracted.

Bush's strategy was to project Saddam Hussein as an extension of bin Laden. To do so he needed convincing evidence to establish a link between Al Qaida and Saddam, and to show that Saddam posed an immediate threat to U.S. security. Those congressional leaders entitled to classified intelligence briefings had so far failed to see or hear evidence that led to either of these conclusions.

But that did not deter Bush from forging ahead with plans to overthrow Saddam's regime by force. Iraq was the subject of talks he had with Blair over the September 6–7 weekend at Camp David. According to Clare Short, a British cabinet minister who resigned in May 2003 in protest of Blair's policy on Iraq, it was at Camp David that the British prime minister entered into "a secret pact" with Bush to go to war the following spring. She based her claim on the information given to her by three unnamed "senior government officials."[4] Since this was apparently a verbal agreement, it would be hard to prove or disprove. Judging by Blair's subsequent behavior, it seems most likely that the two leaders reached a conditional agreement, with Blair promising to join Bush in his war against Baghdad if Bush first sought a UN Security Council endorsement for military action, without ruling out the possibility of a unilateral attack on Iraq, which, with Britain's participation, would become bilateral. (In that sense, it was not just the special pleading by Powell that led Bush to utter those ad-libbed words on September 12 at the United Nations, as Bob Woodward in his *Bush at War* would have us believe.)

Blair would reveal to the Lord Hutton Inquiry a year later that, in the course of a telephone conversation with Bush toward the end of the (British) August break—from the 24th to the 26th— they decided: "Look, we really had to confront this issue [of Iraq's WMD], devise our strategy and get on with it." This was to be done by publishing a dossier to "disclose the reasons for our concern and the reason why we believed this issue had to be confronted." Both governments would publish dossiers, but the main stress would be on the British version: It would be more credible in the Muslim and Arab world than its American counterpart—

especially since Blair never tired of telling his Muslim audience at home and abroad that he always packed a copy of the Quran along with the Bible on his travels.

THE U.K. DOSSIER AND U.S. NATIONAL SECURITY STRATEGY

The starting point for the British dossier was a March 2002 report by the Joint Intelligence Committee (JIC), the clearinghouse for all intelligence agencies, chaired by John Scarlett. It concluded that the JIC had found "no evidence that Saddam Hussein posed a significantly greater threat than in 1991 after the Gulf War." Subsequent MI6 briefings stressed that Iraq's program for WMD had been so disrupted that it was almost utterly redundant.[5]

This document, hurriedly updated, mentioned for the first time Iraq's ability to deploy WMD within forty-five minutes—a claim attributed to a "senior Iraqi officer via a trusted Iraqi agent of MI6." By September 5, the JIC had its first draft ready to discuss with Blair before his weekend trip to Camp David for meetings with Bush. "Iraq has probably dispersed its special weapons, including chemical and biological weapons," it said. "Intelligence also indicates that from forward deployed storage sites, chemical and biological munitions could be with military units and ready for firing within 45 minutes."

Between September 5 and 24, when the dossier was published, its text was changed radically by a small group of bureaucrats, including Alastair Campbell, the prime minister's director of communications, who acted as the conduit for Blair, with the writing assigned to Scarlett.

The following account chronicles the "sexing up" of the dossier, which, over the next year, would escalate into the most severe political crisis faced by Blair, threatening his survival as prime minister.[6]

In the next draft the dossier read, "Intelligence also indicates that chemical and biological munitions could be with military units and ready for firing within 20 to 45 minutes." But by the time the newest version of the dossier was delivered to the prime minister's office on September 10, it read, "Iraq continues to have the capability to produce chemical and biological weapons and has probably already done so." The next day a copy was forwarded to George Tenet in Washington.

On September 13, Scarlett flew to Washington to discuss the document with Tenet. The CIA director reportedly expressed reservations about the statement on the nuclear issue: "Iraq continues to work on developing nuclear weapons. . . . Uranium to be used in the production of fissile material has been purchased from Africa [later narrowed to Niger]." As a result, the final version stated that "recent intelligence . . . indicates" that "Iraq has purchased large quantities of uranium ore, despite having no civil nuclear program that would require it."

On his return to London, Scarlett distributed the latest version to various parties on September 16. *That day Iraq agreed to let UN inspectors return "without any conditions."* As such, the raison d'être for the dossier—to focus world attention on Iraq's WMD and pressure Iraq to allow the United Nations to resume inspections—collapsed. But then, one of the primary, albeit unexpressed, objectives of this document was to actively assist Bush in securing a congressional vote in early October for authority to declare war on Iraq. So, in London the sexing up of the dossier continued unabated.

Among those who were unimpressed by the latest draft was none other than Blair's chief of staff, Jonathan Powell. "First, the document does nothing to demonstrate a threat, let alone an imminent threat from Saddam," he said in his e-mail of September 17, 2002, to Campbell. "It shows that he had the means but it does not demonstrate he has the motive to attack his neighbors let alone the West. We will need to make it clear in launching the document that we do not claim that we have evidence that he is an imminent threat. The case we are making is that he had continued to develop WMD since 1998, and is in breach of UN resolutions. The international community has to enforce those resolutions if the UN is to be taken seriously. Second we will be asked about the connection with Al Qaida. [The following sentence was censored.]"

The next draft materialized on September 19. The earlier sentence, "Intelligence confirms that Iraq has covert chemical and biological weapons programs, in breach of UN Security Council Resolution 687," had been altered to "Intelligence shows that Iraq has covert chemical and biological weapons programs, in breach of UN Security Council Resolution 687, and has continued to produce chemical and biological agents." And "Iraq has chemical and biological weapons available, either from pre-Gulf War stocks or more recent production" was changed to "Iraq has chemical and biological weapons available, both from pre-Gulf War stocks and more recent production."

Finally, and crucially, "The Iraqi military may be able to deploy chemical or biological weapons within 45 minutes of an order to do so" was altered to "Military planning allows for some of the WMD to be ready within 45 minutes of an order to use them."[7]

The document was titled, "Iraq's Programme of Weapons of Mass Destruction: The Assessment of the British Government." But on September 24 it appeared as "Iraq's Weapons of Mass Destruction: The Assessment of the British Government."

In his foreword in the dossier, Blair wrote, "I am in no doubt that the threat is serious and current, that he [Saddam] had made progress on weapons of mass destruction, and that he has to be stopped." And introducing the document to the House of Commons, Blair said, "His [Saddam's] weapons of mass destruction program is active, detailed, and growing. The policy of containment is not working. The weapons of mass destruction program is up and running."

Following Blair's meetings with Bush at Camp David, the two leaders gave a joint press conference on September 7. They showed satellite pictures indicating new construction activity at what appeared to be Tuweitha, the site of the French-built nuclear reactors destroyed by Israel in a daring, clandestine air raid in June 1981. This was the evidence, they claimed, that Iraq was working on a nuclear-arms program. On September 10, Hans Blix said that Unmovic did not draw the same conclusion from the same satellite images.[8]

Blix's assessment was backed up by a group of international journalists who were given a tour of the three buildings in question at Tuweitha. One turned out to be a mere shed. The second was a hulking carcass of a building, which, according to Iraqi officials, was used from 1981 to 1991 to deal with radioactive materials produced for diagnosing and treating cancer, and was bombed during the Gulf War. The third, used for producing chemical agents to treat cancer, was "far from new," according to Amberin Zaman of the (London) *Daily Telegraph*: "Its floors are well worn, its walls grotty and cracked." The complex had been repeatedly scrutinized by Unscom, the escorting Iraqi official told the journalists. Finally came the barnlike structures that had been featured on the Blair-supplied aerial photograph in the British press. "Inside a dark room, white fungi spring from manure-filled plastic bags," Zaman reported. Ali Nadeer, the head of the mushroom unit, picked a few mushrooms and munched them, the (secret) source of his enhanced sexual prowess. "I used to have one American wife; now I have two Iraqi wives," he told the bemused reporters.[9]

Such reports appeared in the Western press on September 11, 2002, the day before President Bush was to address the UN General Assembly. In his speech he emphasized the primacy of America first: "We will use our position of unparalleled strength and influence to build an atmosphere of international order and openness in which progress and liberty can flourish in many nations." He then concentrated almost exclusively on Iraq. "Saddam Hussein's regime is a grave and gathering danger," he asserted. "To assume this regime's good faith is to bet the lives of millions." He claimed that Iraq retained "capable nuclear scientists and technicians and physical infrastructure," and had tried to purchase, unsuccessfully, "thousands of high-strength aluminum tubes for centrifuges to enrich uranium for a nuclear weapon." Once Iraq had fissile material, he warned, it could build a weapon in one year. He presented Iraq with the following demands: disclosure and removal of all WMD; active suppression of terrorism; a halt to the persecution of civilians of all ethnicities; return of the remaining prisoners of war from the Gulf conflict and the Iran–Iraq War; and cessation of any illegal trade outside of the United Nations's oil-for-food program.

Among the audience was Colin Powell, who had lobbied hard at the last minute for Bush to commit himself to taking the Iraq issue to the United Nations by saying in his speech that he would work to get "necessary Security Council resolutions." Bush agreed. Yet it was touch and go. Bush's last-minute promise was not transformed into the appropriate change in the text on the teleprompter. "My nation will work with the UN Security Council to meet our common challenge," Bush said, reading the text. Powell almost stopped breathing. Bush got through the next two sentences, and then realized the reference to the Security Council resolutions was absent. Awkwardly, he ad-libbed: "We will work with the UN Security Council for the necessary resolutions." Powell heaved a sigh of relief.[10] Bush then stressed that "the purpose of the United States should not be doubted," and sketched a guideline for the United Nations: "If Iraq's regime defies us again, the world must move decisively to hold Iraq to account."

Bush's aides later explained that, while acknowledging the United Nations's authority, the president warned that its legitimacy would be at stake if it did not act on Iraq the way he wanted it to. In other words, Bush wanted to have his cake and eat it too.

In Washington that same day, the White House released a twenty-page document on Iraq entitled *A Decade of Deception and*

Defiance. Disarmament experts described it as a recycled compendium of old and circumstantial evidence that Saddam might be concealing the ingredients for WMD and attempting to develop a nuclear capability and weaponize biological and chemical agents. In the one page given to Iraq's support for international terrorism, there was an allusion to an attempt to assassinate Bush Sr. in April 1993. Significantly, there was no reference either to Al Qaida or the purported meeting between Muhammad Atta and Ahmad Ani in Prague.

Behind the scenes, things were not going well between the two English-speaking transatlantic partners. Tenet, after reading a draft of the British dossier, expressed doubt about Iraq's attempt to buy uranium from Niger in 2000 (without giving an explanation, according to British sources), and objected to the claim that some Iraqi WMD were deployable within forty-five minutes of Saddam's orders. Blair ignored Tenet's comments on these issues. Unknown to Blair, Tenet's CIA had concluded by then that the papers pertaining to the alleged attempt by Iraq to buy uranium from Niger were forged. But even if Blair had been told this, he would have stuck to his statement in the draft, since the British government had other "non-documentary" evidence—so claimed his spokesmen ten months later—which, amazingly, was not passed on to the CIA or the International Atomic Energy Agency.

But there were expert skeptics within Blair's own government. One such was Dr. David Kelly, a senior scientific adviser on chemical and biological weapons to the Ministry of Defense (MoD) and the Foreign Office, who had served as an inspector with the United Nations from 1991 to 1998, and who would commit suicide on July 17, 2003, after having given testimony to the British House of Commons Foreign Affairs Committee two days earlier. Writing about the tragic event in the *Mail on Sunday* of July 20, Tom Mangold, a former reporter for BBC-TV's flagship current affairs program, *Panorama,* and a friend of Kelly, revealed the source of the "forty-five minute" claim to be an Iraqi brigadier in Baghdad working for British intelligence MI6—obviously a single, uncorroborated source. "In essence what he [the MI6 agent] said was *not* that biological and chemical weapons could be deployed—that is, fired—within 45 minutes," wrote Mangold. "That's nonsense—and David Kelly and I laughed about it. What the agent probably said was that the Iraqis had created a Command, Control and Communications system (C3) that would enable Saddam . . . to communicate with regional military commanders within 45 minutes, authorizing the use of WMD. And this is not the same thing as deployment." As it was, in his parliamentary testimony, Kelly had called the forty-five-minute scenario "very unlikely," and explained that "it is actually quite a long and convoluted process to go from having bulk agent and munitions to actually getting them to bunker for storage and then issue them and subsequently [load them into missile warheads or even artillery shells or mortars to] deploy them."[11]

As for the material in the dossier released by the White House on September 12, most of it became redundant four days later, when Iraq announced its acceptance of the return of UN inspectors "without conditions." That evening Annan received a letter from Iraqi foreign minister Naji Sabri to that effect. In the Arab world there was a collective sigh of relief. But Bush behaved like a boy who suddenly found his ball taken away.

However, this development left unaffected the "unseen" part of the war, which Bush had initiated in August and Blair had joined the following month, and it had its own momentum. In September, Anglo-American warplanes hit a radar at a remote Iraqi airfield, 240 miles (385 kilometers) west of Baghdad, to open a corridor for the U.S. Special Forces helicopters to enter the western desert undetected from Jordan. During their missions, Special Forces left communications equipment at certain locations to be activated later, and supplied satellite phones to their agents. They were following the precedent set earlier in Afghanistan, when they and the CIA's Special Activities Division (SAD) had dispatched satellite phones and $10,000 in cash to many pro-Taliban tribal leaders and warlords.[12] Taking his cue from the CIA in Afghanistan, Saudi intelligence chief Prince Nawwaf took to bribing the leaders of Sunni tribes in Iraq, giving them sums higher than those they received from Saddam Hussein. On the British side, its MI6 operatives, based in Kuwait since 1991, cultivated Iraqi Shia agents in the south, especially in Basra. They were supplied with secure short-range communications equipment and instructions to go to the city's suburbs at prearranged times to convey the information they had gathered to their MI6 handlers.[13] In the air, U.S.–U.K. aircraft had resorted to dropping propaganda leaflets (eighty thousand at each of the six important locations in the south) warning the Iraqis not to repair fiber-optic links, and advising them to tune in to a certain radio frequency where they could listen to U.S. broadcasts beamed daily for several hours by military aircraft patrolling the no-fly zones.[14]

On the diplomatic front, once Bush had regained his composure, he set out to move the goalposts. Collaborating with Blair, he worked on a draft resolution for the UN Security Council that would propose UN security guards for the inspectors with powers to declare instantly "no-fly/no-drive zones, exclusion zones, and/or ground- and air-transit corridors."

Later that month, when asked if there was "new and conclusive" evidence of Iraq's nuclear-weapons capabilities, Bush cited an International Atomic Energy Agency report saying Iraqis were "six months from developing a weapon." No such document existed. Indeed, in 1998 the IAEA had reported, "Based on all credible information to date, the IAEA has found no indication of Iraq having achieved its program goal of producing nuclear weapons or of Iraq having retained a physical capability for the production of weapons-usable nuclear material or having clandestinely obtained such material." It said that before the 1991 Gulf War, Iraq had been six to twenty-four months from nuclear capability.[15] Bush's statement was based on what Iraqi defector and nuclear scientist

Khidir Hamza had said. Hamza, however, had retired from Iraq's program in 1991, fled to Kurdistan three years later, and left the area in 1995 to settle in the United States with the assistance of the INC. The IAEA later judged the documents submitted by him to be forged.[16]

None of this deflected the White House from getting Congress to give war powers to President Bush before the looming November midterm elections. The White House feared entrusting this decision to the newly elected Congress, whose political complexion was uncertain. It also wanted to impress on Saddam the gravity of the situation. The White House lobbyists focused on the evidence showing the Iraqi dictator's nuclear ambitions. They were helped by *Iraq's Weapons of Mass Destruction: The Assessment of the British Government,* the document Blair released on September 24.

As mentioned earlier, the British government's dossier asserted that Iraq had continued to produce biological and chemical agents and had plans to use them within forty-five minutes of an order being given by Saddam—a statement appearing *four* times in the document. The primary source, who supplied this information to an Iraqi agent of MI6, was probably referring to the command, control, and communications arrangements for using chemical and biological weapons already in place. Also, the dossier alleged, Iraq had developed mobile labs for military use, and it was using clandestine means to procure materials for biological and chemical arms, as well as acquiring technology and materials for nuclear weapons. Furthermore, Iraq had sought significant quantities of uranium "from Africa" and recalled specialists to work on its nuclear-weapons program. Regarding the means of delivery, Iraq had illegally retained up to twenty Al Hussein missiles with a range of 410 miles (650 kilometers) capable of delivering biological and chemical weapons, and were trying to extend the range of the liquid-fueled Al Samoud-2 missile up to 125 miles (200 kilometers), 30 miles (50 kilometers) above the allowable limit. It was starting to produce a solid-fueled Ababil missile,[17] with the aim of also giving it a 125-mile (200 kilometer) range. The report also claimed that Iraq had built a new engine test stand for developing missiles capable of reaching Cyprus—as well as Greece and Turkey and Israel. Finally, taking into account the imminent restart of UN inspections, the dossier claimed that Iraq was concealing sensitive equipment and documents in anticipation of the return of UN inspectors.[18]

By releasing the dossier at 8 A.M. on September 24, 2002, just four hours before the debate in the House of Commons, Blair ensured that parliamentarians would not be able to absorb the full implications of the fifty-page document or draw on the expertise of the specialist journalists or academics. While introducing it to the House, Blair said that "if Saddam were able to purchase fissile material illegally, it would only be a year or two [before Iraq acquired a nuclear weapon]." The next day, a front-page headline in the Rupert Murdoch–owned *The Times* (London) read: "Saddam 'could have nuclear bomb in year,' " while its best-selling tabloid counterpart, *The Sun,* screamed on its front page: "He's got them. Let's get him."

Over the next six months—including four months of inspections by the United Nations—all of these statements would turn out to be false—except the range of the Al Samoud-2 missile, which in many cases exceeded the permissible length by thirteen to twenty miles (twenty to thirty-two kilometers). Seventy of 120 such missiles would be destroyed before the Anglo-American invasion of March 2003 interrupted the destruction of the rest.

"This document is based, in large part, on the work of the Joint Intelligence Committee (JIC)," Blair wrote in his foreword to the dossier. "Its work, like the material it analyses, is largely secret. It is unprecedented for the Government to publish this kind of document." Yet several elements in it were derived from old information already in the public domain. The sources were the declassified CIA report to Congress covering July 1–December 31, 2000, submitted in February 2001; the briefing paper by Clinton's secretary of defense, William Cohen, in January 2001; and a report by the London-based International Institute of Strategic Studies (IISS) published on September 10, 2002. The map showing Cyprus, the site of two British military bases, within the range of Al Hussein missiles (allegedly retained by Iraq albeit in disassembled form), was pinched from Cohen's briefing paper. Paradoxically, although Bahrain, hosting the Pentagon's Fifth Fleet, and Kuwait, hosting many thousands of U.S. troops, were within the range of Al Hussein missiles, the Bush administration did not mention this scenario in any of its documents.[19]

The assertion that Saddam had sought to acquire uranium oxide from Niger came along with the statement that Iraq had tried to import sixty thousand specialized aluminum tubes for centrifuges to enrich uranium—a claim that the White House found effective in getting a substantial body of wavering U.S. lawmakers to accord Bush war powers in October 2002.

Saddam was supposed to have made his Niger move in July 2000, according to the documents that were sold to Italian intelligence sixteen months later. By late 2001 the story had made the rounds of Western intelligence circles. Cheney's office asked the CIA to investigate the matter. In February 2002 the CIA assigned the task to Joseph Wilson. A business consultant, Wilson, during his earlier government service, had been the chargé d'affaires at the American embassy in Baghdad at the time of the 1990 Kuwait crisis,[20] U.S. ambassador to Gabon (1992–95), and the Africa director at the National Security Council (1996–98). He spent eight days in Niger talking to present and past officials and others involved in the uranium business. During his meeting in Niamey with the U.S. ambassador to Niger, Barbro Owens-Kirkpatrick, he learned that the ambassador had already debunked these allegations against Iraq in her reports to the State Department. He discovered that the mining of the ore was done by two French corporations and a consortium of French (the majority shareholder), German, Italian, Japanese, and Spanish companies, which were monitored strictly by the IAEA; and that the Niger government, a minority shareholder in these companies, had no access to the ore, which was exported chiefly to France and Japan—with nothing available for sale at home. The exclusive selling agency was Uranex, which covered all the African French Zone countries (Central African Republic, Gabon, Niger) and France. Any attempt by the Niger government to remove uranium ore from a mine would have required notification of one of the companies and the IAEA, and any sale of the ore by it would have required the signatures of the minister of mines, the prime minister, and the president. In other words, the alleged sale was impossible, and any attempt by Iraq of such a purchase was unthinkable.

On his return to Washington in March 2002, Wilson briefed the CIA at length. (He later briefed the State Department's African Affairs Bureau, too.) The CIA distributed his findings to the Defense Intelligence Agency, the Joint Chiefs of Staff, the National Security Council, the Justice Department, the FBI, and Cheney's office. To be absolutely certain, the CIA's operations and counterterrorism departments conducted their own investigations, as did the State Department's Bureau of Intelligence and Research. They unanimously declared the documents to be forgeries.[21]

Astonishingly, neither the Italian nor the British nor the American government forwarded the Niger documents to the IAEA for verification.[22] It was only after Bush, in his State of the Union speech in late January 2003, had repeated the allegations about Baghdad's attempts "recently" to buy "significant quantities" of uranium in Africa that the IAEA asked the United States and the United Kingdom to pass on the said documents. And only on February 4 did the U.S. State Department hand over the Niger documents to the IAEA along with the letter from Paul Kelly, undersecretary for legal affairs, to the IAEA in Vienna, in which he said, "We cannot confirm these reports and have questions regarding some specific claims." It took the IAEA ten days to conclude that the documents were fake, whereupon it informed Washington. On

March 7, IAEA chief Muhammad el Baradei told the Security Council, "Based on thorough analysis, the IAEA has concluded, with the concurrence of outside experts, that these documents— which formed the basis for the reports of recent uranium transactions between Iraq and Niger—are in fact not authentic."[23]

All the forensic experts at the IAEA did was compare the documents on hand with authentic letterheads from Niger, and conclude that they were dealing with crude forgery. Laughable and childlike errors—noted quickly by the IAEA—had gone unnoticed by the Italian intelligence and British MI6. For instance, the letter of July 2000, from Niger president Tandja Mamadou alluded to 500 tonnes of uranium oxide (out of a total annual output of 2,400 tonnes) to be exported to Iraq. But the signature bore no relation to Mamadou's—what is more, the national emblem on the presidential letterhead was wrong. Another letter dated October 10, 2000 was signed by Allele El Hadj Habibou, minister of mining, and referred to an enclosed "protocol of understanding" for exporting uranium. But Habibou had been deposed eleven years earlier. Moreover, this letter had a date stamp showing it had been received in September 2000—that is, it was received *before* it was written. According to el Baradei, any number of groups, including Iraqi exiles, had an interest in forging the document.[24]

Among those who dismissed the British dossier on Iraq as "propagandist"—at a joint press conference with Blair—was Russian president Vladimir Putin. As a former KGB officer trained in disseminating disinformation, Putin was well qualified to detect material of the kind.[25]

On September 30, the Iraqi foreign ministry published a twenty-nine-page dossier rebutting the charges made in the U.S. and U.K. documents on Iraq's WMD.[26] It would be summarized by Muhammad Douri, Iraqi ambassador to the United Nations, thus: "In December 1998, when the UN weapons inspection team left Iraq on the orders of Richard Butler, it had exhausted all possibilities after seven years of repeatedly examining all possible sites; only small discrepancies existed. . . . Since 1999 we have allowed the IAEA to visit Iraq. . . . Building such WMD weapons costs billions of dollars and huge [electric] power sources. The idea that such projects could be moved around in trucks or stashed away in presidential palaces stretches the imagination."[27]

But this had no impact on U.S. lawmakers, who would be deliberately denied the news by the White House that on October 4, North Korean officials had admitted to James Kelly, U.S. assistant secretary for East Asia, that they were trying to enrich uranium for use as fuel for a nuclear weapon—in order to sway the waverers to vote for giving war powers to Bush.[28]

When Tom Daschle demanded answers to such crucial questions as "Will a major diversion of military resources undermine the war on terrorism?" and "Who will replace Saddam?" before the Senate could discuss the White House's draft "Further Resolution on Iraq," Bush retorted that the (Democratic-controlled) Senate was "not interested in the security of the American people." When Daschle called Bush's remark "outrageous" and demanded an apology, Bush backtracked. "The security of the country is the commitment of both political parties and the responsibility of both elected branches of government," he said.

Unfortunately for Democrats, Bush's anti-Iraq propaganda blitz had paid off. The percentage of those who thought terrorism more pressing than any other issue facing the country rose from 11 to 47, almost equal to those who considered the economy to be the biggest problem.[29]

It was left to Al Gore, who had beaten Bush in the popular vote for the presidency, to attack the White House's policies comprehensively. "President Bush is telling us that the most urgent requirement of the moment—right now—is not to redouble our efforts against Al Qaida and bin Laden . . . but instead to shift our focus and concentrate on immediately launching a new war against Saddam Hussein," he told the Commonwealth Club in San Francisco. "And he is proclaiming a new, uniquely American right to preemptively attack whomsoever he may deem represents a potential future threat." He warned that "the course of action we are presently embarking on regarding Iraq has the potential to seriously damage our ability to win the war against terrorism and weaken our ability to lead the world in this new century." He maintained that Bush and some in his administration were exchanging the tried-and-true practices of "deterrence" and "containment" for a policy of "dominance." If other nations asserted the same preemptive rights that the United States does, "the rule of law will quickly be replaced by the reign of fear . . . by the notion that there is no law but the discretion of the American president." He wondered what precedent that would set, for example, for India facing Pakistan, or China against Taiwan, or Israel confronted by Iran. "If what America represents to the world is leadership in a commonwealth of equals, then our friends are legion; [but] if what we represent is empire, then it is our enemies who will be legion." This was well reflected in an opinion poll in Britain, which showed that 37 percent considered Bush "the greatest danger to world peace"—only six points behind Saddam.[30]

"Irrelevant." That was the White House's dismissive comment on Gore's speech. However, the relevance of Gore's emphasis on focusing on the Al Qaida menace was soon highlighted by the bombing of a disco popular with Australian and European tourists in Bali, Indonesia, on October 12, which killed 202 people.

Straining to link Saddam and Al Qaida, Bush mentioned (in his folksy way) "the danger of Al Qaida becoming an extension of Saddam's madness," and added, "You can't distinguish between Al Qaida and Saddam when you talk about the war on terror."[31] This from the president barely a fortnight after his office had released a document on Iraq that made no mention of Al Qaida!

When erudite multilateralists argued against unilateralism in matters of war and peace by pointing out that the ban on unprovoked—or preventive—offensives against sovereign states has been the foundation of international law since the Treaty of Westphalia in 1648 (which ended the Thirty Years' War between Catholic and Protestant countries in Europe), and that a preemptive attack violated not only the UN Charter but also the NATO Charter, a member of Bush's policy-making team responded, "You can call it preemption, or preventative defense. But it is old-fashioned self-protection, and it comes from the president's gut."[32] This statement tied in neatly with Bush's earlier remark to Bob Woodward, "I'm not a textbook player, I'm a gut player."[33]

Bush's intellectual and linguistic deficiencies stood out. "Washington apes the style of a president who has no capacity for the use of language as a mode of leadership," noted James Carroll, a columnist for the *Boston Globe*. "As a candidate Bush was at a loss for words, and proud of it. Many voters were charmed. Others were appalled. Few understood, however, that this abdication of leadership by the intelligent use of language would be dangerous."[34] However, after his successful war against the Taliban, Bush had come to make a virtue of his incoherence. When Bob Woodward asked Bush if he ever explained his actions, Bush replied, "Of course not. I am the commander—see, I don't need to explain—I do not need to explain why I say things. That's the interesting thing about being the president. Maybe somebody needs to explain to me why they say something, but I don't think I owe anybody an explanation."[35]

However, as president, Bush was required to state—in writing—his strategy on national security. On September 20, a year after 9/11, his office published a thirty-three-page document called *The National Security Strategy of the United States.* It was a mixed bag, with sections reflecting the enlightened approach of Thomas Jefferson, Abraham Lincoln, and George Marshall, the originator of massive aid to Western Europe in the wake of World War II. By and large, though, dominated by a reaffirmation of American power—military, economic, and cultural—it read like the declaration of a Roman emperor or a Napoleon or John Bull—the portly, self-satisfied, and arrogant symbol of the sprawling

British empire. This version of Pax Americana followed in a long line of past empires wherein the imperialist power, believing in its inherently superior values, has preached the doctrine of "civilizing" the "natives" while dominating them, a theme captured aptly in Rudyard Kipling's poem "The White Man's Burden."

Bush's policy paper visualized an overweening United States with a military muscle so strong, any potential adversary would be dissuaded from challenging it. Under this overarching protective canopy, Washington would exercise its self-proclaimed right to strike preemptively any hostile country it believes is developing WMD. The document declared that international treaties were less effective in preventing the proliferation of nuclear arms than the use of military means. This was in line with Bush's earlier go-it-alone policies in foreign affairs—global warming, the international criminal court, biological weapons conventions, tariffs on steel imports, etc.

Having made a friendly gesture toward the United Nations by announcing on September 12 the United States' return to the UN Educational, Social, and Cultural Organization (Unesco) after a gap of twenty years, Bush declared three weeks later that the United Nations would become "irrelevant" if the Security Council did not adopt the resolution on inspections in Iraq his country had submitted in association with Britain—in the face of opposition by China, France, and Russia.

The Anglo-American position hardened when, on October 1, following a two-day meeting in Vienna with the Iraqi delegation led by General Amr al Saadi, special adviser to Saddam on weapons,[36] and Hans Blix and el Baradei, Blix announced an agreement. "The Iraqi representatives declared that Iraq accepts all rights of inspection provided for in all the relevant Security Council resolutions [including 1284]." That meant all sensitive sites, including defense and intelligence ministries and mosques.

To divert attention from this positive development, Washington leaked the draft resolution (on October 2) it had shown to

China, France, and Russia—well aware that Baghdad had said earlier that it would not accept any new resolutions.

The Anglo-American draft began by asserting that "Iraq is still, and has been for a number of years, in material breach of its obligations under relevant resolutions." It called on Baghdad to provide, within thirty days of the adoption of the resolution, "an accurate, complete and full declaration of its programs to develop weapons of mass destruction, ballistic missiles and unmanned aerial vehicles"; it insisted that Iraq provide "immediate, unconditional and unrestricted access to all officials and other persons whom Unmovic or IAEA wish to interview." The motion also sought to establish the following revised procedures:

> Any permanent member of the Security Council may request to be represented on any inspection team with the same rights and protections; Shall have the right to the names of all personnel associated with Iraq's chemical, biological, nuclear weapons and ballistic missile programs and the associated research, development and production facilities; Teams shall be accompanied at the bases by sufficient security forces . . . shall have the right to declare for the purposes of this resolution no-fly/no-drive zones, exclusion zones, and/or ground- and air-transit corridors, which shall be enforced by UN security forces or by members of the Council; Shall have the right at their sole discretion verifiably to remove, destroy or render harmless all prohibited weapons, subsystems, components, records, materials and other related items, and the right to impound or close any facilities or equipment for the production thereof . . . [specified that] of the Council; [and ended with the proviso that] false statements or omissions in the declaration submitted by Iraq to the Council and failure by Iraq at any time to comply and cooperate fully with the provisions laid down in this resolution shall constitute a further material breach of

Iraq's obligations, and that such breach authorizes member
states to use all necessary means to restore international
peace and security in the area.

In his weekly radio address on October 5, 2002, Bush said,
"Iraq has stockpiled biological and chemical weapons, and is
rebuilding the facilities used to make more of those weapons." He
seemed to base his statement on interviews given by Adnan Ihsan
Saeed Haideri, an Iraqi civil engineer who, assisted by the Iraqi
National Congress, fled Iraq in 2001. He claimed to have visited
twenty concealed facilities constructed to produce biological and
chemical weapons, one of which was underneath a hospital in
Baghdad. His information was later conveyed to Unmovic, which
followed up on the tip-off. On the eve of the Anglo-American
invasion of Iraq, Hans Blix told the Security Council that his
inspectors had examined the hospital in question as well as other
venues using ground-penetrating radar. "No underground facilities
for chemical or biological production or storage were found so
far," he reported.[37]

President Bush's claim was a preamble to the speech he delivered in Cincinnati, Ohio, on October 7, the first anniversary of the
Afghanistan campaign. "We've also discovered through intelligence
that Iraq has a growing fleet of manned and unmanned aerial vehicles that could be used to disperse chemical or biological weapons
across broad areas," he said. "We're concerned that Iraq is
exploring ways of using these UAVs for missions targeting the
United States." He claimed that Iraq was reconstituting its nuclear-
weapons program. "Saddam Hussein has held numerous meetings
with Iraqi nuclear scientists, a group he calls his 'nuclear
mujahideen'—his nuclear holy warriors. Satellite photographs
reveal that Iraq is rebuilding facilities at sites that have been part of
its nuclear program in the past. Iraq has attempted to purchase
high-strength aluminum tubes and other equipment needed for
gas centrifuges, which are used to enrich uranium for nuclear

weapons." Bush declared that it would take Saddam's ouster to end the threat of WMD that was growing worse with time and, if left unattended, could lead to another attack on the United States like 9/11. Calling Iraq "an imminent danger," he asserted that it might seek "to strike targets on U.S. territory with the help of terrorist groups or by moving drones filled with germs or chemical weapons close to the U.S."[38]

Bush made the statement about "a growing fleet of unmanned aircraft" that could be used "for missions targeting the U.S." a few days *after* a declassified CIA report had described such a "fleet" as more "an attempt" than an established fact, and as a "serious threat to Iraq's neighbors"—not to the United States. This lie would be exposed by the *Washington Post*'s White House correspondent Dana Milbank—but not before October 21—ten days after Congress had given Bush the war powers he was seeking. In reality, this "fleet" turned out to be a single drone, which, on its discovery at a ramshackle airfield by UN inspectors, would be dismantled by Iraq even though the inspectors were not certain that an unmanned aircraft was a proscribed item.[39]

Bush had aimed his Cincinnati speech at the wavering lawmakers in the vote on war powers on October 10–11. His ploy was aided when George Tenet issued a CIA report on the eve of the crucial congressional vote asserting: "Most analysts assess Iraq is reconstituting its nuclear weapons program."[40] Later, based on the information collected by its members from the current employees of the intelligence apparatus, the Intelligence Professionals for Sanity (IPS) group would reveal that the evidence had been manipulated by the Bush administration to sway Congress before the October vote. "Intelligence used to sell the war was manipulated, forged or manufactured," said Ray McGovern, an IPS member.[41]

As a result, Bush carried the House by 296–133, and the Senate by 77–23.[42] Bush got most of the powers he sought, including the possibility of waging war without UN approval. Referring to the Democrats' dilemma, columnist Maureen Dowd wrote in the *New York Times,* "They did not want to seem weak, so they made the president stronger, which makes them weaker."

One politician who stood out in the debate was eighty-four-year-old Democratic senator Robert Byrd (West Virginia). "This broad resolution underwrites, promotes and endorses the unprecedented Bush doctrine of preventive war and preemptive strikes—detailed in a recent publication, *National Security Strategy of the United States*—against any nation that the president, and the president alone, determines to be a threat," he wrote in the *New York Times* on October 10. "Congress must not attempt to give away the authority to determine when war is to be declared. We must not allow any president to unleash the dogs of war at his own discretion and for an unlimited period of time."

After the congressional vote, the "evidence" that Bush had offered on October 7 was shown to be false. Bush displayed two images of the Nasser Engineering Establishment Manufacturing Facility at Furat, ten miles (sixteen kilometers) southwest of central Baghdad, one taken in 1998 and the other in September 2002, with arrows pointing to a large building, allegedly originally intended to house a centrifuge-enrichment cascade operation. The caption said that the building appeared to be in use again. Later, the Iraqi officials, accompanying two hundred foreign journalists to the site, showed this structure—part of a sun-beaten, dust-blown, ill-kept industrial plant of a dozen buildings—being used as a research center serving the army in the repair and development of communications equipment. General Abbas Saadi, the director of the plant, said that before the 1991 Gulf War there had been a nuclear program at the plant. When asked about the sandbagged bunkers lining the approach road, Saadi said, "It is normal for any country facing military attack to defend its industrial plants."[43]

Bush's assertion that Iraq could attack the United States with terrorist groups "on any given day" was at variance with the CIA testimony to Congress. In July 2002 Democratic senator Bob

Graham, chair of the Senate Intelligence Committee, had asked the CIA director to update the agency's classified National Intelligence Estimate on Iraq's WMD. On October 1, the CIA passed on the revised estimate to the Senate Committee, which later declassified part of it at Graham's request. In it, the CIA said that though Iraq's efforts to acquire WMD were "a serious threat" that could encourage "Iraqi blackmail," Baghdad would refrain from "the extreme step" of assisting terrorists in attacking the United States with WMD if Washington did not invade Iraq, and that Baghdad had no reason to provoke Washington. "For now Baghdad appears to be drawing a line short of conducting terrorist attacks with conventional or chemical or biological weapons against the U.S.," concluded George Tenet. "Should Saddam Hussein conclude that a U.S.-led attack could no longer be deterred, he probably would become much less constrained in adopting terrorist actions." At Graham's insistence, all of the CIA's National Intelligence Estimate on Iraq's WMD was declassified, but only after the Bush White House had edited it and removed all of the qualifying phrases. Even then the CIA's conclusion was that the chances of Iraq using chemical weapons were "very low" for "the foreseeable future."[44]

By October 2002, the reports of the Office for Special Plans (OSP)—whose staff had mushroomed tenfold, to 110—vied with those of the CIA and the DIA as the chief source of intelligence for Bush on Baghdad's possible possession of WMD and links with Al Qaida. Pressured by Cheney, Libby, and Gingrich, CIA analysts had stopped discarding anything that came in from the field, however unsubstantiated and incredible. Yet, according to Gregory Thielmann, a freshly retired director at the State Department's Intelligence and Research Bureau, "Normally when you compile an intelligence document, all the agencies get together to discuss it. But the OSP was never present at any of the meetings I attended." The chief reason for holding these meetings was to examine the various interpretations on a piece of raw intelligence. For example, according to Thielmann, CIA analysts said the sixty thousand aluminum tubes that Iraq had bought could be used for gas centrifuges to enrich uranium, whereas the best experts at the Energy Department disagreed. Yet Condoleezza Rice asserted publicly that they could be used only for centrifuges. She was proved wrong when UN inspectors found these tubes being used in rocket engines for permissible missiles.[45]

Thielmann also revealed that Rumsfeld "went around" his own "massive DIA," suggesting that the defense secretary paid more attention to the OSP documents than those from his departmental intelligence agency. And the OSP was so insulated from the rest of the Defense Department that a senior Pentagon official who left during the war planning period said, "Nobody from the military staff ever heard, saw, or discussed anything with the OSP staff."

Small wonder that an investigation by Democratic congressman David Obey led him to conclude that "information collected by OSP was in some cases not even shared with established intelligence agencies, and in numerous instances was passed on to the NSC and the president without having been vetted by anyone other than the political appointees."[46] These high officials then used some information to illustrate the failures of CIA and State Department analysts, and pressured them to follow up OSP leads. At other times they leaked information to the press. For example, a report attributed to an unnamed U.S. official stated that the reason WMD were not found in Iraq was that they had been smuggled into Syria. Following vehement denials by the Syrian government, it emerged that the story had originated in Ariel Sharon's ad hoc intelligence unit in Jerusalem.

Not surprisingly, the Bush Jr. administration earned the reputation of being "the most secretive in living memory"—a contrast to the preceding administration, which leaked frequently and profusely.

It also proved to be uncommonly impervious to popular opinion. Its obsession with attacking Iraq remained unaffected by the antiwar demonstrations in the United States over the October

26–27 weekend, with 200,000 marching in Washington, and with the polls showing a drop (in two months) of 14 percent to 50 percent for those in support of sending troops to topple Saddam, with only 27 percent favoring a unilateral action as well.

With Bush armed with war powers, the Pentagon set up the Doha army base in Kuwait, which had openly and consistently sided with Washington since the expulsion of the Iraqis from the emirate by the U.S.-led coalition in 1991. Soon U.S. forces began conducting war exercises in the Kuwaiti desert. Before long, they were joined by British troops.

At the same time, Bush escalated his threats against Baghdad, partly to patch up his splintered inner circle of advisers who differed on how much to rely on the UN Security Council, and partly to scare most of the world into thinking he was intent on war, thus improving his chances of getting a stiffer UN inspection regime than the one that seemed possible in August.

At the UN Security Council, behind-the-scenes negotiations continued on the U.S.–U.K. draft resolution. Facing opposition to the idea of using UN armed guards for inspectors from various parties—including Blix, who argued that the arrangement would expose the governments to the possibility of low-level firefights that could escalate out of political control—Washington agreed to drop it. France and Russia also objected to the automatic authorization of force by UN member-states in case of Iraq's failure to fully comply with the new resolution. When the Bush administration refused to budge on the subject, Paris threatened to submit its own draft resolution. The Chirac government also stressed the need to win unanimous backing for the draft to give "a clear and strong message to Iraq," and added that "for France the use of force cannot be automatic and is only the last resort."[47]

In Baghdad it was business as usual. The referendum on Saddam Hussein's presidency took place on October 15 as scheduled. The preordained outcome was published the next day, with a record

100 percent of the voters backing Saddam—an improvement of 0.04 percent over the previous referendum! The Iraqi dictator probably reckoned that this unique result would impress the outside world and discourage war planning by Bush and Blair—a fantasy. In any case, on the following Friday, October 20, he released all prisoners in celebration, with thousands pouring out of Abu Ghraib penitentiary, the largest of the fifty jails nationwide.[48] On November 1, the Annual International Trade Fair opened with the largest participation yet, with Saudi companies taking part for the first time since the 1991 Gulf War.

On November 3, in an interview with the Cairo weekly *El Osboa*, Saddam Hussein declared that Iraq was ready for the war, which could break out "any time," and warned that "it would be no picnic for the American and British troops." Believing that "time is on our side," Saddam said, "We must buy more time because the U.S.–U.K. alliance will disintegrate for internal reasons and because of the world opinion." He urged fellow Arabs as well as Iran "to defend Iraq" as "America will not be content to seize Iraq but will seek control of Egypt, Syria and Iran."[49]

Two days later, American voters gave the thumbs-up to Bush. In the House the Republicans enhanced their plurality by five, and in the Senate they displaced the Democrats as the majority party by improving their strength by two. This was a reversal of the tradition whereby the party occupying the White House loses seats in the first midterm congressional elections. The party functionaries were cock-a-hoop. So too was Bush. He had succeeded in exploiting tax cuts and terrorism to divide and demoralize the Democrats, who failed to unite around alternative policies. The other major factor was the imbalance between the election expenses of the two parties, with the Republicans spending 50 percent more than the Democrats.[50]

On November 6, Bush's step acquired a new spring. Even though the nation had rallied around him after 9/11 and his ratings had soared to 91 percent—the same as his father's in the afterglow of the 1991 Gulf War—transforming him from a diffident politician, prone to dyslexia, into a resolute leader, what continued to gnaw at him was Al Gore winning the popular vote in November 2002. The Republican Party's unprecedented success in the midterm election gave him the kind of electoral legitimacy he craved.

GEORGE W. BUSH

As the Republican candidate challenging the incumbent vice president, Al Gore, George W. ("Dubya") Bush had considerable difficulty overcoming his lack of solemnity, of a grasp of foreign affairs, and of political experience at the federal level, something his well-traveled father, George Herbert Walker Bush—having served as vice president from 1981 to 1989 and as director of the CIA and U.S. ambassador to China before that—had in abundance. What Dubya shared with his father was Phillips Academy, in Andover, Massachusetts, and Yale University, where he majored in history in 1968.

He joined the Air National Guard in Texas, the base of his father's oil business—thus avoiding military service in Vietnam—with a six-year commitment. After two years of training he began serving as a part-time pilot while based in Houston. In that role he was required to attend regular drills. Official records show his absence from these drills for a year starting in May 1972. During that time he was in Alabama assisting the Senate campaign of Winton Blount. He claimed that he fulfilled his Air National Guard service locally, on weekends, but his Alabama base commander had no recollection of him being present at the compulsory drills. When asked about his Air National Guard attendance record, Bush described it as "spotty." He also acknowledged that he was granted special permission to fulfill part of his Air National Guard service in Alabama, and that he was given an early release—by a year—to enroll at Harvard University Business School.

After graduating with a master's degree in Business Administration from Harvard, Bush returned to Midland, Texas, where his father had migrated in 1947 to become a self-made, successful oil businessman. Following in the footsteps of his father, Bush Jr. set up Arbusto (Spanish for "bush") Energy, Inc. with $20,000 in 1977. But soon after, he changed direction—by contesting a U.S. House of Representatives seat in his district that opened up. He lost to Democrat Kent Hance, who scornfully portrayed him as "an Ivy League carpetbagger." Dubya then took a crash course in oil drilling, leasing, and other basics of the industry. He got rich friends to invest in several oil-drilling ventures, most of which failed. Yet, thanks to tax loopholes, Arbusto Energy generated more than twice as much in tax deductions as in profits.

In 1982, facing a bleak future, Bush Jr. changed Arbusto Energy to Bush Exploration, believing, rightly, that with his father installed as vice president in the White House, "Bush" would attract more investors than the Spanish "Arbusto." Two years later, friendly investors arranged a deal in which Bush Exploration was acquired by a drilling company called Spectrum 7. Bush Jr. became its chairman and chief executive officer. When petroleum prices crashed in 1985, investment in the industry dried up. Spectrum 7 faced collapse, but Harken Energy, Inc., a Dallas-based company aggressively buying up troubled oil firms, noticed the Bush name at Spectrum 7. A deal, finalized in September 1986, brought Dubya $500,000 worth of Harken stock, a seat on the board of directors, and a consulting contract worth $60,000 to $120,000 a year.

But the rough-and-tumble of the oil business—both psychological and physical, as Bush worked at times as a driller—took its toll, turning Bush Jr. into an alcoholic, a matter of deep concern to his parents and to his wife, Laura. His various attempts to kick the bottle failed. What finally came to his rescue in 1986, at the age of forty, was a moving religious experience, buttressed by studying the Bible along with friends in an environment of "small group evangelicalism"—a process initiated by evangelist Billy Graham, who would be rewarded for his spiritual services with an invitation by Bush Sr. to give him benediction at his inauguration as president three years later. It was, therefore, unsurprising to learn from former Bush speechwriter David Frum's book *The Right Man* that the study of the Good Book was part of the routine at the president's office, and that "attendance at the Bible study at the White House was, if not compulsory, not quite uncompulsory."

"This kind of born-again epiphany is common in much of America, and it creates the kind of faith that is not beset by doubt because the believer knows that his life got better in the bargain," noted Bill Keller in the *New York Times*. "By church affiliation Bush is a Methodist. In theological terms he is a pietist in a tradition in which religion is more a matter of heart than of intellect. . . . Bush's faith entails a direct relationship between the believer and God. . . . According to those who travel in evangelical circles, Bush's faith is therefore highly subjective. It enjoins him to try to do the right thing. . . . Perhaps the most important effect of Bush's religion is that it imparts a profound self-confidence once he has decided on a course of action."[51] The key question is, Who decides "the right thing": a mortal like Dubya following his "gut instincts," or God Almighty who then communicates it thus? If the latter, how does this communication occur? Equally important, does Karl Rove run this divine message through his jumble of assorted toy magnets of varying electoral weight? What admirers call Bush Jr.'s superb self-confidence and serenity, his critics dismiss as bone-headedness combined with tunnel vision.

Dubya's conversion to born-again Christianity was so thorough that his father put him in charge of reaching out to evangelical Christians, a very substantial and motivated electoral constituency, during his election campaign for presidency in 1988. In the course of that assignment, which put Bush Sr. into the White House, Dubya became friends with Franklin Graham, son of Billy, who would take up his father's mantle after his death. In that role Franklin Graham would deliver the invocation at the inauguration of the presidency of George Walker Bush. Graham would remain close to Bush Jr., despite such declarations in his book *The Name* (2002) as "Christianity and Islam are as different as light and darkness," and that the two religions are destined to fight each other until the Second Coming of Christ, which is imminent.[52] "It wasn't Methodists flying into those buildings, it wasn't Lutherans," Graham told NBC-TV after 9/11. "It was an attack on this country by people of the Islamic faith."[53]

With his father as chief executive of the United States in January 1989, Dubya had little difficulty assembling a group of investors to buy the Texas Rangers baseball franchise. After five years with the Rangers as managing general partner, he won the gubernatorial election in Texas with a slim majority, with Karl Rove as his chief election campaigner. In office he showed a bipartisan spirit and was reelected governor in 1998.

During his campaign for the presidency his malapropisms—dubbed "Bushisms"—acquired nationwide currency. A few examples: "Rarely is the question asked, 'Is our children learning?' " Once in a speech he got confused between "deflation" and "devaluation." Another time he warned Iraq about "weapons of mass production." Addressing an economic forum in Texas, he said, "I promise to listen to what was said here, even though I wasn't here." And, "This must be a budget. There are lots of numbers in it."[54]

His choice of Dick Cheney as his running mate brought some maturity to the election campaign, which focused on presenting Bush Jr. as "a compassionate conservative." After his election he personally chose Powell (who had campaigned for him actively) and Rice as his secretary of state and national security adviser, respectively, leaving the rest of the selections to Cheney. He ended up with a powerful, experienced team of senior advisers—a contrast to what Bill Clinton had done. But this was not enough to mask his inexperience and his lack of a grasp of the details of the weighty issues he faced.

Bush's lackluster presidency was transformed by 9/11. On

September 12, 2001, he reinvented himself as a latter-day Teddy Roosevelt. In late October, during a war cabinet meeting to discuss the ongoing Afghanistan campaign, he declared that the anti-Taliban coalition was held together not by consultations among Washington's allies and partners as much as by strong American leadership that would force the rest of the world "to adjust." In his interview with Bob Woodward the following August, he elaborated: "We are the leader. And a leader must combine the ability to listen to others, along with action. I believe in results. . . . Confident action that will yield positive results provides kind of a slipstream into which reluctant nations and leaders can get behind and show themselves that there has been—you know, something positive has happened toward peace."[55] This "adjusting" by the rest of the world meant kowtowing to the will of the Bush White House, as the deliberations at the UN Security Council in early 2003 would show.

Bush Jr., who during his election campaign had dismissed the ideas of nation-building overseas and having an overarching vision, now confidently talked about his vision—in the simplistic terms his mind could handle. "I will seize the opportunity to achieve big goals. There is nothing bigger than to achieve world peace."[56] He seemed oblivious of the fact that the five major victors of World War II—the United States, the Soviet Union, Britain, France, and China—had set up the United Nations in 1945 precisely for that purpose, "to achieve and maintain world peace," and that such a colossal task could only be achieved collectively, with the United States working actively with its friends and allies. But no; according to Woodward, Bush's vision included "an ambitious reordering of the world through preemptive and, if necessary, unilateral action" to "reduce suffering and bring peace."[57]

In all of these monumental self-imposed missions, Bush was guided not by history, facts, knowledge, study, and reflection, but by his instinctive reactions. "During the [140-minute] interview, the president spoke a dozen times about his 'instincts' or his 'instinctive reactions,' " wrote Woodward. "It's pretty clear that Bush's role as a politician, president and commander-in-chief is driven by a secular faith in his instincts—his natural and spontaneous conclusions and judgments. His instincts are almost his second religion."[58]

In Woodward's words, in August 2002, Bush, guided by his gut instincts, "wanted Saddam out." The crucial question was, "How?" Multilaterally through the United Nations, or unilaterally? On November 7, the good news reached the White House that the U.S.–U.K. resolution on disarming Iraq, which had been much debated and refined during intense negotiations among the Permanent Members at the UN Security Council, was adopted unanimously.

NOTES

1. *Guardian,* July 10, 2003.
2. *The Times* (London), September 2, 2002.
3. Cited in *Sunday Times,* February 16, 2003.
4. *Independent,* June 2 and 18, 2003; *Guardian,* June 18, 2003.
5. *Guardian,* June 28, 2003. The British intelligence agencies were: domestic, MI5; foreign, MI6; and Defense Intelligence Staff.
6. *Independent,* August 19, 26, and 27, 2003; *Guardian,* August 29, 2003; *Independent on Sunday,* September 14, 2003.
7. By "some of the WMD," the authors meant biological and chemical weapons, not nuclear.
8. *Washington Post,* September 11, 2002.
9. *Daily Telegraph,* September 11, 2002.
10. Bob Woodward, *Bush at War,* p. 348.
11. *Guardian,* July 31, 2003. The reference to Box 850—the insiders code for British Intelligence Service MI6—in one of David Kelly's letters produced during the Hutton Inquiry showed that he had ongoing contacts with MI6.
12. See further Dilip Hiro, *War Without End,* p. 289, p. 295.
13. Michael Smith, *The Spying Game: The Secret History of British Espionage,* Politico's Publishing, London, 2003, p. 249.
14. *Washington Post,* December 22, 2002.
15. Ibid., October 21, 2002.

16. In the United States Khidir Hamza became a senior fellow at the Institute for Science and International Security (ISAIS), a Washington disarmament group whose president, David Albright, was a former Unscom inspector. In 1998 he and Hamza sent publishers a proposal for a book tentatively entitled *Fizzle: Iraq and the Atomic Bomb*, which described Iraq's failure to produce an atom bomb. No publisher was interested in this undramatic truth. So Hamza resorted to spinning yarns. He left the ISAIS. In 2000, collaborating with Jeff Stein, a Washington journalist, he published *Saddam's Bombmaker*, saying that during the run-up to the 1991 Gulf War, Iraq was much closer to manufacturing a nuclear weapon than had been known.

17. The correct name for this missile was Al Fatah, The Victory—the other missile was Al Samoud-2, meaning The Steadfast-2.

18. Iraq announced its decision to let in UN inspectors on September 16. The British government finalized its dossier on September 19. How it managed to collect raw information about Baghdad's concealment plans, assess it, and draw a conclusion within three days must remain a matter of wonderment and awe in the annals of intelligence.

19. In his briefing paper, William Cohen said, "Although Iraq claims it destroyed all the specific equipment and facilities for developing nuclear weapons, it retains sufficient skilled and experienced scientists as well as weapons design information that could allow it to restart a weapons program." *Independent*, July 12, 2003.

20. For Joseph Wilson's meetings with President Saddam Hussein in 1990, see Dilip Hiro, *Desert Shield to Desert Storm*, pp. 114, 268.

21. *International Herald Tribune*, May 7, 2003; *New York Times*, June 14 and July 6, 2003. In late September 2002, when Joseph Wilson read in the papers that Britain had issued a dossier mentioning Iraq seeking to buy uranium "in Africa," he contacted the CIA headquarters and asked them to find out if the dossier referred to Niger. He heard nothing in return. *Independent on Sunday*, June 29, 2003. Any attempt to smuggle uranium would have meant handling tons of ore across the barren stretch of the Sahara to reach a North African port, and would have been exposed. Tony Blair's spokesman's later statement that Iraq had bought 270 tons of uranium oxide from Niger in the 1980s was wrong (to put it politely) or a lie (to put it bluntly). Niger's current mining minister, Rabiou Hassane Yari, told the *Independent on Sunday* that "The Iraqis asked [for uranium oxide] but there was never any transaction. The request was officially made and officially turned down." July 20, 2003. Why Blair's office did not contact the government of Niger to check its claim—as the *Independent on Sunday* did—must remain a mystery.

22. The British government's explanation in July 2003 that it did not pass on the information to the IAEA because the intelligence originated elsewhere was at odds with the fact that the U.S. administration—which was not the originator of the intelligence either—had forwarded the papers to the IAEA five months earlier.

23. *Independent,* July 10 and 11, 2003.

24. *New York Times,* March 10, 2003; *Sunday Times,* March 16, 2003.

25. *The Times,* October 12, 2002.

26. For the text, visit www.uruklink.net/iraqnews/enews20.htm.

27. Referring to the economic sanctions, Muhammad Douri said, "These [economic] sanctions have caused the death of more than 1.7 million of our citizens," and added, "Three U.S. presidents have stated that these sanctions could not be lifted as long as our president Saddam Hussein remains the nation's leader." *New York Times,* October 17, 2002.

28. The White House released this sensational news only after Congress had given Bush war powers on October 11. *New York Times,* October 17, 2002.

29. *Washington Post,* September 29, 2002.

30. *Observer,* September 29, 2002.

31. *Washington Post,* September 27, 2002.

32. *New York Times,* September 11, 2002.

33. Bob Woodward, *Bush at War,* p. 342.

34. Cited in *International Herald Tribune,* September 6, 2002.

35. *Washington Post,* November 20, 2002.

36. After obtaining a doctorate in chemistry at a British university, Dr. Amr al Saadi took training courses at British weapons factories before returning home in the mid-1970s and becoming a top military scientist.

37. *New Yorker,* May 12, 2003.

38. *International Herald Tribune,* October 9, 2002.

39. Ibid.

40. Cited in *New York Times,* June 28, 2003.

41. *Washington Post,* June 5, 2003.

42. In the House, of the 296 voting for the war powers for Bush, 215 were Republicans, the rest Democrats; and in the Senate, forty-eight were Republicans, the rest Democrats. The divide among the opponents was: in the House, 126 Democrats and the rest Republican; in the Senate, twenty-two Democrats and the remaining one, Republican.

43. *New York Times,* October 14, 2002.

44. Ibid., October 10, 2002; *Independent on Sunday,* April 27, 2003.

45. *Guardian,* July 10, 2003. They could also be used for bomb shells.

46. Cited in *Guardian,* July 17, 2003.

47. *New York Times,* October 28, 2002.

48. Most arrests were made in 1980 (when the Iran–Iraq War started), 1987 (when Basra was threatened), 1991 (after the Gulf War), 1992 (after a coup attempt), and 1999 (after Operation "Desert Fox"). More than fifty thousand prisoners, including two thousand political detainees, were released.

49. Reuters, November 3, 2002.

50. The actual figures were: Republicans, $530 million; Democrats $340 million. *Washington Post,* November 7, 2002.

51. *New York Times,* May 18, 2003.

52. During the book tour, Franklin Graham said that Islam posed "a greater threat than anyone is willing to speak."

53. Cited in *International Herald Tribune,* April 22, 2003.

54. *Metro* London, December 30, 2002.

55. Bob Woodward, Ibid., pp. 340-41.

56. Ibid., p. 339.

57. Ibid., p. 341.

58. Ibid., p. 342.

CHAPTER 3

RESOLUTION 1441 TO POWELL'S PERORATION

"Every statement I make today is backed up by sources, solid sources. These are not assertions. What we are giving you are facts and conclusions based on solid intelligence."
—Colin Powell, U.S. secretary of state, to the UN Security Council,
February 5, 2003

"We went to a great many sites that were given to us by [U.S.–U.K.] intelligence, and only in three cases did we find anything—and they did not relate to weapons of mass destruction. That shook me a bit. I thought, 'My God, if this is the best intelligence they have had and we find nothing, what about the rest?'"
—Hans Blix, executive chairman, UN Monitoring, Verification and
Inspection Commission (Unmovic), in a BBC interview, June 6, 2003[1]

ACCORDING TO UN SECURITY COUNCIL RESOLUTION 1441, passed under Chapter VII of the UN Charter, Iraq had not provided "an accurate, full, final, and complete disclosure of all aspects of its programs to develop weapons of mass destruction and ballistic missiles with a range greater than 150 km," had "repeatedly obstructed immediate, unconditional, and unrestricted access to sites designated by Unscom and IAEA," and had finally ceased all cooperation with Unscom and the IAEA in 1998. After declaring that Iraq "has been and remains in material breach of its obligations under relevant resolutions," the resolution gave Iraq "a final opportunity to comply with its disarmament obligations under relevant resolutions of the Council" under "an enhanced inspection regime" to bring about full disarmament. It required Baghdad to provide the Council "a currently accurate, full, and complete declaration of all aspects of its [above-stated] programs" within thirty days, and warned Iraq that "false statements or omissions in the declarations submitted by Iraq and failure by Iraq at any time to comply with, and cooperate fully in the implementation of, this resolution shall constitute a further material breach of Iraq's obligations which will be reported to the Council for assessment in accordance with paragraphs 11 and (replacing the earlier 'or') 12 below."

Paragraph 11 directed the heads of Unmovic and the IAEA to report immediately "any interference by Iraq with inspection activities, as well as any failure . . . to comply with its disarmament obligations, including its obligations regarding inspections under this resolution." Paragraph 12 required the Council to convene immediately upon receipt of a report to "consider the situation and the need for full compliance with all of the relevant Council resolutions in order to secure (replacing the earlier 'restore') international peace and security."[2] Paragraphs 11 and 12 were crucial. The latter paragraph specified a discussion of the inspectors' report before any military action was decided. Its importance was stressed by Russian deputy foreign minister Yuri Fedotov as well as Arab League secretary-general Amr Moussa.

Syria's stance was equally important. Washington had apparently taken into account some of its concerns while drafting the final version. In fact, Colin Powell wrote to his Syrian counterpart, Farouq al Sharaa, emphasizing the importance of a unanimous vote, which, in his view, "would serve to avoid a future military confrontation." The implication was that if Syria, the only Arab member of the council, abstained or cast a negative vote, Saddam would feel encouraged to defy the council, thus making a war inevitable. France also had leaned heavily on Syria, with President Chirac visiting Damascus in October after the forty-nation Francophone conference in

Beirut, insisting that a "Yes" vote would help Syria end its political and economic isolation. Syria was keen to prevent an attack on Iraq, which would very likely hurt its economy by halting the $1 billion worth of trade in Iraqi oil. Damascus also calculated that the overthrow of Saddam would encourage Washington to target Iran and Syria next. These considerations—protecting Syrian interests, restraining the only superpower, and putting U.S. hawks on the defensive—led Syria to do what it did.

Among the obligations Iraq was required to meet under Resolution 1441 was to provide Unmovic and the IAEA "immediate, unimpeded, unconditional, and unrestricted access to any and all areas, facilities, buildings, equipment, records, and means of transport which they wish to inspect, as well as immediate, unimpeded, unrestricted, and private access to all officials and other persons whom Unmovic or the IAEA wish to interview in the mode or location of Unmovic's or the IAEA's choice pursuant to any aspect of their mandates; Unmovic and the IAEA may at their discretion conduct interviews inside or outside of Iraq, may facilitate the travel of those interviewed and family members outside of Iraq."

It gave Baghdad seven days to accept the resolution, and instructed Unmovic and the IAEA to resume inspections no later than forty-five days following the resolution's adoption and to update the council sixty days thereafter.

Unmovic's chief, Hans Blix, considered Unscom head Rolf Ekeus, a fellow Swede, heavy-handed and held him partly responsible for tarnishing Unscom's image. "In the end, Unscom was frankly no longer a UN operation," Blix told the *New York Times*.[3] Consequently, Blix retained only 30 percent of Unscom veterans.

Subsequently, those whom Blix didn't rehire accused him of naiveté. Blix retorted, "We have the most intrusive inspection system ever created."

Under the Unmovic scheme, senior scientists and engineers were given five weeks of secret training in skills required to penetrate and expose Iraq's secrets, while three hundred personnel from sixty countries were put through a training process their contracts prevented them from disclosing.[4] This was a marked contrast from what Unscom had done. Two-fifths of its inspectors were American or British. Unscom staffers also kept their jobs at home, and their respective governments paid their salaries. Unmovic's inspectors and their supporting staff, however, were required to quit their original jobs and were put on the UN payroll. This was done to diminish the chance of Unmovic staffers spying for their respective governments, as had happened with many of Unscom's American and British staff.

On the day Resolution 1441 was adopted, the Pentagon released a map of the Gulf region showing where the U.S.–U.K. forces were stationed, a step designed to warn Saddam that the alternative to total cooperation with the United Nations was an attack by the Anglo-American alliance. A fortnight later, the U.S. Centcom, amid great media fanfare, set up its operational headquarters at Al Udaid air base in Qatar—calling it Al Saliyah base—the first time the Pentagon had established a command center outside of America. Again, the Pentagon was sending Saddam a clear message.

Most people outside the Gulf region associated Qatar with Al Jazeera satellite TV (established in November 1996), which, with its editorial independence, had blazed a new trail in the electronic media of the Arab world. Al Jazeera had the blessing of Qatar's ruler, Shaikh Hamad ibn Khalifa al Thani (r. 1995–), whose government was a minority shareholder. The Shaikh's open alliance with Washington puzzled many. The explanation lay in the coup he had mounted against his father, Shaikh Khalifa al Thani, while the latter was in Geneva, Switzerland, in June 1995. The only way the ruler could consolidate his seizure of power was to secure the Clinton administration's backing. He got it, apparently on the understanding that he would gradually establish relations with Israel (which was then making peace with the Palestinians under the 1993 Oslo Accords). Thus Shaikh Hamad allowed Israel to open a trade mission in Doha, which ultimately acted as a conduit for talks between the Israeli government and Qatar General Petroleum Company on supplying Israel with natural gas. In 1997 Qatar hosted the U.S.-sponsored Fourth Middle East and North Africa (MENA) Economic Conference—it was largely boycotted by Arab states—which aimed at fostering economic ties between Israel and the Arab world. In any event, the outbreak of the Second Palestinian Intifada in September 2000 killed the prospect of Qatari gas flowing to Israel. And on the eve of Qatar assuming chairmanship of the fifty-seven-member Islamic Conference Organization (ICO) in December, the government ordered Israel to close down its trade mission in Doha.[5]

Qatar's open alliance with Washington removed the pressure that Donald Rumsfeld had been exerting on Riyadh to lend its land bases to the Pentagon—a step the Saudi government could not afford to take for obvious political and religious reasons. But Rumsfeld had succeeded in getting King Abdullah of Jordan to let the Pentagon use its air bases and station its Special Forces (as well as Britain's Special Forces) on Jordanian soil with the proviso that Washington and London would officially deny they were doing so while letting the monarch warn the United States vocally of the risks involved in attacking Iraq—an elaborate charade that would allow the Jordanian king to appear to be voicing the popular opinion of his people while the United States and Britain got what they wanted.

As for Turkey, a formally democratic state since 1924, only its parliament could permit a foreign power to station its troops on Turkish soil. And the Turkish parliament underwent a peaceful revolution on November 3, 2002. On that day only the Islamist Justice and Development Party (JDP) and the Republican People's Party passed the necessary electoral threshold to win seats in parliament, thus breaking with the past, which had been dominated by unwieldy coalition governments. So the Pentagon would have to wait until the victorious JDP formed its new administration.

Centcom's forward base at Al Salilya Camp near Doha reported directly to four-star General Tommy Ray Franks. Born in Wynnewood, Oklahoma, he grew up in Midland, Texas, a preeminent oil town. After graduating from the University of Texas, he joined the Army and was commissioned in 1967. He saw combat in Vietnam as an artillery officer, was wounded three times, and won two Purple Hearts. He returned to the university and got a postgraduate degree in business and public administration, then rejoined the Army in a cavalry division. He rose through the ranks, winning a Bronze Star, and served in the 1991 Gulf War. By then he had acquired the reputation of a "muddy boots" soldier, or a "soldier's soldier," one who made a special point of making himself accessible to the lower ranks and mixing with them. He once summed up his career and life's philosophy thus: "The military infrastructure grew in me. My faith in God is important, my belief in my country is important, my relationship to my family is important." Given such beliefs, it was not surprising that he climbed the career ladder higher during the 1990s and succeeded General Anthony Zinni as commander-in-chief of Centcom at MacDill Air Force base near Tampa, Florida. It was the 9/11 outrage that put him in the limelight, as the Bush White House prepared to attack the Taliban regime in Afghanistan in double-quick time. And it was during that war that his aversion to public speaking and television cameras came to light. "The operations we undertake go on twenty-four hours," he announced at one press conference. "They go on from the air, they go on day, they go on night." During the Iraqi invasion of March–April 2003, he would explain the war strategy thus: "Sometimes air, sometimes ground and sometimes special forces; sometimes a combination of the above two, sometimes all three."[6] Behind closed doors, though, he was said to be opinionated and an extrovert. Not that such behavior made him immune to Donald Rumsfeld, who pressured him to keep trimming his original "troop heavy" war plan—until it was down to five-eighths of its initial size of 400,000—and integrate the high-tech weaponry, the Special Forces, and the CIA into the final plan. Whether such an innovative scheme would work or not depended on how Saddam Hussein's forces would fare, "an unknown unknown," in the words of Rumsfeld.

For now, the Iraqi dictator had seven days in which to accept or reject Resolution 1441. Judging by his past behavior, he was most likely to declare his hand only at the very last moment, and to try to cover his retreat or defeat with as much dignity as he could muster. So, while the state-run Iraqi TV described the new resolution as unjustified, since Iraq had already agreed to the unconditional return of UN inspectors, accusing the United States of getting it passed to provide "groundwork for the legitimacy of moving into Iraq in the name of the UN and launching aggression against a founder member of the UN," the *Babil* (Babylon) newspaper, owned by Uday Saddam Hussein, said: "The most important thing is the awareness of our wise leadership which . . . will seek to deny the Bush administration a chance to exploit any circumstances or situation to implement its designs against Iraq." In the end, Saddam accepted the resolution—on the very last day.

He followed up the formal acceptance with concrete action. On December 6, the eve of the Eid al Fitr (Festival of Breaking the Fast)—at the end of the holy month of Ramadan—Saddam held a closed-door meeting of high-level military and political officers and told them to cooperate fully with UN inspectors in order to "keep our people out of harm's way."[7] He also seemed to have been seized with a rare feeling of self-examination—even atonement, of sorts. The gist of his long statement on Kuwait and the Kuwaitis, read on TV by Information Minister Muhammad Said al Sahhaf, went beyond outlining the background of the Kuwaiti ruler and the United States conspiring to lower oil prices in 1990 to hurt Iraq economically. Saddam said, "We apologize to God about any act that has angered Him in the past, and was held against us, and we apologize to you [the Kuwaitis] on the same basis." He added, "What we wish for you is what we wish for your brothers in Iraq—to live free from foreign rule and intervention in your wealth and future." He then accused the neighboring Arab rulers of conspiring with "the infidel forces" preparing to attack Iraq. Calling on Kuwaitis to "remain free and faithful by not allying yourself with the aggressors," he warned them that "America will steal your wealth and turn you into slaves working for them and turn your leaders into the agents for American oil companies." Therefore, he continued, "The faithful in Kuwait should join hands with brothers in Iraq to defeat evil, instead of joining forces with London and Washington." Then he referred to "the new conspiracy between the U.S. and the Iraqi opposition in exile—an unsavory band of characters—which was really for the region's oil." Finally, using Islamic terms, he talked of "jihad against the occupiers," and appealed to God for "the faithful to be victorious against this new conspiracy."[8] There was, as expected, no response from the Kuwaiti government. And the impact of his statement on ordinary Kuwaitis remains unknown. In any case, it had taken Saddam twelve long years to offer something approaching an apology for his grotesquely vicious and brutal invasion and occupation of Kuwait.

FRESH UN INSPECTIONS

UN inspections started on November 27, with the number of inspectors reaching nearly one hundred by mid-December. Given the history of espionage by Unscom inspectors from the United States and Britain, Blix had drastically reduced the size of the Anglo-American contingent. Headed by Miroslav Gregoric, a Yugoslav, the new team had a list of seven hundred inspection sites. Among the first sites that Unmovic and IAEA inspectors visited were Al Tawhidi Scientific Research Center, twelve miles (nineteen kilometers) northeast of Baghdad, a factory housing graphite equipment, and a missile-testing facility at Rafa, sixty miles (one hundred kilometers) southwest of Baghdad. Within a week they had checked out not only Khan Bani Saad airfield, north of Baghdad—where they found a mere nine of the twenty-five aging helicopters airworthy—in search of the devices allegedly to be used for spraying biological weapons, but also Saddam's Sijood Palace in central Baghdad. After the inspectors had departed, the officer in charge of the palace let hundreds of foreign journalists with TV cameras enter the building. "Intricately carved wooden doors were inset with a gold seal bearing the initials 'SH' while, inside, the white marble lined walls of the entrance hall were inscribed in gold with a poem singing the praises of SH, lit by a glittering gilt-and-crystal chandelier," reported one correspondent.[9] Iraq's chief liaison officer, Lieutenant General Hosam Muhammad Amin, reckoned that inspections would take about eight months, after which, he insisted, the Security Council should suspend sanctions while continuing its monitoring program.

The smoothness with which the UN inspections progressed had no impact on the course that Bush and Blair had decided on three months earlier. Among other things, Blair kept up his steady output of dossiers, including one on Iraq's violations of human rights, a regurgitation of old facts that had been in the public domain since the 1980–88 Iran–Iraq War, when the West backed Saddam.[10]

Equally, Bush and Blair remained impervious to public opinion in Europe as well as in the Arab and Muslim world. A survey of forty-four countries, fourteen of them Muslim—involving thirty-eight thousand interviewees—conducted by the *International Herald Tribune* and Pew Research Center in mid-November showed that a war on Iraq was opposed by 79 percent of Russians, 71 percent of Germans, 64 percent of the French, and 47 percent of Britons. The corresponding figure for the United States was 26 percent, with 62 percent favoring force. In the Muslim world, 80 percent of Turks opposed the Pentagon's use of their military facilities in its war on Iraq, believing that the United States was punishing a Muslim country, and not trying to bring about stability in the region.[11] Given Washington's indulgent attitude toward Israel in contrast to its hard line on Iraq, and the anti-Muslim statements made by conservative American Christian leaders (Franklin Graham called Islam "an evil religion"; Pat Robertson described the prophet Muhammad "an absolute wild-eyed fanatic, a robber and a brigand"; and according to Jerry Vines, former president of the Southern Baptist Convention, the prophet Muhammad was "a demon-possessed paedophile"), it came as no surprise when a poll by the U.S. State Department found 67 percent of Pakistanis opposing the Pentagon's attack on Iraq *even if* Saddam blocked UN inspections. In reality, however, Iraq was being cooperative.

As required by Resolution 1441, on December 7 Baghdad submitted a 11,790-page dossier on its past and present WMD programs to the Security Council, which had decided a day earlier that the Iraqi document would remain with Blix, whose experts would analyze it over the weekend and excise elements that might provide arms-making recipes to the reader, and then be given to all fifteen members. But the Council's Colombian president, Alfonso Valdivieso, handed over the document solely to the U.S. mission (after Colin Powell, then in the Colombian capital of Bogotá, had pledged $200 million in aid to Colombia): It promised to make "copies," but only for the four other Permanent Members. This sleight of hand was condemned by UN secretary-general Annan: "The approach, and the style and the form was wrong because the Security Council had decided on Friday that nobody would get it [on its own]." Iraq described the arrangement as extortionist. Blix was miffed, too. He gave the Permanent Members a week to remove whatever they wanted and then hand over the document to the other members.

The reason for this skullduggery was that the Iraqi document listed the foreign companies that had provided it with materials and equipment to make WMD before the 1991 Gulf War. In the bioweapons field, Iraq's two suppliers were American Type Culture Collection, located in Manassas, Virginia, and the Pasteur Institute, located in Paris. These two companies supplied all seventeen types of biological agents to Iraq, which used them for weapons—including anthrax and the bacteria needed to make botulinum toxin. Two U.S. corporations were also involved in supplying Iraq with chemical agents and precursors, the bulk of which came from European companies. In the nuclear field, ten U.S. companies either made or sold equipment to Iraq. Washington wanted the American names withheld, but the only way to do so was to withhold the names of all 150 companies implicated, eighty of which were German—with thirty involved in the nuclear program, which took up 2,100 pages (in Arabic) in the Iraqi dossier. In the nuclear field, eleven British companies were involved and a handful of Brazilian, French, Italian, Japanese, Swiss, and Swedish firms. Most of the sales, made from the early 1980s up to the 1991 Gulf War, were legal and made with the respective government's knowledge and approval. Despite Washington's wishes, three months later the names of the involved American companies would become public anyway, when Gary Pitts, a Houston lawyer suing the Pentagon on behalf of 1991 Gulf War veterans for exposure to biological and chemical weapons, released the relevant papers on the U.S. suppliers of biological and chemical warfare agents to the *New York Times*.[12]

Meanwhile, the excising of the Iraqi dossier was so extensive that the abridged version constituted less than a third of the original. The ten non-permanent members of the United Nations got the attuned document on the evening of December 17. (Syria was so incensed by this treatment that its ambassador returned his copy, saying, "Either we take a full copy or we don't take anything.") The next morning—when the capitals of the non-permanent members had not even yet received the dossier—Powell announced that the council members shared the U.S. assessment that the Iraqi declaration contained "troublesome gaps and omissions," which were tantamount to "a material breach" of Resolution 1441. The French ambassador to the United Nations disagreed. Referring to the pertinent clause in 1441, he pointed out that "missing data and less than candid statements are not enough to cause a material breach if there is no other pattern of defiance by Baghdad."

Powell's ploy was in line with the predetermined policy of the White House. Commenting on the first week of inspections, Bush said he was "not encouraged" by the work of UN inspectors, and suggested that his administration might not abide by the inspectors' findings. "The issue is not the inspectors," he added. "Saddam says he doesn't have any WMD. He has got them. The choice is his—he could voluntarily disarm and avert a war."[13] To say that inspections were not the issue was a clear hint from Bush that he considered the United Nations a sideshow and that he would press on with his war plans irrespective of what UN inspections teams found or did not find. Here he was at odds with public opinion in the United States. A Gallup poll in mid-December showed two-thirds of Americans saying the United States should wait until UN inspectors found hard evidence that Saddam Hussein had lied about WMD.[14]

An important element in Bush's political strategy was to impress the American public with the size and variety of the Iraqi opposition to Saddam. However, despite frantic efforts by his senior aides, the movement on that front had been tardy. An opposition gathering was originally scheduled for September as a follow-up to the meeting that the leaders of the six U.S.-approved groups—including the Tehran-based Supreme Council of Islamic Revolution in Iraq (SCIRI)—had with Cheney in mid-August in Washington.[15] Washington's objective was to get these factions to form a steering committee to speak as the unified voice and adopt an agreed statement of principles to govern Iraq in the post-Saddam era—summarized in the phrase "a democratic, multi-ethnic, unified state," with the Kurdish groups insisting on inserting "federal" after "unified."

Brussels was to be the venue for the conference in late November, but the disagreements on whom to invite became so acute that a delegation of State Department, Pentagon, and NSC officials had to fly to London to resolve them. As a result, the list of those invited tripled, to three hundred. Then the Belgian government said to the conference organizers that the UN resolution was about disarming Saddam, whereas they wanted to meet to topple him, which was unacceptable."[16] So the organizers moved the meeting to London.

The continued inclusion of SCIRI in the forthcoming conference was deeply puzzling. Ahmad Chalabi, a Shia, seemed to be playing the role of intermediary, as Washington lacked direct contact with Iran. The Bush administration accepted SCIRI in order to demonstrate wide support among a diverse array of factions, and to reassure Iraq's Shia majority that they were adequately represented in the opposition ranks. Also, by co-opting SCIRI's leader, Ayatollah Muhammad Baqir al Hakim, the United States prepared the ground for Iran's neutrality in its war on Iraq. From a military viewpoint, it helped to have Hakim on the U.S. side, as Shias are predominant in the south, the Pentagon's planned invasion route. But Washington refused to incorporate in its war plans SCIRI's ten- to twelve-thousand-strong Badr Brigades—recruited from among the Iraqi exiles as well as POWs who refused to return home—who were trained and armed by Iran. From SCIRI's viewpoint, it was important to pave the way for a share of power in a democratic, post-Saddam Iraq in order to safeguard the rights of Shias. At the same time, Hakim was clear about the role of the United States once Saddam had been ousted. "I see no need for American forces to remain in Iraq, because no external forces threaten Iraq," he told the *New York Times* in late November.

Just then, the United States released a ninety-eight-page document entitled *The Transition to Democracy in Iraq,* prepared by a group of Iraqis led by Professor Kanan Makiya of Brandeis

University, as a platform around which diverse opposition factions could unite. It endorsed the principles of democracy, federalism, and the rule of law. Its authors agreed on the separation of religion and state but were unclear about the relationship between the two. It specified a transitional period of three years to culminate in elections in which Iraqis would vote on a constitution and the structure of the new government. (Differences arose however on whether to establish a transitional government immediately after Saddam's overthrow.)

On the eve of the conference in London in mid-December 2002, however, the opposition leaders received written instructions—signed by Paul Wolfowitz, Richard Armitage, deputy secretary of state, and I. Lewis Libby, Cheney's chief of staff—telling them that all that was expected of them was to establish an advisory committee selected by the conference to work alongside the U.S.-led coalition.

But there were divisions in the American camp. The State Department backed the Iraqi National Accord (INA), led by Iyad Muhammad Alawi, a heavy-set, balding, mustached Shia physician living in London, which—claiming covert links with disaffected military officers in Saddam's regime—favored a coup or a limited military engagement by the Pentagon, thus leaving intact most of Saddam's government and providing a virtually seamless transition. This was opposed by Cheney's office and the Pentagon's civilian hawks (who, in the interagency warfare, were winning, with the DIA putting the CIA on the defensive by openly accusing it of not debriefing Iraqi defectors, and the CIA denying the charge while repeating its overall assessment that most of them exaggerated to underscore their own importance), who reckoned that such a regime would prove less malleable than one led by their favorite, the INC's Chalabi.

Among the Iraqis, the INC was intent on creating a transitional government immediately after Saddam's ouster, a proposition rejected by all other factions. It failed to win the conference's

backing. What the assembly achieved after four days of deliberations was the creation of a sixty-five-member Advisory Council,
with Shias getting thirty seats (half of these to going to SCIRI),
and Kurds fifteen. For the post-Saddam era, it settled for a transitional national assembly and a three-person sovereignty
council, with a maximum transitional period of two years,
during which a new constitution would be adopted and parliamentary elections held.[17]

In New York, in his first report to the Security Council, Blix stated
that access to sites had been promptly given and the Iraqi assistance had been expeditious, with inspections averaging six per day.
Commenting on the Iraqi dossier, he said that in terms of biological weapons, what it had provided was "essentially" a rehash of
Iraq's previous declaration to Unscom in September 1997. The
unanswered issue remained the lack of supporting evidence (docu-
mentation, personal testimony, physical evidence) for Iraq's
claimed unilateral destruction of anthrax during 1988–91. In
terms of chemical arms, the present document updated the 1996
declaration, further explaining its account of the material balance
of chemical precursors. Also, Baghdad had submitted the previously withheld air force documents relating to munitions used
during the Iraq–Iran War[18], and that would help resolve questions
about the material balance of chemical weapons.

At his weekly press conference, General Amr al Saadi said it was
unrealistic to expect Iraq to account on paper for all the chemical
and biological weapons it had destroyed in the 1990s. "Can anyone
reach zero, having gone through a war, a devastating war, and a
month of disturbances [in 1991]?"[19]

Regarding missiles, the Iraqi dossier had updated the 1996 submission, describing fresh projects, including a new liquid
oxygen–ethanol propellant engine and replacement of the guidance
systems. It contained information about a short-range rocket with
eighty-one-millimeter aluminum tubes (at the center of the

U.S.–U.K. allegation of Iraq's revival of its nuclear-arms program). It also said that Iraq had used a missile with a diameter of 760 millimeters, much larger than the standard 500 millimeters. In thirteen test flights, its Al Samoud-2 missile had covered 114 miles (182 kilometers)—twenty miles (thirty-two kilometers) above the allowed limit.

Washington gave its own assessment of the Iraqi dossier. Regarding biological weapons, information was missing on about two thousand kilograms of growth media as well as the facilities Iraq calls "refrigeration vehicles and food-testing labs" but which really are mobile biological-warfare-agent facilities. Regarding chemical arms, Baghdad had not furnished enough information on VX,[20] and there was no accounting for thirty thousand empty munitions. The United States wondered why Iraq was attempting to produce more energetic fuel, such as oxygen–ethanol.[21]

When Washington and London persisted in their allegations against Iraq, Blix said, "If the U.S. and the U.K. are convinced, and they say they have evidence, well then, one would expect that they would be able to tell us where is this stuff." There was no public response from the American or British government. In Baghdad, Saadi said, "Since the U.S. does not believe us, let the CIA agents accompany the UN inspectors and go where they want to go; we will allow that. . . . Let the CIA agents guide the inspectors to the suspect sites." To this, Rumsfeld responded, "This is all a stunt. Iraq is a large country, and there are bunkers and underground facilities."

Once Baghdad provided Unmovic with a list of more than five hundred scientists on December 28, the Bush administration pressured the United Nations to interview them outside the country. "How many scientists; how do you take them out; and do you send them back if they don't give us any useful information?" asked Ewen Buchanan, the Unmovic spokesman. Also, the information promised might prove to be less valuable once the Iraqis' objective (to leave Iraq) had been achieved, as had proved to be the case with past information (often of "questionable value") from defectors, Buchanan explained. A further complicating problem was how to determine whether the scientists themselves did not want to leave the country, or were being pressured by their government to say so. Soon afterward, Mark Gwozdecky, the IAEA spokesman, announced that the IAEA had started one-on-one interviews with the scientists, and that they were being conducted efficiently.[22]

These retorts aside, the unremitting U.S. pressure on the United Nations made the inspectors aggressive. During their fourth visit in a month to the Al Samoud-2 missile factory, twenty-five miles (forty kilometers) west of Baghdad, for instance—according to Hussein Muhammad, the works manager— "As soon as they entered the site, they spread out like gangs. They went to all the workshops and buildings inside the site. They prevented anyone from entering or exiting. They behaved in a provocative manner."[23]

During one month, UN inspectors had visited Mosul, Basra, and Akashat near the Syrian border, and had checked 150 sites. They had checked out Al Thuwaita, the former nuclear facility site, *six* times. "Schooled by Iraq's past record of concealing its weapons programs in 'dual use' sites, the inspectors have visited plants producing baby formula, cement, steel, fiberglass, ceramics, automobile parts, commercial electronics, and industrial chemicals such as chlorine and sulfuric acid," reported John F. Burns in the *New York Times*. "They have pulled lecturers out of classes at universities, demanding access to labs. They have taken gamma radiation readings all over Baghdad, and drawn water, sediment, and vegetation samples from drainage basins along the Tigris and the Euphrates, rivers along whose banks many of Iraq's 22 million people, and much of its industry, is clustered. Iraqi officials have been punctilious, so far, in meeting their obligations to grant immediate and unhindered access to any sites the inspectors choose, opening access gates, labs and workshops, offices and filing cabinets almost on demand."[24]

None of this changed Bush's mind. In his weekly radio address on December 28, 2002, he said, "The burden now is on Iraq's dictator to disclose and destroy his arsenal of weapons. If he refuses, for the sake of peace, the United States will lead a coalition to disarm the Iraqi regime and free the Iraqi people."[25] This left many politicians and commentators in the United States and abroad wondering about Bush's ulterior motive. "Bush's priorities are baffling to me," said Heidemarie Wieczorek-Zeul, German development minister, in an interview with *Der Speigel* (The Mirror). "War must not be the extension of politics or the economy by other means. . . . It is depressing that the U.S. administration is preparing for war apparently regardless of the result of weapons inspections." Just then Israeli prime minister Ariel Sharon declared that he had been briefed on a tentative date for the American attack on Iraq.[26]

Those on the inside track in Washington knew that the first phase of the "unseen" war against Iraq, activated in August with Operation "Southern Focus," had been in full swing by the end of the year, and that the Pentagon's Special Forces units were now implementing the second phase of the "unseen" war by infiltrating Iraq and depositing telecommunications equipment at selected sites in the western desert and other sparsely populated areas to be activated once the hot war started. It was noteworthy that in the first three weeks of December 2002, the Pentagon struck targets nine times in the south—at Amara, Basra, Kut, and Nasiriya—using precision bombs.

The third phase of the "unseen" war—known as psychological warfare operations, or "psy-ops"—was launched with a broad hint from the Pentagon in mid-December that it was "actively considering" covert operations to influence public opinion and policy makers in "friendly and neutral countries."[27] Soon afterward, stories appeared in the German and Saudi press about Saddam's plans to flee and take refuge in a foreign country, which varied from Egypt to Saudi Arabia to Russia, Belarus, and Libya. Contradicting these fanciful tales, Libyan leader Colonel Muammar Gaddafi said, "Don't delude yourself into believing such legends. Saddam will never leave Iraq and he will die a martyr there."

At home, however, the news was not to the liking of the Bush administration. A CNN/*USA Today* Gallup poll showed Bush's approval rating down to 58 percent, one of the lowest ratings since 9/11. The approval rating on his handling of the economy was down to 48 percent at a time when the most important issue for Americans was the economy (53 percent), not terrorism (32 percent).[28]

On the street, opposition to the war was rising. Despite the bone-chilling weather, an antiwar demonstration in Washington on January 18, 2003, drew upward of two hundred thousand people, with the Metropolitan Police Chief saying that the march was "bigger than [last] October's," which was estimated by the *Washington Post* at one hundred thousand. "Tens of thousands of antiwar protesters converged on Washington today, braving the bitter cold in thunderous numbers and assembling in the shadow of the Capitol dome to voice their opposition to a U.S. military strike against Iraq," reported the *Post.* On the West Coast, the *San Francisco Chronicle* claimed fifty-five thousand to two hundred thousand protesters (quoting the police and the organizers, respectively) in San Francisco.[29] A national effort to mobilize the antiwar movement was led by groups such as MoveOn.org and TrueMajority.com. In a letter to the *Wall Street Journal,* the Business Leaders for Sensible Priorities said, "We supported the Gulf War. We supported our intervention in Afghanistan. We accept the logic of a just war. But Mr. President, your war on Iraq does not pass the test." If this group was looking for solid evidence, it could find it in an Associated Press dispatch of January 18: "In almost two months of surprise visits across Iraq, UN arms monitors have inspected 13 sites identified by U.S. and British intelligence agencies as major 'facilities of concern,' and reported no signs of revived weapons building." (These sites included all the satellite images that Bush and Blair had published since their first joint press conference at Camp David on September 7, 2002, and any further information their governments had passed on privately to Unmovic and the IAEA.) The Business Leaders for Sensible Priorities would have drawn succor from a poll in Britain in which 68 percent said that Prime Minister Blair had not convinced them that a war in Iraq was justified.[30]

None of this mattered to Bush or Rumsfeld. Following a pre-planned schedule, the Pentagon moved on to its fourth phase in the "unseen" war against Iraq on January 9. In a concerted move, it sent hundreds of e-mail messages to Iraqi military and Baath Party leaders, urging them to dissent or give up—instructing them to contact the United Nations in Baghdad if they wanted to defect! Actually, almost everyone with an e-mail account in Iraq received such a message. It was not until January 11 that the Iraqi authorities started to block these e-mails. Soon the whole e-mail system in Iraq broke down, and it took the authorities a week to restore it.[31] Several weeks later, the roles were reversed in the United States. As a "virtual" march on Washington, hundreds of thousands of antiwar protesters simultaneously phoned, faxed, or e-mailed the White House and Congress, paralyzing the telephone lines for several hours on February 26.[32]

In New York the Security Council continued to receive reports on UN inspections in Iraq. In one such submission, the IAEA's Muhammad el Baradei informed the council that while eighty-one-millimeter aluminum tubes could be modified for the manufacture of centrifuges, they are not directly suitable for it, and that they were used for a rocket program, thereby rebutting one of the major charges in Bush's *Decade of Deception and Defiance*.[33] That day, January 10, North Korea withdrew from the Nuclear Non-Proliferation Treaty and expelled IAEA inspectors while one million people in Pyongyang demonstrated against the United States. Bush responded to North Korean leader Kim Jong Il's defiance with promises of food and oil for his country while thundering: "I am sick and tired of games and deception by Saddam." North

Korea would go on to reactivate its nuclear facilities on February 5, and announce, three weeks later, that its nuclear reactor at Yong-byon complex was operational.[34]

In a dramatic move, on January 15 seven carloads of Unmovic inspectors arrived suddenly at the Republican Palace, the main presidential site, in central Baghdad. They checked out two office complexes with high walls and two fences—which turned out to be residential sites and a war veterans agency. They checked safes, but took away nothing. The next day there was much excitement at the White House when the news came in that eleven empty 122-millimeter chemical warheads had been discovered at the Ukhaidar Ammunition Storage Area, 105 miles (170 kilometers) southwest of Baghdad. This was the smoking gun the Bush administration had been hoping for. Alas, it was not to be. Unmovic accepted the explanation of the head of the Iraqi National Monitoring Directorate, General Hussam Muhammad Amin, that "the rockets had expired and were packed in closed wooden boxes that we had forgotten about," and challenged anybody to prove otherwise. Dispassionate observers held up the discovery of these warheads as evidence that the inspections were working.

Further progress was assured when, during their visit to Baghdad on January 19–20, Blix and el Baradei signed a ten-point agreement with Baghdad. Iraq agreed to conduct its own investigation regarding the eleven empty 122-millimeter warheads for delivering chemical weapons and to encourage its scientists to be interviewed without the presence of official Iraqi minders. But there was no agreement on U-2 flights marked with the UN symbol. "How can we guarantee the safety of U-2?" asked a top Iraqi official. "How can our air defense people distinguish between U-2 and other U.S.–U.K. planes [in the no-fly zones]?"

At the end of two months of inspections, when a third of the seven hundred sites had been visited, Blix and el Baradei reported to the Security Council that, overall, Iraq had cooperated well, giving them access to all sites. On the chemical front, Iraq's statement that it had produced a few tonnes of VX that was not weaponized did not tally with the information Unmovic had. Whereas the Iraqi Air Force document showed Iraq using 13,000 chemical bombs between 1983 and 1988 (during the Iran–Iraq War), elsewhere Iraq had stated that it had used 19,500 munitions. On the biological front, Iraq had yet to show evidence that it had unilaterally destroyed 8,500 liters of anthrax. Also, 650 kilograms of bacterial growth media were unaccounted for. In the missiles area, Al Samoud-2 (using liquid fuel) and Al Fatah (using solid fuel) may have exceeded the limit of ninety-three miles (150 kilometers). El Baradei reported that his inspectors had visited presidential compounds and private residences but had discovered no evidence that Iraq had revived its nuclear-weapons program since its elimination in the 1990s.

While noting that Blix and el Baradei had been fair generally, General Amr Rashid, who liaised with the IAEA and Unmovic at the highest level, added that they had failed to mention that their inspections did not support U.S. and British allegations of forbidden weapons work at specific sites.[35]

For Saddam, offering full cooperation to the United Nations went hand in hand with making preparations to defend his country against a U.S. invasion. His defense strategy rested on four pillars: regular armed forces; the Baath Party militia (called the Jerusalem Army) and the Firqat Fedayeen Saddam (lit., Saddam's Self-Sacrificers Division); tribal leaders and their armed followers; and ordinary citizens.

In the army, Saddam paid particular attention to the eighty-thousand-strong Republican Guard—which included the twenty-thousand-strong Special Republican Guard, charged with safeguarding Baghdad and eight presidential complexes in the country.[36] He dispersed the six Republican Guard divisions to save them from U.S. air strikes, with a plan to deploy them later in two defensive rings around Baghdad.

An official indication of the role to be played by the Baath Party militias came on December 26, when *Al Qadissiya* reported that they had practiced fighting in rural and urban areas in Babylon and had rehearsed "techniques of distracting the enemy in different directions by using light and medium weapons." Equally important was the Firqat Fedayeen Saddam—popularly called Fedayeen, plural of *fedayee,* self-sacrificer. During Iraq's crisis with the United States in October 1994 in the wake of Iraqi troop maneuvers in southern Iraq, Saddam Hussein's elder son, Uday, set up a volunteer force of young men, called Firqat Fedayeen Saddam, which soon became twenty-thousand strong. Its task was to assist the regime in suppressing subversion. It assisted the forces of the Special Republican Guard and the General Security in quashing the riots that erupted in Ramadi, seventy miles (110 kilometers) west of Baghdad, a stronghold of the (Sunni) Dulaimi tribe, in May 1995, following the execution of General Muhammad Madhlum al Dulaimi for his alleged involvement in a plot to assassinate Saddam.[37] It would play a leading role in offering resistance to the invading Anglo-American forces eight years later.

By early 2003, Saddam Hussein had charged local clan and tribal leaders to defend their own areas and armed them accordingly. Initially opposed to fostering tribal loyalties, Saddam had changed his policy in the 1980s when tribal leaders provided him with men to wage the war with Iran. Again, after the end of the 1991 Gulf War, the tribal leaders had rallied around Saddam to help him quash the uprisings by the Shias in the south and the Kurds in the north. Shaikh Talal al Khalidi, head of the Bani Khalid tribe in the north, for instance, told Neil MacFarquhar of the *New York Times* that in March and April 1991 his armed men protected a seventy-mile (110-kilometer) section of the highway in the south. "We protect the nation's land, and we would consider killing Americans a jihad in the service of God if they come here as aggressors," he said. "The Quran says an eye for an eye and a tooth for a tooth."[38] Finally, the government handed out guns to citizens to help them conduct urban warfare.

Meanwhile, to keep up public morale, the Iraqi media gave much publicity to the periodic downing of a U.S. unmanned vehicle originating in Kuwait. And, starting in mid-January, Saddam began appearing almost daily on state-run television to discuss war preparation and strategy. On January 31, for instance, he discussed with senior military commanders the most likely American offensive strategy: land in the desert and then advance to capture Baghdad. This was one of several scenarios—including the one where U.S. troops parachuted into Baghdad and then fanned out—that were debated. The government had made contingency plans assuming a total breakdown of communications systems. The fact that these plans had worked during and after the 1991 Gulf War gave confidence to Saddam's regime. At the administrative level, it had appointed a shadow government, with parallel civil servants and advisers to the ministers.[39]

Saddam's overall strategy was to stretch out the inspection process over the next four or five months by providing the evidence for the claimed unilateral destruction of the WMD soon after the 1991 Gulf War in bits and pieces—well into late spring and early summer, when it gets unbearably hot in the desert and elsewhere—and turn the U.S.–U.K. military buildup into a waiting game. Also, he reckoned that the Anglo-American alliance would wither with time as the antiwar movement in Britain and America gathered steam.

In a long television interview with Tony Benn, a former British Labor minister and a veteran peace campaigner, aired on Britain's Channel 4 on February 4, Saddam went on record. "It's not surprising that there might be complaints relating to some details of the inspections," he said. "When Iraq objects to the conduct of those implementing the Security Council resolutions, that does not mean that Iraq wishes to push things to confrontation. . . . It is in our interests to help them to reach the truth. The question is whether the other side wants to reach the truth or wants to find a pretext for aggression." Referring to the WMD, Saddam said, "These weapons do not come in small pills that you can hide in your pocket. These are weapons of mass destruction, and it is easy to work out if Iraq has them or not. . . . I tell you Iraq has no weapons of mass destruction whatsoever. We challenge anyone who claims we have them to bring forward evidence and present it to the world opinion." Asked about Iraq's links with Al Qaida, he replied, "If we had a relationship with Al Qaida and we believed in that relationship, we wouldn't be ashamed to admit it. Therefore I would like to tell you directly . . . that we have no relationship with Al Qaida." Addressing the importance of oil, Saddam said, "Those [pro-Israeli] people and others have been telling the various U.S. administrations, especially the current one, that if you want to control the world, you need to control oil. And one of the most important requirements for controlling oil is to destroy Iraq. One of the main reasons for the aggression that the U.S. administration is engaged in is to control the world. . . . This hostility [to various major powers] is a trademark of the present administration and is based on its wish to control the world."[40]

In the petroleum business, Saudi Arabia, possessing 25 percent of the global reserves—twice as much as Iraq's—remained the primary player. And, occupying four-fifths of the Arabian Peninsula, its geostrategic position was unrivaled. Saddam knew this. He had moved steadily to normalize relations with Riyadh. In mid-December the two neighbors reestablished telephone links after a break of twelve years.

The following week, discussing the kingdom's policy toward Iraq in an interview with CNN, Saudi foreign minister Saud al Faisal said, "If it is a war that is through the United Nations, with consensus on it, we will have to decide on that—based on the national interests of Saudi Arabia." In other words, Riyadh would not participate in a war unauthorized by the United Nations. Given that the Pentagon had set up a state-of-the-art air operations command center at the Prince Sultan base in the kingdom, Riyadh's stance on the war mattered greatly. In the end, the Pentagon revealed that the Saudis would let them use their bases for "fly support missions such as surveillance, refueling trips and cargo transport," but would not allow its strike aircraft to take off from their bases.[41]

With the predetermined date for invading Iraq approaching, Bush used his annual State of the Union address to Congress on January 28, 2003, to ratchet up pressure not only on Iraq but also on the United Nations. "From intelligence sources we know thousands of Iraqi security personnel are hiding documents and materials, sanitizing inspection sites, and monitoring inspectors themselves," he said. *"The British government has learned that Saddam Hussein recently sought significant quantities of uranium in Africa."* [Italics added][42] On the crucial Israeli-Palestinian conflict, Bush had just eighteen words to say: "In the Middle East, we will continue to seek peace between a secure Israel and a democratic Palestine."

In a two-hour interview with Judith Miller and Julia Preston of the *New York Times* on January 30, Blix challenged the assertions of Bush and Powell. Referring to Powell's claims at the Security Council in late January that UN inspectors had found that Iraqi officials were hiding or moving illicit materials within and outside of Iraq, Blix said, "Inspectors have reported no such incidents." Regarding Bush's statement in his State of the Union speech that Iraqi agents were posing as scientists, Blix said, "Inspectors have reported no such instances." On the claims by "Bush's top officials" that Iraq was sending its weapons scientists to Syria, Jordan, and other countries to prevent them from being interviewed by the UN inspectors, Blix said, "I have seen no convincing evidence to this effect." Blix made a similar statement when faced with allegations by Bush's officials that Unmovic had been penetrated by Iraqi agents and that sensitive information might have been leaked to Iraq, thus compromising the inspections.

On Bush's repeated assertions of Al Qaida links with Iraq, Blix stated that he had had not seen "any persuasive evidence" to that effect; nor had he received any intelligence from member states of the United Nations to that effect. Lastly, Blix challenged Bush's argument that military action was needed now to avoid the risk of a 9/11-style attack by terrorists wielding biological, nuclear, or chemical weapons. "The world is a far less dangerous place today than during the Cold War when the Soviet Union and the U.S. threatened each other with thousands of nuclear-tipped missiles," he said. As head of the IAEA from 1981 to 1997, Blix was on the inside track of that aspect of the Cold War.

This point-by-point rebuttal by Blix was ignored by a White House bent on pushing its preconceived agenda. Bush's January 28 statement on Iraq was a curtain-raiser for Powell's upcoming presentation to the UN Security Council.

POWELL'S PERORATION

For all practical purposes, Powell's much-trumpeted seventy-five-minute presentation to the UN Security Council, on February 5, with CIA director George Tenet by his side, signaled the end of the Bush administration's support of continued UN weapons inspections and set the scene for an invasion of Iraq.

The highlights of Powell's peroration, and the facts established within the next few days to few months, were as follows:[43]

IRAQ–AL QAIDA LINK:

Nearly two dozen Al Qaida terrorists based in Baghdad were active; prominent among them was Abu Mussab Zarqawi, a senior associate of Osama bin Laden. He and the Iraqi Ansar al Islam (Helpers of Islam), based in Khurmal, Kurdistan, operated a poison factory where Zarqawi taught how to make ricin and other chemical poisons. "Baghdad has an agent at the most senior levels of the radical organization Ansar al Islam, which controls this corner of Iraq." This agent had offered Ansar members haven in 2000. All this proved a link between the Iraqi government and Al Qaida.

> *Fact:* Even though Zarqawi was described as bin Laden's senior associate, he was not on the CIA's most-wanted list.

Born in a village near Amman, Jordan, Zarqawi traveled to Afghanistan in the late 1980s to join the anti-Soviet jihad. Following the Taliban victory in 1996, he stayed on with thirty members of the Muslim Brotherhood of Jordan in the Afghan city of Logar. Following the fall of the Taliban in December 2001, he escaped to neighboring Iran, where he was arrested. Since Jordan did not want him back, the Iranian government expelled him—to Iraq. There he reportedly went to Baghdad for treatment of his injured leg. He then somehow ended up in Khurmal in that part of Iraqi Kurdistan administered by the Patriotic Union of Kurdistan (PUK), part of the U.S.-recognized Iraqi opposition. The Ansar's founder, Mullah Mustafa Kreikar, had fled the area and was living in Oslo as a refugee. His colleague Abu Wael was supposed to be the Iraqi intelligence liaison to Ansar, according to Powell. But Kreikar said that the Iraqi agents tried to poison Abu Wael in 1992 and would kill him now if they knew his whereabouts. In an interview with Don Vat Natta of the *New York Times* in Oslo, Kreikar said, "Saddam Hussein is my enemy. I have never met a member of Al Qaida." Kreikar denied ever meeting bin Laden or allowing his organization to become a safe haven for Al Qaida members on the run. "Powell's information is propaganda, it is very odd and very weak," he said.[44]

Regarding the satellite picture of the alleged poison factory shown by Powell, Kreikar remarked that it looked like a village. Luke Harding of the (London) *Observer,* who was one of the twenty foreign journalists allowed into the area by the Ansar's Victory Brigade, described the alleged "poison factory" as "a derelict dump"; and C. J. Chivers of the *New York Times* cited a commander of the brigade thus: "This place is an isolated place, and we just have our weapons."

Within the U.S. intelligence community, the head of the National Security Project, Melvin Goodman, an ex–CIA officer, said, "I have talked to my sources at the CIA and all of them are saying the evidence [of a link] is simply not there."[45] There was also the need for remaining focused on the UN Security Council mandate, which pertained in this case to disarming Iraq. "Even if certain terrorists could have been able to find refuge in Iraq, we must not mix up the issues," French president Jacques Chirac told *L'Orient-Le Jour* (The Orient Today) in Beirut. "The first objective of action by the international community is Iraq, and that means disarmament."

WEAPONS OF MASS DESTRUCTION AND THE MEANS OF DELIVERY:

Missiles:

While the Security Council was debating a resolution authorizing renewed weapons inspections in early November, the United States "knew from sources that a missile brigade outside Baghdad was dispersing rocket launchers and warheads containing biological warfare agents . . . to various locations in western Iraq." Powell added that "most of the launchers and warheads had been hidden in large groves of palm trees and were to be moved every one to four weeks to escape detection."

> ***Fact:*** Until April 25, 2003, none of those weapons had been found, a senior administration official admitted to the *Washington Post*. Searches had been conducted in western Iraq without any success. During the invasion, U.S. forces attacked the missile brigade along with the Iraqi Special Republican Guard units that Bush administration officials told reporters in the weeks before the war had received chemical weapons. "We don't know where those people are," the official admitted to the *Post*, adding that U.S. military personnel in Iraq might be looking for them.
>
> Since then there has been no word on the subject from the Bush administration.

Mobile labs to produce chemical or biological weapons:
Powell detailed Iraq's use of mobile laboratories to produce chemical or biological weapons as a way of avoiding discovery. He displayed diagrams to show their interiors. The information came from an Iraqi chemical engineer who had seen one of them and witnessed an accident in which twelve technicians died from exposure to biological agents. This defector and three others presented independent information (said Powell) that proved Iraq had "at least seven of these mobile biological agent factories" and that each of the truck-mounted factories had at least two or three trucks—all told, eighteen trucks (according to Prime Minister Blair).

> *Fact:* In April and May 2003, when two truck trailers that held the possibility of being the alleged labs were discovered in northern Iraq, it created much frisson in Washington and London. Three different U.S. groups checked out the truck trailers. Of these, the last team, consisting of senior analysts, was highly skeptical. But that did not stop the U.S. administration issuing a "white paper" analysis detailing its case for "mobile bio-weapons labs" while conceding both discrepancies in the evidence and lack of "hard" evidence. According to the briefing given to the (London) *Observer* in early June by Dr. David Kelly, a leading British expert on biological weapons at the Ministry of Defense, after his examination of the tractor trailers in Iraq, the following facts militated against the trailers being bio-weapons labs. They contained no pathogens. They had canvas sides, an oddity for a vehicle where technicians would be handling dangerous germ cultures. There was a shortage of pumps required to create vacuums for working with such cultures. They did not have an autoclave for steam sterilization. Finally, they lacked an easy way to remove germ fluids from the processing tank. The Iraqis said that the units were for

hydrogen production to fill artillery balloons, part of a
system originally sold to them by Britain in 1987 during the
Iran–Iraq War.[46]

This dovetailed with what Brigadier General Dr. Ala Saeed told
Christina Lamb of the *Sunday Times*. "Those were mobile detection units which we used for field tests," he said. "We would use
artillery bombs with [hydrogen] gas or fire them with plastic explosives and then take samples from the air and ground." Saeed, possessing a doctorate in analytical chemistry from Britain's Sussex
University, was in charge of quality control at the Muthanna State
Establishment, where the military manufactured mustard gas,
tabun, and sarin. He was the author of the three reports on chemical weapons that Iraq submitted to Unscom, the first one in 1994
(by which time, according to him, all chemical arms had been
destroyed), and later the section on chemical weapons in the
dossier that Baghdad submitted to the UN Security Council in
December 2002.

He took Lamb to the destroyed site of the Muthanna State
Establishment and told her that munitions dropped on the Iraqi
Kurdish town of Halabja in March 1988 contained a mixture of
tabun, sarin, and mustard gas—used earlier on Iranian troops—
killing 3,200 to 6,800 people, mainly civilians.[47] "VX that we
produced deteriorates within a week," Saeed said. "To be useful
it had to have a shelf life of two years. We produced two batches
in 1990 which were not weaponized." He told Lamb that at the
end of 1991 the Special Security Organization ordered the officials in charge of the biological, chemical, and nuclear programs
to hand over all the documents pertaining to it. At the
Muthanna State Establishment they handed over fifteen wooden
crates of documents. When in 1994 Iraq was asked to submit a
full report on its WMD, Saeed asked the Special Security for
documents, only to be told that they had been destroyed. So the
staff at the Muthanna State Establishment fell back on their

memories. "Maybe some numbers were not right," he conceded. However, after the August 1995 defection of Hussein Kamil Hassan, the elder son-in-law of Saddam, Saeed said, "They [Unscom] found 150 wooden boxes on his chicken farm including all our documents."[48] Until Hussein Kamil Hassan's defection, Iraq had denied having anything to do with VX. "We had lied to them from 1991–95 about VX program, which they only found out when Kamil defected," said Saeed. "So they [Unscom] didn't trust us."[49]

Iraq trying to conceal evidence:
Powell alluded to an electronic intercept of a conversation between two Republican Guard Corps commanders "just a few weeks ago," where they talked about removing the discussion of "nerve agents wherever it comes up" in wireless instructions, in anticipation of the UN inspectors' arrival. He played several audiotapes prepared by the electronic eavesdroppers of the U.S. National Security Agency. The most dramatic one featured a colonel in the Second Republican Guard Corps ordering one Captain Ibrahim to sanitize communications.

> *Fact:* U.S. intelligence knew the locations of the two commanders and their names. Yet on April 25, an administration official told Walter Pincus of the *Washington Post*: "We don't know where they are." The sites they were talking from were on priority lists for searching, another senior analyst told Pincus.

Iraq cleaning up sites and removing contraband in anticipation of UN inspections:
Powell claimed that the military site at Taji, north of Baghdad—one of sixty-five such facilities—had fifteen active munitions bunkers, and that soldiers relocated munitions just before inspectors arrived, showing they had advance knowledge. "We have

observed such housecleaning at 30 military sites," he added. He displayed two satellite pictures, one showing a "chemical deconta-mination truck" and the other without the vehicle, concluding that the truck in question had removed contraband.

> *Fact:* Encouraged, privately, by several Security Council members to respond to this and other allegations by Powell, Blix noted that the two satellite images were taken several weeks apart, and that the reported movement of munitions at the site could have been a routine activity. Also, the alleged chemical decontamination truck turned out to be a fire engine.[50]

Iraq moving missile parts:

Pointing to a satellite picture, Powell said, "At this ballistic missile site on November 10, we saw a truck preparing to move ballistic missile components."

> *Fact:* Two days after Powell's presentation, Karim Yusuf, manager of the plant, run by Al Rashid Company, showed off the empty inside of the truck and said it had been used to move "mechanical parts" allowed under UN regula-tions. "Nothing unusual was happening in November. Any day they would see constant activity here. Powell could say any day that there is activity." At the second site, Al Rafah plant, fifty miles (eighty kilometers) west of Baghdad, Ali Jassim, the plant's manager, showed a new testing stand for rockets. Powell had alleged that a new testing stand for rockets was for "long-range missiles that can fly 750 miles (1,200 kilometers). These are missiles that Iraq wants in order to project power, to threaten, and to deliver chem-ical, biological and, if we let him, nuclear warheads." The new stand (still unfinished) is fifteen meters high and the vent, at thirty-five meters, is longer than the old stand, a

few hundred meters away. Jassim explained that the old stand was for rockets to be tested vertically, and the new stand was for testing horizontally, which was safer; so the vent had to be longer. Regarding the range of the missile, Jassim said that UN inspectors had visited five times and had not complained about its range. The aluminum roof that Powell alleged was designed to conceal activities from satellites was "to protect the stand from rain and dust."[51]

Powell said that Iraqi scientists had been threatened with death if they talked about weapons activities to UN inspectors, and that a dozen experts had been placed under house arrest, albeit not in their residences.

Fact: That information had come from human intelligence sources, a senior Bush official told the *Washington Post* on April 25, 2003, but to date none of those informants has been produced in public.

Powell played a tape of a Mirage jet retrofitted to spray simulated anthrax, and a model of Iraq's unmanned drones capable of spraying chemical or germ weapons within a radius of at least 550 miles (880 kilometers).

Fact: This was a less scary version of the subject Bush had mentioned in his October 7, 2002, speech in Cincinnati, and which had been debunked in a report by Dana Milbank in the *Washington Post* on October 21, citing a CIA report declassified in early October.

On March 12, 2003, Iraq displayed a drone to reporters near Baghdad, insisting it was a prototype reconnaissance plane that had never gone into production. It was later destroyed by the UN inspectors even though they were not certain it constituted a proscribed weapon.

Powell claimed Iraq had one hundred to five hundred tons of chemical agents.

> *Fact:* UN inspectors, working from Iraq's declarations, supervised or obtained evidence of the destruction of about 80,000 munitions and several thousand tons of chemical precursors by 1998. The Iraqi officials had not been able to prove they had unilaterally destroyed 550 artillery shells containing mustard gas, 30,000 *empty* munitions that could be filled with chemical agents, 6,500 bombs missing from the Iran–Iraq War of the 1980s, and possibly 25,000 liters of anthrax material, *not* weaponized anthrax.
>
> On June 6, 2003, CNN aired a summary of the DIA's report of September 2002, which said, "There is no reliable information on whether Iraq is producing and stockpiling chemical weapons or where Iraq has or will establish chemical weapons warfare agent production facilities," adding that while Iraq "appeared" to have stocks of mustard gas, the agency had detected no clear indications of other deadly agents.
>
> Four months after the end of the war on Iraq, the Anglo-American forces had failed to find the one hundred to five hundred tons of chemical agents mentioned by Powell.

Finally, Powell referred to British prime minister Tony Blair's nineteen-page dossier, Iraq: Its Infrastructure of Concealment, Deception and Intimidation, *which he had seen on January 31 during Blair's visit to Washington, as "an exquisite piece of evidence." Blair had presented it to the House of Commons on February 3, thus: "I hope the people have some sense of the integrity of our security services. They are not publishing this, and giving us this information, and making it up."* [52]

> *Fact:* Ninety percent of this dossier, praised by Powell and hyped by Blair in the House of Commons as providing "up

to date details of Iraq's network of intelligence and security,"
had come from three articles published between 1997 and
2001, each of which relied in turn on open sources and was
available on the Internet, from where the authors of the
"intelligence" dossier, working under Blair's communications director, Alastair Campbell, had copied them by using
a search engine and typing in "Iraq" and "intelligence." Two
of the articles had originally appeared in *Jane's Intelligence
Review* (one in mid-1997, the other in November 2001),
and the third, "Iraq's Security and Intelligence Network" by
Ibrahim Marashi, a Shia Iraqi-American doctorate student
at the Center for Nonproliferation Studies, Monterey, California, in the September 2001 issue of the *Middle East
Review of International Affairs* (published in Herzliya, Israel;
its editor, Michael Leeden, was a well-known American
neoconservative). The plagiarizing was so blatant that the
authors of the dossier reproduced even the original spelling
and punctuation errors in the government document. On
the other hand, they, or their boss, Campbell, had no
qualms about falsifying the original statements in order to
"sex up" the document.[53] As Marashi would explain to the
British House of Commons Foreign Affairs Committee in
London in June, whereas his article, summarizing his doctorate thesis, had stated that Iraq was backing foreign—
chiefly Syrian—opposition groups, including dissident
(secular) Syrian Baathists, the Blair dossier had implied
that the Iraqi government was supporting Islamist terrorist
groups outside Iraq. "By changing the words they were distorting the meaning, and it looks like they [the Iraqis] are
supporting [foreign] groups like Al Qaida," he would tell
the committee.[54] Here was a glaring example of those
accusing Saddam Hussein of deception being caught red-
handed in their own lie.

Iraq's evaluation of Powell's presentation was summed

up by Amr al Saadi thus: "A typical American show: full of stunts and special effects."

At the Security Council, Powell's peroration changed no minds. After all, such council members as China, France, Germany, and Russia had their own, generously funded intelligence agencies, and none of them had discovered any link between Iraq and Al Qaida. Since Hans von Sponeck, a German who had been the head of the UN Office of Humanitarian Coordinator in Iraq from 1998 to 2000, had kept up his interest in Iraq, visiting the country in recent weeks to make a television documentary, the German people and government were particularly well informed on the subject. "The UN inspectors have found nothing which was in the Bush and Blair dossiers of last September," von Sponeck told the *Mirror,* a British tabloid. "I have seen facilities [broken] in pieces in Iraq which U.S. intelligence reports say are dangerous. The Institute of Strategic Studies [in London] referred to the Al Falluja's three castor oil production units and the Al Daura foot and mouth center as facilities of concern. In 2002 I saw them and they were destroyed, there was nothing. All that was left were shells of buildings. This is a classic example of manipulating allegations, allegations being converted into facts."[55]

Those U.S. officials at the Security Council who were sensitive enough to notice Powell's diplomatic failure let it be known that President Bush would himself deliver the *coup de grâce,* the decisive evidence to justify military intervention. He did nothing of the sort.

In any case, Powell's presentation went down well at home, and that is what ultimately mattered to Bush. In the view of Richard Murphy, former assistant secretary of state for the Near East, "Powell will have carried his American audience further towards supporting military action." Indeed, a poll showed that 70 percent agreed with Powell that Iraq was practicing deception. Powell's job was made even easier thanks to a Gallup poll in mid-December, where 52 percent would believe the White House's statement that it had evidence of Iraq's WMD program even if the UN inspectors found nothing.[56]

The reason for this is that most Americans get their news from television. And, for months, the leading cable channels, Fox News and CNN, had abandoned their expected role of providing a forum for debate to weigh the pros and cons of invading Iraq, and instead accepted the White House's apparent decision to attack Iraq as a given. They saw their self-imposed mission to be preparing the American public for a war. As such, the mainstream electronic media almost invariably presented Powell's claims as facts, dispensing with the standard journalistic practice of saying "Powell claims" or "Powell alleges."

This was all the more ironic given that—as would later transpire—Powell himself seemed unsure of the veracity of the "facts" he was presenting to the Security Council. According to the *U.S. News and World Report* of June 9, 2003, the Pentagon gave Powell a first draft of his speech that ran for two hundred minutes. It was, in the words of a senior official, "over the top," running the gamut "from Al Qaida to human rights to weapons of mass destruction," and full of "unsubstantiated assertions." While perusing this material, Powell reportedly became so angry at the lack of adequate sourcing of intelligence claims that he said, "I'm not reading this; this is bullshit." He set up his own team to scrutinize the first draft, and later, working with a CIA team led by George Tenet at the Waldorf-Astoria Hotel, New York, they removed from the Pentagon's draft dozens of pages about Iraq's WMD and its ties to terrorists.

Still Powell was apparently far from satisfied. On the eve

of the presentation to the Security Council, he and his British counterpart, Jack Straw, discussed the validity of their governments' intelligence reports. According to the leaked transcript of this meeting—which circulated in NATO diplomatic circles in late May—Straw said there was a lack of "corroborative evidence to back up the claims. Much of the intelligence was assumptions and assessments not supported by hard facts or other sources." Powell expressed doubts especially about the assessments offered by the Pentagon's Office of Special Plans. He told Straw that he had "moved in" with U.S. intelligence to prepare his UN Security Council presentation, but had left the meetings feeling "apprehensive" about "at best circumstantial evidence that was highly tilted in favor of the assessment drawn from them rather than any actual raw intelligence. I hope the facts, when they come out, will not explode in our faces."[57]

In stark contrast to how Powell's presentation had been received in the United States, in the Arab and Muslim world there was almost total disbelief in Powell's peroration, which came in the aftermath of the crash of the U.S. space shuttle *Columbia* over central Texas.

NOTES

1. Cited in *Guardian*, June 7, 2003.

2. As a result of two days of intense negotiations between France and Russia and the Anglo-American allies, the earlier word "or" was changed to "and,"and the earlier word "restore" was altered to "secure." France and Russia wanted to ensure a meeting of the Security Council to discuss the inspectors' report before any military action was contemplated.

3. "In the end"—meaning when Unscom was headed by Richard Butler, who succeeded Rolf Ekeus in July 1997. Hans Blix's implication was that Unscom had by then become a U.S. operation. See further Dilip Hiro, *Iraq: In the Eye of the Storm*, Nation Books, New York, 2002; and *Iraq: A Report from the Inside*, Granta Books, London, 2003, pp. 123–24; p. 127.

4. *Observer*, November 17, 2002.

5. Saudi Arabia and Iran refused to attend the ICO summit in Doha, where Israel's trade mission was based.

6. *Independent*, March 31, 2003. His most colorful statement so far was: "Sudan is a basket case, and Somalia is a basket case with government."

7. *New York Times*, December 14, 2002.

8. Cited in *Observer*, December 8, 2002.

9. *Washington Post*, November 28, December 2 and 4, 2002.

10. *New York Times*, December 3, 2002.

11. *International Herald Tribune*, December 5, 2002.

12. *Washington Post*, December 9, 2002; *Guardian*, December 11, 2002; *Independent*, December 12, 2002; *The Times* (London), December 12, 2002; *USA Today*, December 17, 2002; *International Herald Tribune*, January 15, 2003; *New York Times*, March 16, 2003. The list of twenty-four U.S. companies supplying Iraq with nuclear, chemical, biological, and missile technology included Bechtel, DuPont, Eastman Kodak, Hewlett Packard, Honeywell, Rockwell, and Spectra Physics. Also, the U.S. Departments of Agriculture, Commerce, Defense, and Energy were listed as suppliers. *The Nation*, January 13, 2003, p. 8. The credit for securing the original Iraqi dossier and publishing the names of leading American, British, and German companies as suppliers to Iraq's WMD program went to the Berlin-based *Tageszeitung* (Daily News), just before Christmas 2002.

13. *The Week*, December 13, 2002, p. 4. Obviously, a preprogrammed Bush had no interest in registering reality if it clashed with his set scenario.

14. *Financial Times*, December 21–22, 2002.

15. It was only after Iran's Supreme National Security Council had agreed to let SCIRI participate in the Iraqi opposition groups' meeting in Washington that SCIRI's delegates flew to Beirut to collect their U.S. visas. Telephone interview with a senior Iranian journalist in Tehran, December 2002.

16. *International Herald Tribune*, November 21, 2002.

17. *Financial Times*, December 18, 2002.

18. See further Dilip Hiro, *Iraq*, pp. 108–9.

19. *Washington Post*, December 20, 2002.

20. VX, invented by British scientists at Porton Downs, near the English town of Salisbury, is ten times deadlier than Sarin nerve gas. A teaspoonful of VX applied to the skin is enough to kill a person.

21. *New York Times*, December 20, 2002.

22. Mark Gwozdecky said, "First, we need to have reliable information that there is someone who has information and cannot give it to us inside Iraq. Second, we must know that the person is willing to leave. Third, there is a country willing to provide him protection and asylum." *International Herald Tribune*, December 24–25, 2002.

23. Agence France-Presse, December 30, 2002.

24. December 28, 2002.

25. *Observer*, December 29, 2002.

26. Israel's military intelligence chief, Major General Aharon Farkash, told a parliamentary committee, "If there is an attack it will be in the first week of February." Reuters, December 25, 2002. This showed Farkash's ignorance of the fact that this date clashed with the annual hajj pilgrimage, due to start on February 7, with more than 1.25 million foreign Muslims arriving in Saudi Arabia from February 1 onward, and that no U.S. administration in its right mind would start bombing a neighbor of the Saudi kingdom with nearly 2 million foreign and local Muslims gathered in Mecca.

27. *New York Times*, December 16, 2002.

28. *The Times* (London), January 15, 2003.

29. *Observer*, November 10, 2002. The antiwar demonstration in Florence, Italy, was four-hundred-thousand strong.

30. *Sunday Times*, January 26, 2003.

31. Interview with an Iraqi exile in London whose young nephew and niece, both university students, received messages from the Pentagon.

32. *USA Today*, February 27, 2003.

33. *International Herald Tribune*, January 11–12, 2003.

34. *USA Today*, February 27, 2003.

35. Associated Press, January 28, 2003.

36. Of the eight presidential complexes of Saddam Hussein, three—Republican, Sijood, and Radawaniye—were in Greater Baghdad, and the rest in Tharthar, Tikrit, Mosul, Jabal Makhbul, and Basra.

37. See further Dilip Hiro, *Neighbors, Not Friends: Iraq and Iran after the Gulf Wars*, Routledge, New York and London, 2001, p. 91.

38. January 7, 2003.

39. Interview with an Iraqi exile in London, January 2003.

40. *Independent*, February 5, 2003; *New York Times*, February 6, 2003.

41. *Guardian*, December 30, 2002.

42. After the Anglo-American invasion of Iraq, these sixteen words would become a source of contention between Washington and London, and among various U.S. agencies—even though Bush had attributed the information to "the British government"—after it emerged that CIA director George Tenet had advised the Blair government to remove altogether its reference to Iraq seeking to procure uranium "in Africa" in its September 2002 dossier. After much transatlantic consultation, a senior Bush aide said, "Knowing all that we know now, the reference to Iraq's attempt to acquire uranium from Africa should not have been included in the President's State of the Union speech." *Independent*, July 9, 2003.

43. Most of Colin Powell's points items appeared in the *New York Times* of February 6, 2003.

44. February 7, 2003.

45. *Observer*, February 2, 2003.

46. *New York Times*, June 7, 2003; *Observer*, June 8 and 15, 2003.

47. For the bombing of Halabja in March 1988, see further Dilip Hiro, *The Longest War: The Iran-Iraq Military Conflict*, HarperCollins, London, 1989/Routledge, 1991, p. 201; and Dilip Hiro, *The Essential Middle East*, p. 176.

48. See further Dilip Hiro, *Iraq*, p. 65, p. 68.

49. *Sunday Times*, June 8, 2003.

50. *Independent*, February 15, 2003; *New York Times*, March 2, 2003.

51. *New York Times*, February 8, 2003.

52. Such a statement by a British prime minister showed a poor grasp of the history of Britain's domestic and foreign intelligence. "Over the last thirty years or so . . . continuous wave of spy scandals has been a feature, a succession of traitors, weirdos and bunglers engaged in clumsily executed plots of one kind or another," noted columnist Richard Ingram in the *Observer*. "In Northern Ireland in particular we have seen these intelligence services engaged in dirty tricks to discredit Labor politicians, not to mention covert assassination plots aimed at unfriendly (Irish) republicans."

53. *Independent*, June 16, 2003. It was an Internet search by Dr. Glen Rangwala, a lecturer in political science at Cambridge University, which showed that the authors of the "British Intelligence" dossier had pinched most of their text, word for word, by using a search engine. He informed some friends, and his findings ended up with a couple of enterprising teenagers, who e-mailed them to journalists in London.

54. *New York Times*, February 8, 2003; and *Guardian*, June 20, 2003. The three books that Marashi drew on were Kanan Makiya's *Republic of Fear* (1990), Scott Ritter's *Endgame: Solving the Iraq Problem—Once and For All* (1999), and Dilip Hiro's *Neighbors, Not Friends: Iraq and Iran After the Gulf Wars* (2001).

55. February 15, 2003.

56. *Financial Times*, December 21–22, 2002.

57. *Guardian*, May 31, 2003. Jack Straw insisted that he had not seen Colin Powell at the Waldorf Hotel on the morning of February 5 as noted by the leaked minutes of their meeting. However, it was not a question of a single meeting. Powell said, "I had conversations with the British, with Jack Straw, constantly during the period . . . so he had a sense of how the presentation was coming together and what I would be saying. . . . I was in constant communication with Jack."

CHAPTER 4
THE RUSH TO WAR

"When I talk about the war on terror, I am not just talking about Al Qaida, I am [also] talking about Iraq."

—George W. Bush on February 14, 2003[1]

"The JIC assessed that any collapse of the Iraqi regime would increase the risk of chemical and biological technology or agents finding their way into the hands of terrorists."[2]

—"Iraqi Weapons of Mass Destruction—Intelligence and Assessments," Intelligence and Security Committee of the British Houses of Parliament report

"The time needed is not the time it takes for inspectors to discover the weapons. They are not a detective agency. The time is the time necessary to make a judgment: Is Saddam prepared to cooperate fully or not?"

—Tony Blair on February 18, 2003[3]

FOR SEVERAL DAYS the Arab and Muslim world was rife with rumors and speculation about the crash of the U.S. space shuttle *Columbia* over a town named Palestine in central Texas on the morning of Saturday, February 1, which killed seven astronauts, including an Israeli colonel. Many in that part of the world saw the hand of God in this disaster. It showed, in the words of the *New York Times*'s John F. Burns, reporting from Amman, how visceral anti-American feelings had become, spreading "beyond mosques and other strongholds of conservative Islamists, Arab nationalists and others across the whole spectrum of Arab society."[4] According to a prominent columnist in the Saudi daily *Al Yom* (The Day), the United States had become an arsenal of weapons in advance of a military campaign across the entire globe: "The world has become a map of targets for the American arrows, represented by the Trinity of War—Bush, Rumsfeld and Rice—and behind it, the famous 'quiet' man, Dick Cheney." However, anti-American feeling was not limited to the Arab and Muslim world. An Internet poll conducted by the European edition of *Time* magazine recorded the feeling in Europe. Of the 318,000 people responding to the question, "Which country poses the greatest threat to world peace in 2003?" 84 percent said "America."[5]

Finding the moment opportune, as he had done in the past, Osama bin Laden intervened—from his hideout somewhere along the Afghanistan–Pakistan border. On February 11, at the high point of the Muslim hajj pilgrimage, Al Jazeera TV aired his audiotaped statement. Washington's intent was "to occupy the former capital of Islam (Baghdad), to pillage the wealth of Muslims and install a puppet government there," bin Laden said. He then laid out a broad strategy to fight the United States. "To wage this war of infidels, we say: 'Firstly, the fighting should be in the name of God only, not in the name of national ideologies, nor to seek victory for the ignorant governments that rule all Arab states, including Iraq . . . Thirdly, the American enemy depends mainly on psychological warfare and intense aerial bombing . . . so the most effective way to deplete the air power of the enemy is to dig armed and camouflaged trenches in large numbers. In Afghanistan America spent a great deal of its air power and did not dare to storm our bases. So, our Iraqi brothers, don't be afraid of the American propaganda and its smart bombs. These bombs have no sizable effect in mountains, trenches, and forests. So drag the enemy's forces to a long, exhausting, and continuous battle. Their worst fear is street and city fighting. Also we stress the importance of martyrdom [meaning suicide attacks] against the enemy."

Bin Laden called on "honest Muslims" to incite and mobilize the Islamic nation (umma) especially in Jordan, Morocco, Nigeria, Pakistan, Saudi Arabia, and Yemen:[6]

> This Crusade war is primarily aimed at the people of Islam regardless of the removal or survival of the socialist government [of Iraq] or Saddam. The Muslims as a whole and in Iraq in particular, should carry out jihad against the oppressive offensive. It does not hurt that in the current circumstances, the interests of Muslims coincide with those of the socialists in the war against the Crusaders, taking into account our belief and declaration of the apostasy of socialists. The socialists and their rulers lost the legitimacy of their rule a long time ago, and socialists are infidel wherever they are, whether in Baghdad or Aden.

Significantly, Powell broke the news of the bin Laden tape hours before Al Jazeera announced it had it.[7] It was noteworthy that Fox News aired the whole tape, not just sound bites, forgetting Condoleezza Rice's diktat during the Afghanistan campaign not to broadcast bin Laden's statements, as they could contain hidden messages to his followers.

Since its inauguration as a commercial channel in November 1996 at the behest of the Qatari government, its part-owner, Al Jazeera had followed its brief of being an independent twenty-four-hours-a-day news and current-affairs station, acting as the British Broadcasting Corporation (BBC)—an independent public-service organization financed by television license fees—does in Britain. It is funded by a Qatari state subsidy, advertising revenue, and its contracts with the likes of the BBC, CNN, and Sky TV. Its reporting staff consists almost wholly of BBC-trained journalists who lost their jobs in April 1996 when, angered by the BBC's interviews with Saudi dissident Muhammad al Masaari and a documentary on capital punishment in Saudi Arabia, the Rome-based Orbit TV, owned by Saudi Prince Khalid bin Abdullah, canceled its contract with the BBC's Arabic Service to produce news for it. Al Jazeera's leading weekly features—"The Opposite Direction" and "The Other Opinion"—debate such controversial issues as religion and politics, Arab relations with Israel (with Israeli officials and commentators participating), women's status in society, and the role of monarchy in the Arab world—with viewers joining in with phone calls and e-mails. Because of its iconoclastic policies, Al Jazeera bureaus have been closed down in Jordan, Kuwait, Libya, and Tunisia (which complained that too much time was given to the opposition), Bahrain (for being pro-Israeli), and the Palestinian Territories (for showing "an unflattering image" of Yasser Arafat during the 1982 Lebanese civil war). Over the years the Qatari foreign ministry has received nearly four hundred official complaints, which it has passed on to Al Jazeera management with a note to the complainant: "If Al Jazeera has said something wrong, you always have the right to reply." In a region where rulers rigidly control broadcasting media, the arrival of Al Jazeera was greeted as an oasis in a desert. It built up a worldwide audience of thirty-five million, mostly in the Middle East and North Africa, but also extending to the Arabic-speaking communities in Western Europe, North America, and Latin America.

Al Jazeera, it should come as no surprise, won the plaudits of the U.S. State Department in its 2000 report on human rights as "a beacon of free speech in the Middle East." Within a week of the 9/11 attacks, Al Jazeera had interviewed Colin Powell, Donald Rumsfeld, and Condoleezza Rice. During the Afghanistan war, it was the only channel with a permanent base in Kabul, run by bearded Syrian-born journalist Tayseer Alouni. Washington accused him of being pro-Taliban, and bombed the Al Jazeera office, the last place to be hit in the Afghan capital. Once bin Laden went into hiding in December 2001, taped statements from him arrived at Al Jazeera's head office in Doha, but the management aired the tape only when it concluded that it had news value.

Five days after the bin Laden broadcasts, the Arab League foreign ministers meeting in Cairo passed a nonbinding resolution calling on member states to "refrain from offering any kind of assistance or facilities for any military action that leads to the threat of Iraq's security, safety and territorial integrity."

Egyptian president Hosni Mubarak urged Saddam to cooperate 100 percent with UN inspectors. Saddam did. During his visit to Baghdad, where he signed another ten-point agreement with the government, Blix noticed a "change of heart by Iraqis." Iraq agreed to flights by U.S.-made U-2 reconnaissance planes as well as unmanned Russian and German aircraft; it handed over eleven documents on the nuclear program and twenty-four on the unaccounted-for biological and chemical weapons and missiles; and it expanded its own committee to search for the WMD and related documents, and to legislate against the WMD.[8]

In Blix's third report to the Security Council, on February 14, he said there had been 177 inspections at 125 locations, and that the results of more than two hundred chemical and one hundred biological samples had been consistent with Iraq's declaration. "[W]e have obtained good knowledge of the industrial and scientific landscape of Iraq, but as before we do not know every cave and corner," he said. "We are aware that many governmental intelligence agencies are convinced that proscribed weapons and programs continue to exist. Governments have many sources of information that are not available to inspectors." He explained that "the inspectors must base their reports only on the evidence they can examine and present publicly. Without evidence, confidence cannot arise." While pointing out that some prohibited arms—including 8,500 liters of anthrax and VX nerve gas material—were still unaccounted for, he said, "One must not jump to the conclusion that they exist. However, that possibility is also not excluded. If they exist they should be presented for destruction. If they do not exist, credible evidence to that effect must be presented."9 He confirmed that the Al Samoud-2 missile exceeded the permissible limit, and added that the number of empty chemical shells found was small. Muhammad el Baradei basically repeated his statement of the previous fortnight.

The overall impression given by both Unscom and the IAEA chiefs was that Iraq was cooperating satisfactorily. In the subsequent Security Council debate, the French foreign minister, Dominique de Villepin, made a mark. Rejecting Powell's call for "serious response" to Iraq's "temporizing," de Villepin proposed strengthened inspections, with their results to be debated a month later, the foreign ministers of the five Permanent Members attending. "The option of inspections has not been taken to the end," he said. "The use of force would be so fraught with risks for people, for the region and for international stability that it should only be envisioned as a last resort. In this temple of the United Nations, we are the guardians of an ideal, the guardians of a conscience. This message comes to you from an old country, France, from a continent like mine, Europe, that has known wars, occupation and barbarity."10 When he finished, the chamber burst into spontaneous applause, a rare event at the Security Council.

A tall, slim, silver-haired man of forty-nine, and a published poet, Dominique de Villepin is often described as a "diplomatic pinup." The Moroccan-born son of a powerful French senator, he joined the French diplomatic service and by the 1980s was the press spokesman at the French embassy in Washington, where he forged close ties with the U.S. media and Congress, and gained insight into how they function, an asset that would help him convey the French viewpoint to the American media in 2003. In between, he served as an aide to then foreign minister and later the prime minister Alain Juppe. In 1995 he became an adviser to President Jacques Chirac, who promoted him to foreign minister after his reelection in 2002. Accused of anti-Americanism, he said, "We are so convinced that America is taking risks for its future with this Iraqi cause. To act like we do, you have to know how much I love America."11

Such sentiments failed to pacify senior Bush officials, who found his speech infuriating. Instead of witnessing the February 14 session of the Security Council turn into what Powell had described as "the moment of truth" for Iraq, the Bush team saw it transformed into what Maureen Dowd of the *New York Times* called "the St. Valentine's Day massacre of America."

The next day, February 15 (Saturday), brought further bad news for the Bush White House. An estimated fifteen to twenty million people marched against the war on Iraq in 600 towns and cities—150 of them in the United States—in sixty countries, an unprecedented event in world history. Rome, London, and Barcelona witnessed the largest demonstrations in their illustrious histories, with estimates of the participants at 1.8 million, 1.5 million, and more than 1 million, respectively—thus illustrating a tension between popular opinion and the official, pro-Bush policy of Italy, Britain, and Spain. At an estimated 500,000, the demonstration in New York was the second-largest ever, despite below-freezing temperatures. In the Middle East, with 200,000 joining the antiwar march in Damascus, that city was the leader, with Baghdad far behind. "The phenomenon on the streets of the world may not be as profound as the people's revolutions in Eastern Europe in 1989 or Europe's class struggles in 1848, but politicians and leaders are unlikely to ignore it," noted Patrick Tyler in the *New York Times*. Indeed, Italian prime minister Silvio Berlusconi was sufficiently shaken by the size of the marches to declare that any military action on Iraq would be taken only under UN auspices. Later, while supporting Washington, he refused to send a single combat soldier to join the "Coalition of the Willing." The most high-profile opponent of the war against Iraq to emerge was his wife, Veronica Lario, a former actress with ravishing blonde hair and striking blue eyes. In an interview with *Micro Mega* (Small & Big), an Italian magazine opposed to Berlusconi's party, Forza Italia, Lario praised the antiwar camp, saying, "I believe the pacifist movement serves to re-awaken our consciences." After the invasion, she would refuse to accompany Berlusconi on his trip to Crawford, Texas, in late July to meet Bush, and declared in another newspaper interview that "the development of the situation [in postwar Iraq] has confirmed my convictions."

The response of Tony Blair was less public—but more effective. He had senior intelligence officials brief his cabinet colleagues—separately or in small groups—on the seriousness and iminence of the threat of Iraq's WMD, a move that would pay him back hand-somely a month later, when he had to struggle to secure the support of a majority of Labor parliamentarians.

What counted most, however, was the impact of the antiwar marches on the White House. That, in turn, depended very much on how they were reported by the media, especially the television channels. Fox News, for example, described the antiwar demon-strators in New York as "the usual protesters" and "serial pro-testers." The headline on the CNN website was "Antiwar rallies delight Iraq," and the accompanying picture showed a demonstra-tion in the Iraqi capital. Frank Magid Associates, a leading media consulting company, warned its TV-station clients that covering antiwar demonstrations might harm their standing. Such advice ignored the fact that the protests had support from leading Chris-tian denominations, including Roman Catholics, Presbyterians, Baptists, the United Methodists (to which Bush belonged), and mainstream evangelicals. Only ultraconservative evangelists like Franklin Graham, the Southern Baptist Convention, and some Pentecostal leaders supported a war. Despite repeated requests, Bush, a devout Christian and a regular Bible reader, refused to meet the protesting church leaders.[12] Among the retired military generals who expressed concern about the war were Generals Norman Schwartzkopf (who commanded the U.S.-led coalition forces in the 1991 Gulf War), Wesley Clark (who commanded NATO during the bombing campaign against Serbia in Kosovo in 1999), and Anthony Zinni, the immediate predecessor of Tommy Franks. "If the U.S. intends to solve this through violent action, we are on the wrong course," said Zinni. "I don't see that is necessary, and second, war and violence are the very last resort."[13]

Invited to comment on the size of the protest in his country, Bush replied, "Size of the protest. It is like I am going to decide policy based upon a focus group," adding that "the role of the leader is to decide policy upon the security of the people." Equating a mass march with a focus group showed staggering ignorance. As every American politician and chief executive officer knows, a focus group consists of a handful of people carefully chosen to reflect widely divergent views, selected to help a politician or businessperson devise a strategy to sell a policy or a product. Led by a facilitator, the participating members are encouraged to air their likes and dislikes freely while policy/product strategists eavesdrop behind a one-way mirror. In the general scheme of policies and products, focus groups are a means to find the reasons behind the public's view of a certain issue or product, whereas opinion polls are the means to quantify these views. Dismissing Bush's bravura, Alan Simpson, a former Republican senator from Wyoming, said, "The Bushies do as much polling as the Clinton administration. The fact that these were the biggest demos in three decades does say something about underlying public opinion around the world. You don't have to accept it or follow it, but you can't ignore it."

However, it was not just ordinary citizens protesting around the world; their governments were doing so, too. And not just France, Germany, Belgium, and Russia, but also—most disappointingly for Bush—Canada, a long-standing loyal ally of the United States.[14] Bush's response was unchanged. He instantly rejected the Franco-German plan, backed by Russia, to increase the number of inspectors and send in UN military observers. Its proponent was Jacques Chirac. Ignoring Bush's rebuff, the 22nd Franco-African summit in Paris unanimously endorsed France's position on Iraq. Its final communiqué declared that "there is an alternative to war," and added that fifty-one African leaders were expressing their support for continued inspections and for substantially reinforcing "the humanitarian and technical capacities of the inspectors."[15]

With this, Chirac's prestige at home and abroad rose to new heights, with his approval rating rising to 65 percent. Elected to the French parliament at thirty-five and promoted to minister the following year, Chirac, a tubby man of medium height with a quizzical expression, has all along been a right-of-center politician. A Parisian, he had a strong base in the capital, where he was elected mayor in 1977 after two years as prime minister (1974–76), and reelected twice for six-year terms. From 1986 to 1988 he again served as prime minister. In 1995 he won the presidential election, and was reelected seven years later on a record 82 percent vote in the second round against the neo-Fascist Jean Marie le Pen, after his Socialist rival Lionel Jospin, widely expected to win, failed to come in second in the first round of elections.

When the English-speaking Chirac took a firm stand against Washington's rush to war, he was accused of anti-Americanism, a charge he denied vigorously. After all, he reminded his critics, he belonged to the generation that had fond memories of the Americans arriving in France as liberators in 1944–45, when he was in his teens. In his early twenties, he traveled and worked in the United States—as a forklift operator in St. Louis, a barman at a Boston restaurant, and a journalist in New Orleans. "I know the U.S. better than most French people, and I really like the United States," he told *Time* magazine in late February 2003. He was the first foreign leader to visit Ground Zero after 9/11, and it was at his initiative that the French president of the UN Security Council called a meeting within a day of 9/11 to pass Resolution 1368 affording the United States any action it deemed necessary to punish those who had perpetrated the terrorist attacks. "I've always worked toward and supported transatlantic solidarity, and that unity is a major element in global equilibrium."[16] The reason for his opposition to war lay in his belief that the consequences of ousting Saddam by force would be far worse than any benefits. He was also wary of the impact of invading Iraq on France's five million Muslims, fearing that the wave of anti-Americanism in the Muslim world at large would translate into a wave of anti-Westernism that would affect France adversely.

None of this registered on the minds of the senior Bush administration officials, who had resorted to denigration, locker-room taunts, and bullying in their crusade to compel all other nations to follow Uncle Sam unquestioningly. Those European leaders unwilling to abandon deeply held beliefs and convictions for the preemptive doctrine of the U.S. neocons were pilloried as pathetic Lilliputians trying to tie down the Gulliverian United States. What compounded the Bush team's frustration was the realization that their attempts to sideline their critics—spreading malicious rumors about the sexual or moral indiscretions of troublesome Democrats and journalists, for example—did not work in the case of the leaders of "old Europe," whose citizens tend to pay scant attention to salacious gossip about their politicians. Bush's team could not escape the fact that the Franco-German bloc was just too large an economic and cultural force to ignore. The supreme irony was that the condescending description of the French, Germans, and Belgians as "Nervous Nellies" came from an administration whose leading lights—with the exception of Powell—had all been draft dodgers.

Foremost among those hurling insults was Rumsfeld, a born bruiser and the administration's chosen rottweiler. "They [the French] are frequently recalcitrant about a lot of things," he told a TV interviewer in Chicago. "Any given day or week, they seem to be the country that disagrees with a lot of other countries." He gave similar short shrift to Germany when, in testimony before a congressional committee, he lumped it with Libya and Cuba as countries that did not want to take part in a war against Iraq and also did not want to rebuild Iraq after the war. This angered German politicians. "Rumsfeld's remark is beyond impertinent," said Peter Struck, German defense minister. "It is out of order. It is even un-American when you consider that fairness is practically an American virtue."[17] Those horrified by Rumsfeld's statements included not only Europeans but also an embarrassed U.S. State Department. Its spokesman told the (London) *Observer*: "Bullying countries to follow the U.S. line will further exacerbate anti-Americanism and alienate those countries wishing to side with the U.S."

However, the number of UN member-states wishing to ally with Washington was thin on the ground, judging by the drift of the debate at the Security Council when, after it was petitioned by South Africa, it opened its chamber to non-members on February 18. Over the next three days *all* of the sixty-four speakers—from Canada to South Korea, and from Egypt to Indonesia—voiced opposition to war.[18] At the same time, UN inspectors reported that they were making steady progress. By now they had chalked up nearly six hundred inspections at four hundred sites out of a total of seven hundred. The IAEA had interviewed twelve Iraqi scientists, and Iraq had offered a fresh list of scientists. And the U-2 reconnaissance flights had started.

This was the backdrop to the draft resolution, proposed by the United States and Britain (and co-sponsored by Spain), that was submitted to the Security Council on February 24. Bush declared, "It's a moment . . . to determine whether or not it [the Security Council] is going to be relevant as the world confronts the threats to the 21st century."

In practice it made no difference to the Pentagon's war plans. The fifth phase of the "unseen" war was under way. The Pentagon's 250-strong Intelligence Support Activity (ISA) unit—the most secretive of the U.S. Special Forces (now 2,000 strong in northern Iraq alone)—called the Gray Fox, working closely with Delta Force and the CIA, operating as TASK FORCE 20, had slipped into Iraq from Kuwait and Jordan and was firmly inside the country. This was a xerox of Pentagon tactics from the eve of the Afghanistan war, except that then, America, the victim of outrageous attacks—had carte blanche from the UN Security Council. During that campaign, at least two thousand troops from Centcom's Special Forces Regiment, who were already posted at several air bases in Pakistan, Uzbekistan, and Tajikistan, had by the third week of September 2001 already penetrated Afghanistan by helicopter in small teams, where they hid during the day and waited for the sunset, when, using night-vision equipment, they pinpointed command posts, supply depots, training headquarters, etc. They were supplemented by the CIA's Special Activities Division units, carrying, among other things, huge bags of cash.[19] In Iraq, cash bribes would play a more crucial role than they had in Afghanistan, ending up as *the* decisive factor in swaying the commanders of the Iraqi Republican Guard to abandon Saddam Hussein.

ISA personnel specialize in languages, intelligence gathering (recruiting local agents with money), and electronic surveillance (using small U-21 Beechcraft planes with eavesdropping antennas fitted inside the wings). They were also charged with tapping into Iraq's underground fiber-optic cables, used for air defenses, and breaking the encryption of British-made Racal military radios used by top Iraqi leaders.[20] Some members of the Gray Fox were assigned to Task Force 20—consisting of the CIA, Delta Force, and Navy Seals—and were charged with investigating sites suspected of being storage depots for long-range Scud missiles or chemical and biological weapons. They too infiltrated Iraq earlier than Operation "Iraqi Freedom," which was launched on March 20. However, "They came up with nothing," a former high-level intelligence official told the *New Yorker's* Seymour Hersh after the invasion. "Never found a single Scud."[21]

The latest U.S.–U.K. draft recalled that Resolution 1441 (November 2002) had "repeatedly warned Iraq that it will face serious consequences as a result of its continued violations of its obligations," and noted that Iraq had submitted a declaration [on December 7, 2002] "containing false statements and omissions" and had "failed to comply with, and cooperate fully in the implementation of, that resolution." Therefore, the proposed resolution concluded, "determined to secure full compliance with its decisions," the Security Council resolves that "Iraq has failed to take the final opportunity afforded to it in Resolution 1441."

Washington was active behind the scenes, too, exerting strong pressure on UN inspectors to behave in such a way as to guarantee their expulsion or to present material to the Security Council that could be used as a pretext for military action, claimed Russian foreign minister Igor Ivanov. Hans Blix would confirm this after the Anglo-American invasion, when Washington refused point-blank to let in UN inspectors. "Towards the end," he told the *Guardian*, "the [Bush] administration leaned on us to ratchet up the language in the inspectors" report to the Security Council in the hope of winning more votes." But he resisted: "We were in nobody's pocket." He also resisted American suggestions to declare Iraq to be in "material breach" of its international commitments under disarmament resolutions, stating that such a political decision—amounting to a declaration of war—rested with the Security Council.[22]

France, Russia, and Germany presented a joint memorandum to coincide with the publication of the U.S.–U.K. draft resolution. "Our priority," it stated, "should be to achieve this [disarmament of Iraq] peacefully through the inspection regime." It acknowledged that Iraqi cooperation was improving "as mentioned by the chief inspectors in their last report," but it proposed increasing pressure on Iraq through a precise program of action by inspectors, with each task clearly defined and made precise; reinforced inspections; and a timeline for inspections and assessment, with the chief inspectors reporting progress every three weeks, and an overall report by Unmovic and the IAEA to be submitted 120 days after the adoption of this program—as mentioned in Resolution 1284 (December 1999).

In a speech at Tufts University, George Bush the Elder seemed to favor a peaceful resolution when he said, "The more pressure there is [on Iraq], the more chance the matter will be resolved in a peaceful manner." He was in tune with public opinion in both the United States and Britain, where 59 percent and 76 percent, respectively, wanted to give more time to inspectors.[23]

At the Security Council, Blix listed "positive elements," which included the destruction of small quantities of mustard gas; Iraq disclosing documents dealing with its unilateral destruction of chemical weapons; and by digging up bombs and fragments, in the course of which Unmovic had found two bombs at a bomb disposal site, one of which being R-400, contained a liquid that appeared to be a biological agent. Overall, though, Blix cautioned: "We have a long list of disarmament issues and it will require a big effort in order to clarify all of those."

Returning to the missile issue, Blix said that in thirteen of the forty test flights the Al Samoud-2 missile exceeded the permissible limit by twenty miles (thirty-two kilometers). The Iraqis countered that the missiles had been tested without payloads or guidance systems, and with these in place, their range would be reduced to the allowable limit of ninety-four miles (150 kilometers). While France, Russia, and Germany urged Baghdad to destroy all 120 Al Samoud-2 missiles, Bush declared that the "illegal" missiles were just "the tip of an iceberg." Iraq soon agreed to destroy the missiles, but that made no difference to Bush.

Bush was getting restless, for a variety of reasons. He had postponed the invasion, originally set for mid-February, due to the belated realization that, with two million Muslim pilgrims making the four-day hajj in mid-February, still in Mecca or Medina, it would be highly inflammatory to start bombing Iraq next door. Second, the steady progress made by the United Nations, reported by Blix, was not to his liking. Third, and most important, the U.S. opposition to war was rising sharply, almost doubling in a month—from 20 percent at the end of January to 37 percent toward the end of February.[24]

After the initial sniping, Bush's officials began gunning for Blix, who had failed to turn out to be a clone of Richard Butler, the

Australian disarmament expert who, as Unscom chief from 1997 to 2000, did Washington's bidding.[25] "Blix Now More a Dead End than a Guide Post" ran a headline in the *New York Times* on March 2. The report said that Bush officials had "hoped Blix— former Swedish foreign minister and director-general of the IAEA—would aggressively carry out inspections and then report with absolute clarity whether or not Iraq had complied." Instead, complained a senior U.S. official: "Inspections have become a false measure of disarmament in the eyes of the people *(sic)*. We are not counting on Blix to do much of anything for us." The *New York Times*'s interlocutor revealed that Cheney and Rumsfeld had warned that Blix would not deliver what they wanted. This was an extraordinary statement to make, revealing as it did how American officials had come to expect those engaged by the United Nations to act as virtual employees of the United States.

In response, an unnamed associate of Blix said, "The Americans have been very heavy handed, obvious and clumsy in their dealings with him." Blix's meeting with Condoleezza Rice on February 11 went badly when she insisted he make his reports more specific. Later, she would dismiss his idea of creating benchmarks for disarmament, saying that this would become a diversion. "Our job is to accurately and objectively assess whether or not Iraq is complying with its obligations," said Blix's spokesman. "We don't tailor our reports for anybody." In private, Blix said he wanted more time for inspections, but he did not say this publicly—unlike el Baradei, who did, and who reaffirmed his earlier conclusion that Iraq had not reactivated its nuclear-weapons program. That, however, did not prevent Cheney from asserting in an NBC-TV interview on March 16 that "we believe he [Saddam] has, in fact, reconstituted nuclear weapons."

Outside of the Bush team, there was much respect for Blix. In Britain, 83 percent trusted him against the 43 percent and 23 percent who trusted Blair and Bush, respectively. A seasoned diplomat, Blix had concluded, quite rightly, that the best way to gain Iraq's cooperation lay in avoiding anything that Saddam might find humiliating. There was much respect too, especially among Arab leaders, for el Baradei, an Egyptian lawyer who had served the IAEA as its top legal officer for many years before being promoted to director-general.

Arab leaders regarded the prospect of a Security Council resolution authorizing force as a *sine qua non*; only with such a resolution could they justify assisting the United States openly, as part of their international obligation. Their summit at the Egyptian resort of Sharm al Shaikh ended on March 1 with a declaration strongly opposing an American-led attack on Iraq, describing it as "a threat to Arab national security," calling for a peaceful solution, and saying that "the neighbor countries will not participate in any military operation against Iraq." However, it fell short of denying Washington facilities in the Arab countries, as demanded by Syria—a position that longtime U.S. allies were not prepared to consider. The communiqué welcomed the steps Iraq had taken to cooperate with the United Nations, while urging Iraq to increase that cooperation. It added that inspectors must be given more time.[26] The Arab leaders were hoping against hope to avert an invasion of Iraq, but Syrian president Bashar Assad had no illusions. "No matter how much Iraq cooperates, the [U.S.] response will be, 'This is not enough,' because the [American] goal is clear," he told the newly elected parliament on March 9.

Bush's goal, decided in principle a year earlier, was to invade Iraq. Saddam Hussein knew it too. He combined his defense strategy with appeals for Islamic solidarity beyond Iraq's national borders. When he moved the Adnan Republican Guard division south from Mosul to Tikrit, the northern headquarters of the Republican Guard, the Pentagon interpreted this as a move to set up two defensive rings around the capital, which was guarded by four Special Republican Guard (SRG) brigades (the remaining SRG brigade had the task of safeguarding the five presidential complexes outside Greater Baghdad). The consensus at the Pentagon was that Saddam would make his last stand in Baghdad, well aware that a prolonged siege of the city, and the resulting suffering of its nearly six million residents, would likely inflame feelings on the streets of the Arab world and Europe, to the extent of frustrating Bush's plan to overthrow his regime. Saddam was also in the habit of exploiting Islamic sentiment for the benefit of Iraq when it suited him. He used the Islamic New Year, on March 4, to call for a jihad against the United States in a television message read out for him. "What is the right path to defeat him [Bush]?" he asked. "The despot imagines that he is like God, capable of controlling the universe and doing whatever he wishes, but the Devil has pushed him in the abyss of blasphemy. The tyrant thinks that he is capable of enslaving people and besieging their freedom, their decisions and their legitimate choices." That "tyrant" had been defied a few days earlier by Turkey, whose parliament had refused to let the United States use its air bases for invading Iraq, thus scuttling the Pentagon's plans to deploy its Fourth Infantry Division from the north in a drive to Baghdad while the Third Infantry Division raced to the capital from the south. The news was received by the Iraqi regime with much satisfaction. The Pentagon did its best to downplay the impact of the Turkish decision on its plans. It would transpire later, though, that General Franks argued that the invasion date be delayed by three to four weeks to enable him to bring in the Fourth Infantry Division through Kuwait, a proposal summarily rejected by an impatient Rumsfeld. As the secret report for the U.S. Joint Chiefs of Staff, published six months later, would reveal, postponement of the invasion by four weeks would have given the Pentagon generals badly needed time to make proper preparations for coping with the massive problems in post-Saddam Iraq.[27]

"Saddam Hussein has had his last chance, we have to take action," an equally edgy Powell told British Channel 4 News on March 4. "Public opinion will come around [once the war starts]. We want to see a second resolution at the United Nations, but in our view 1441 is enough anyway."[28] Yet both the United States and the United Kingdom were so intent on getting their draft adopted at the Security Council that their intelligence services had resorted to intercepting the telephone conversations of the six undecided Security Council members as their ambassadors to the United Nations communicated with their respective governments for instructions—a fact embarrassingly exposed by the (London) *Observer* on March 2. The newspaper revealed that Frank Koza, defense chief of staff (Regional Targets) at the NSA, had sent a memorandum ordering an "intelligence surge" at Angola, Cameroon, Chile, Bulgaria, and Guinea, with "extra focus on Pakistan's UN matters" in order to win favorable votes at the UN Security Council. This memo was sent to "a friendly foreign intelligence agency" (that is, Britain's Government Communications Headquarters [GCHQ]), where it leaked. It was authorized by Rice. But it was so important that it would have involved not only NSA chief General Mike Hayden, but also CIA director George Tenet and defense secretary Rumsfeld—with President Bush being informed at his daily intelligence briefing. The leak was the result of anger felt by intelligence staffs on both sides of the Atlantic after being pressured to doctor information linking Iraq to Al Qaida.

Such shameful behavior by the Bush and Blair governments went hand in hand with imperviousness to well-considered advice from prestigious institutions such as the *New York Times*. "The threat of force should not give way to the use of force until peaceful paths to Iraqi disarmament have been exhausted and the Security Council gives its assent to war," it said editorially on March 4. "Even if there is a quick military triumph, many things could go wrong over the long haul." In reality, after the Pentagon's swift victory in Iraq, things would go wrong within a few months.

The chances of the "second resolution" getting adopted disappeared when the French, German, and Russian foreign ministers meeting in Paris on March 5 issued a nine-paragraph statement. It criticized the United States for delays in publishing and implementing a road map to settling the Israeli-Palestinian crisis that had been agreed to jointly by the United States, Russia, the European Union, and the United Nations. It pointed out that the international system was at "a turning point" on establishing the rules of diplomacy in the post–Cold War era. And it said categorically that their countries would not allow the U.S.–U.K. draft resolution to pass at the Security Council. The next day, Chinese foreign minister Tang Jixuan backed the tripartite declaration. In New York, the Russian ambassador to the United Nations, Sergei Lavrov, said that a U.S.-led invasion of Iraq would be a clear violation of international law. "No country has the right to send its troops into the territory of another state to achieve regime change—which Bush has said would be the leading U.S. war aim."[29]

Bush remained intransigent. "It is time for people to show their cards and let the world know where they stand with respect to Saddam Hussein," he said in a television address on March 6. "Inspectors do not need more time or personnel. All they need is . . . the full cooperation of the Iraqi regime. Token gestures are not enough."

What Baghdad offered was hardly "token," according to Blix. Starting March 1, the Iraqis had begun taking UN inspectors to the sites where they said their government had unilaterally destroyed biological weapons. Iraq's cooperation, Blix told the Security Council on March 7, had become "pro-active," and it was involved in "real and very fine disarmament." In recent days Iraq had promised to provide information on missing anthrax and VX within a week; the UN inspectors had conducted "unimpeded interviews" with seven Iraqi scientists; and Blix had an agreed Iraqi schedule for destroying its missiles.

On top of that, el Baradei told the council that the IAEA's forensic experts had concluded that the papers concerning the Iraqi delegation's mid-2000 visit to Niger to purchase uranium were forged.[30] The chief inspectors' reports demolished Bush's position as far as disarming Iraq was concerned.

But for Bush, "disarmament of Iraq" was just a ruse to bring about "a regime change," which he had decided upon nearly a year before. Appropriately enough, it was during the course of a February 26 dinner speech at the American Enterprise Institute (AEI) in Washington, the font of neoconservatism, that he unfolded his "vision" of Iraq after Saddam. "We will provide security in post-Saddam Iraq," he promised, adding, "We will remain in Iraq as long as necessary, and not a day more." He unveiled too his concept of "trickle-down democracy" in the Middle East, music to the ears of the AEI fraternity, which had concocted the idea in the first place. "A new regime in Iraq will serve as a dramatic and inspiring example for other nations in the region," Bush predicted. "Success in Iraq could also begin a new stage for a Middle Eastern peace, and set in motion progress towards a truly democratic Palestinian state."[31] In essence, the U.S. president talked about using warfare as a tool of sociopolitical engineering, a novel doctrine that he adopted without having discussed it with his senior advisers. He had done the same with his "axis of evil" doctrine.

In contrast, it would take Bush's loyal ally, Tony Blair, a few weeks to mention the phrase "regime change" for the first time (in Parliament), albeit in the context of disarming Iraq through the UN Security Council. Domestic opinion had made Blair stick with the United Nations. His foreign secretary, Jack Straw, airily predicted that the U.S.–U.K. draft resolution would get the necessary vote at the Security Council, then presided over by Mamady Traore of Guinea, a member of the French Commonwealth. This was a vain hope, since only four members (the two sponsors, Bulgaria, and Spain) supported this document and five (China, France, Germany, Russia, and Syria) were opposed, requiring the United States and Britain to win all of the remaining undecided six members, including Pakistan.

Blair was in a tight spot. A private poll commissioned by his office showed hostility toward Bush among both the public and Labor parliamentarians, who disliked his language and manner. Blair invited Bill Clinton to his official weekend home at Chequers over the March 8–9 weekend to discuss Iraq (though this would only be revealed six weeks later, when Patrick Wintour broke the story in the *Guardian* on April 25, 2003). Blair felt that he could get the vote of Chile's Socialist president, Ricardo Lagos, to back the second resolution if it set a specific new deadline for Saddam to cooperate "fully" or face military action. This again was a vain hope. The revelation that the United States and Britain had been spying on the undecided six Security Council members had angered and alienated Lagos, who had telephoned Blair three times to protest and demand an investigation. At The Chequers, Clinton promised to help Blair. In a speech in Washington three days later, Clinton proposed that Hans Blix should set the timetable for compliance by Iraq: "I hope the United States would agree to that amount of time, whatever it is." He said that Bush was sincere in his pursuit of UN support, but added, "The question is, 'Do they [the Bush administration] want the [UN] support bad enough to let Mr. Blix finish his work and give him enough time to do that?'" The plain answer to that was, "No." For starters, Bush was *not* sincere in his pursuit of UN backing.

As for Blair, the forty-minute TV interview President Chirac gave on March 10, a Monday, came in handy later for spinning, an activity in which he and his communications director, Alastair Campbell, were well versed. In this interview, Chirac made his opposition to war abundantly clear, giving a dispassionate assessment of what had been achieved and the risks of invading Iraq. "The Americans have already won," he declared. "I said that to President Bush not very long ago. It is highly probable that if the Americans had not deployed these large forces, and the British had not deployed these large forces, Iraq would not have produced this more active cooperation that the inspectors had demanded and are now getting.[32] So . . . insofar as their strategy for disarming Iraq goes, the Americans have already reached their objective." Therefore there was no need to attack Iraq. "It would set a dangerous precedent if the United States went ahead with a war unilaterally," he said. "I promise you that France will not participate in such a fight. It would end the international coalition against terrorism, and the first victors will be those who want a clash of civilizations, cultures and religions."[33] With the polls showing 80 percent of the French opposing the war even with a UN endorsement, Chirac was expressing popular opinion. At 67 percent, his popularity rating was ten points higher than it had been a month earlier.

The French position had the backing of Chris Patten, the European Union's commissioner for external relations. He told the EU parliament in Strasbourg that an American military campaign that lacked the authority of the United Nations would do "enormous damage" to the authority of the United Nations, NATO, and relations between Europe and the United States.

Encouraged by Patten's support, and miffed by Bush's rejection of a summit meeting of the leaders of the five Permanent Members at the United Nations to discuss the Iraq issue, Chirac decided to work actively against the adoption of the U.S.–U.K. draft resolution. His foreign minister, de Villepin, toured the African member-states of the Security Council—Angola, Cameroon, and Guinea. On the eve of his visit, a top Cameroon official said, "France and Cameroon are old friends." What he did not say was that Cameroon's currency was backed by France. De Villepin's arrival in Guinea's capital of Conakry was greeted with the announcement by the state-run radio that Guinea might abstain on the U.S.–U.K. draft. In between, Pakistani prime minister Mir Zafarullah Khan Jamali said on television, "It will be very difficult for Pakistan to support a war in Iraq." Earlier, the Pakistani government had been hurt and disappointed by the news that the Anglo-Americans were monitoring its communications.

The situation in the Western Hemisphere also looked bleak for the Anglo-American alliance. When asked (on March 13) if Chile would vote for the U.S.–U.K. draft, President Lagos said, "No"—even though Chile's free-trade agreement was pending at the U.S.

Congress.[34] Even the conservative president Vicente Fox of Mexico, the first foreign country Bush visited after becoming president, refused to back Washington on this issue. He was disappointed with Bush's failure to keep his promise to legalize the status of undocumented Mexican immigrants, and said (as early as May 2002) that there would be no privileged U.S.-Mexican relationship unless this "substantive issue" was resolved. His opposition to war had the backing of more than 80 percent of Mexicans.

In an attempt to find an acceptable middle ground, on March 11 the six undecided, non-permanent members of the Security Council proposed to give Unmovic and the IAEA just forty-five days—compared to the 120 days proposed by France—to wrap up their work. But the Bush White House rejected this summarily, just as Russia repeated its threat to veto any resolution calling for a military action against Iraq, even indirectly. The six neutrals at the Security Council were not the only ones to be humiliated. That day, Rumsfeld announced in his lordly way that the United States "can go to war" without Britain, if necessary. He might have said this to underline Washington's resolve.[35] But the impact of this on Blair was devastating. Here he was—ignoring a poll that showed that merely a quarter of Britons favored joining a unilateral U.S.-led attack on Iraq—and going out on a limb to stick with Bush, only to be told that his help was easily dispensed with. An urgent message was fired off to Bush. And several hours later Rumsfeld, unaccustomed to eating his words, did precisely that.[36]

However, Rumsfeld's brush-off to Britain was based on the Pentagon's achievements so far in its "unseen" war against Iraq. Operation "Southern Focus," for instance, had by now resulted in 606 precision-guided weapons being fired at 391 targets—most of them being above–ground cable-repeater stations, thus decapitating Iraq's air defenses—in the course of 21,736 sorties since August.[37]

Though silence on the unseen war was almost mandatory, there was no need to be tight-lipped about the possible length of the conflict. Here Rumsfeld would fob off questions on this vital issue with answers such as:

> As you know,
> There are known knowns.
> There are things we know we know.
> We also know
> There are known unknowns.
> That is to say
> We know there are some things
> We do not know.
> But there are also unknown unknowns,
> The ones we don't know we don't know.[38]

The war's expected length was of primary concern to Bush, as shown in a report in the Iraqi National Congress's mouthpiece, *Al Mutamar* (The Congress), in mid-March. During his meeting with Professor Kanan Makiya and two other leaders of the INC, Bush asked, "What reaction do you expect from the Iraqis to the entry of U.S. forces into their cities?" Makiya explained that "each of us [were] agreed that all Iraqis of all sects would welcome these forces from the very first moment," and added, "The Iraqis will welcome the U.S. forces with flowers and sweets when they come in." Bush's second question was, "If the initial bombardment of Iraq is severe, will the reaction be the same? I mean, will they still welcome the U.S. army?" Makiya "stressed" to President Bush his "personal opinion" that "the regime will be destroyed with the first blow," adding that he expected "no real fighting right from the start of the war."

In Baghdad, while paying close attention to the diplomatic goings-on abroad, Saddam prepared his country for war. He had taken to holding consultations daily with his military officers, where his performance as a defiant commander-in-chief was a curious blend of avuncular preacher and folksy, overgrown farm boy, his imagery derived from his rural, tribal upbringing. "I don't need to say that Iraq is attached to your mustache, because after all it is your country," he told a group once. (The phrase "attached to your mustache" means "something entrusted to you.") He also showed an extraordinary grasp of names, telling local commanders to pass on his salutations to particular tribal leaders in their areas. As usual, his statements were peppered with historical and religious references. In one such televised session on March 7—flanked by his son, Qusay, General Supervisor of the Republican Guard—Saddam told his audience that each of the U.S. aircraft carriers was nine stories high and served twenty thousand meals a day. "But does this aircraft carrier have wheels that enable it to come to Baghdad?" he asked. Besides these televised meetings, there were Saddam's very private confabulations with senior Republican Guard and Special Republican Guard commanders. If these officers had any qualms about their commander-in-chief's assessment of the situation, they kept them strictly to themselves. As Colonel A. T. Said of the Republican Guard would later reveal to Kim Sengupta of the *Independent*, "Saddam would tell them [senior Republican Guard and Special Republican Guard commanders] how the Iraqi forces could defeat anybody in the world, including America. Afterwards some of them, who trusted each other, would say the man can't mean this. Our immediate superiors knew that, but they said we must humor Saddam [otherwise he would execute us]. No one believed that we could hold Baghdad for more than a few days without any air cover and with American superiority in military equipment." [39]

As for the televised sessions, there were multiple motives behind this exercise. Saddam wanted to reassure ordinary Iraqis that they would not be overrun by the Americans. He tried to mobilize and rally his troops by assuring them that the high-tech U.S. weaponry could be overcome by Iraqi resolve to defend their homeland. He was keen to project a calm, assured face by displaying a certain camaraderie with his commanders. His instructions covered all facets of military life. He told the commanders to ensure that their troops bathed, slept well, and read books: "The more you deal with soldiers as humans the greater their ability to give their best." His bottom line on the defense strategy was, "The battlefield should be wherever there are people," out of which grew his classic hit-and-run tactics.[40] Since almost every household in Iraq owned at least one gun, there was ample scope for guerrilla activities. Reflecting Saddam's views, the imam of the prestigious Abdul Qadir Gailani Mosque in downtown Baghdad declared, "Any believer who has dust on his feet from the field of battle [with infidels] will never enter hell on the Judgment Day. Prophet Muhammad said, 'Fight the infidels with everything you have.' "

At the same time, Saddam's government increased its cooperation with the United Nations. On March 14, it handed over a twenty-page document detailing how it had destroyed 3.9 tons of VX nerve agent, adding that a similar report about its destruction of anthrax stores would follow in "a few days." As part of its ongoing disarmament process, the United Nations had by now destroyed seventy Al Samoud-2 missiles.[41] Two days later, Iraq handed over videos of the alleged "mobile bio-weapons labs," saying they showed that Iraq had not violated UN resolutions.

On March 16, Saddam Hussein held his last publicly displayed meeting with his commanders. Denying that Iraq had WMD, he said, "Are weapons of mass destruction a needle that you can conceal in a head cover or the scarf of an old woman that inspectors cannot find?" His final words of defiance were: "Well, give us time and the necessary means and we will produce any weapons they want and then we will invite them to come and destroy them." [42]

The same day, a Sunday, soldiers and civilians dug trenches furiously as tankers poured oil into long lines of the trenches on the outskirts of Baghdad. This was part of a plan to encircle the city with fire and smoke, thereby hindering the bombing missions of the Pentagon by denying pilots visibility and/or misleading the guidance systems of the precision bombs. To protect fuel tankers, the troops buried them under sand. They also buried tanks, leaving only their turrets exposed so they could be deployed as artillery guns.

Fear and apprehension gripped the civilian population. At the behest of the (London) *Sunday Mirror*, Thuraya al Kaissi, an intelligent, articulate schoolgirl of seventeen with almond-shaped eyes and jet-black hair, living with her parents and a brother in the Adhamiya neighborhood of Baghdad, started keeping a diary. *"I am not worried about dying,"* she wrote. *"But I am worried I will live and my family will die."*

That day, Bush, Blair, and Jose Maria Aznar of Spain—the three co-sponsors of the draft resolution at the Security Council— had a meeting on the Portuguese island of Terceira in the Azores. They declared that they would abandon the draft resolution at the Security Council unless the council, during the next twenty-four hours, backed their moves to disarm Iraq immediately. "Three men meeting on an [isolated] Atlantic island seems an apt symbol for the failure of the Bush administration to draw the world around its Iraq policy," wrote the *New York Times* aptly. What was just as remarkable was that despite being a co-sponsor of the draft resolution at the Security Council, Aznar, keenly aware that 70 percent of Spaniards opposed war, refused to send a single combat soldier to join Bush's "Coalition of the Willing." On his part, what mattered most to Bush was not opinion abroad, but at home. There the *New York Times*/CBS poll showed that 42 percent of Americans believed that Saddam Hussein was "personally" responsible for 9/11, and an ABC News survey showed that 55 percent believed he gave direct support to Al Qaida.[43]

Before leaving for the Azores, Blair had received counsel from British attorney general Lord Goldsmith that war would be legal under UN Security Council Resolution 1441, which called for immediate, unconditional cooperation by Iraq—as well as under Resolution 678 (November 1990), which authorized the use of "all necessary means" by UN members to expel the Iraqis from Kuwait, and Resolution 687, which "in effect" said that a cease-fire was conditional on Iraq's disarmament. But the purpose of 678 was the expulsion of Iraq from Kuwait, not the overthrow of the Iraqi regime. Also, said the critics, Resolution 1441 mentioned "serious consequences" if Iraq did not comply with its provisions, whereas the sanction of war flows from the statement that "all necessary means" will be used to secure compliance.[44] Crucially, Lord Goldsmith added that if the sponsors of the U.S.–U.K. draft resolution sought a vote at the council and failed to get it, serious doubts would be cast on the legality of military action against Iraq.[45] This explained the joint decision of Blair, Bush, and Aznar to withdraw their draft resolution from the council.

Among those who disagreed with Lord Goldsmith's interpretation was UN secretary-general Kofi Annan, who said that he believed war without the second resolution by the Security Council would break international law.[46] Earlier, Anne-Marie Slaughter, dean of Princeton University's School of Public and International Affairs, had reckoned that eight out of ten international lawyers would consider a U.S. attack on Iraq without a new resolution a violation of international law. "That view would be supported by the legal advisers of most other countries in the UN," added Steve Ratner, a professor of international law at the University of Texas. To that list could be added Elizabeth Wilmhurst, deputy legal officer at the British Foreign Office, who resigned in protest at Lord Goldsmith's advice to the British government.[47] Others who would challenge Lord Goldsmith's ruling included Professors Philippe Sands QC (Queen's Counselor), director of the Center on International Courts and Tribunals, University College, London; James Crawford, Whewell Professor of International Law, Jesus College, Cambridge; and Robert Black, professor of Scots Law, Edinburgh University. "The real test of any legal argument is whether a court would accept it," said Professor Black. "I challenged the Attorney General [Lord Goldsmith] to say what he thought the odds were of the International Court of Justice in The Hague accepting his argument. [But he did not respond.] In my view, the odds against were greater than 10 to 1."[48]

At the Security Council, nobody paid attention to the twenty-four-hour deadline mentioned by Bush, Blair, and Aznar. President Bush declared in a television address to the nation on March 17 that "intelligence gathered by this and other governments leaves no doubt that the Iraq regime continues to possess and conceal some of the most lethal weapons ever devised." He said that the United Nations had failed to discharge its responsibility. "Now we must discharge ours." He gave Saddam Hussein and his (unnamed) sons forty-eight hours to leave Iraq, failing which his administration would mount military operations "at a time of our own choosing." Saddam rejected the ultimatum.

Bush's deadline added a new dimension in the eyes of many Iraqis. "Before, it seemed to be about biological and chemical weapons, but now it is clear they want to get the president out," said Oil Ministry administrator Ammar Khadham al Habibi, a squat, powerfully built, fleshy-faced man in his early forties. "At work everybody talked about the war and the [Bush] speech, and how their preparations were going—getting gas or water and all of that. . . . Tonight we shall have dinner as a family and listen to the BBC in Arabic. But we have little hope. . . . We prepared everything about a month ago. We taped all the windows and we bought lanterns. But we will get our water across the street at the mosque."[49]

In contrast, for an Iraqi Airways ticket agent, Suha Abdul Rahman al Azi, a bulky woman of fifty-four with a chubby visage and short hair, water was stored in a big tank on the roof. "I was out buying vegetables and extra mineral water in Mansour [neighborhood]," she said. "I work at Saddam [International] Airport on the computers taking tickets. I have worked there since 1978. There were flights to Basra and Mosul today. And one to Syria. . . . We love our president, and don't know why Bush wants to get rid of him. . . . When I see Bush on TV I want to bite him or kill him. Mr. Bush used to talk before about [Iraqi] guns and missiles but now he just talks about Saddam, only Saddam. Are we asking Bush to leave America? How can they ask that? I watched the TV with my husband and three sons. My husband is a doctor at the University of Baghdad. He is in Mansour now for the demonstrations. He is a member of the Baath Party. . . . We are not afraid. Bush should know that there are Kalashnikovs behind every Iraqi door."[50] The veracity and significance of al Azi's last sentence would dawn on the U.S. forces only after they had occupied Iraq.

Both al Habibi and al Azi had been in Iraq before and during the 1991 Gulf War, during which thirteen members of al Habibi's family were killed in a U.S. bombing raid on Najaf, where they had gone from Baghdad to stay at his uncle's house, thinking that Najaf, a religious city, would be spared. They were thus "battle-hardened." But not Thuraya al Kaissi.

"Today at school, we were half way through our morning classes when the headmistress came into our class," she wrote in her diary on March 17. *"Pointing at my best friend Meena, she told her that her mother and father had arrived. They had decided to go to Syria. The headmistress told Meena to go immediately. Meena and I were crying. All other girls in the class were crying too."*

On March 18, there was panic on the streets of Baghdad. The wide boulevards, normally crammed with cars and buses, emptied quickly as residents rushed to stock up on food, bottled mineral water, and flashlight batteries and candles. Lines for gasoline stretched for blocks. The Iraqi dinar fell precipitately, from 2,000 to a dollar to 3,000.

Perhaps a rumor had spread about the withdrawal of about a quarter of the Central Bank's total foreign cash reserves of $4 billion. At 4 A.M. that day, Qusay Saddam Hussein and the Iraqi president's personal secretary, Abid Hamid Mahmoud, had arrived at the Central Bank with a letter from Saddam Hussein authorizing the "removal of $900 million in U.S. $100 bills and $100 million in Euros." It took two hours for a team of workers to load the cash onto three tractor trailers.[51] It was assumed by the U.S. authorities after the fall of Baghdad that Saddam and his sons fled with the vast public treasure. However, most of this money was later found at one of Saddam's palaces and other official residences. So, it seems, removing the cash was possibly part of Saddam's hastily conceived contingency plan.

"They say the war could start tonight," Thuraya al Kaissi noted in her diary on March 18. *"My father tells me to stay at home. . . . I am sad to miss school because I have an English examination soon. I must have top marks. But how can you get top marks when you worry about war all the time? I was five when the Gulf War happened in 1991. My father took us to a cousin's orchard by the Tigris about half an hour's drive from here for a few days. We have cracks in the wall on both sides of our living room from the last war. The Americans bombed the telephone exchange which is a kilometer from here. They bombed it three times and all the houses shook. I am worried they will bomb it again."*

As part of the sixth phase of the Pentagon's "unseen" war, unexpected faxes in Arabic arrived at government offices in Baghdad urging Iraqis not to resist the invasion and providing frequencies for "the information radio" to which the recipients were advised to tune in. Elsewhere in the country, leaflets rained from the sky in an enormous military air drop. One informed Iraqi soldiers that they as well as the invading troops could be victims if Saddam Hussein used chemical weapons. Another urged them to refrain from torching oil wells. This exercise had started a few weeks earlier in the southern no-fly zone, when Centcom aircraft dropped hundreds of thousands of leaflets in a day calling on soldiers not to fight in case of war.

Following a night curfew imposed in Baghdad on March 18, local Baath leaders were put on around-the-clock alert. The small sandbag emplacements that appeared were there more to impose the curfew than to defend the capital. At main crossings, small clusters of troops stood, while at most street corners defensive positions emerged, manned by middle-aged and older men wearing a variety of uniforms and carrying an assortment of weapons, including AK-47 Kalashnikovs.

While Bush had armed himself with war powers in October, Blair needed parliamentary approval to attack Iraq. Noticing that the latest poll, published in the right-wing tabloid *The Sun,* showed only 15 percent favoring war without a second UN Security Council resolution, the government-sponsored motion in the 659-member House of Commons on March 18 read: "The United Kingdom must uphold the United Nations' authority as set out in Resolution 1441 and many resolutions preceding it, and therefore supports the decision that the U.K. should use all means to disarm Iraq." So, while Bush declared that the United Nations had failed to act, implying thereby its "irrelevance," his close ally Blair called on his fellow parliamentarians to authorize his government to actually implement the latest UN Security Council resolution. What was absent from his speech was any reference to the JIC's February 10 report, "International Terrorism: War with Iraq," in which it warned that the threat from Al Qaida "would be heightened by military action against Iraq"—a report that he had not submitted to his cabinet colleagues for discussion.[52]

Had this fact been known then, rather than six months later, the disquiet among governing Labor ranks would have been deeper and more widespread. As it was, there were reports that as many as 200 members of Parliament (MPs) out of 411 might vote against the government motion. This was the most severe crisis that Anthony Charles Lynton Blair had faced in his political career—which stretched back to 1983, when he was elected Labor Member of Parliament for Sedgefield constituency in northern England at thirty. He was then a practicing barrister in London, having graduated in law from St. John's College, Oxford, in 1972 after attending the elite Fettes College in Edinburgh, Scotland, where he was born and where his father, a Conservative politician, was a university lecturer on law. An outgoing student at Oxford, he was the bass guitar player and lead singer for a rock band named the Ugly Rumors.

In Parliament he joined the Tribune group, named after the

leftist *Tribune* weekly. He rapidly advanced to Labor's front benches during the Conservative government of Prime Minister Margaret Thatcher (r. 1979–1990), becoming, first, the Labor opposition's spokesman on Economic Affairs (1984–87), and then Trade and Industry, Energy, and Employment. He shed any leftist tendencies he had had and moved firmly into the centrist section of the Labor Party. Following the 1992 general election, Labor's new leader, John Smith, promoted Blair to Shadow Home Secretary, dealing with domestic issues of law and order. As a highly successful lawyer who was qualified to plead in court, Blair was well versed in advocacy, sounding vigorous and sincere, and absolutely convinced about whatever case he had taken up. He was also known to be a devout Anglican Christian. Initially, his semireligious air of righteous conviction appealed to many Britons, especially the young, who often viewed politicians as insincere and self-serving. But through overuse, this Blair style would begin to pall, especially after the fiasco of failing to find WMD in occupied Iraq.

Following Smith's sudden death in 1994 due to heart failure, Blair won the leadership contest by a large majority. It was believed that, as a moderate, he would attract new voters for the party, which had been out of office since 1979. He de-emphasized the party's traditional ties to trade unions in order to widen its appeal.

This policy paid off, with Labor winning a landslide victory in 1997; Blair became the youngest British prime minister since Lord Liverpool in 1812. He devolved power to Scotland and Wales, reformed the welfare state, and improved relations with the European Union. He got along famously with U.S. Democratic president Bill Clinton. Later, to the surprise of many, he quickly established rapport with the newly elected, and still very diffident, George Walker Bush. Following 9/11, his relationship with Bush deepened. His government participated actively in the U.S.-led campaign against the Taliban regime in Afghanistan, which had the sanction of the UN Security Council. In the case of Iraq, the absence of such a sanction did not deter Blair from backing the United States by supplying a large British force to the Pentagon's war plans—the only non-American leader to do so—from September 2002 onward, soon after his momentous September 6–7 meetings with Bush at Camp David. By now, Blair, a nominal social democrat, had fully embraced the U.S. neocons' unilateralist doctrine based on the assumption of Islamist terrorists acquiring WMD from a rogue state in the future. This was a matter of considerable angst not only among Labor MPs but also in the country at large.

As the House of Commons began its two-day debate on Iraq on March 17, Blair found himself assured of the almost total backing of the opposition Conservative Party, with its 166 MPs. His problem lay with his own party. Desperate to secure their bare majority support, he drafted his wife, Cherie Booth, a practicing lawyer, to lobby Labor MPs. In a closed-door meeting he told his party MPs, totaling 410, that if he failed to win their majority backing he would resign—a clear case of bluff. Nobody really believed that, having dispatched nearly a third of the British armed forces and one aircraft carrier to fight the impending war, Blair would step down.

In his one-on-one meeting with Clare Short, cabinet minister for international development, to dissuade her from resigning, Blair told her that French president Chirac had said in a TV interview that France "will vote 'no' on the second resolution at the Security Council" because it considers that "there are no grounds for waging war in order to achieve the goal we have set ourselves—to disarm Iraq." In reality, going by the transcript of the TV interview that Short would read later (after receiving a copy from a member of the public), Chirac's stance was laid out in three phases: allow the inspectors to finish the job (in 120 days, as provided for in Resolution 1284 of December 1999); if the inspectors find WMD and Iraq refuses to destroy them, then the Security Council should consider the matter; and then it must specifically authorize the use of force.[53] Putting his spin on Chirac's position, Blair would tell the House of Commons that France had made it clear it would not accept any resolution that had allowed automatic use of force in the absence of compliance by Saddam.

On March 17, Robin Cook, leader of the House of Commons and a cabinet minister, resigned; his lead was followed by two non-cabinet ministers. In an eleven-minute resignation speech, he skillfully demolished the argument for war. "If we believe in international community based on binding rules and institutions, we cannot simply set them aside when they produce results that are inconvenient to us," he said. "I cannot defend a war with neither international agreement nor domestic support." Now that the attempts to secure a second resolution at the Security Council had failed, "we cannot pretend that getting a second resolution was of no importance." Alluding to the argument of some that Iraq's forces were "so weak, so demoralized, and so badly equipped that the war will be over in days," he said, "We cannot base our military strategy on the basis that Saddam is weak and at the same time justify preemptive action on the claim that he is a threat."

As foreign secretary from 1997 to 2001, Cook was the boss of the British Secret Intelligence Service, MI6, and as a cabinet minister he had access to classified documents. So he spoke on the core issue of Baghdad's possession of WMD with an insider's knowledge. "Iraq probably had no *weapons of mass destruction in the commonly understood sense of the term—namely, a credible device capable of being delivered against strategic city targets* [italics added]," he said. "It probably does still have biological toxins and battlefield chemical munitions. But it has had them since the 1980s, when the U.S. sold Saddam anthrax agents and the then British government built his chemical and munitions factories. Why is it now so urgent that we should take military action to disarm a military capacity that has been there for [nearly] 20 years and which we helped to create?" He failed to see any logic in going to war "this week when Saddam's ambition to complete his weapons program is frustrated by the presence of UN inspectors."

While the British public had "no doubt" about Saddam being

"a brutal dictator," they were "not persuaded that he is a clear and present danger to Britain. . . . They are suspicious that they are being pushed hurriedly into conflict by a U.S. administration that has an agenda of its own."[54]

Later, weeks after the invasion of Iraq, Cook would explain that to produce "a credible WMD" requires quite a large industrial infrastructure and a large workforce. "It is inconceivable that such factories exist in Iraq, and we've not found them," he said. "There is no part of the globe that has been more managed by aerial surveillance [than Iraq]. It is also inconceivable that anybody working on that program hasn't come forward to tell us where it is: We've had the top people under interrogation for weeks now."[55]

In the House of Commons, winding up the debate for the government on March 18, Blair did not address the specific points raised by Cook. Instead, he focused on the WMD and the credibility of Saddam Hussein. "We hear exactly the same claim as before: that he [Saddam] has no WMD," he said. "Indeed, we are asked to believe that after seven years of obstruction and non-compliance finally resulting in the inspectors leaving in 1998 . . . he then voluntarily decided to do what he had consistently refused to do under coercion." (But, "under coercion," Iraq had destroyed 90 to 95 percent of the WMD, according to Scott Ritter, an American naval intelligence officer who worked as Unscom's chief inspector from May 1991 to August 1998, and later published *Endgame: Solving the Iraq Problem—Once and for All*.) Now, said Blair, "We are asked to accept [that] Saddam decided to destroy those weapons. I say such a claim is palpably absurd." Then he read selectively from the latest UN inspectors' report. "What is perfectly clear is that Saddam is playing the same old games in the same old way," he said. (This contradicted the facts provided by Hans Blix and his statement to the Security Council that Iraq had become "proactive" in its cooperation with the United Nations.) Finally, "the possibility of the two coming together—of terrorist groups in possession of WMD," he concluded, was "now in my view a real and present danger." (He ignored the rather obvious fact that 9/11 had not involved WMD, and that the six North Africans arrested in London in January for possessing ricin had made it from castor beans, for which they did not have to journey to Baghdad.) "To retreat [now] would put at risk all we hold dearest," Blair declared.

The U.K. House passed the war motion by 412 votes to 149—with the Conservatives voting for it. When the antiwar amendment to the motion was put to a vote, it received 219 votes, including fifty-three left-of-center Liberal Democrats, sixteen Conservatives, and eleven others. The 139 Labor MPs who voted for the amendment formed a majority of the backbenchers—that is, those MPs who were not cabinet or non-cabinet ministers (eighty-eight of them) or their personal parliamentary secretaries (fifty-eight of them). This was the largest "backbench rebellion" in British parliamentary history. It is not something for which Blair would like to be remembered.

In contrast, he would certainly like to be noted as the only foreign leader to be privy to the Pentagon's secret "1003 Victor" Plan, based on Rumsfeld's doctrine of "Rolling Invasion."[56] At the strategic level it boiled down to "Baghdad First," ignoring all other cities and towns. At the tactical-operational level of battalion and brigade strength, the plan followed the principle of "Inside Out," with the battalion or brigade securing a foothold and then spilling out. The overall function of these units was to degrade the subsidiary sectors without losing their main focus on Baghdad. As it was, the Pentagon's Plan 1003 had a head start, because twelve years of periodic bombing in the northern and southern zones, covering three-fifths of Iraq, had degraded the Iraqi defenses considerably. "Our aim was to be aggressive and dominate and keep driving for Baghdad," said Colonel Bryan McCoy of the U.S. Marines after the fall of the capital. "That way the enemy was always on the back foot and we had the whip hand." As far as capturing Baghdad, the plan was to do it "sector by sector"—to encircle the city and launch armed and armored raids inside. These were expected to last seven days. But they lasted only three days because of the success the U.S. intelligence officials had in bribing the Republican Guard generals. During that period, the U.S. Third Infantry Division would launch three armored raids.[57]

The overarching concept was to use speed and firepower and combine them with intelligence pinpointing the location of the enemy. Intelligence came from two major sources—round-the-clock drones unimpeded by sandstorms or smoke, and human intelligence (HUMINT) gathered mainly by U.S. Special Operations Forces (SOFs), who were deployed on their largest scale yet. The latter relayed the information to the encircling aircraft, armed with precision-guided munitions. The job of the Centcom headquarters was to combine the latest real-time tactical information about the enemy's position and strength with the previously completed strategic analysis to determine which target to hit in order to do maximum damage to the enemy.

U.S. regular forces were equipped with the high-tech weaponry that was deployed against the Taliban in October 2001, as listed on pp. 23. As before, B-52 bombers were to be used to drop 2,000-pound bombs during the night at dug-in defense lines of the enemy's elite forces. Tomahawk cruise missiles were to be launched from ships or submarines to hit static prestigious ground targets such as the Defense Ministry or a presidential palace. Cruise missiles were meant to be fired from aircraft at civilian infrastructure sites, like phone exchanges, to destroy the command and control capability of the Iraqi military. Unlike radio and satellite telephone systems, land lines cannot be tapped into. So the American arms industry had devised an "e-bomb" (electronic bomb) to be launched inside a cruise missile. Such a bomb converts the energy from an explosion into a surge of microwave energy, which destroys all electronic circuits—such as radar and missile systems—and blankets a large area. There was also the Blackout Bomb, a missile without a warhead that breaks open to shower graphite filaments, short-circuiting power grids, and thus depriving large areas of electricity. The Joint Direct Attack Ammunition (JDAM), a conventional free-fall bomb weighing 2,500 pounds (1,125 kilograms), turned precision-guided weapon, uses a Global Positioning Satellite (GPS) system to find the target, thus allowing the pilots to fly at higher, safer elevations. A bunker buster bomb, weighing 4,000 pounds (1,800 kilograms) and using enhanced GPS to destroy targets in deep bunkers, penetrates twenty feet (six meters) of concrete or ninety-five feet (thirty meters) of earth. The Massive Ordnance Air Blast Bomb (MOAB), also called Big Blu, weighing 21,500 pounds (10,000 kilograms)—the successor to the Daisy Cutter, weighing 15,000 pounds (6,800 kilograms)—the size of a passenger bus and guided by satellite, is dropped from the back of a C130 cargo plane and destroys everything within 1,900-feet (600-meter) blast radius. The Paveway bomb, weighing 1,000 pounds (450 kilograms) and equipped with both laser and satellite guidance systems, is dropped from U.K.-made Tornados.

There had also been advances in military satellites and reconnaissance planes. Military radar satellites now have infrared cameras that can see through darkness or bad weather. They also monitor enemy mobile and satellite phone conversations. And JSTAR (Joint Surveillance and Target Attack Radar) surveillance aircraft has six different types of radar and provides real-time imaging of moving targets for the Special Forces and Command and Control units on the ground.

On the human side, the Pentagon this time came up with the idea of "embedding" journalists with different units. The journalists agreed to live with the units whose activities they would report once the hot war started, within the limits set by the Pentagon. Altogether, some seven hundred journalists from several countries, including Israel, would be embedded—not only with the ground forces, but also with those stationed on aircraft carriers.

Many of the regular troops in the American and British forces assembled in Kuwait and on aircraft carriers were new to warfare.

On March 19, reporting from the British military headquarters in Kuwait, Ben Brown of the BBC said, "The atmosphere here is very tense. There is some trepidation and apprehension among the troops as this long-awaited and debated war is about to begin. Some of the troops are young and have not been in battle before. The hour is almost upon us and there is no doubt it will be utterly terrifying in its intensity. Tonight the troops have been allowed to make one last phone call to their loved ones before they move forward."[58]

Britain was the only country to contribute combat forces in large numbers—45,000, to be exact, under its own Operation "Telic" (Arabic for "Comfort")—to what Washington grandly called the "Coalition of the Willing,"[59] led by the United States with 255,000 troops. The others were: Australia (2,000); Czech Republic (200); Poland (200); and Slovakia (200). The Anglo-American forces were equipped with 920 tanks, 600 warplanes, 300 combat helicopters, and 50 unmanned aerial vehicles. The U.S. Navy deployed five aircraft-carrier battle groups out of its total of nine, and the U.K. Navy, one.

In the "unseen" war, too, Britain was the only other participant, having maintained agents in Iraq, especially in the south, over several years, and then initiating a program of developing more once British troops had begun training with their American counterparts in Kuwait in October. The clandestine activity involved the British defense ministry, working with MI6's Arabic specialists, nicknamed the "Camel Corps," infiltrating its two hundred commandos of the Special Forces—specifically Special Air Services (SAS) and Special Boat Services (SBS)—into the south. For instance, two SBS men dressed in local Arab clothes arrived in Basra and called on an Iraqi agent called "Karim" who had earlier been supplied with a short-range communications system and given the times when he was to send reports to his MI6 handler.[60]

The Anglo-American alliance faced 389,000 Iraqi troops, including just over 80,000 in the Republican Guard (within which the Special Republican Guard was 20,000 strong). They were equipped with 2,200 tanks and 100 combat helicopters, backed by 300 combat aircraft, only half of which were serviceable. Iraq's active paramilitary force included 5,000 armed personnel of the Special Security Organization, 18,000 members of the Fedayeen Saddam—and some 6,000 non-Iraqi Arab volunteers who had gravitated to the country in the past few weeks from the rest of the Arab world, driven by a blend of religious fervor and Arab nationalism. The government had hurriedly set up training camps for them around Baghdad.

Saddam Hussein wanted to keep the war going for twenty days or more. He had decentralized the command structure and set up an alternative communications system. He wanted to lure the Allies to Baghdad for long, debilitating urban warfare. The Allies were equally determined to avoid this.

NOTES

1. *Independent,* February 15, 2003.
2. Cited in *Guardian*, September 12, 2003.
3. Cited in *Independent on Sunday*, September 14, 2003.
4. February 17, 2003.
5. *International Herald Tribune*, February 1–2, 2003.
6. Morocco, Pakistan, and Saudi Arabia would become targets of terrorism soon after the Anglo-American invasion of Iraq.
7. It transpired later that Qatar's ruler, Shaikh Hamad al Thani, had intervened personally to see that Powell got the audiotape before Al Jazeera broadcast it.
8. On February 14, 2003, the Iraqi parliament unanimously approved—as it was so often accustomed to do—Saddam Hussein's decree banning the WMD.
9. *New York Times*, February 15, 2003; *Daily Mirror*, February 15, 2003.
10. *New York Times*, February 15, 2003.
11. *International Herald Tribune*, March 8–9, 2003.
12. *New York Times*, March 11, 2003. What probably mattered to him was the instruction he received directly from Almighty God rather than the opinion of those whose vocation was to interpret the Bible and provide moral guidelines to believing Christians.
13. *International Herald Tribune*, February 8–9, 2003.

14. Later, to teach Canada "a lesson," President Bush "postponed" a scheduled visit to the country in May.

15. Reuters, February 20, 2003.

16. *Time*, February 24, 2003, p. 24.

17. *International Herald Tribune*, February 8–9 and 14, 2003.

18. Washington pressured South Africa, the leader of the 114-member Non-Aligned Movement at the United Nations, to desist from calling for a General Assembly session on Iraq. In a fax to the South African foreign ministry in Pretoria, the U.S. embassy said: "Given the current highly charged atmosphere, the United States would regard a General Assembly session on Iraq as against the U.S. . . .Please know that this question as well as your position on it is important to us."

19. Indeed, the inexperienced President Bush, feeling the popular urge for action against the Taliban, broke the protocol of never officially divulging the activities of secret services, and announced on September 28 that U.S. Special Forces were already inside Afghanistan. See further Dilip Hiro, *War without End*, p. 321.

20. *Sunday Times*, April 13, 2003.

21. May 12, 2003.

22. *Financial Times*, February 21, 2003; *Guardian*, June 5, 2003; *Independent*, June 30, 2003. In his interview with the *Guardian*, he referred to vilification by "my detractors in Washington; there are bastards who spread things around, of course, who planted nasty things in the media."

23. *New York Times*, February 23, 2003.

24. *USA Today*, February 28, 2003, reporting the *USA Today*-CNN-Gallup poll, conducted during February 24–26.

25. See further Dilip Hiro, *Iraq*, pp. 105–7, 113, 123–24.

26. Reuters, March 1, 2003.

27. *Washington Times*, September 3, 2003.

28 That evening, when asked by David Dimbleby of BBC-TV what justification he had to take military action against Iraq in the absence of WMD, all Donald Rumsfeld had to say was, "Saddam Hussein has learned to live in an inspections environment. He does things underground. He is very skillful at denial and deception." *Independent*, March 5, 2003.

29. Reuters, March 6, 2003.

30. *New York Times*, March 10, 2003. According to Muhammad el Baradei, any number of groups, including Iraqi exiles, had an interest in forging the document.

31. *Financial Times,* February 27, 2003; *USA Today*, February 27, 2003.

32. Subscribing to the strategy of using serious threat of force to achieve the disarmament of Iraq, President Chirac had dispatched a French aircraft carrier to the Gulf in early February.

33. *International Herald Tribune*, March 11–12, 2003.

34. *New York Times*, March 14, 2003. Later the Bush administration held up Chile's free-trade agreement.

35. In Rumsfeld's words, Britain's role in Iraq was "unclear," and America could do "workarounds" without Her Majesty's boys.

36. *Observer*, March 16, 2003.

37. *Washington Post*, July 20, 2003.

38. Cited in *Guardian*, May 3, 2003.

39. April 17, 2003.

40. *New York Times*, March 8, 2003.

41. Associated Press, March 16, 2003.

42. Ibid.

43 Cited in *International Herald Tribune*, March 12, 2003.

44. In the past, the Security Council had often translated its threat of "serious consequences" against Iraq into banning the country's top officials from traveling abroad.

45. *Observer*, March 16, 2003.

46. Ibid.

47. Reuters, March 6, 2003; *Independent*, March 23, 2003.

48. *Independent*, May 25, 2003.

49. *Guardian*, March 19, 2003.

50. Ibid.

51. *New York Times,* May 6, 2003.

52. Cited in *Independent*, September 12, 2003.

53. *Independent*, June 2, 2003.

54. *Guardian*, March 18, 2003. Bearing in mind those who remembered Robin Cook backing military action in Kosovo in 1999 without UN support, he said, "There was no doubt about the multilateral support [in NATO] we had for military action in Kosovo. It is precisely because we have none of that support that it was all-important to get the Security Council on board as the last hope of demonstrating international agreement."

55. *Guardian*, July 7, 2003. Electric power cables leading to a factory producing WMD would provide a telltale sign to spy satellites and to reconnaissance planes.

56. The only other foreign leader to be shown the Pentagon's plan—in February—was Israeli prime minister Ariel Sharon. *Washington Times,* September 3, 2003.

57. *Independent*, April 12, 2003.

58. Cited in *Independent on Sunday*, April 13, 2003.

59. The phrase "Coalition of the Willing" was a glaring example of tautology, since the term "coalition" implies willingness on the part of its constituents.

60. Michael Smith, *The Spying Game: The Secret History of British Espionage*, Politico's Publishing, 2003, p. 141.

PART II · OPERATION "IRAQI FREEDOM"

CHAPTER 5

WEEK ONE: ALLIES' DASHED HOPES

"The streets of Baghdad and Basra are sure to erupt in joy."
—Vice President Dick Cheney, on NBC's *Meet the Press,* March 16, 2003

"I was woken at 5:30 A.M. by the air raid sirens. It is a horrible noise. I was very scared the night before, so I got in bed with my mum. When the sirens started, we both woke up and hugged each other. After half an hour we hear the explosions. After two hours, we have the all-clear. All day I feel tired."
—Thuraya al Kaissi, in her diary on March 20, 2003

THURAYA WAS TYPICAL of Baghdad's 5.7 million residents, huddled in their beds in fear. The opening U.S. salvo coincided with dawn prayers, with the muezzin's rousing call to the faithful mingling with the wailing of sirens and the rising din of antiaircraft fire directed at the cruise missiles that came hailing down on assorted Iraqi targets. Barking street dogs filled the silent gaps between the rattle of antiaircraft guns.

The Pentagon's Operation "Iraqi Freedom" started at 2:33 A.M. GMT (5:33 A.M. Iraqi time) on March 20, Thursday, targeting the farmhouses of two of Saddam's three daughters—the youngest, Hala, married to Jamal Mustapha al Tikriti, and the eldest, Raghad, a widow—along the southern bank of the Tigris in the Daura district of Baghdad. According to reliable information conveyed by a CIA informer, Saddam had arrived at this site at about

1:30 A.M. local time for a meeting with his two sons, Uday (b. 1964) and Qusay (b. 1966), in a bunker, and would stay there for four hours. Nearly two hours later, Bush ordered the strike. It was another two hours before the Pentagon's B1 Lancer Stealth bombers dropped four 2,000-pound (950 kilogram) bunker-busting bombs and fired cruise missiles at the target.

Bush's aides immediately informed U.S. congressional leaders, and even the rulers of Kuwait, Qatar, Bahrain, and Saudi Arabia, of the start of the war. It was originally planned to commence fourteen hours later, according to the Pentagon's plan "1003 Victor," which was known to British prime minister Blair. But, embarrassingly, no one at the Bush White House bothered to tell Blair of the change. So he and his war cabinet heard the news on radio or television *after* the event.

Nor did the early strike achieve the desired result. Three searches of the bombed site after the end of the war by the CIA and a search team led by Colonel Tim Madare revealed that every structure had been destroyed except the main palace, hidden behind a wall topped with electrified barbed wire, and that there were no bunkers or corpses. It was, however, possible that those who perished evaporated, given the massive firepower of the bunker-busting bombs.[1] In any case, none of them could have been Saddam Hussein or either of his two sons. According to twenty-eight-year-old "Abu Tiba," a tall, broad-shouldered man with a crew cut and stubble, who served Uday Saddam Hussein as a bodyguard for six years, Uday and his brother and father were "on the other [northern] side" of Baghdad in "one of the dozens of safe houses of trusted friends and relatives."[2]

After the initial, unplanned salvo, the U.S. Central Command (Centcom) implemented its preplanned firing of Tomahawk missiles from American warships and cruise missiles by warplanes.

In Washington, where it was still Wednesday, March 19, Bush addressed the nation on television at 10:15 P.M. EST (3:15 A.M. GMT Thursday). "Now that conflict has come, the only way to limit its duration is to apply decisive force," he declared. By 11 P.M. EST, he was asleep, smug in the knowledge that the American bombs had killed the Butcher of Baghdad and his equally vicious sons.

But, alas, no, the Butcher was far from finished. It was as if, on cue, he had crept into Bush's sleep and turned into a nightmare at 12:30 A.M. EST on Thursday, 8:30 A.M. Iraqi time. There he was, on Iraqi TV in military uniform, a black beret over his head, but (unusually) wearing large dark-rimmed glasses, reading from a notepad, not a teleprompter. "At the time of dawn prayer on this day 20 March 2003," Saddam Hussein began, deftly dating his speech, "the enemy wanted to make the war short, but we hope, God willing, to make it long and heavy. Iraq will carry out jihad against the invaders with the heroic army in the Iraq of civilization, history and belief. We will fight the invaders and drive them out, God willing. Iraq will be victorious. Long live Iraq and Palestine." In between his lines, he recited a poem, which read in part: "Draw your sword and make it gleam/ No winner but the determined man/ Make the banner fly on each pole/ Pray to God, the wound will heal."

Three hours later, while Bush still slept, a Chinese spokesman said in Beijing, "This war is violating the norms of international behavior." Russian president Vladimir Putin called it "a big political mistake." And President Jacques Chirac of France expressed "regrets" at what was happening, while his prime minister, Jean-Pierre Raffarin, would say in a TV interview, "The U.S. has erred in going to war, morally, politically, and strategically. There was an alternative to war. Going to war was a moral error when one can disarm in other ways." There were protest marches in London, Rome, Berlin, Athens (one hundred thousand strong), and Melbourne (forty thousand strong). Cairo witnessed its most outspoken antigovernment protest in recent times, with thousands of mainly Islamist students shouting slogans against President Hosni Mubarak and chanting, "Americans and Israelis, one enemy; Iraq and Palestine, one cause." The armed police beat up hundreds and arrested hundreds more. The following Monday, however, the Arab League foreign ministers, meeting in Cairo, called for an end to the attack on Iraq and the withdrawal of foreign troops, and renewed its earlier call that no member-state should take part in the war, which had been described by Iranian president Muhammad Khatami as "satanic." Saud al Faisal, the Saudi foreign minister, announced that he had sent specific cease-fire proposals to Washington and was awaiting response. It came. "No question of a cease-fire," replied Donald Rumsfeld publicly.[3]

Anticipating an attack, the Iraqis at the Rumeila oil field west of Basra set ablaze about thirty oil wells, a small part of the total. At night, when U.S. Navy SEALs and Royal Marine commandos under British command tried to capture oil and gas platforms in Iraq's Fao Peninsula, they encountered resistance.

That night in London, BBC-TV's ten o'clock news stated on twelve separate unattributed occasions that Scud (surface-to-surface) missiles had been fired by the Iraqis at Kuwait, the first of many false reports aired by the Anglo-American media during the invasion. While in general the BBC's news managers jealously guard their independence and rebuff governmental pressures, in the case of the run-up to the Anglo-American invasion of Iraq and the war itself, they failed the independence test. Their problem stemmed from a disjunction between the mainly prowar political elite and the largely antiwar public. The BBC's top management stepped in with a confidential memorandum on February 6— about a week before the largest demonstration in London's history against the war—to senior news managers, instructing them to be "careful" about broadcasting dissent, as "we will pay a high price for getting this wrong." Once the invasion started, the limits of acceptable dissent contracted further. Little wonder that a study of five countries by the Frankfurt-based *Frankfurter Allgemein Zeitung* (Frankfurt General Newspaper) revealed that the BBC's 2 percent level of dissenting content was even lower than the American ABC's 7 percent. The BBC always prefaced the dispatches of its correspondents in Baghdad with the statement that "their reports are monitored" and/or "the reporters are sometimes restricted in their movements." But it never prefaced the dispatches of the journalists embedded with Centcom, each of whom had signed a contract requiring him/her "to follow the direction and orders of the [respective] government."[4]

At 9:10 P.M. Iraqi time, the bombing of Baghdad started. The targets included the foreign and planning ministries and presidential compounds in central Baghdad, a fact noted by Thuruya al Kaissi. *"I go to bed very early, but I am woken at 9 p.m. by the sirens again,"* she wrote. *"More bangs, but far away. In 1991, the blasts at the telephone exchange [in our Adhamiya neighborhood] broke all our windows. May be this time we will be Okay. How would the people of Britain or America like it if someone was doing this to them? My father, who is 60, was at the University of Essex [in Britain] for two years in the 1970s, and had a wonderful time. I get back to sleep but have very bad dreams. In one I run up the street and I am chased by two American rockets."*

The next morning (Friday, March 21) at 7 A.M. local time, Centcom mounted a four-pronged ground attack on Iraq from Kuwait. One, moving sharply to the northeast, was aimed at the Umm Qasr–Basra–Zubair triangle, with the British taking the leading role in a joint operation alongside the U.S. Marines, through the border town of Safwan. The Marines dropped napalm bombs on the Iraqi observation post at Safwan Hill, the first of many such bombs to be fired during the four-week invasion. "Safwan Hill went up in a huge fireball and the observation post was obliterated," reported the *Sydney Morning Herald* correspondent. "I pity anyone who is in there," a Marine sergeant said. The Pentagon denied deploying napalm, saying it had used Mark 77 Firebomb—an example of cynical sophistry. Napalm, first invented in 1942, is a mixture of jet fuel and polystyrene that sticks to skin as it burns, whereas Mark 77 Firebomb, a more recent invention, is a mixture of kerosene and polystyrene, and equally lethal.[5] "The generals love napalm," Colonel James Allen, commander of Marine Air Group 11, told the *San Diego Union-Tribune*. "It has a big psychological effect."[6]

Of the remaining three prongs—all manned exclusively by Americans—the extreme western prong was destined for the Shia holy city of Karbala (population 572,000), the burial place of Imam Hussein (d. 681 A.D.), through Najaf (population 550,000), a communications center served by an airfield. Najaf is also the city where the road running parallel to the Euphrates from Nasiriya (population 350,000) meets the road coming up from the west of the Euphrates, and from then on, the highways run parallel on both sides of the Euphrates to Baghdad. The eastern counterpart of this prong was directed at Kut (on the Tigris) connected to Nasiriya (on the Euphrates) by Highway 7, which cuts through the fertile land between the two rivers, called Mesopotamia (Greek, land between the rivers). The final prong was focused on reaching Diwaniya through Samawa.

At 1 P.M. local time, Group Captain Al Lockwood, spokesman for the British forces in the Gulf, said, "Hopefully, we'll be in Baghdad in the next three or four days." A rosy prediction like this had been preceded by such news stories as the one by Kuwaiti News Agency released twelve hours earlier that the Allies had overrun the port of Umm Qasr (population 45,000), a claim confirmed the following day by Centcom. The Allies' westerly flank, advancing through the sparsely populated desert, would make rapid progress, while its easterly counterpart, running through the fertile, populated area between the Euphrates and the Tigris, would encounter resistance. The Iraqis had two options. One was to ambush the Americans with small arms. The other was to attack them with their tanks, but for this they would need air cover—which was not forthcoming, because Saddam kept all his warplanes and combat helicopters grounded, probably reckoning that deploying them would lead to their almost instant destruction. Lacking air cover, Iraqi armor was an easy target for the Pentagon's tank-busting A10 aircraft. On top of that, the possession of night-vision and other surveillance equipment, which turned night into day, gave the Americans an unbeatable advantage over their Iraqi adversaries.

Such advantages were obvious as British and American Special Forces infiltrated Iraq from Jordan, and claimed the capture of Iraq's H2 and H3 airfields in the western desert.

However, Centcom's quick and surgical strikes on the government buildings and presidential compounds in Baghdad, combined with a torrent of e-mails and cell-phone calls to Iraqi generals to defect, failed to bring about the expected collapse of the regime—the "Instant Victory" scenario.

So Centcom geared up for its next move.

"When the siren goes off my whole body feels numb," noted Thuraya al Kaissi. *"My brother (aged 23) and my dad go outside to watch the rockets, but my mother and I hide under the stairs. My face goes totally white. Now another siren goes off."*

At 8:20 P.M. Iraqi time, the Centcom unleashed its "Shock and Awe" strategy, with a series of staggering explosions, most of them in the Republican Presidential Palace Complex, in an "awesome," murderous fireworks display unlike any witnessed before. "Cruise missiles and bombs heaped devastation on Baghdad, sending enormous mushroom clouds of smoke wafting hundreds of feet into the air," reported Hala Jaber of the (London) *Sunday Times*. "Giant fires raged fiercely all over the city as wave after wave of missiles slammed into government ministries and military command centers. A huge series of ear-splitting explosions rocked the banks of the Tigris. White pinpricks of exploding anti-aircraft shells seemed to offer little defense against the barrage as fireballs lit up the sky." The images shown on television—Al Arabiya, the BBC, CNN, Fox, Al Jazeera, MSNBC, et al.—were terrifying. It seemed as if all of Baghdad were ablaze. The fires at the Republican Presidential Palace and the Ministry of Armaments Procurement continued well into the next morning. *"Why does this have to happen to Baghdad?"* asked Salam Pax, the *nom de plume* of the Iraqi blogger from Baghdad who would later turn out to be a twenty-eight-year- old European-trained architect who had lived in Vienna from 1988 to 1996.

That is the question many asked in Greece, the current chair of the European Union, where 90 percent were opposed to war, and where a daylong antiwar strike brought the country to a standstill. Outside Europe and the Middle East, there were protest marches in Bangladesh, Indonesia, and Australia. In the Arab world, Yemen, Egypt, and Jordan witnessed large demonstrations as Arab leaders gathered for an Arab League summit in Sharm al Shaikh, Egypt, to forge a common stand on the war. The title of the resolution they would adopt on March 24—"The American/British aggression against fraternal Iraq and its implications for the security and safety of neighboring Arab States and Arab national security"—would leave little doubt about their stance. Describing the invasion of Iraq as a threat to Arab security, the resolution declared that the league members would not participate in any such war, but left open the option of the Anglo-American alliance using their soil and/or military facilities in its invasion of Iraq. This sleight of hand did not fool many inside or outside the Arab countries. In Amman, the capital of Jordan—adjoining Iraq as well as the Palestinian Territories—one hundred thousand people gathered on March 25 in the largest demonstration in the Arab world since the start of the war, with protesters denouncing King Abdullah as "Zionist."

However, the answer to Salam Pax's question about the shocking fate of Baghdad lay with Donald Rumsfeld, who, in the aftermath of the first night of the "Shock and Awe" bombing, confidently declared that Saddam's regime was "about to fall."

As it was, this round of bombardment had included targets in Mosul and Kirkuk in the north—just as the Kurdistan Democratic Party (KDP) and the Patriotic Union of Kurdistan (PUK) agreed to put their seventy-thousand-strong militia, called *peshmargas* (Kurdish, those prepared to die) under Centcom command. Since the KDP and the PUK had been running Iraqi Kurdistan for many years, independent of the central authority in Baghdad—protected by an air umbrella provided by the Anglo-Americans, whose warplanes patrolled Iraq above the 36th Parallel around the clock—the subordination of their forces to Centcom went ahead smoothly.

On the first two days of the invasion, March 20–21, Centcom undertook one thousand combat missions and fired six hundred cruise missiles. To the Anglo-American soldiers and politicians, these were mere statistics. What lay at the end of each of these missiles and bombs only Iraqis knew.

"I'm so afraid," wrote Thuraya al Kaissi in her diary. *"Please, God, save us. Save the children of Iraq. Oh my God, it's getting heavier and heavier. I don't know where to hide. God help me. How long is all this going to last and how many people will have to die? I wish that Bush lived in the same situation that we are in. How would he feel? [Later I] looked through the kitchen window. The sky was just red. Red and red and red. Our beautiful country. Why are they doing this?"*

Another perspective was provided by Rageh Omaar, an Arabic-speaking Somalia-born reporter for the BBC in Baghdad. "Think of what it must have been like for the families living near these targets, huddled indoors as their neighborhood was torn apart," he said on March 22. "The main concern of ordinary Iraqis is just to survive. Even in the calm of the day, when the bombs are not falling, the markets are deserted. Now everyone feels it is too dangerous to leave their homes, even to buy food."[7]

That day the British troops fired cluster artillery projectiles L20A1 at the Five Miles and Gah Ashab districts of Greater Basra, with each shell containing forty-nine bomblets. (See Map, "Week ending March 26, 2003.") All told, during the next fortnight, they would launch at least seventeen cluster munitions strikes in the area, using 2,100 cluster shells, and drop sixty-six cluster bombs.[8]

Overall, though, the BBC, like its American counterparts, presented the "War in Iraq" or "War against Iraq" by the "Coalition forces" largely as a grand fireworks display and tank parade inter-spersed with press conferences at Centcom's Al Saliyah headquar-ters. The absence of blood was noteworthy, with nothing more shocking shown than hand or foot injuries normally sustained in sports. When asked about the absence of gory images of the war, a CNN spokeswoman explained to the *Wall Street Journal*: "It is news judgment where we would of course be mindful of the sensi-bilities of our viewers." It was not just CNN. "All American net-works and much of print journalism have made a similar decision [as CNN], even though some on-air correspondents, notably ABC's Ted Koppel, have questioned it," Frank Rich would note in the *New York Times* on April 12. Commenting on this, Tim Rob-bins, the actor and antiwar protester, said, "As we applaud the hard-edged realism of the opening battle scene of *Saving Private Ryan*, we cringe at the thought of seeing the same on the nightly news. We are told it would be pornographic. We want no part of reality in real life. We demand that war be painstakingly realized on the screen, but that war remain imaged and conceptualized in real life."[9]

By contrast, Arab networks, especially Al Jazeera TV and Abu Dhabi TV, among a dozen channels,[10] provided straight news that in many ways gave their viewers a more rounded picture—from the inside—than the Anglo-American networks did. While the Anglo-American networks tended to show Allied medics treating injured Iraqi civilians tenderly while their armed colleagues handed out drinking-water cans to thirsty Iraqi POWs, the Arab media, while airing the briefings and sound bites coming from London, Washington, and Doha, and charting the advances made by the Anglo-American forces (Al Jazeera, for example, had a reporter embedded with Centcom troops), also showed the devas-tating consequences of war: charred Iraqi bodies by wrecked vehi-cles, grievously wounded civilians, dead Allied troops and injured Iraqi soldiers, hospitals choked with wounded and burned Iraqis. Away from the battle zone, the Arab networks showed Iraqi suffering, humiliation, and panic—distraught families held up at Anglo-American military checkpoints, hooded Iraqi POWs, thousands fleeing the capital, and civilians, deprived of food and water, driven to begging or looting. A photograph of three women in black robes and veils being body-searched by a young American (male) soldier, displayed on the front pages of the Arabic newspapers, shocked and angered millions of Arabs. When it came to commenting on the conflict, the Anglo-American channels almost invariably had the Bush and Blair administrations' civilian and military officials or prowar academic experts as talking heads, whereas the expert commentators on Arab channels were usually skeptical of Centcom claims and its political masterminds' intentions.

Since Arab networks often had better camera positions, they gave a much fuller—and grislier—picture of what those brilliant explosions lighting up television screens did to the hapless Iraqis living in those neighborhoods, though Iraqi armed guards often made no exception for them in blocking access to areas in which missiles had struck targets the night before. An insight into the damaging consequences of being in the targeted area was provided by Subhy Haddad, a Baghdad-based Iraqi correspondent of the BBC World Service Radio: "My eldest child, eleven, is scared to death. In 1998 [during Operation "Desert Fox"] a missile passed by the entrance of our house. Now when she is asleep and hears a door banging she wakes up shouting."[11] A visit to a Baghdad hospital by a correspondent of the *Independent* showed that 85 of the 101 wounded were civilians.

Unsurprisingly, the sanitized version of the bloody warfare broadcast by the Anglo-American channels was criticized by the Arab networks. "War has victims from both sides," said Al Jazeera's chief editor, Ibrahim Hilal. "If you don't show both sides, you are not covering [it]." So the Arab and Muslim networks—which, besides Al Jazeera and Abu Dhabi, included Dubai-based Al Arabiya, Beirut-based Al Manar, Beirut-based Lebanese Broadcasting Corporation-Al Hayat, and Tehran-based Islamic Republic of Iran

Broadcasting—were not squeamish about showing corpses, charred bodies by burnt vehicles, blood-soaked pavements, blown-out brains, screaming infants, and wailing women. Al Arabiya TV punctuated its telethon on March 24 for "our kin in Iraq" with images of the children wounded by U.S. cluster bombs, and raised more than $1 million. Al Jazeera had no qualms about showing the gruesome result of the U.S. bombing of the suspected positions of the armed militant group Ansar al Islam (Helpers of Islam, allegedly linked to Al Qaida), in Iraqi Kurdistan, when all but two of the thirty-five killed were civilians, a fact glossed over in a hurry by the Anglo-American channels.

They were foremost too in transmitting images of Iraqi defiance and resistance. On March 21, a Friday, the Muslim holy day of the week, a few of them showed Iraqis in the thousands assembled at the Mother of All Battles Mosque, where Shaikh Abdul Latif Homeim urged the congregation to "surround the Americans and kill them wherever you find them," thus underscoring the official line that Iraqis were fighting for both Islam and Iraq. His lead would be followed by the Sunni Grand Mufti of Syria, Shaikh Ahmad Kiftaro, who issued a *fatwa*, (religious decree) on March 26: "All Muslims have to use all possible means of defeating the enemy, including martyrdom operations against the invading soldiers." Senior Shia clerics in Lebanon did the same, as did their counterparts in Iran, prohibiting cooperation with the Anglo-American invaders and calling it treason.[12]

Indeed, Al Jazeera had its first scoop on Saturday, March 22, when it successfully challenged Centcom's claim that the U.S. Fifteenth Marine Expeditionary Unit under British command had captured Umm Qasr by showing that the fighting was still going on. For this audacious act of reporting, it found itself punished. Two days later its website, aljazeera.net, went down. "Few here doubt that the provenance of the attack is the Pentagon," wrote Faisal Bodi in an article in the *Guardian*. "Our hosting company, the U.S.-based DataPipe, has terminated our contract."[13]

Al Jazeera's other major scoop would be in Basra (population 1.37 million), the headquarters of the Iraqi Southern Command under General Ali Hassan al Majid (b. 1938), a tough-looking beefsteak of a man with the mandatory Iraqi mustache, who was a first cousin of Saddam Hussein. Centcom's initial plan was to bypass Basra on the assumption (based on the "intelligence" supplied by the Iraqi National Congress), that the predominantly Shia city would offer nominal resistance, if any. Centcom's claim that the Iraqi Fifty-first Division had surrendered wholesale was faithfully aired by the Anglo-American channels. The U.S. Third Infantry Division, charged with reaching Baghdad in the shortest time possible, rushed to Nasiriya (130 miles/210 kilometers from Basra) with its four bridges, two on the Euphrates and two on the nearby Saddam Canal, leaving it to the British Seventh Armored Brigade—fondly called "Desert Rats" by the media—to capture Basra. Nasiriya is an ancient settlement where the syllabic alphabet and the first mathematical system centered around the number sixty, still the world's measurement of time, were developed six millennia ago.

That evening (March 22), they marched up to the city's outskirts, expecting minimal resistance. Instead, the Iraqis, entrenched on both sides of the bridge of the canal Shatt al Basra (i.e., Basra Waterway), attacked them, using tanks, artillery, and rocket-propelled grenades. The British called for U.S. air strikes with Apache attack helicopters to fend off the assault. Then they advanced toward a military complex south of the Shatt al Basra, against a background of seven burning oil-processing facilities polluting the air with thick plumes of smoke and acrid fumes. At the complex, they had to engage in room-to-room combat for several hours. Finally, they crossed the bridge, whose foundation had been packed with one and a half tons of explosives—which, they claimed, the retreating Iraqis did not have time to blow up. The long and bloody encounter left seventy-seven civilians dead and hundreds injured. Al Jazeera showed the wounded being treated on a hospital floor, capping its footage with a harrowing image of a boy with the back of his head blown off—an apt illustration of the horrors of war from which the Anglo-American viewers were punctiliously shielded.

As for Iraqi TV, its major aim was to present Saddam Hussein in the best possible light—relaxed, engaged in consultations with his senior advisers. That was the main fare in the evening bulletin as the troops set fire to oil-filled trenches around Baghdad. They hoped that the resulting thick smoke clouds would mislead the cruise missiles' guidance systems and obscure targets from the U.S. pilots dropping dumb bombs. *"I went up to the roof to take a look and saw that there were too many of them [fires],"* said Salam Pax on his website. *"Now you can see the columns of smoke all over the city."*

At the Centcom headquarters near Doha, Qatar, Brigadier-General Vincent Brooks and other Pentagon sources said that U.S. paramilitary intelligence forces—meaning the CIA's Special Activities Division (SAD) and the Pentagon's Special Operations Forces (SOF), now brought together into U.S. Task Force 20—were inside Baghdad, and that they "may be" involved in talks between the United States, represented chiefly by the Iraqi exiles belonging to the Iraqi National Accord (which had all along favored a military coup against Saddam), and Republican Guard generals. The State Department also reported that "contacts had intensified in the past 24 hours regarding mass surrenders and surrenders higher up the chain of command."[14] The release of such sensitive information, part of the psychological warfare, was designed to demoralize the Iraqi armed forces and civilians. At the same time, a serious American effort involving recognized Iraqi opposition groups had been afoot for several weeks before the invasion to neutralize the Iraqi military by getting the Iraqi generals either to sit out the war or leave the country in exchange for a very large bribe—in the range of $1 million—and/or a promise of a job in the post-Saddam army. In some cases, the defecting generals had signed letters addressed to General Tommy Franks saying, "I now work for you," the Centcom commander-in-chief would claim publicly after the war. The Pentagon would describe bribing the Iraqi generals as "a cost-effective way of fighting the war," resulting in low casualties and zero collateral damage. "How much does a cruise missile cost?" asked a senior Pentagon official. "Between $1 million and $2.5 million."[15] What was missing from these statements was the actual number of Republican Guard generals who either did not turn up at their postings or actively asked their subordinates to go home—crucial information, given that the eighty-thousand-strong Republican Guard had more than 180 generals in contrast to the eighteen that a force of the same size would have in the U.S. army.[16]

In the first three days of the invasion, the number of cruise-missile strikes reached one thousand as Centcom hit targets in Mosul and the U.S. Special Forces moved in to secure oil fields around Kirkuk in the north.

On March 22, the first Saturday after the start of the war, there were protest marches not only all over Europe but also in south and southeast Asia—as well as in Manama, Muscat, and Cairo in the Middle East. In Damascus, the leaders of Syria's ruling National Progressive Front demanded "an immediate end to the barbaric aggression against Iraq," warning that it would "have grave ramifications on the security of the region," and calling on the United Nations "to assume its role in addressing this dangerous situation."

Such demonstrations had no impact on the Bush White House, which was buoyed by the rise of 19 percent in Bush's approval rating—to 70 percent—in ten days. At the same time, 85 percent thought that the United States would be a victim of a major attack on its soil "in the very near future." In Britain, the only other country to field a large number of troops in the invasion of Iraq, a poll showed 56 percent saying the Anglo-American alliance was "right to go to war," whereas 36 percent otherwise—a reversal of the figures just before the war.[17]

On Sunday, March 23, Centcom's claim of the capture of the

Zubair naval base—three miles (five kilometers) from Basra's municipal boundary—remained suspect in the absence of confirmation by Al Jazeera.

But U.S. Marines did arrive at Nasiriya where, unknown to them, General Ali Hassan al Majid had reinforced the regular army with Republican Guard units from its Baghdad Division based in Amara (population 350,000).

On the night of March 23–24, the 507th Maintenance Company, following the armored unit ahead of it, took a wrong turn near Nasiriya. The company, which included maintenance clerk Private Jessica Lynch, a slim blonde, aged twenty, from the tiny Appalachian village of Palestine in West Virginia, was ambushed by the Fedayeen Saddam irregulars. In the firefight that ensued, the Humvee that Lynch was traveling in crashed into a jack-knifed truck. Her MI-16 semiautomatic gun jammed. She suffered multiple fractures—both legs broken, a head wound, and other injuries—and passed out. By the time the fighting ended, eleven U.S. soldiers and an unknown number of Fedayeen were dead, and six American troops, including Lynch, were taken prisoner. Her Iraqi captors rushed Lynch in an ambulance to Saddam Hospital in Nasiriya. Though the city's main infirmary, it lacked running water and electricity, and was indescribably filthy, with malodorous corridors, wet floors awash with grime, and plastic bed cover sheets splattered with dried blood. With hundreds of people with shattered limbs—punctured by shrapnel released by ground combat and relentless U.S. air strikes—needing urgent attention, the hospital staff were unbearably overworked. Yet they treated Lynch with uncommon care, giving her the best private room in the hospital—in the cardiology ward—and the cleanest bed, according to British-trained Dr. Ahmad Jassim.

The death of eleven soldiers pushed the total U.S. fatalities on March 23 to thirty, the highest daily figure during the war.

Farther northwest, Centcom's westerly flank met heavy resistance as it approached Najaf. When its attack helicopters assaulted the Republican Guard's Medina al Muanora (The Shining Medina) Division, they encountered "the hornet's nest"—a well-orchestrated barrage of small arms and machine-gun fire that badly damaged thrity-four helicopters, downed one, and left most of the surviving machines unfit for battle.

Consequently, three days into the war, Luke Baker of Reuters, embedded with the U.S. Third Infantry, reported, "The impression I get talking to several officers is that they are surprised at the level of [Iraqi] resistance and that more Iraqis have not surrendered."

That night (at 10:33 P.M. GMT), a *Jerusalem Post* journalist, also embedded with the U.S. Third Infantry Division, reported that his unit had discovered a "chemical weapons factory" near Najaf. Immediately ABC News did so too, citing an unnamed official who said that an Iraqi general captured at the site was "a potential gold mine of evidence about Saddam's weapons of mass destruction." Later, however, Centcom began backpedaling, saying merely that tests were being carried out. A few days later, General Tommy Franks, when questioned on the subject, characteristically replied, "It would not surprise me if there were chemicals in the plant and it would not surprise me if there weren't. We'll have to wait for the days ahead." Months later, the world was still waiting to hear about the WMD in Iraq.[18]

The next day (March 24), the Centcom claimed that its middle flank, manned by U.S. Marines, had captured one bridge over the Euphrates in Nasiriya in the morning, followed by another after three hours of bitter combat. That left two bridges under Iraqi control, and made the U.S. forces vulnerable as they covered a 1-mile (1.5-kilometer)–long "ambush lane" of houses, schools, and mosques between the two captured bridges. After his 100-mile (160-kilometer) drive to Nasiriya from the Kuwaiti border, Sergeant Chris Merkle, thirty-one, told a *Washington Post* reporter, "Each unit takes its turn being sacrificed. Everybody gets torn apart the same way. It's a turkey shoot."

The nightly bombing of Baghdad continued while the city

remained shrouded in smoke from the burning oil. Gigantic, earth-shattering explosions meant that the Pentagon had unleashed its Massive Ordnance Air Blast (MOAB) bomb, the size of a passenger bus, to devastating effect.

"Today was the worst day yet of bombing," noted Thuraya al Kaissi in her diary. *"I close my eyes and think for a moment that if I open them I will find myself dead. I imagine that death is waiting for us at every moment. Then I open my eyes and I am still alive, and I thank God."*

On Monday, March 24, came reports of Iraqi resistance to the invading forces in Zubair. In Umm Qasr, Royal (British) Marines, specializing in urban warfare, took over from the U.S. Marines, and the two hundred Polish Special Forces—Poland's total contribution—joined the British, suggesting that the invaders were encountering stiff resistance. Also, with armed Iraqis reappearing in the Rumeila oil field, the Centcom declared it a "no-go area."

That day, after meeting heavy resistance in Basra, the British troops retreated and settled for a siege of the city.

On the night of March 24–25, the five-hundred-vehicle convoy of the U.S. Seventh Cavalry engaged in a thirty-hour battle along the Euphrates at the village of Faisaliya, south of Najaf, when it was attacked by the Fedayeen militia and regular soldiers with mortars and rocket-propelled grenades. To repulse them, the American forces called in tank-busting A10 aircraft.

The Fedayeen Saddam—conspicuous by their tight, head-to-toe black uniforms, with openings only for the eyes—emerged as a crucial element in the Iraqi resistance to the invasion. This came as a pleasant surprise to their commander, Uday Saddam Hussein, a tall, slim man with a crew cut, closely trimmed beard, and large, expressive eyes. Before the war, Uday had not taken the Fedayeen job seriously. As chairman of the Iraqi National Olympic Committee and owner-manager of *Babil* (lit., Babylon), the Youth TV and Radio, this playboy had plenty of other things to do. Not that he worked hard, or even worked at all. According to his bodyguard, "Abu

Tiba," he slept during the day and spent his evenings and nights cruising around Baghdad in search of pretty women or boozing with his cronies in posh nightclubs.

But once the U.S. bombing started, forcing him to abandon his favorite palace—part of his father's Republican Palace complex—he changed dramatically. He stopped drinking and seeing his girl-friends. Emulating his younger brother, Qusay—a moon-faced tubby man sporting a mustache who supervised the Republican Guard and ran the Special Security Organization—and his worka-holic father, he took active command of the Fedayeen Saddam. He changed his safe house every few days, sometimes staying in a modest home in a residential district, and sometimes staying with close friends. Abandoning his flashy, expensive cars, he now drove a Toyota or Kia, his face covered in a red Arab *kaffiyeh* (head and face dress) to disguise himself, and carried a machine pistol, while his six bodyguards were armed with Kalashnikov assault rifles. He slept only for a few hours each night and worked until two in the morning, issuing orders to the commanders of the six-hundred-strong battalions of the Fedayeen, which were passed on to them by messengers all over Iraq, including the predominantly Shia south.[19]

A glimpse of what it felt like to be in the landscape of southern Iraq came from Terri Judd of the *Independent*, embedded with the British forces in that region. "At night the light disappears as fast as the temperature drops," she reported. "Without the moon, darkness seems impenetrable, with only the incandescent orange of the burning well heads of the Rumeila oil fields on the sky line. Hot days are but a fond memory when the sandstorms descend from nowhere. The winds create rivers of sand, snaking across the ground before building into ferocious gales. Sudden bursts send grains swirling and stinging, grazing the skin like giant emery paper. A fog descends, cutting sights of the horizon and turning the sun into a watery moon. The invasive [sand] grains permeate every pocket, every unprotected gap, Teeth grind with sand, hair mats with dry filth, hands rarely feel clean."[20]

Baghdad remained covered in smoke from the burning oil. But that brought no respite from the nightly bombing. On its outskirts, U.S. and British Special Forces were active, painting targets with lasers to guide the Joint Direct Attack Munitions (JDAM) bombs. *"More bombs,"* wrote Thuraya al Kaissi. *"They sound so close. But none of us leaves the house so we don't know where they are falling. The windows shake and the floor moves. It is like having an earthquake on our street about three times each hour."*

That night Mother Nature intervened, with thirty-five-knot gales causing such a virulent sandstorm that visibility was reduced to a few yards. "The aid workers are taking the tents down because the wind is so strong the canvas is tearing," reported Martin Asser of BBC-TV at the Kuwaiti–Iraqi border. "The wind is absolutely freezing and there is sand in our mouths. At one point my camera froze up and I had to warm it up in the Jeep."[21]

Taking advantage of the sandstorm, and aware that Centcom could not use its air force, Qusay Saddam Hussein, instructed by Saddam, ordered the Republican Guard to counterattack at dawn. Iraqi TV announced that the "heroic Republican Guard" had carried out the first devastating operation against the invaders, creating "fear and panic among the enemy," without giving any details of the location or time. Realizing that the sandstorm and poor visibility ruled out the use of attack helicopters or A10 tank-busting aircraft, Centcom ordered the Pentagon's B-52s, stationed at Fairford, England, to be deployed. These bombers hit the Iraqi Republican Guard, with bomb blasts echoing in a radius of twenty miles (thirty-two kilometers).

As before, Thuraya al Kaissi provided a personal touch. *"No one in my family has known a sandstorm like it,"* she wrote. *"All the windows are shut, but they leak, and I am gasping for air. For lunch my mum makes my favorite dishes. She thinks it will tempt me to eat. I try but I can't."*

In Nasiriya, only by forming an armored corridor along the mile-long "ambush lane" could the U.S. Marines secure the passage of hundreds of tanks, Bradley fighting vehicles, and trucks to cross the bridge over the Euphrates to Kut on their way to Baghdad. But just fifteen miles (twenty-four kilometers) along Highway 7, at Daghara, the American convoy got ambushed by Iraqi irregulars.

Unlike the drizzle in Baghdad, torrential rain in southern Iraq was followed by thunder—loud enough to drown artillery fire—and lightning, which illuminated the night sky, turning communications masts into red-hot pokers. The resulting damp seeped into the sleeping bags and clothes of the troops and the embedded journalists.

In the Shia holy city of Najaf, where the Iraqis were engaged in a fierce ground battle with U.S. forces, Grand Ayatollah Ali Husseini Sistani (b. 1930; grand ayatollah since 1999), the spiritual leader of Iraqi Shias, issued a *fatwa* calling on Muslims worldwide to "help us in a fierce battle against infidel followers who invaded our homeland." In this calamitous hour, he added, "it is imperative for the Iraqi people to be united, preserve public order and Iraq's territorial integrity." This extremely significant event, which spiked any chance of Shia uprisings in the south against the Saddam regime—the core of the Pentagon's much-flaunted scenario, based on "intelligence" provided by the Iraqi National Congress—went unreported. Not only did the Anglo-American electronic media ignore Sistani's momentous religious decree, but so did the news agencies. Only the Chinese Xinhua news agency put the story on the wire.

That evening (March 25), BBC News 24 in London began broadcasting the news of an uprising against the Saddam regime in Basra, based on a report by the London-based GMTV's Richard Gaisford, embedded with the British troops. The BBC showed a video of the Anglo-American forces firing backup artillery into the city to help the uprising. "Don't look now, but the Shiites have hit the fan!" shouted Neil Cavuto on Fox News in the United States. British defense secretary Geoff Hoon even went so far as to declare that Saddam's regime "had lost control of southern Iraq," a view echoed by his American counterpart, Rumsfeld.

Once again it was Al Jazeera that pricked this bubble. Its correspondent in central Basra was stationed at the Sheraton Hotel. The images he sent from inside the city showed it to be fairly calm: orderly streets with some groups chanting pro-Saddam slogans. Any lingering doubts were quashed by a statement by the Tehran-based SCIRI, part of the U.S.-recognized Iraqi opposition: "Some people shouted slogans against Saddam Hussein. But it was not widespread and it was not an uprising."[22] Apparently, efforts by members of the Arabic-speaking British Special Forces in traditional Arab dress who had infiltrated into Basra, and their cohorts—the local agents of the British Secret Intelligence Service's Arabic specialists, called the "Camel Corps"—to foment an uprising had failed.

The Iraqi resistance in Nasiriya continued, as U.S. Marines, supported by attack helicopters and artillery, charged their way across the Euphrates after heavy street fighting in which Iraqi snipers, operating from homes, shops, and schools, participated.

This was the backdrop against which hundreds of thousands of antiwar protesters once again poured into the streets of Amman, Beirut, and Damascus.

The next day, March 26 (Wednesday), Centcom had its latest claim of Umm Qasr being "open and secure" confirmed by both Al Jazeera and Iranian TV—five days after its original claim had been proven false.

In the south, fighting continued in Zubair while Centcom claimed full control of the Rumeila oil field. Iraqi resistance continued in Nasiriya, with U.S. Marines facing constant sniping. At the same time, the troops that followed the advance force were ambushed by Iraqi guerrillas as the Americans moved from Kuwait to reinforce their front line. During the sandstorm, the U.S. troops were ambushed near Najaf. And in Karbala, there was hand-to-hand fighting as the U.S. Third Mechanized Infantry tried to consolidate its positions around the city.

In Baghdad, a U.S. warplane fired two missiles at a busy market in the poor northern Shia suburb of Shaab, killing forty-eight. Centcom said that it was aiming at the missile launchers posted in the neighborhood. "The ambulances are still taking people away," reported Paul Wood of the BBC. "There are four or five cars that are completely flattened by the blast. This is a row of shops and a row of workshops. People were working on repairing cars. There is a mood of anger here. A lot of people have said to me in bewilderment: 'Give a message to Bush and Blair that this has got to stop.' " It was hard to overstate the adverse impact of such a bombing on the public in the Arab and Muslim world, where people often watch television in cafés and restaurants. "As Iraqis pulled the mutilated dead from the rubble and the cameras lingered on a boy with blood streaming from his head," reported a *Time* correspondent, describing a scene at a restaurant in Amman, "a taxi driver said, 'This blood must be avenged. We will see pictures of American children bleeding like that, God willing.' "[23]

On the southern outskirts of the capital, the Anglo-American Special Forces continued painting targets with lasers to guide precision JDAM bombs. Centcom also bombed the dug-in Iraqi troops of the Special Republican Guard. It hit the TV Center, but domestic TV was back within hours, albeit with reduced strength. The regime commissioned a stand-by unit, which worked.

"My mother and I have decided to move in with my aunt on the other side of Baghdad," wrote Thuraya al Kaissi in her diary on March 26. *"We think there are no targets there. My father and my brother are staying at our house. They are not scared like us. Every night they are out on the roof watching the explosions."*

In the first week of its invasion of Iraq, Centcom mounted 5,700 air sorties, dropped two thousand JDAM guided bombs, and fired five hundred Tomahawk missiles and seven hundred cruise missiles. This was a record, a plus for the Pentagon and its high-tech war machine.

But the minuses, though not quantifiable, were far more numerous, and weightier. For starters, the Pentagon's plan to assassinate Saddam Hussein at the very start failed. Then the much-vaunted "Shock and Awe" bombing scenario failed to deliver the collapse of Saddam's regime. Those who had dreamt up this outcome had forgotten that during the one-hundred-hour blitzkrieg of Iraq under Operation "Desert Fox" in December 1998, the Pentagon had fired 415 cruise and Tomahawk missiles—ninety more than in the 1991 Gulf War—and dropped six hundred laser-guided bombs,[24] and that such a fearsome experience had made the Iraqi military and civilians less afraid of a repeat performance by the United States.

The Pentagon's next rosy scenario was more specific. Based on the intense hatred of Saddam by Shias who, in the immediate aftermath of the 1991 Gulf War, had mounted uprisings in the south, where the U.S.–U.K. alliance had maintained full air control since mid-1992. In the months preceding the invasion, the Allied aircraft had dropped hundreds of thousands of leaflets calling on the Iraqi troops to desert. This was followed by their intelligence agencies activating their Iraqi agents, supposedly in contact with senior army commanders. "In the south, where there are six Iraqi divisions, 50 percent of their officers are planning to surrender once the campaign opens," predicted a U.S. intelligence officer. Little wonder that within twenty-four hours of the Allied invasion, Pentagon sources claimed that the Iraqi army was "breaking from within." On March 22, Admiral Sir Michael Boyce, chief of the U.K. defense staff, claimed that Iraq's Fifty-first Division had surrendered and that "we have many thousands of prisoners of war." His civilian boss, Geoff Hoon, the U.K. defense secretary, claimed that the Fifty-first Division's commander and deputy commander had surrendered along with eight thousand soldiers. The *New York Times* reported that the Fifty-first Division had "melted away." It turned out that a junior officer (probably in the pay of the Anglo-American intelligence agencies), masquerading as the divisional commander, had surrendered, and that the total number of all Iraqi POWs so far with Centcom numbered fewer than four thousand.[25]

Ironically, this phantom Iraqi Fifty-first Division would return to Basra and keep the surrounding British troops at bay for many days.

This scenario, of Iraqi troops and their commanders surrendering in droves and agreeing to accept the command of the Pentagon while Iraqi civilians showered their Anglo-American liberators with sweets and flowers, had been concocted by the Iraqi National Congress, based on its "intelligence," and bought wholesale by the Bush and Blair administrations. Under such rosy conditions, the Bush team saw no need to augment U.S. troops for peacekeeping in the immediate post-Saddam period, since the bulk of Iraqi soldiers and policemen would maintain law and order—albeit under the exclusive supervision of Washington.

All in all, therefore, the first week of the invasion of Iraq failed to produce either the instant victory or the "Shock and Awe" triumph that the Bush and Blair governments had led their respective citizens to expect. They had convinced themselves that the Shia-dominated south would welcome their forces as liberators while the Iraqi Army changed sides or collapsed. Instead, they found the Shia cities of Basra and Nasiriya emerging as places of resistance, with Najaf and Karbala not far behind, and the Iraqi irregulars ambushing the long supply lines of U.S. forces rushing toward Baghdad. Their intelligence sources had led them to believe that the Fedayeen Saddam and the Baath Party militia (called the Jerusalem Army), with their pickup trucks equipped with heavy machine guns and air-defense weapons, would stay in Baghdad and not deploy in the south. This was not to be. Equally, the intelligence supplied by the Iraqi National Congress that members of the Republican Guard were not deployed in the south would turn out to be wrong.

Equally, and embarrassingly, wrong, was the BBC. In addition to the nonexistent Iraqi Scuds, it aired false stories about the capture of Umm Qasr and Nasiriya and an uprising in Basra, all of which had originated with the U.S. or U.K. militaries.[26] So too did the major American television channels.

NOTES

1. Centcom also hit two houses in a street in the Daura district. Judging by the arrival of a convoy of Land Cruisers at the suspected site, it seemed that five VIPs arrived there, but their identities could not be verified. Interview with an Iraqi expert at the Royal United Services Institute, London, June 2003.

2. *The Times* (London), July 25, 2003; *Newsday,* July 25, 2003.

3. *Independent,* March 26, 2003; Reuters, March 27, 2003.

4. Op-ed by David Miller of Stirling Media Research Institute at Stirling University, Scotland. *Guardian,* April 2, 2003

5. The United States is the only country in the world that has used napalm, and continues to do so.

6. August 5, 2003.

7. Cited in *Independent on Sunday,* April 13, 2003.

8. *The Times* (London), September 11, 2003.

9. *Observer,* April 20, 2003. Because of his opposition to war, actor Martin Sheen found his credit-card commercial canceled. Ed Gernon, the CBS producer of four mini-series on Hitler's rise to power, scheduled for May, said in an interview with *TV Guide* magazine, "It basically boils down to an entire nation gripped by fear, who ultimately chose to give up their civil rights, and plunged their nation into war. I can't think of a better time to examine this history than now." This led to his dismissal by the CBS chief executive officer Leslie Moonves. *Independent,* April 21, 2003.

10. Other Arabic-language TV channels were ANN (Arab Network News), Al Arabiya, Al Manar (lit., The Tower), Lebanese Broadcasting Corporation-Al Hayat, *Al Mustaqabil* (The Future), as well as the state-run channels of Egypt, Jordan, Kuwait, and so on.

11. Cited in *Independent on Sunday,* March 23, 2003.

12. *Observer,* March 30, 2003.

13. March 28, 2003. The New York Stock Exchange and Nasdaq ejected Al Jazeera reporters from their premises.

14. *Observer,* March 23, 2003.

15. *Defense News,* May 19, 2003.

16. Promotion in the military was the sole prerogative of Saddam Hussein, who used it more for personal and political gains than for military reasons. Even a few of his personal bodyguards held the rank of general.

17. *Observer*, March 23, 2003; *Sunday Times*, March 23, 2003. Once a government commits combat troops to a conflict, it sways a certain proportion of the population to the war camp, which feels that patriotism demands that they back the fighting soldiers, who are staking their lives in the battlefield—a historical phenomenonon of which both the Blair and Bush administrations were complacently aware.

18. *Independent,* March 29, 2003; *Guardian*, March 29, 2003.

19. *The Times* (London), July 25, 2003; *Newsday*, July 25, 2003.

20. March 27, 2003.

21. Cited in *Independent on Sunday*, April 13, 2003.

22. *Independent,* March 29, 2003; *Guardian*, March 29, 2003.

23. April 7, 2003, p. 69.

24. See Dilip Hiro, *Neighbors, Not Friends: Iraq and Iran after the Gulf Wars*, Routledge, New York and London, 2001, p. 163.

25. *Independent,* March 29, 2003; *Guardian*, March 29, 2003.

26. Op-ed by David Miller of Stirling Media Research Institute at Stirling University, Scotland. *Guardian*, April 22, 2003.

Chapter 6
WEEK TWO: A DECISIVE PERIOD

"After a week of intense and unremitting bombing, no Baghdadis I talked to spoke any more of being liberated by the coalition, however strong their desire to see the end of Saddam's rule. There is a pent-up anger here against the Americans for the cruelty to ordinary Iraqis of sanctions and a deep distrust of American motives for invading Iraq, reinforced by the rising civilian casualties and increasingly senseless destruction of their city."
—Jon Swain, a veteran British war correspondent[1]

"The enemy we are fighting against is a bit different from the one we war-gamed against [which did not take into account irregular fighters outside the control of the military's central command]. We knew they [the paramilitaries] were there, but we didn't know they would fight like this. Long supply lines and guerrilla actions had reduced the chances of a swift victory that the planners had hoped for."
—Lieutenant General William Wallace, commander of U.S. ground forces in Iraq[2]

THE SECOND WEEK of the war started with continued resistance from Saddam's forces, which, being unexpected, was all the more disconcerting to the Allies. This, along with the failure of the much-vaunted scenario of the quick fall of the Saddam regime, resulted in a volley of criticism aimed at Donald Rumsfeld, the sole architect of the U.S. military plan based on his doctrine of "rolling invasion."

This turn of events was reminiscent of what had happened during the U.S.-led Afghanistan campaign, which started on October 7, 2001. Relying totally on the "intelligence" of the opposition Northern Alliance, Rumsfeld had predicted confidently that there would be massive defections from the Taliban ranks and that the campaign would be over in a few weeks. In reality, though, well into the third week of armed hostilities, the Taliban suffered virtually no defections while withstanding the relentless American bombing with remarkable fortitude. Having announced earlier that the Taliban's combat power had been "eviscerated," the Pentagon now expressed "surprise" at their ability to regroup, disperse, and conceal troops and equipment while reorganizing resistance. U.S. rear admiral John Stufflebeem, who on October 17 had said that "we are pulling away at the legs underneath the stool that Taliban leadership sits," now conceded: "They [the Taliban] are proving to be tough warriors."[3] It was at this juncture that President Bush is reported to have told his war cabinet not to be swayed by the critics and the media, and to prosecute the war as originally planned.

Now Bush found himself having to play the same role—publicly—after only one week, because his senior officials had made the American people and media believe that the overthrow of Saddam Hussein would be accomplished in days rather than weeks. When, following his meeting with Blair at Camp David on March 27, he was asked at a joint press conference whether the war would "last months, not weeks," he could hardly wait for the journalist to finish his question. "However long it takes to win," he declared. A little later he repeated the message—slowly, deliberately: "However. Long. It takes." Bush's fidgeting and frowning, coupled with his scowling at questioners, betrayed the anxiety of a man puzzled by the failure of his message to the Iraqi people—conveyed in millions of leaflets and countless radio broadcasts, exhorting them not to fight for "a dying regime"—and visibly nervous at the prospect of having to face the consequences of his overconfident predictions, based more on his much-vaunted "gut instincts" than reliable, dispassionate intelligence and analysis.

Luckily for him, though, around the middle of the crucial second week, March 30–31, the tables began to turn in his favor—but only after the Anglo-American forces resorted to dropping cluster bombs and firing cluster munitions from howitzers with a twenty-mile (thirty-kilometer) range, and using napalm. Altogether, 1,566 cluster bombs and countless munitions would be deployed all over Iraq, including in the north. Use was also made of the Israeli-manufactured BLU 108, an antiarmor bomblet with a sensor that spews out four smaller units with parachutes, each of which discharges four circular discs. Though intended for enemy tanks, BLU 108s would be found on farmland after the war.

The change in the overall situation was summed up aptly by what happened to the Iraqi Air Defense unit on the eastern approaches to Baghdad under Lieutenant Colonel Adil Abdul Jabar, who commanded 250 men, handling 57-millimeter antiaircraft guns, in the area. "We shot down some cruise missiles initially and the morale was high," he told Jonathan Steele of the *Guardian* after the invasion. "But on 24 March a missile had a direct hit on an underground bunker, killing four soldiers. Many deserted as they went home for food and clean clothes. After one week my unit was down to 175. On 4 April a cluster bomb landed on part of the air defense force at Daura [a neighborhood of Baghdad], killing or wounding two officers and 19 soldiers [10 of whom later died]. You could not approach the injured because of the unexploded bombs lying on the ground. The wounded were dying where they were. This frightened the men." Further desertions followed, reducing his unit to thirteen officers and one soldier five days later.[4]

On the other hand, Washington's diplomatic and political slide continued—both in the Middle East and elsewhere. "The war is in danger of rocking global stability and the foundations of international law," said Vladimir Putin the day after the Bush–Blair press conference. "The only correct solution is the immediate end to military activity and resumption of a political settlement in the UN Security Council." By contrast, Donald Rumsfeld, reflecting Bush's impatient hard line, demanded "an unconditional surrender" of Iraq.[5] Knowing Saddam Hussein, that was out of the question.

In the Middle East, the slowing or stopping of the Allied advance was portrayed as cause for celebration by both Arab nationalists and Islamic militants, who applauded every single downed American helicopter or drone, wrecked tank or Humvee, or captured soldier, and lamented every Iraqi dead as a family member. "Muslims of Iraq greet the Crusaders with bullets not flowers" was a typical headline even in state-controlled newspapers, regarded by Islamists and nationalists as mouthpieces of their puppet-rulers, manipulated by Uncle Sam. The prestigious *Al Ahram* (The Pyramids), the official newspaper of Egypt, lambasted Mubarak's government to an unprecedented degree. It and other mainstream Arabic papers published close-ups of dead and wounded Allied soldiers and crying POWs as well as destroyed Allied military hardware on their front pages. Such images ended up an the websites run by Islamists or Arab nationalists. The term "Crusader" used for Westerners, first mentioned in a statement by Osama bin Laden five years earlier, gained currency.

BATTLES IN THE SOUTH: BASRA AND NASIRIYA

The battle for Basra was tough for the British. On March 27, when U.K. forces tried to infiltrate the city from their line of containment eight hundred yards from the Shatt al Basra Bridge, they got involved in—according to the Centcom's description— "the heaviest tank battles since World War II." The casualties were heavy, as could be seen by the footage of local hospitals shown by Al Jazeera.

The British then decided to stage surgical raids into the city, with their Special Forces dressed in traditional Arab robes slipping behind Iraqi lines at night to arrest and kill Fedayeen Saddam commanders themselves—or have them killed in air strikes directed by them. The political-psychological objective was to show residents that Saddam Hussein's officers were no longer in control, and thus encourage them to mount a popular uprising that had, to their distress, failed to materialize. Some of the British assaults failed, as could be inferred from the footage of local residents crowding around a captured British military vehicle inside Basra, shown by Al Jazeera—the only TV station with a reporter inside the besieged city.

On March 28, working in coordination with the local British agents and Special Forces commandos disguised in traditional Arab dress, Centcom directed its delayed-action JDAM bombs at the Baath Party headquarters on Al Jumhuriya Street. This was done in the belief that the notorious General Ali Hassan al Majid, the regional commander—who earned the nickname of "Chemical Ali" due to his use of chemical weapons against the Kurds in 1987–88, then fighting the Saddam regime—was there, along with some two hundred Fedayeen. He was not. Many Iraqis were killed, but it was unclear whether or not they were Fedayeen.

At dawn the following day, U.K. tanks and armored personnel carriers crossed the Shatt al Basra into the city, with different units targeting General al Majid's mansion, the two-hundred-foot transmission tower, and a huge statue of Saddam in the city center park. They succeeded in their missions—except the one of capturing or killing General al Majid, whose mansion was empty.

The British, now desperate, resorted to frequent firing of cluster shells from howitzers into Basra to demoralize the Iraqis, as did their American allies, deploying M42 cluster shells, each containing eighty-eight bomblets. The Anglo-American forces also targeted electricity pylons and cut off fresh water supplies from the vicinity of the airport. This, along with the relentless British shelling and bombing, angered the people of Basra and eliminated any prospect of a popular uprising against the Baathist regime.[6]

At Nasiriya's Saddam Hospital, the Iraqi military officers pondered the case of Private Jessica Lynch, who had undergone successful surgical operations. On the night of March 27 they decided that one of them would accompany her in an ambulance, execute her, and then burn the vehicle, thus making it appear an accident. But this plan did not take into account the opinion or feelings of the ambulance driver, Sabah Khazal, a young man of conscience. While driving the ambulance, he appealed to the accompanying military officer not to shoot the innocent Lynch. The officer relented because (in Khazal's words) "he feared God." Indeed, he ran away never to report for duty again. Left to himself, Khazal decided to deliver Lynch to an American checkpoint—as he would tell the Arabic-speaking Nicholas Kristof of the *New York Times* during his visit to the city nearly three months later—but there were firefights on the streets, so he returned her to the hospital.[7]

In fact, the street fighting was so intense, and the need to capture the strategic Nasiriya to secure a safe passage for U.S. forces northward to Baghdad so urgent, that the Centcom headquarters diverted several hundred combat troops to the city on March 28. By now the U.S. forces had been drawn into the kind of street fighting their generals feared might be the forerunner of the battle for Baghdad. "Nasiriya was supposed to be a six-hour fight," gunnery sergeant Tracy Hale, thirty-two, told the *Washington Post*. "It has already been five days [from March 23]. Five days of non-stop, 24-hour fighting."

Reflecting this reality, embedded journalists in Nasiriya and elsewhere in the south started reporting that the level and intensity of resistance from Iraqi soldiers, and more particularly from the Fedayeen Saddam paramilitary force, had been dispiriting. "From talking to quite a few U.S. Marines here they are admitting that the way this conflict has been going has worn them down," said an embedded BBC correspondent. "It was not the kind of fighting they had been expecting and it had worn them down." The Iraqi tactics had left them puzzled and anxious. "Every time these U.S. Marines engage Iraqi units they often find these units change into civilian clothes and melt away," reported another embedded journalist. "The next thing the Marines know they are being hit from behind by guerrilla fighters."[8] One lethal Iraqi tactic that struck terror into U.S. combat troops was the stringing of wire across roads at a height where it would decapitate machine gunners standing on top of moving military vehicles.

The innovative and spirited resistance offered chiefly by the Fedayeen boosted the standing of Uday Saddam Hussein. He regained the approval of his father, which he had lost when he bludgeoned to death Kamal Hanna Jajjo, a food taster and bodyguard of the president, during a drunken bout at a party in November 1988. Jajjo had acted as a messenger between Saddam and Samira Shahbandar, a young beautiful divorcée, thereby distressing Uday's mother, Sajida Talfa.[9] Now Saddam wrote a personal note of congratulations to Uday praising him for the Fedayeen's performance. Overcome by emotion, Uday published the letter in his newspaper, *Babil*. At last he had garnered some of the favor showered on his younger brother, Qusay, who had supplanted him as the heir-apparent after 1988. "For the first time [in his life] Uday had a sense of purpose," said "Abu Tiba," his bodyguard. "He was doing something for his country."

In the beginning, regular Iraqi soldiers performed fairly well in the south too. "Our own [regular] troops were fighting in the south much better than around Baghdad," an unnamed brigadier-general would tell Robert Fisk of the *Independent* after the war. "They had help from the people in the villages, the tribal people. The Americans and the British [wrongly] thought these [Shia] people would support them, not fight them."

BATTLES IN THE CENTER: NAJAF AND KARBALA

In the central Euphrates military sector, commanded by Mizban Khidir al Hadi, a civilian member of the Iraqi Revolutionary Command Council, the regular army did well in the early days. In the fighting near Najaf on Friday, March 28, 1,500 Iraqi troops claimed to have destroyed thirty-three U.S. tanks and fighting vehicles. If true, such a loss by Centcom was unprecedented.

However, in the Karbala area, U.S. troops started consolidating their positions outside the city. Their aim was to close the Karbala Gap—twenty miles long and twenty miles wide (32 kilometers by 32 kilometers)—between Lake Razaza and the Euphrates, which provided the most direct passage to Baghdad. "It is a choke point," a senior U.S. officer told the *New York Times*. "Once we go through [it], it will allow us more freedom of movement between Najaf and Karbala."[10] But cutting through the Karbala Gap was proving difficult for the Americans, who faced six thousand Iraqi soldiers from the regular army and the Republican Guard.

More generally, small bands of Iraqi irregulars harassed the thinly defended 300-mile (480-kilometer)-long U.S. supply lines. Using rocket-propelled grenades and automatic rifles, they wrecked an unspecified number of American tanks and fighting vehicles daily.

While the Iraqis operated in familiar terrain and were accustomed to the harsh desert conditions, their American adversaries were at a severe disadvantage. None of the troops had had a shower for ten days, and there were no hot meals, only "ready to eat meals" (REMs). "The other day the unit I was with was engaged in some action when some Iraqi forces tried to ambush them," reported Gavin Hewitt of the BBC in central Iraq on March 28. "The Americans tried to use their guns, but some of those guns didn't work in the sandstorm. For both the soldiers and for everybody, it's a hard and unforgiving environment. One of them said to me, 'There's no mercy in the desert.' "[11]

Centcom's problems increased when, on March 29, Ali Hammadi Numani—a Shia Iraqi soldier in civilian dress—killed himself and four soldiers of the Third Mechanized Division at a military checkpoint in a suicide attack near Najaf.[12] Among those who witnessed the event was twenty-one-year-old Jamie Betancourt, a sergeant in the U.S. Third Infantry. It shook him deeply. "It was the most scary thing—trusting civilians, especially after the car bomb," he told Steven Lee Myers of the *New York Times*. Later, as he guarded a hospital, manned a checkpoint, or patrolled streets bustling with people in Baghdad, even children would terrify him. "At the end it was like, 'Get that kid away from me.'"[13]

By now, Centcom's operational headquarters at Al Saliyah, Qatar, had gotten the message. "I think coalition commanders, led by General Tommy Franks, have realized they are facing much tougher resistance than expected, and they are fighting an unconventional war," reported Michael Voss of the BBC from Centcom headquarters in Doha on March 30. "I think the suicide bombing has shocked them to a degree." Actually, more than "to a degree." As Lieutenant Colonel Wes Gillman, commander of Task Force 130 of the Third Infantry Division, told his men, "If you see an Iraqi in civilian clothes coming toward you—even with a stick—shoot him." It was a practical application of the "force protection" doctrine that now applied to all military checkpoints—according to the order issued immediately by Centcom headquarters (but not publicized).

The strict application of this command led, inevitably, to the deaths of many innocent civilians. Mark Franchetti of the *Sunday Times* described how "one night [in Nasiriya] we listened a dozen times as the machine guns opened fire, cutting through cars and trucks like paper." The next morning he saw fifteen vehicles, including a minivan and two trucks, riddled with bullet holes, and counted twelve dead civilians in the road or nearby ditches. "All had been trying to leave overnight, probably for fear of being killed by U.S. helicopter attacks and heavy artillery," he reported.

"Their [fatal] mistake had been to flee over a bridge that is crucial to the coalition's supply lines and to run into a group of shell-shocked Marines with orders to shoot anything that moved. One man's body was still in flames. Down the road, a little girl no older than five lay dead in a ditch next to the body of a man who may have been her father. Half his head was missing. A father, baby girl and boy lay in a shallow grave. On the bridge itself a dead Iraqi civilian lay next to the carcass of a donkey."[14]

Like their British allies, the American forces had resorted to dropping cluster bombs. The first reports of such bombing came in on March 29 from the village of Manaria in the Muhammadiya area, thirty miles (fifty kilometers) south of Baghdad, a prime target of the Pentagon and its civilian boss, Donald Rumsfeld. Ignoring deliberately, or unwittingly, the religious decree issued by Grand Ayatollah Ali Sistani on March 25 calling on the faithful to resist the invading infidels, Rumsfeld remained plugged into his scenario of the Iraqi Shias turning into the nemesis of Saddam. On March 27 he expressed the hope that the Shias in Baghdad, forming a third of the city's population, would rise up against the regime, thus sparing the Pentagon the task of invading the capital.[15]

BAGHDAD

The bombing of the city after dark continued. On the night of March 27–28, Centcom bombed the military command and control communications center with two bunker-busting bombs, along with the Mimoun International Communications Center (telephone exchange) in a central shopping area of the al Salam compound. From that point, the bombing of the telephone exchanges accelerated, so that by March 30 most of the capital's twenty-two exchanges were wrecked.

"The beat of the bombardment has become the soundtrack of our lives," noted Salam Pax on March 27. *"You wake up to the sound of*

bombardment; you brush your teeth to the rhythm of the anti-aircraft rat-tat-tats. Then there is the attack, which is timed exactly with our lunch time. The first two days we would hurry inside and listen with worry; now you just sigh, look up at the sky, curse and do whatever you have to do."

That night, in a unique antiwar gesture, the management of the Alhambra Palace in the Spanish city of Granada—symbol of the Islamic past of Spain, which had expelled all the Muslim Moors in 1492—switched off its lights, while in Barcelona firemen sounded their sirens in protest.

That same night, after prolonged delay, one thousand members of the U.S. 173rd Airborne Division parachuted into northern Iraq to open a second front.

On March 28, a missile struck a market in Baghdad's northwestern suburb of Shuala, killing at least fifty-five, including fifteen children. Graphic pictures showed people scrabbling through rubble to reach the dead and injured. Rumsfeld and Geoff Hoon, the respective U.S. and U.K. defense secretaries, asserted that it was an old Iraqi missile without a guidance system that had caused the massacre. Their claim was repudiated by the indefatigable Robert Fisk of the *Independent*. He said that a foot-long shard of the missile's fuselage (either Harm, High Speed Anti-Radiation Missile, or Paveway laser-guided bomb) was computer-coded 3003-70ASB-7492, followed by the Lot # MFR 96214 09, supplied by Raytheon Corporation's plant in Mckinney, Texas, to the U.S. Navy. A further inquiry by the *Independent* established that the missile or a laser-guided bomb was fired or dropped by an EA6B prowler jet flying in from a warship, which fired at least one missile to protect two U.S. fighter aircraft from an Iraqi SAM battery in the area.[16] As for the comparison of the weaponry used by Iraq and the United States, an unnamed Iraqi Lieutenant-General would tell Fisk after the invasion that "the U.S. planes could detect Iraqi radar and fly faster than my [Soviet-made Sam-2, -3, -6 and -9] missiles, and then turn around and bomb my crews. So I would send only one battery [out of thirty] to engage an American aircraft and keep the rest safe."[17]

Thuraya's entry in her diary that day read: *"As usual, just a couple of hours of sleep. We have our breakfast in the kitchen. Afterwards we sat in the garden because the weather was so nice. I noticed a small nest on a tree with two birds which had astonishingly survived the sandstorm."* And the following day: *"Everyone is talking about the civilians who died at the Shuala market. Today I am so depressed it is hard to write. Then I listen to my favorite song, "CRAZY" by Britney Spears. I feel much better."*

In the north, to the apparent satisfaction of the Patriotic Union of Kurdistan (PUK), Centcom bombed the suspected positions of the Ansar al Islam, inside the PUK-controlled Kurdistan. The result was pretty gruesome—as shown by Al Jazeera—with thirty-three of the thirty-five dead being civilian.[18] Farther north, along the Iraqi-Turkish border, the government of Turkey amassed forty thousand troops ready to march into Iraq for "humanitarian purpose or to prevent terrorism [read Kurdish separatism]," represented, in its view, by the militia of the Iraqi Kurdistan Democratic Party.

On Saturday, March 29, there were worldwide antiwar demonstrations in Europe—including Sofia, the capital of Bulgaria, which had backed the Anglo-American draft resolution on Iraq (later withdrawn) at the Security Council—South Asia, East Asia, North Africa (in Morocco, 150,000 marched, shouting, "Suicide attacks lead to freedom"), and the Middle East, including one by ten thousand people in Port Said, Egypt, organized by the ruling National Democratic Party. This unprecedented event showed that popular resentment in the Arab and Muslim world was rising so fast that the solidly pro-American president Hosni Mubarak thought it prudent to channel the protest through an official organization, of which he was the head. This was also true of another pro-American ruler, King Abdullah of Jordan.

RUMSFELD ON THE DEFENSIVE

With his much-heralded military Plan "1003 Victor" getting unstuck, Rumsfeld found himself at the center of criticism from various quarters—civilian, intelligence, and military. Faced with this flak, he took to saying "our country's military plan." This was not correct. Two months earlier, in a flattering profile of Rumsfeld, *Time* writers had described him poring over Deployment Order 177, a sheaf of documents each ten to twenty pages long and containing the details of where, how, and when U.S. Army and Marine battalions, Navy carrier groups, and Air Force combat aircraft were to be shipped overseas or deployed for attacking Iraq. "He has been demanding to know which units are going where and why. He got deeply involved in operational planning, normally the province of the generals."[19]

Rumsfeld's armored rush to Baghdad—with tanks advancing at full speed, well ahead of the slower fuel tankers and other supplies—could only be accomplished by leaving the southern cities unsecured. This proved disastrous. The Iraqi Republican Guard and the Fedayeen allowed the American tanks to pass and then ambushed the lightly armed supply convoy in the rear. This left the U.S. advance force—fifty thousand combat troops of the Army's Third Infantry Division and the First Marine Expeditionary Force—stretched ahead, drained and perplexed, and deficient in food, water, and fuel.

"Rumsfeld thought he knew better," an unnamed senior Pentagon planner told Seymour Hersh of the *New Yorker*. "He was the decision-maker at every turn. This is the mess Rummy put himself in because he didn't want a heavy footprint on the ground." Furthermore, he had overruled advice from General Franks to delay the invasion by four weeks so that the troops denied access through Turkey on March 1 could be ferried in by an alternate route. This would have given much-needed time to the generals to prepare properly for the post-Saddam Hussein operations under Phase IV of the Plan "1003 Victor" by working out the details of the command and communications relationships and responsibilities—the absence of which would lead to glaring failures in the post-Saddam period, much to the embarrassment of Rumsfeld—as the secret report entitled " 'Operation Iraq Freedom' Strategic Lessons Learned" would reveal after the invasion.[20] Furthermore, Rumsfeld had underestimated the level of Iraqi resistance due to his uncritical acceptance of the intelligence supplied by the Iraqi National Congress (INC) and his failure to distinguish between a nation and a regime, with many Iraqis deciding to fight for Iraq rather than for Saddam.

"He [Rumsfeld] was so focused on proving his point—that the Iraqis were going to fall apart," that he ignored any advice or assessment that clashed with his vision, an unnamed former high-level intelligence official told Hersh. Conversely, he unquestioningly accepted the "intelligence" that fitted his pet scenario—such as the absence of any Republican Guard or Special Republican Guard in the south, as claimed by the INC.

Rumsfeld's critics highlighted his fraught relations with the U.S. Army's top brass, especially the chief of staff, General Eric Shineski, and his partiality toward U.S. Special Operations Forces, a key element in his Plan "1003 Victor." He let it be known as early as April 2002 that General Shineski would retire in July 2003! (He would go on to ignore Shineski's estimate that the United States would need to deploy four hundred thousand to five hundred thousand troops in post-Saddam Iraq to maintain law and order.) Resolved to make the invasion by the Army less "tank heavy," instead of adding First Cavalry and First Armored divisions to the Army units, he injected Marines and Airborne troops.

Suddenly, all those people whose toes Rumsfeld had trodden on before (they were legion) got a chance to speak their minds in public. They accused him of being flagrantly abusive toward senior soldiers. Summing up a generally held view, a high-ranking officer with thirty years' service said, "Rumsfeld is a bully; he is arrogant and truculent; and he has a huge ego."

A few unnamed senior Bush administration officials tried to put a brave face on the situation. "People are seeing firsthand that there are some fierce battles going on," one such official told *Time*. "It's steeling the public. We're seeing a hardening and steeling of the troops [as well]." The Pentagon rushed to say that it would have one hundred thousand more soldiers in the region—albeit by the end of April.

Print and electronic media commentators took to citing the neocons' confident predictions of instant victory. Here was Ken Adelman, former U.S. ambassador to the United Nations and former assistant to Rumsfeld, on February 13: "I believe demolishing Hussein's military power and liberating Iraq would be a cakewalk." There was Richard Perle speaking seven months earlier: "Support for Saddam, including within his military organization, will collapse at the first whiff of [American] gunpowder."

Now Perle, never short of glib explanation or interpretation, fell deafeningly silent. And so did his fellow neocons.

The resulting vacuum was filled by senior soldiers. General Tommy Franks listed Centcom's successes, including securing all southern oil fields, Iraq's coastline, and main port; and the U.S. Army's "dramatic advance," which had brought it to within striking distance of the three Republican Guard divisions defending Baghdad, and enabled it to attack north of Karbala. "The air force has worked 24 hours a day across every square foot of Iraq; and every day Iraq loses more of its military capability," he said. "We are in fact on plan."[21]

British prime minister Blair summed up the Allies' progress with assured eloquence as his office outlined the three phases of the Anglo-American invasion. Phase 1: Getting a strategic grip on Iraq in the first few days—securing oil fields; isolating urban centers in the south; ensuring that western Iraq was not turned into a staging area for attacking "neighboring states" [read, "firing Scud missiles at Israel"]; and advancing rapidly toward Baghdad. "The decision to rush armored forces north to Baghdad in the first hours of the invasion was an example of the commanders taking one of the windows of opportunity sometimes presented during a war," said the Downing Street statement. Phase 2: Steady advance; wearing down the enemy; and beginning the process of changing the military profile, where Allies take control. This would culminate in Phase 3—an attack on Baghdad to remove Saddam Hussein and his regime.[22]

But this did not satisfy the critics. They alluded to the hype that the Pentagon had disseminated during the run-up to the invasion. It would be a "war like none before"—with civilians plying the liberating Allied troops with sweets and flowers and Iraqi soldiers and policemen placing themselves under U.S. command in an orderly fashion. After twelve days of sieges, blockade, and "bite and hold" (seize a small area, ensure the forward edge is secure, and clear it of any remaining resistance), it was "a familiar war," concluded Professor Christopher Bellamy, a British military expert.

An example of the "bite and hold" tactic came from the Karbala area. Here U.S. troops fought a bloody battle to seize the airfield near Karbala—as a precursor to capturing the city. Centcom applied a similar strategy at Najaf, the scene of fierce fighting between the U.S. Third Infantry Division, backed by a fleet of Apache attack helicopters, and the Iraqis, armed with mortars and rocket-propelled grenades, on the outskirts of the city. Meanwhile, the paratroopers of the U.S. 101st Airborne Division focused on capturing the airfield near Najaf. They did so following bitter combat. But the task of dislodging the Iraqi forces from Najaf proved daunting. "U.S. troops have been forced into street fighting which could become more difficult as they get closer to the center," an American intelligence officer told the *Washington Post* on April 1. According to him, some two thousand Iraqi fighters, made up of the Fedayeen and the Baath Party's Jerusalem Army militia, were putting up stiff resistance, and there were intense artillery exchanges, with the Americans firing thirty cannons at a time.

In Nasiriya, despite eight days of almost nonstop fighting, U.S. forces had failed to secure the city for themselves. So great was the pressure on them from the Centcom headquarters to unclog the supply lines to the troops northward that they started building an extra bridge over the Euphrates.

Baghdad was now bombarded around the clock. Defended on the outside circle by Republican Guard divisions, and on the inside circle by four Special Republican Guard brigades, the capital was still shrouded in smoke from burning oil trenches.

"Thank God, we are still here and everyone in our family is well," Thuraya al Kaissi said in her diary on March 30. *"We are still talking about the market bomb [in Shuala] on Friday which killed so many civilians. What must it be like for their families?"*

In the north, as a result of heavy U.S. bombardment, the Iraqi troops under the command of Izzat Ibrahim al Douri, vice president of the Revolutionary Command Council, retreated on March 28 from Kirkuk's outer defense line twelve miles (twenty kilometers) east of the city at Chamchamal to the inner defense line two miles (three kilometers) east in an orderly withdrawal. But the subsequent advance of the Kurdish troops was slow due to the dense minefields left by the retreating Iraqi forces. Farther down, in southeastern Kurdistan, the Centcom, aided by the U.S. Special Forces on the ground, destroyed the six villages held by Ansar al Islam on March 30. These developments took place against the backdrop of Centcom's relentless bombardment of the Iraqi positions.

"The pounding is becoming unbearable for Iraqi recruits," reported John Simpson of the BBC in northern Iraq on March 31. "They could die if they stayed and be shot [in theory] if they try to desert. Increasingly, they are taking the risk of escaping. The battle is going on as I speak. You wonder how long the Iraqis can take this sort of punishment." Later, the British unit that Simpson was embedded with would become a victim of "friendly fire" by U.S. warplanes, and his Kurdish translator would die.

A day later, another British unit in the north suffered a setback.

The landing mission of the British Special Forces commandos went awry. Once again it was Al Jazeera that had the scoop. It showed footage of captured British vehicles and military equipment at the village of Khirbat al Waar, west of Mosul, saying the Iraqis had foiled a landing attempt by the British.

In the south the British Marines had a success when, following a bitter fifteen-hour battle, they seized the Abu al Qassib suburb of Basra on March 30. But their claim to have discovered protective suits at a military facility near Basra—thereby proving that Iraq possessed WMD—proved false when it was later established that the suits were for defensive purposes, and that it was the Iraqis who feared that the Allies would assault them with WMD—not the other way around. "The gas masks, anti-contamination suits and atropine injectors had been intended to protect Iraqis rather than for offensive use," explained an Iraqi general to the *Guardian* after the war.

A similar conclusion would be drawn in the case of the U.S. troops finding protective suits for the Iraqis near Nasiriya on March 31.

Overall, though, in Nasiriya the Americans had by now gotten over the hump, with the Iraqis losing out. Among the signs was the disappearance of all Iraqi military officials at Saddam Hospital, whose many scores of patients included Private Jessica Lynch, by the morning of March 31. The medical staff told Lynch they would hand her over to the Americans the following day. However, just past midnight, the U.S. Army's Delta Force commandos—accompanied by a military television cameraman equipped with a night sight—arrived by Blackhawk helicopter. The deputy director of the hospital, Saad Abdul Razak, welcomed them with some relief. But the commandos were all hyped up. When the staff could not find the keys for Lynch's room instantly, they kicked open the door. In the words of Nicholas Kristof of the *New York Times*, who visited the Saddam Hospital after the war, "The staff members all said there was no resistance and that they all welcomed the Americans."[23] As such there was no need for the theatrics of the commandos firing blanks and the TV cameraman recording the "rescue" of a badly injured young female soldier who had killed a number of Iraqis while "fighting to the death" as her ammunition ran out. She had received "stab and bullet wounds" from her Iraqi captors (as U.S. intelligence officials claimed in anonymous briefings at the time), and would later be plucked behind enemy lines by U.S. commandos braving firefight. Nor was there any truth in the statement of Army Brigadier-General Vincent Brooks, chief Centcom spokesman, that "some brave souls put their lives on the line for this to happen. Loyal to a creed that they will never leave a fallen comrade."[24]

While the seven thousand U.S. Marines deployed in Nasiriya had yet to make the city secure for the American forces and welcomed the Centcom headquarters' decision to dispatch five thousand Army troops to bolster their ranks, in general the balance started shifting toward the Pentagon. This happened on March 30–31, and it had to do primarily with the redeployment of the Republican Guard.

ONSET OF THE PRO-ALLIES SHIFT

"Our regular southern troops [army and Republican Guard] were in real fighting in the south in the first days of the war but on about 30 or 31 March, the Republican Guard were ordered out of the deserts [in central Iraq] and back into Baghdad," said an unnamed brigadier-general after the war in his interview with the *Independent*. "The order came from Qusay. We don't know why. We then learned that many of their Republican Guard soldiers, along with other fighters, were told to leave their duties and stay at home. When the regular army in the south heard the same news, their resistance which had hitherto prevented the capture of a single city by the American or British forces began to collapse."[25]

A hint of this redeployment had come a couple of days earlier, when Iraq's defense minister, Sultan Hashim Ahmad, said (in a televised press conference on March 28) that the enemy must come inside Baghdad, and that Baghdad would be its grave. Inside the capital, the government had vacated obvious military targets and moved soldiers to apartment blocks, schools, and social clubs. The ring around the capital was about twenty-five miles (forty kilometers) from the city, where a visitor could see camouflaged tanks, sandbagged bunkers defended by machine-gun emplacements, and mobile antiaircraft trucks near military checkpoints.

Heavy air raids on Baghdad continued, with the increasing participation of low-flying U.S. aircraft, which improved the Centcom's targeting. One of its missiles scored a direct hit on Uday's favorite palace, where he entertained female visitors amid indoor fountains and erotic murals; stored his extensive gun collection; kept his collection of expensive cars in an underground car park; and maintained a private menagerie of exotic animals, including tigers and cougars. Suspecting that some friends of his had passed on its location to the Americans, he became very tense. His tension was shared by millions of Baghdadis—for altogether different reasons.

"The sky is red at night from all the missiles, and black during the day from the smoke," Thuraya al Kaissi noted in her diary on March 31. *"Two rockets fell close to our neighborhood today and now the floor is shaking. My mother is by my side, praying to God to save us. We have decided to move to Baquba, north-east of Baghdad. My mother has family there, and we think it will be safer."*

Not every Baghdad family had such an option. Most had to stay put and draw some succor from the periodic pep talks that Saddam Hussein dished out with his characteristic blend of Iraqi nationalism and Islamic terminology. In his April 1 statement, read by his sixty-two-year-old information minister, Muhammad al Sahhaf, he referred to the United States and Britain as "evil, accursed by God," and described Iraqis as "the victors" who will vanquish them. He urged Iraqis to "fight them everywhere the way you are fighting them today. And don't give them a chance to catch their breath until they withdraw from the land of the Muslims, defeated and cursed in this life and the afterlife. The invasion that the aggressors are carrying out is an aggression on the religion, wealth, honor, and soul of the Land of Islam." Therefore, jihad is a duty and "those who are martyred will be rewarded in heaven. This is what God requested of you."[26]

That Saddam did not deliver this speech himself led the White House to take seriously an intelligence tip that he was hiding in his native village of Auja, near Tikrit. Centcom bombed two houses in Auja—belonging to distant cousins of Saddam allegedly providing him a safe haven—killing twenty-one civilians, including four children, during the night of April 1–2.[27]

On April 1, some protesters in Alexandria, Egypt, marched dressed as suicide bombers with fake dynamite sticks. The phlegmatic President Mubarak had become so agitated by the conflict that, addressing the Third Army in Cairo, he said, "When it is over. . . . this war will have horrible consequences. Instead of having one Osama bin Laden, we will have 100 bin Ladens." He warned that an ancient Arab civilization (in Mesopotamia) would be destroyed if no solution was found to safeguard international will while protecting Iraq's control of its land and national dignity. A similar view would be expressed by the moderate Iranian president Muhammad Khatami in a televised speech a few days later: "With this war, you [Americans] are giving a green light to extremist movements and violence seekers to answer back your violence with violence."[28]

"We didn't have much bombing [in Baghdad] and the weather was so nice," Thuraya al Kaissi noted in her diary on April 1. *"We went back to our own house [from Baquba] to clean it. My father and brother are living there on their own. Later, back at my aunt's we all sat around listening to music. We painted our faces with the slogan, 'No war.' "*

After trudging along Highway 7, infested with Iraqi hit-and-run paramilitary units, for nearly five days, the U.S. First Marine Expeditionary Unit manning the easterly flank of the Centcom's drive to Baghdad reached the outskirts of Kut, 115 miles (185 kilometers) from Nasiriya, on April 1. It faced the combined forces of the Republican Guard's Baghdad Division, the regular army, and the Fedayeen Saddam. The battle lasted four days nonstop. On their way to Namaniya via a bridge over the Tigris River in central Iraq, the Marine jets dropped several napalm bombs on the Iraqi positions before approaching the bridge. Napalm was also used to the southwest of this site near the bridge over the Saddam Canal. "We napalmed both those [bridge] approaches," Colonel James Allen, commander of Marine Air Group 11, based at Miramar Marine Corps Air Station in California, told the *San Diego Union-Tribune* four months later. "Unfortunately there were people there because you could see them in the [cockpit] video. They were Iraqi soldiers. It's no great way to die."[29]   (See Map, "Week ending April 2, 2003.") Allen's commanding officer, Major-General Jim Amos, told the same newspaper that napalm was used on "several occasions" in the war. Such an important fact was withheld by Centcom during the war.

In their rush to reach Baghdad, both the U.S. Marines and the Army often bypassed the recently abandoned Iraqi arms dumps, leaving it to the follow-up units to destroy them or have them bombed by warplanes. But by the time the latter arrived on the scene, most of the arms had been looted by the nearby Iraqis, who buried them in their backyards and fields. This would have baneful consequences for the Anglo-American occupation forces after the invasion.

The westerly flank of Centcom's advance to Baghdad, manned by the U.S. Third Infantry Division, finally succeeded in encircling Najaf. Farther north, it clashed with Iraq's Nebuchednezzar Republican Guard Division at Hindiya. There was also combat around Hilla, where the Centcom dropped cluster bombs on the nearby village of Mazarak, killing thirty-three people, including at least nine children, and wounding more than three hundred, according to Dr. Nadhim Adali, a British-trained surgeon. A twenty-one-minute video taped by a Reuters correspondent in a hospital in Hilla showed the tiny corpse of a baby "wrapped up like a doll."[30] In another instance, cluster bombs dropped on the Nada neighborhood of Hilla killed scores of civilians.

As had happened in Afghanistan, Centcom's frequent use of cluster bombs and ammunition demoralized the Iraqi soldiers. The result was a series of successes for the Americans. The westerly flank finally succeeded in encircling Karbala on April 2. Its middle flank reached Sarbanbdi, forty miles south of Baghdad (sixty-five kilometers) from Baghdad. And the U.S. Third Mechanized Infantry moved north with the aim of crossing the Euphrates to reach Iskandariya, thirty miles (fourty-eight kilometers) south of Baghdad.

In the capital, the government tried to bolster public morale by showing a relaxed Saddam Hussein on Iraqi TV chairing a cabinet meeting on April 2, with the implicit message of "business as usual—almost." But reality was much too fraught for any such public-relations exercise to work. That day there was heavy bombing, with low-flying aircraft swooping over the city, and several missiles striking the Baghdad Trade Fair complex, the shrapnel and shattered glass hitting the maternity hospital across the road.

"Bombing is back," noted Thuraya al Kaissi on April 2. *"At 10 a.m. we heard very loud explosions [in Baquba], and the windows and doors were shaking. My father came over to say hello at tea time . . . my mother started crying as she wants to be with my father."*

By now, Salam Pax, a sophisticated diarist, had reached the end of his tether. *"Actually too tired, scared and burned-out to write anything,"* he wrote at the end of the second week of the war. *"Yes, we did go out again to see what was hit. Yes, everything just hurts. I can't stand the TV or the lies on the news any more. No good news wherever you look."* Except at Centcom headquarters, near Doha.

Centcom could now claim—rightly—that it was in Phase 2 of its invasion (as described earlier by the Downing Street statement in London), and that the overall military profile was changing in favor of the Allies—with the Iraqi soldiers drifting away from their units or failing to turn up for duty the next day, discarding their uniforms and going home—paving the way for the final, triumphant phase.

A *USA Today* poll published on April 1 showed 70 percent of Americans supporting the war. But a breakdown revealed that only 40 percent were firmly behind it, twice those who were against it. "War supporters tend to get their news from television, especially the Fox News channel, and tend to believe what they are told by the Pentagon," noted Andrew Gumbel of the *Independent*. "Opponents are more likely to surf the Internet for foreign newspaper reports and alternative news sites, discounting what the government says as empty propaganda." In Britain the prowar figure had dropped eight points to 48 percent, while the opposition had stayed steady at 38 percent.[31]

Opinion surveys in France and Germany provided a contrast. A *Le Monde* poll on April 2 showed that 78 percent were opposed to the war and that 33 percent did not want an Allied victory. The popularity of President Chirac—who, while opposed to the war, reaffirmed his denunciation of the dictatorial regime in Iraq—soared to 90 percent, the highest since surveys were started in 1938. In Germany a poll published in *Der Stern* (The Star) on April 2 showed that 90 percent of Germans had lost their respect for the United States and that 89 percent expected it to emerge weakened from the conflict. In Spain, opposition to the war stood at 91 percent. An opinion survey in Russia showed that while 45 percent sympathized with Iraq, only 5 percent backed America.[32]

At the end of the first fortnight of its military campaign, the Centcom had flown eighteen thousand air sorties, launched 725 Tomahawk missiles, discharged twelve thousand precision-guided munitions, dropped fifty cluster bombs, and fired an unknown number of cluster shells and mortars. It claimed to have seized six hundred of the one thousand Iraqi oil wells and refineries in the south and the center. But no weapons of mass destruction had been found. The claim by U.S. Special Forces arriving at the abandoned Ansar al Islam camps in Kurdistan on April 2 that they had come across documents "indicating [the] presence of chemical and biological weapons" turned out to be baseless. The death toll was: 1,251 Iraqi civilians (Baghdad's estimate); 61 U.S. troops; 27 U.K. soldiers; and 34 troops killed in friendly fire. The Allies had 8,023 Iraqi POWs. The U.S. Congress had set aside $80 billion for the war, and the British budget for it was $5.6 billion (£3.5 billion).

NOTES

1. *Sunday Times*, March 30, 2003.
2. *Washington Post*, March 26, 2003.
3. See Dilip Hiro, *War Without End: The Rise of Islamist Terrorism and Global Response*, Routledge, New York and London, p. 351.
4. Altogether, of the 250 soldiers, 25 died, 11 were injured, and the rest defected. *Guardian*, May 28, 2003.
5. *International Herald Tribune*, April 2, 2003.
6. *Independent*, March 31, 2003; *Guardian,* April 4, 2003.
7. June 21, 2003.
8. *Independent*, March 29, 2003.
9. See Dilip Hiro, *The Longest War: The Iran-Iraq Military Conflict*, p. 282, note 49.
10. *Independent*, March 29, 2003.
11. Cited in *Independent on Sunday*, April 13, 2003.
12. Saddam Hussein rewarded Ali Hammadi Numani posthumously by promoting him in the military hierarchy and giving his family a substantial sum.
13. June 15, 2003.
14. March 30, 2003.
15. Associated Press, March 28, 2003.
16. March 30 and April 2.
17. *Independent,* May 29, 2003. Yet he claimed that his men shot down twelve American planes around Baghdad by using only two hundred antiaircraft missiles, and that he lost only thirty missile crew members.
18. *The Week*, April 5, 2003, p. 11.
19. January 27, 2003, pp. 18–25.
20. *Washington Times*, September 3, 2003.
21. *Independent*, March 31, 2003.

22. Ibid., April 2, 2003.

23. June 21, 2003.

24. Nor indeed was there any need for the Centcom to give the sole credit, much publicized, for her rescue to Iraqi lawyer Muhammad Odeh al Rehaief, who "risked his life" to tell the Americans where Jessica Lynch was, and who was quickly granted asylum in America and awarded a $300,000 deal for a book entitled *Return to Nasiriyah,* retitled *Because Each Life is Precious.*

25. May 27, 2003. Indirect confirmation of this came in a statement by the Centcom on April 3: "In the last 24 hours the U.S. has insisted that there is no longer any coherence in the moves by the Republican Guard, whose divisions have crumbled into small units, and have either melted away into the country-side or pulled back into Baghdad." *Guardian,* April 4, 2003. The Centcom also knew why: It had made deals with many Republican Guard generals who had been assured that the Centcom would destroy the Iraqi military's communica-tions system so thoroughly that Saddam Hussein would be unable to reach them, thus inadvertently freeing them from any governmental control.

26. *Independent,* April 2, 2003.

27. These deaths and the bombing, unannounced by the Centcom, came to light four months later when Robert Fisk chanced upon these graves during his trip to see the burial site of Uday and Qusay Saddam Hussein. *Independent,* August 5, 2003.

28. Ibid., April 1 and 4, 2003.

29. August 5, 2003. The Pentagon could not say how many Iraqis died.

30. Reuters, April 1, 2003.

31. *Guardian,* April 4, 2003

32. Ibid.

CHAPTER 7

WEEK THREE: THE FALL OF BAGHDAD

"The key [to quick American victory] was doing what Saddam didn't expect."
—Senior Pentagon official[1]

"On April 11, outside the Abu Hanifa Mosque in Adhamiya, Baghdad, an old woman asked Saddam, 'What have you done to us?' Smacking his forehead with an open palm, Saddam replied, 'What could I do? I trusted my commanders. They have broken the oath they took upon themselves to protect Iraq. We hope we will be back in power, and everything will be fixed.'"
—"Abu Tiba," bodyguard to Uday Saddam Hussein[2]

DURING THIS WEEK, Centcom progressed to the final phase of its Plan "1003 Victor": besieging Baghdad, smashing the regime's command and control system, and defeating or destroying its leadership. Its overriding objective was to avoid urban warfare, which usually results in a 30 percent casualty rate for the attacking combatant. Even if the improved training given to U.S. troops over the past decade could reduce this figure by half, the casualties would still have run into the thousands, a politically unacceptable figure.

Of the eight options that the Pentagon planners had listed—isolation siege; remote strikes; reducing Baghdad to rubble; frontal ground assault; segment and capture; soft point capture and expansion; nodal isolation; and nodal capture—the first three were ruled out, as they would entail heavy U.S. military and/or Iraqi

237

civilian casualties. What followed was a combination of the last five options.[3]

The "segment and capture" option is a variant of the "frontal ground assault," where the invading force focuses on those neighborhoods of a city most likely to welcome it. This is what the troops of the opposition Northern Alliance in Afghanistan, consisting of ethnic Tajiks, did in Kabul when they approached the Tajik section of the city. Now the Pentagon focused on Saddam City, a predominantly working-class district home to a million Shias on the northeastern edge of the capital. Despite various calls and attempts made by U.S. agents in Saddam City, the Shias there remained quiescent.

In the "soft point capture and expansion" strategy, the invading troops seize unprotected city segments where military opposition is known to be weak, and then use them as bridgeheads to expand into heavily contested parts.

The remaining two options were more focused. The "nodal isolation" option involves using air and ground forces to isolate the enemy's command centers and focal points in the capital by separating the leadership from the civilian population. This is what the Centcom tried to do in Baghdad. However, its planners had failed to take into account the active presence of the irregular Iraqi forces—the Fedayeen Saddam and the foreign volunteers—who were not taking day-to-day orders from the regular military command centers. Finally, "nodal capture" means physically seizing the enemy command and control centers while leaving the rest of the military infrastructure intact. That is what the U.S. troops did on April 5 and 6, with a lot of low-level bombing on the western bank of the Tigris, with considerable success.

In the event, Centcom deployed a combination of these options within the general framework of cordoning off Baghdad with a loose chain of troops equipped with 325 Abrams tanks, two hundred Bradley fighting vehicles and one hundred attack helicopters, after cutting off the city's electricity supplies and disabling its communications systems.

NASIRIYA, NAJAF, AND KARBALA

After eleven days of the war's most bitter and bloody combat yet in Nasiriya, Centcom declared the city "secure" and under its control on April 3—which, in practical terms, meant that looting and lawlessness erupted. "The streets of Nasiriya are littered with the evidence of the struggle that raged for 11 days," reported Andrew Buncombe of the *Independent*. "Along the main roads, strewn with rubble and cartridge shells, lie burnt-out Iraqi armor and T-55 tanks, destroyed by the U.S. forces as they advanced through the city. There are also the upturned remains of at least two U.S. vehicles, the result of an ambush on logistical support personnel. Many of those are still missing, and up to 20 troops were killed in the fight for Nasiriya." In contrast was the figure of the Iraqi dead: 1,117, according to Andrew North of the BBC, who later returned to the city to make a radio documentary.[4]

Under the Centcom's control, Nasiriya was neither safe nor secure. That became apparent when Ahmad Chalabi of the Iraqi National Congress and his five-hundred-strong Free Iraqi Army were ferried into the city in U.S. helicopters. Their arrival sparked renewed fighting.

Word of Chalabi's shady background and his lack of religious piety had reached the residents of Nasiriya before his actual appearance in the war-torn city. Born into a rich banking family in Baghdad, Chalabi and his Shia parents fled the city in the wake of the antiroyalist coup in 1958. After a university education in Beirut, he enrolled at the Massachusetts Institute of Technology, and subsequently obtained a doctorate in mathematics at the University of Chicago. He became a mathematics professor at the American University in Beirut and stayed there until 1977, when, due to the escalating Lebanese civil war, he moved to Amman. He established Petra Bank there and, within a decade, it became the third-largest bank in Jordan—only to be seized by the Central Bank of Jordan in August 1989 due to underhand foreign-exchange transactions that resulted in its collapse. His reported flight in the trunk of a friend's car to Damascus damaged his reputation. He moved to London, where he later became a British citizen. In 1992 the State Security Court in Amman convicted him in absentia in two cases for embezzlement, fraud, and breach of trust, and sentenced him to two jail terms, one for three years and the other for twenty years. The Jordanian government claimed that the Petra Bank debacle had cost it $300 million in deposits that went missing. Chalabi is believed to have gotten away with some $70 million from the scam.[5]

In the wake of Iraq's invasion of Kuwait in 1990, he carved out a niche for himself in Iraqi opposition circles in London. The CIA recruited him as an asset partly because he lacked any constituency inside Iraq, which meant he was the least threatening to other opposition groups, each of which had some contacts at home. In June 1992, at a convention of three hundred opposition delegates in Vienna bankrolled by the CIA, Chalabi was elected leader of the Iraqi National Congress (INC), an umbrella body that gained the affiliation of nearly twenty groups. He moved to Salahuddin in Iraqi Kurdistan, the headquarters of the INC, with a plan to develop the region as a launching pad for overthrowing the regime of Saddam Hussein. But his plan in March 1995 to combine a military coup against Saddam with a popular uprising in the area adjacent to Kurdistan failed when the United States withdrew its support for it, preferring to back an alternative plan by the Iraqi National Accord (INA).

In September 1996, following intra-Kurdish fighting in which the Kurdistan Democratic Party successfully secured Saddam's military assistance to defeat its rival, the Patriotic Union of Kurdistan, the CIA decided to pull out all of its 5,500 Arab and Kurdish agents, including Chalabi, from Kurdistan. After the passage of the Iraq Liberation Act in October 1998, the INC was recognized as one of six factions that qualified for official U.S. assistance.[6]

The hawks in the Bush administration warmly adopted Chalabi, who had by then developed close relations with influential pro-Israeli lawmakers, the American-Israeli Public Affairs Committee, the Jewish Institute for National Security Affairs, and American Enterprise Institute, and visited Israel.[7] At the Iraqi Open Opposition Conference in London in December 2002, his proposal for a transitional government in post-Saddam Iraq was rejected.

A fortnight after Centcom had installed Chalabi in Nasiriya, the *Guardian* reported that London-based Jawad Chalabi, one of Ahmad's brothers, had confirmed that he and his other brother, Hazim, had been given six months' suspended prison sentences by the Swiss authorities in September 2000 on charges of false accounting. This was related to the collapse of Socofi, an investment company that was part of Ahmad Chalabi's financial empire, which also included Associated Software Co. and Middle East and Trading Investment Co. Jawad Chalabi confirmed that Mebco, run by the Chalabi brothers, had had its banking license revoked by the Swiss banking commission in April 1989 and that the bank had failed. This revelation came after news in the Swiss press that the authorities had accused Jawad and Hazim Chalabi's Socofi of lending millions of dollars to Ahmad Chalabi's companies.[8]

Such shenanigans contrasted sharply with the spartan lifestyle of Grand Ayatollah Ali Sistani. Born into a Shia religious family in the Iranian city of Mashhad, Sistani pursued his theological studies in Qom and Najaf, where he studied under Grand Ayatollah Abol Qasim Khoei, who was the preeminent figure of the Hawza al Ilmiya (lit., Center of Learning), encompassing both teacher-clerics and students, located behind a gray metal door in the chief seminary of Najaf. He then began teaching Islamic jurisprudence. Like his mentor, Khoei, he belonged to the quietist school of Shia clerics, who wanted to focus exclusively on providing succor to the community in its spiritual life and social welfare—quite apart from those clergy who favored intervention in the affairs of the state. This distinction became all the more important after the coup by the secular Baathist Party in 1968, and the repression of the Shia religious establishment that followed when Saddam Hussein became vice president in 1975, and which intensified in the aftermath of the Islamic revolution in Iran four years later. Following the revolution, the Iranian-born Shia clerics came under suspicion, which increased during the early period of the Iran–Iraq War, but subsided when most Iraqi Shias proved loyal to their country and fought against Iran. By the time the war ended in 1988, Sistani had acquired the status of an ayatollah and gained popularity due partly to his simple lifestyle.

Following the death in 1992 of Khoei, whose funeral prayer was performed by Sistani, the mantle of the *marja-e taqlid* (Arabic, source of emulation) passed not to him, as had been widely expected, but to the younger Ayatollah Muhammad Sadiq al Sadr, due to Saddam's intervention. But a breach occurred between Grand Ayatollah al Sadr and Saddam in 1998 when al Sadr issued a religious decree calling on Shias to attend Friday prayers in mosques, a step disapproved of by the Iraqi leader, who was apprehensive of large religious gatherings. Saddam viewed this decree by al Sadr as a sign of the latter's leaning toward the interventionist school within Shia Islam. In February 1999, al Sadr and his two sons were shot dead as they left a mosque in Najaf. After blaming "foreign countries" for the assassinations, the Iraqi government appointed Sistani as the *marja-e taqlid*, entitling him to the honorific of grand ayatollah.

Sistani lived near the shrine of Imam Ali, whose caretaker, Shaikh Dr. Haidar Muhammad Hussein al Kalidar, had recently gone into hiding. Now, just as U.S. forces prepared to take armor into the center of Najaf on April 4 by using smoke canisters to mask their advance and directing artillery fire at sniper positions in alleyways and on rooftops, Sistani issued a *fatwa* saying Muslims should stay at home and refrain from looting and revenge killing. But Abdul Majid Khoei, a son of the late Grand Ayatollah Abol Qasim Khoei who had been airlifted into the Najaf area by U.S. Special Forces in early April from London—where he had lived for thirteen years while running the Khoei Foundation—had taken to acting as Sistani's mouthpiece in the latter's contacts with Centcom, primarily due to his fluency in English. Khoei twisted the words of Sistani's decree to say that he had called on Muslims not to impede the progress of the U.S. forces. Centcom exploited this version, ignoring the assertion by Sistani's son, Muhammad Rida Sistani, that his father had made no mention of the American troops in any context in his decree.[9]

Khoei was part of an American plan to make the Shias in the south welcome the invading American forces. On April 6, a Special Forces unit videotaped an interview with Khoei dressed in clerical robes in Najaf, witnessed by Charles Clover of the *Financial Times*. Urging local residents to receive the U.S. troops with open arms, he called on the citizens of Najaf and other Shia-majority cities to rise up against Saddam's regime. The idea was to broadcast the videotape from an American aircraft, which would jam Iraqi TV and replace the channel with Khoei's tape. But the covert Centcom plan to get a pro-American authority installed in Najaf and other cities by popular demand went awry when, on April 8, an armed battalion, claiming to belong to the Iraq Coalition for National Unity (ICNU), arrived in the city on U.S. Special Forces trucks and showed no interest in what Khoei said or did. Two days later a worse fate would befall him.

In Karbala, another Shia holy city, the Iraqis continued to resist the Americans. Fighting flared up on the night of April 5, when the Iraqis retaliated against U.S. artillery attacks with rocket-propelled grenades, mortars, and Kalashnikov firings. "They certainly are persistent," said Sergeant Jeremiah Sample of the U.S. First Armored Division. "These guys will take our fire, wait for us, and when we're underneath their positions, they will fire straight at our turrets." Sporadic fighting continued on April 6, a Sunday morning. It was only on Monday, after ten days of bitter combat, that the Centcom could rightly claim victory in Karbala when three battalions of the U.S. 101st Airborne Division.

The British struggle to capture Basra lasted longer. The fact that on the night of April 5–6 U.S. warplanes struck certain targets painted by the British Special Forces commandos who infiltrated Basra—including the Baath Party head office and a villa in central Basra that belonged to General Ali Hassan al Majid—did not mean the end of hostilities. The next day, a three-pronged attack by two thousand British troops backed by forty tanks aimed for the College of Literature near Shatt al Arab. Three miles (five kilometers) from their front line, the college was thought to be the headquarters of the Fedayeen and Baath Party's militia. This was the climax of relentless pounding by the British of populated areas in and around Basra, using more than two thousand cluster shells.[10] When the British finally reached the city center, they were received by the residents as a relief from fourteen days of bitter fighting, during which they had often been deprived of water and electricity.

MARCH ON BAGHDAD

Centcom's race to Baghdad continued as Saddam daily exhorted Iraqis to fight "the infidel invaders" with "bare hands" if need be—though not always in person, as he more often than not instructed Muhammad al Sahhaf to read his speeches, as on April 3.

"The desert sky is black with smoke [emanating from fifty oil-filled trenches around Baghdad burning]," reported David Willis of the BBC in central Iraq. "I saw dozens of Iraqi tanks engulfed in flames as the [U.S.] Marines traveled towards Baghdad. The wreckage of war was strewn across the highway. The battles have left many communities along the Tigris deserted. Other than a few farmers who came out to wave at the convoy on its way, it seemed everyone else had left."[11] These troops would soon reach the village of Furat near Saddam International Airport, located nine miles (fifteen kilometers) from downtown Baghdad. (See Map, "Greater Baghdad, April 3–11.")

That night, Iraqi TV showed a calm Saddam Hussein chairing a cabinet meeting, smiling and laughing, discussing the troops' battle-readiness. His military strategy consisted chiefly of placing three lines of defense around the capital—the first two lines being basically arcs between the Euphrates and the Tigris: the outer one from Karbala to Kut, 100 miles (160 kilometers) long, manned by four Republican Guard divisions, and the inner one from Yusufiya to Suwaira, the Guard's southern regional headquarters, thirty miles (fifty kilometers) long, manned by the remaining two Republican Guard divisions—and the third line around Baghdad manned by four Special Republican Guard brigades. They were to be complemented by the emplacement of huge explosive charges, which were designed to kill the advancing U.S. troops and wreck their tanks. Soon after the TV news ended, however, as a dramatic sign of the unexpected events to come, Baghdad plunged into darkness after sixteen bombs—both conventional and "black-out," which showered power cables with graphite filament—had short-circuited part of the national grid in the capital and the adjoining Babylon and Qadisiya provinces.

However, the damage was repaired quickly. On April 4, speaking to the residents of the capital in his television address, Saddam urged them to "hit them [the invading Americans] with force, resist them, oh people of Baghdad, whenever they advance upon your city, and remain true to your principles, your faith, and your honor." The capital was (in theory) safeguarded by four brigades of the Special Republican Guard—whose commanders had had considerable difficulty communicating by telephone with the central command since March 29, when the communications towers were destroyed—and an unknown number of the Fedayeen Saddam and foreign volunteers under the command of Uday. Both he and his brother, Qusay—who now acted on his father's behalf (he had not used the telephone for many years)—had resorted to communicating with their unit commanders in Baghdad and else-where through messengers, a cumbersome process. This manifested itself in a certain incoherence of movement by the Republican Guard, which the Centcom noticed on April 3–4.

Saddam tried to put a brave face on a deteriorating situation. Alluding to the American tactics, he said, "The enemy avoids fighting our forces when they find out that our troops are steadfast and strong. Instead, the enemy drops some troops here and there in small numbers."[12] This was an apparent reference to the Pentagon's extensive use of Special Forces, which in effect erased the traditional "static front line"—the basic doctrine for combat by armies globally—and instead came up with flexible front lines, which no army in the world knew.

Some hours later, a tired and somewhat distracted Saddam appeared in the upmarket neighborhood of Mansour in military fatigues and a black beret, surrounded by a cheering crowd. (See Map, "Greater Baghdad, April 3–11.") He held up a child for the cameras and clenched a fist as the chanting grew louder. This was shown on Iraqi TV at night.

THE REGIONAL RESPONSE

The political temperature was rising fast in adjoining Jordan. Ninety-five prominent Jordanians, including several parliamentarians and centrist and leftist politicians, called on King Abdullah to condemn not just the bombing of civilians in Iraq but the invasion itself: "Moral, national, and legal duty obliges all Arab governments, including Jordan's, clearly to denounce the aggression on Iraq as illegitimate," the petitioners said. The Islamic Action Front described the monarch's having given permission to American troops, including Special Forces units, to enter Jordan as "a grave sin and a violation of national principles and interests." Summing up the general feeling, Taher al Masri, a former Jordanian prime minister, said, "There is bitterness across the board, among the rich, the poor, the young, the old, the U.S.-educated. There will be more extremism, more introversion and more suspicion of the West [i.e., the United States and Britain]." Responding to the popular pressure, King Abdullah condemned Washington's plans for regime change in Baghdad. "Jordanians' loyalty, their national feelings and their pride make them absolutely reject and condemn what is happening to their brothers in Iraq, the killing and destruction," he said.[13]

"Stop the war," urged Saudi foreign minister Saud al Faisal. "Let's have a breather, after we have seen the destruction [in Iraq]. Let's have diplomacy work." Such statements by moderate, pro-Western rulers indicated the breadth and depth of the feelings against the Anglo-American alliance in his country. But none of this affected Bush or Blair—who were undoubtedly anxious to see the war end quickly.

In radical Syria, the state-run TV station regularly showed an American bomber taking off from an antiaircraft carrier, with the after-burn of its exhaust turning into the letters "Children"—in red—then morphing into the burst of an explosion, concluding with a heavily bandaged child. Such images both reflected and fueled public fury.

Belatedly, Palestinian leaders, religious and political, expressed their views. The Mufti of Jerusalem, Shaikh Ekrima Said Sabri, issued a *fatwa* at a Palestinian Authority (PA)–sponsored press conference in Ramallah saying that Muslims were obliged to rise in the face of the Anglo-American aggression, and that all Muslims were forbidden to aid the Anglo-American war effort. The PA endorsed the Mufti's *fatwa*. Earlier, the Greek Orthodox bishop Panaritos of Bethlehem told his congregation that Bush and Blair were "murderers" and therefore could not enter the house of God, and that their place was in prison. "They would never be allowed to enter the Church of Nativity in Bethlehem," he declared.

Summing up the regional mood, Mustafa Hamarne of Jordan's Center for Strategic Studies said, "There is pride in Iraqi resistance and anger at their own governments who are either sitting on the fence or collaborating with the U.S."

FALL OF SADDAM INTERNATIONAL AIRPORT

Along with racing to Baghdad, the American forces were also focused on finding the WMD, the proverbial "smoking gun." At Al Qaqaa, south of the capital, the U.S. 101st Airborne Division found suspicious white powder in boxes at the Latifiya explosives plant on April 4, and were confident that it was a chemical explosive. It was not: It turned out to be a nonchemical explosive. Likewise, there was much excitement when the Americans found a bottle marked "tabun" at an abandoned military training center in the western desert on April 4. "That was the only sample; this was not a weapons site," said the Centcom's General Vincent Brooks.

All along, the fighting was taking its toll of human life, most of it Iraqi—a fact noted by Thuraya al Kaissi on the fifteenth day of the invasion in a very personal way. *"I was woken by the lady who lives in the house opposite us,"* she wrote in her diary. *"Her son, an army officer, has been killed. She is crying and pulling her hair."* The next day was special for Thuraya. *"Today is the wedding anniversary of my parents,"* she noted. *"Each year we have a big party. But not this year. We hear the Americans are at the airport, which makes us even more frightened."*

Indeed, after a day's heavy combat, the U.S. troops captured, on April 4, the Saddam International Airport, to the southwest of the capital. The chief of staff of the Republican Guard, General Saifuddin Hassan Taha al Rawi, leading a 1,000-strong brigade outside the airfield, contrived to get out an announcement that he had died—followed by a fake funeral within twenty-four hours, as required by Islam.[14] In the fight, involving another 950 Iraqi Air Force troops guarding the perimeter and 1,000 infantry of the regular army posted inside, about 100 soldiers died.

As it was, al Rawi was not the only one to create a fiction about himself. Increasingly, information minister Muhammad Saeed al Sahhaf, the Iraqi government's face on the world's TV screens—always dressed in the standard Baath Party functionary's khaki uniform and black beret and wearing rimless spectacles—turned into a Panglossian character at his daily noon press conference. After the Iraqis had lost Saddam International Airport to U.S. forces on April 4, Sahhaf declared: "The Americans have no foothold in Iraq. We will welcome them with bullets and shoes." Later, describing the combat at the airport, Sahhaf said, "[At the airport] the Americans came in and we pushed them back and pounded them with our artillery, and they disappeared back to Abu Ghraib. But when we stopped, they came back." He added, "The American occupation of the airport was for filming and propaganda."[15]

Sahhaf had made a point of accusing the Anglo-American alliance of lying, and some of its claims were indeed found to be baseless—particularly during the first week of the invasion. But as the Allies began to prevail in the battlefield while Sahhaf stuck to his earlier mode of defiance and denial—very much like the master, Saddam Hussein—he lost his credibility with the media in the non-Arab world. His daily outpouring of unverified claims and braggadocio left ordinary Iraqis dangerously ill-informed. An English teacher by training and a longtime member of the Baath Party, he secured the radio and TV stations in Baghdad during the 1968 Baathist coup. Later he was put in charge of the state-run radio and TV, which enabled him to hone his propaganda skills. He rose through the party hierarchy and served as foreign minister from 1993 to 2001, where his confrontational style went down badly even in Arab chancelleries.

In comparison with al Sahhaf's blatantly inflated claims, the one made by the British that day (April 4) that, in their surgical strike on a Baath Party office inside Basra, their Special Forces commandos had killed General Ali Hassan al Majid and his body-guards, seemed rather measured. All British newspapers dutifully published long obituaries of the general, commonly known as "Chemical Ali." However, the report would turn out to be false, as it was al Majid who on April 6 would order the regular army to move northward to defend Baghdad. Some months later, on August 21, Centcom headquarters near Tampa, Florida, would announce the capture of the very alive General al Majid at an undisclosed location in Iraq.

On April 4, central Baghdad was relatively quiet, with little evidence of troops, roadblocks, or other defenses. Most of the city was without power or water after another night of bombing. Yet the Iraqi government managed to show on its television station Saddam Hussein in military fatigues at a large table, laughing and chatting with his sons, Uday and Qusay.

Overnight, the U.S. Third Infantry Division repulsed two Iraqi counterattacks on the Saddam International Airport. *"Still in the Greater Baghdad area and wondering whether we should leave,"* wrote Thuraya on April 5. *"The bombing continues."*

That day, after making the airport secure from the south overnight, an armored column of sixty-five tanks and thirty armored vehicles of the Second Brigade of the U.S. Third Infantry Division, covered by tank-busting A10 aircraft equipped with depleted-uranium rounds, rolled along Highway 8 through a southeastern corner of Baghdad to conduct a "Thunder Run"—an exercise designed to intimidate the capital's residents—around an arc in the southwest of the city leading to the Saddam International Airport via Qadisiya Expressway. In the course of this show of force, Centcom claimed, the column destroyed one hundred Iraqi military vehicles and killed one thousand soldiers—with no mention of any civilian casualties.

The experience of the Baghdadi civilians who encountered the "Thunder Run" and lived to talk about it was altogether different. At 6 A.M. that morning, Shahad al Majid, thrity-two, set up his cigarette stall at the Qadisiya road junction as he had been doing since he was sixteen. "They [Americans] came from nowhere—at about 7 A.M.," he told Ed Vulliamy of the *Observer Magazine*. "Suddenly shooting everywhere. I didn't think the Americans were in Baghdad after what I had heard on television. And there were some Fedayeen between the houses. But I didn't expect the Americans to come into Baghdad like that. When I saw what was happening, I grabbed my cigarette packages and ran into the supermarket over there. The Americans were firing at anything that moved." Majid pointed to the bus-stop shelters, one on each side of the road. "There was an American military vehicle, and the soldiers ran into the bus shelter over there. They shot it up. Then a bus came down the road, and the passengers ran off it to hide behind the other bus shelter. The Americans fired at that one too. I could hear people screaming as they died even with the noise of the guns. . . . [Later] I myself helped get 30 bodies into the supermarket. What a smell they made." In short, the U.S. troops shot dead not one thousand Iraqi soldiers, as had been claimed, but several hundred innocent civilians at random.[16]

The U.S. 101st Airborne Division, a companion of the U.S. Third Infantry, claimed to have circumvented Baghdad and swung into the north to cut off Highway 7 to Tikrit. The U.S. First Marine units, approaching to take over Al Rashid military airport in the east, clashed with the non-Iraqi Fedayeen.

Iraqi TV showed Saddam at a meeting with his son Qusay, top aides, and military commanders, laughing and chatting. Black-uniformed Fedayeen Saddam appeared on the streets of central Baghdad for the first time. Earlier, on the eve of the invasion, Uday had ordered the Fedayeen in the capital to maintain a strong vigil in the Shia working-class areas of Saddam City, Shuala, Shaab, and Kadhimiya on the edges of the capital, to nip in the bud any sign of an uprising. Small groups of Fedayeen patrolled these areas in pickup trucks with PK heavy machine guns mounted on the roofs. Their orders were to fire in the air if they saw a gathering of more than five men and to look out for the agents of U.S. forces who were active in these neighborhoods and on whom Rumsfeld had pinned his hopes of an uprising against Saddam's regime. The arrival of the American troops took the Fedayeen by surprise— they had been indoctrinated to believe that, despite their superiority in weaponry, U.S. forces would lose their resolve in battle. "We thought we would be honored as defenders of the fatherland,

and rewarded by Uday with money or a new car," said "Ali," twenty-two, a soft-spoken, stocky member of the Fedayeen. "We were shocked when we realized that the Americans were at the city doors. The army betrayed us."

Now Uday Saddam Hussein ordered the Fedayeen—armed with AK-47 assault rifles, heavy machine guns, rocket-propelled grenades, pistols, and knives—to retreat into central Baghdad to ambush the invaders and engage in urban warfare. "Ali" became part of a forty-man group that received its orders directly from Uday. Driving a Land Cruiser, Uday, his face covered in an Arab head-and-face scarf, would inquire about the American positions and exhort "Ali's" Fedayeen unit not to let the American attackers seize a nearby highway bridge over the Euphrates leading to the city center.[17]

On April 6, a Sunday morning, no newspapers appeared in Baghdad. The Second Brigade of the U.S. Third Infantry Division mounted an armored raid in the capital to seize control of a narrow strip of land on the Tigris's west bank, while seven thousand U.S. troops defended the Saddam International Airport, the scene of determined counterattacks by the Iraqi Republican Guard and regular army units, which were also trying to block the American line of advance to the city center.[18]

"Today I returned to my home," wrote Thuraya al Kaissi in her diary on April 6. *"I have been living with my mother at my aunt's place. But my aunt lives near the airport where all the fighting has been. Now all we can do is sit in the house."*

The Iraqis managed to blow up the headquarters of the Second Brigade of the Third Infantry. But this went largely unnoticed in the Anglo-American media, because Centcom deliberately mentioned it in a scattered fashion as details to other events and not in its own right. The short clips of TV footage that the Centcom allowed to be transmitted, and which the Anglo-American channels broadcast many times, provided very little hard information, and the battlefield reporters were seldom in a position to cobble together different bits to present a comprehensive picture.

The U.S. First Marine Expeditionary Force, forming Centcom's easternmost prong, advancing from the south to the eastern side of Baghdad to reach Al Rashid military airport, found that the bridges across the Diyala Tributary of the Tigris had been made insecure by the Iraqis, who had destroyed two other bridges. That was when the Centcom again ordered the use of napalm bombs.

None of the napalm bombing appeared in the clips that Centcom allowed to be aired. Most Americans who followed the war did so by switching on cable networks, with regular network TV news, local TV news, newspapers, and the Internet trailing behind. A *Los Angeles Times* survey conducted on April 5–6 showed that 69 percent turned to Fox News (3.1 million), CNN (2.65 million), and MSNBC (1.4 million), with the three main regular networks—ABC, NBC, and CBS—losing about 2 million viewers a night to cable, an unprecedented phenomenon during a war. Fox News had pioneered a school of journalism that discarded traditional notions of objectivity and balance, along with healthy skepticism of government, and, showing undisguised contempt for dissent, reveled in liberal-baiting put-downs. Its morning magazine program, "Fox & Friends," overtook CBS's "Early Show," a disturbing challenge to those who still believed in some sort of balance in news reporting. It was in January 2002 that Fox News became No. 1 in cable TV as a result of covering the Afghanistan war, with its reporters and anchors, covered in Stars and Stripes, referring to the Pentagon fighting "terror goons"—a style it repeated in the Iraq war. "The conveying of actual news [on TV] often seems subsidiary to the anchors' mission to out-flag-wave one another and to make their own personnel the leading actors in the drama," noted Frank Rich in the *New York Times* on April 12. "For anchors like Brian Williams and Wolf Blitzer, Kuwait City is a backdrop that lends a certain amount of gravitas, but couldn't they anchor just as well from New York? It's not that they are vying to interview the locals." As for the natives of the country that had been invaded, noted Rich, "Iraqis are the better-seen-than-heard dress extras in this drama, alternately pictured as sobbing, snarling or cheering. Even Saddam remains a villain from stock." Little wonder that in a speech in London, the BBC's director-general, Greg Dyke, revealed that the BBC World Service Radio was attracting 4 million American listeners every week, while almost 1 million were watching BBC news bulletins on cable and PBS networks. Referring to his recent trip to the United States, Dyke said, "I was amazed by how many people just came up to me and said they were following the war on the BBC because they no longer trusted the American electronic news media."[19]

A rare glimpse of the total picture could only be provided by a print journalist fluent in Arabic. Such was the case with Nadim Ladki of Reuters News Agency, who traveled by car from Baghdad to Jordan on April 6. "Despite U.S. claims that its forces had nearly encircled Baghdad, I did not see any U.S. troops on the road toward Falluja, due west," he reported. "That area belonged to the Iraqi military, who are dug in along the road, concealed by greenery, their tanks and trucks camouflaged with mud. There were Iraqi trucks towing anti-aircraft guns until Ramadi, more than sixty miles (one hundred kilometers) from Baghdad. Only after a further fifty miles (eighty kilometers) did the situation change. Here Iraqi military positions were manned by the American and British Special Forces speaking Arabic with a non-Iraqi accent—all the way to the Jordanian border town of Trebil."

Beneath the surface, however, the situation was very much in flux. "It was on 6 April that the southern military commander General Ali Hassan al Majid ordered the regular army to abandon the south of Iraq and redeploy north for the defense of Baghdad," the unnamed brigadier-general in charge of the antiaircraft batteries in Baghdad told Robert Fisk of the *Independent*. As for the Republican Guard around Baghdad, the American version, that they had abandoned their positions due to heavy B-52 bombardment, was false:

They had experienced worse bombing during the 1991 Gulf War. No, they had just left their nearly eight hundred tanks on the roads, in the fields, in the desert; all the equipment of the Medina al Muanora Hammurabi, Nebuchednezzar, and Baghdad just abandoned, said the unnamed Iraqi officer. "The result was chaos."

The redeployment by the regular army, whether in the Baghdad area or elsewhere, gave an opportunity to those who wanted to desert to do so. The case of the artillery unit at the Taji air base in the northern outskirts of the capital was illustrative. In early April, when the Americans began to approach Baghdad, the unit was ordered to move to the western outskirts. Half of them slipped off. In theory, every Iraqi had signed a declaration saying he understood that he would be executed if he deserted. But so far, no Iraqi interviewee had known of any such execution. "On 5 April U.S. planes attacked, hitting seven of our 18 guns in one hour," said Private Abbas Ali Hussein. "About 10 of us were killed. Our guns were in the civilian areas on the main road. We quickly moved the remaining guns under palm trees. I experienced bombing as a child during 1991 but had never been near anything like this. It was terrible. Two of my close friends were killed. So I felt I had to carry on to avenge them. Also my father is a retired army officer and Baath Party member. By 8 April, my unit was down to six. In my unit 20 were killed, 20 injured, and the rest deserted."[20]

According to "a high-ranking Republican Guard officer" (most probably a general, of whom there were 180-plus) who, on April 6, was dispatched by the Central Command to resupply various commanders in Baghdad with ammunition and other items, "I saw with my own eyes a group of high-ranking [Republican Guard] officers moving through different units, asking them to leave their arms and go back home. I saw staff colonels and staff brigadiers telling anti-aircraft units not to use weapons against enemy warplanes."[21] These Iraqi officers acted with impunity because they knew that the Central Command no longer had control over them, due to the breakdown of the communications system, and that without air cover it was impossible to defend the capital. Several weeks before the invasion, they had apparently been approached by U.S. Task Force 20—which had worked in conjunction with Iyad Alawi of the Iraqi National Accord (which had all along favored a military coup against Saddam); the Amman-based Muhammad Abdullah Shahnawi, a former brigadier-general in the Republican Guard's helicopter force;[22] and the Jordanian intelligence—and had agreed either to keep their forces out of combat or desert in return for a promised role in the post-Saddam military and/or a large sum of cash, along with an air flight out of the country—or a simple pledge of being left alone under the new regime.[23] In return, the officers were assured that, unlike what had happened in the 1991 Gulf War when the Pentagon bombed and killed tens of thousands of unarmed, retreating Iraqi troops, the Pentagon would not target the deserting Iraqi soldiers. It kept its word. It is noteworthy that the total number of Iraqi POWs never exceeded eight thousand. The downside of the lack of communication between the Iraqi Central Command and its subordinates, for the Pentagon at least, was that there could be no formal surrender. The U.S. military had refrained from bombing the Defense Ministry in the vain hope of securing a formal surrender, which would have been a glittering political prize, and would have obviated the immense problems that cropped up in the post-Saddam period.

Colonel A. T. Said of the Republican Guard, who deserted as the U.S. tanks rolled into Baghdad (on April 7) and threw away his uniform, described how unit after unit of the Republican Guard "melted away," and said that the Baath Party commissars attached to the Special Security Organization were the first to desert. "The U.S. bombing of the communications systems meant that messages had to be relayed orally from the Republican Guard's Central Command in Baghdad to the Southern Regional Command at Suwaira, 30 miles [50 km] south of the capital, and to the Northern Command at Tikrit 110 miles [175 km] north, and that system collapsed as the officers at the regional headquarters failed to report for duty."[24] As a result, Saddam's elaborate plan of safeguarding Baghdad with three lines of defense, and detonating large explosive charges to destroy the approaching American armor, collapsed.

Initially, most officers of the regular army and the Republican Guard felt that it was their duty to protect the sovereignty and integrity of their fatherland, and made a distinction between fighting for Iraq and fighting for Saddam. But when they found themselves the primary targets of Centcom's airborne firepower— receiving nearly half of the twenty-eight thousand bombs and missiles during the war,[25] they had second thoughts. They were flabbergasted by the Pentagon's massive high-tech weaponry as they witnessed tanks parked under freeway overpasses hit sideways by laser-guided munitions and armor hidden under palm trees blasted by bombs, with pilotless drones doing the reconnaissance. They realized that defeat was inevitable. So they took a pragmatic view to save themselves as well as their soldiers, and spare the block-by-block destruction of Baghdad—as envisaged by Centcom's plan, which was to sever supplies of water and food to compel civilians to abandon the city, especially its downtown area, to the soldiers, whereupon it would be subjected to air strikes, long-range artillery, and surgical commando raids. That this in turn would have raised the political temperature in the Arab and Muslim world to the extent of destabilizing Jordan and Pakistan did not enter the officers' estimation. In the final analysis, the commanders of the Republican Guard and the Special Republican Guard did not have undying loyalty to the Baath Party or to Saddam Hussein and his sons, and were not willing to sacrifice their lives for either. Because of this, the usual tactics of blowing up bridges, etc., to hinder the enemy's advance did not take place. Only one bridge over the Diyala River to the southeast of the capital was wrecked. The Americans moved fast, and there was no time for the Iraquis to implement the necessary tactics of slowing down the enemy's advance.

The aforementioned agreement did not apply to the irregulars, Iraqi and non-Iraqi, and they continued to fight. Nor did it apply to the north, where the one-hundred-thousand-strong regular army, under Izzat Ibrahim al Douri, the Revolutionary Command Council's vice-chairman, held on in Mosul and Kirkuk.

PRELUDE TO THE FALL OF BAGHDAD

"The TV says Baghdad is totally besieged by the Americans," noted Thuraya al Kaissi on April 7. *"In the afternoon, my uncle saw U.S. troops and tanks [go] past his street [in the southwest]."*

At 7 A.M. on April 7, Iraqi TV went off the air, never to return. A large statue of Saddam Hussein was pulled down in Karbala. Wide-scale looting broke out in Basra and continued unabated the next day. The ransacking of public buildings extended to Basra's Museum and Library, and the Basra University, whose library of two million volumes, including some dating back to 1015, was reduced to hundreds of meters of blackened, twisted metal shelves and smoldering ashes from books torched by looters. "There's a crowd of men gathered outside," Kylie Morris of the BBC reported from Basra outside a police station. "They're carrying plastic chairs, ceiling fans. Some have rather large sticks. Parts of the courtyard are on fire. There are filing cabinets; there are lounge chairs; a lot of frenetic activity."[26]

That day, Abdul Karim Mahoud al Hattab, better known as Abu Hatim, leader of the eight-thousand-strong Hizbollah militia, liberated Amara, near the Iranian border. He was an integral part of Washington's prewar strategy who had met with CIA officers in Kuwait in February. Immediately after his capture of Amara, he received a call on his satellite phone from a CIA officer in Kuwait, called "Daoud," who ordered him to leave Amara within an hour. He was puzzled. He called Kanan Makiya, his earlier conduit to the CIA, in Washington to use his influence to get the order reversed. It took many hours to get this done. By then the city was thoroughly ransacked.[27] But when his Hizbollah militia took over the local governor's headquarters, Centcom's Special Operations Force ordered Abu Hatim to leave under threat of bombing. He withdrew his men. Later, in June, he would resurface to conciliate the British with the locals, and in the following month he would be appointed a member of the Iraqi Governing Council.

The drip-drip of claims that U.S. forces had discovered WMD continued. According to an embedded National Public Radio (NPR) journalist, U.S. troops had found a cache of twenty medium-range missiles armed with sarin and mustard gas near Baghdad. No official comment followed, and there was no further mention of this story. The same day, the U.S. 101st Airborne Division units found two dozen suspicious barrels at an empty military training camp at Hindiya near Karbala, claiming that they contained sarin, tabun, and mustard gas. This was followed by a report that the findings were "inconclusive." The sickness experienced by the U.S. troops at the site was ascribed to fatigue, with Centcom spokesman General Benjamin Freakly saying the barrels might simply contain pesticide. After so many false alarms, even Rumsfeld was compelled to concede: "Almost all first reports turn out to be wrong." Yet the ever-confident Blair assured his audience in Britain that coalition forces would be led to the WMD as Saddam's regime collapsed.

Despite the artillery exchanges between the Iraqis and the U.S. 101st Airborne units at Saddam International Airport, now called Baghdad International Airport,[28] C130 and C17 transport planes brought in supplies. The Centcom deployed more troops to set up cordons and block the road going north to Tikrit. The Iraqis destroyed the bridge over the Army Canal and held up the progress of the U.S. First Marine force, engaging them in street battles.

Baghdad Airport was the base from which an American armored column of seventy tanks and sixty fighting vehicles, with an air cover of tank-busting A-10 aircraft equipped with depleted-uranium rounds, staged its second "Thunder Run," more ambitious and deadlier than the first, penetrating the city this time from the southwest, along Saddam International Airport Road and then Qadisiya Expressway, with special mine-sweeping tanks clearing its path in advance.

After rolling along Qadisiya Expressway, the armored column split—with its left prong going past the Parade Ground to the prestigious Rashid Hotel, and its right prong passing under the Victory Arches (built to mark the "victory" in the 1980–88 Iran–Iraq War). Sections of the column broke off to attack the governmental Tigris Compound and the vast Republican Presidential Palace Complex (140 buildings in 1.7 square miles/4.4 square kilometers) located along the Tigris—both of which had been softened up earlier by artillery fire—and the remainder surrounding the Information Ministry near the Sinak Bridge, between the Jumhuriya and Liberation bridges, after silencing the sniper fire. Along the way, the U.S. armored column overpowered the resistance it had met at the barracks of the First Brigade of the Special Republican Guard at the junction of Airport Road and Qadisiya Expressway, the Baath Party headquarters also on Qadisiya Expressway, and the barracks of the Republican Presidential Palace Guard. (See Map, "Greater Baghdad, April 3–11.")

The American forces rolled across the parade ground and blew up the forty-foot (thirteen-meter) statue of Saddam in Zawra Park. Having seized the Republican Presidential Palace, the attackers filmed its bathrooms and lavatories, with their twenty-four-carat-gold fittings, and rested on its lawns. The left prong of the armored column shelled the Rashid Hotel—popular with foreign journalists, and known for its floor mural of George Bush Sr. in the lobby near the entrance, for guests to walk over—and briefly surrounded it. Its armed personnel opened fire outside the hotel on civilians and Iraqi militiamen, blasting a motorcyclist and shooting at a Reuters photographer in his car. From there the journalists could hear the whining A-10 aircraft on the far banks of the Tigris firing their depleted-uranium-coated rounds at Iraqi tanks.

By sunset, confident of having destroyed the Iraqis' antiaircraft gun batteries, the U.S. F/A-18 fighters—providing close support of the ground forces—were cruising in pairs in the capital. Along the edges of the city, F/A-18 fighters blasted the dug-in positions of the Iraqis while the latter used oil fires to ease their escape.

The human toll of the two "Thunder Runs" by Centcom was enormous, as hundreds of Iraqi men, women, and children were rushed to hospitals—victims of bullets, shrapnel, and cluster bombs. The wall in the reception hall of Yarmouk Infirmary in southwest Baghdad, for instance, carried a list of the dead—740, all civilian—and the missing—1,200, among whom only a few were soldiers.[29]

Elsewhere in this vast, sprawling city, the local municipality's red double-decker buses were running. While most shops were closed, stalls were open. Men in tea houses talked about the invasion, while at every street corner Baathist militiamen with Kalashnikovs lounged with seeming leisure.

This was enough to provide a pretext to the Iraqi Information Minister al Sahhaf to remain firmly locked in his "denial" mode at his daily noon press conference. He accused Al Jazeera of being in cahoots with Centcom, and the Americans for using the lounges and halls of President Saddam Hussein's palace to make cheap propaganda. "With the U.S. tanks rolling into Baghdad and sound of artillery fire reverberating around the city, and the sound of sirens and gunfire"—reported Suzanne Goldenberg of the *Guardian*—"and the sight of the Iraqi troops running for cover on the other side of the Tigris, Sahhaf declared, on the roof of the Palestine Hotel: 'Baghdad is safe. The battle is going on. The infidels are committing suicide by the hundreds on the gates of Baghdad. Don't believe those liars. As our leader Saddam Hussein said, "God is grilling their stomachs in hell."'"

At around 3 P.M. local time, the Pentagon's B1 bombers, already airborne in search of "targets of opportunity," directed two satellite-guided JDAMs and two bunker-busting bombs at *Al Saah* restaurant in the Mansour neighborhood, following an intelligence tip-off an hour earlier that Saddam Hussein and his two sons were meeting about forty senior aides in a bunker at the back of the building, connected to the restaurant. The bombs left the restaurant and three other building's razed in a sixty-foot (twenty meter) crater and killed fourteen—but not Saddam or any of his close aides. It turned out later that the meeting took place at the house of General Saifuddin Hassan Taha al Rawi, chief of staff of the Republican Guard, and that Saddam and others had left the bombed building ten minutes before the strikes, which left al Rawi's house intact.[30]

It later transpired that this had been a sting operation by Saddam to catch an American agent among his bodyguards, whose existence he came to surmise after noticing that several of the safe houses he had used had been attacked subsequently by Centcom. He asked the suspect, a captain, to prepare a safe house behind Al Saar Restaurant in the Mansour neighborhood for an urgent meeting. Saddam and his two sons arrived at the site and left again, almost immediately, by the back door. "Ten minutes after they went out of the door, it was bombed," said "Abu Tiba," one of Uday Hussein's bodyguards. Saddam had the captain executed summarily by one of his loyal bodyguards.[31]

"Since the day the airport was seized [on April 4], we have no electricity and water is not reliable," wrote Salam Pax on April 7. *"We turn on the generator for four hours during the day and four at night mainly to watch the news. Today, my father wanted to turn on the generator at 8 am because of the news of an attack on the center of Baghdad. We sat for two hours watching the same images until Kuwait TV showed footage taken from Fox News of American soldiers in Al Sijood Palace. Totally dumbstruck. Right after that we saw Muhammad Said al Sahhaf denying once again what we have just seen minutes ago. He kept insisting that there are no American troops in Baghdad, and for some reason kept insisting that Al Jazeera has become 'a tool of the American media.' Idiot. I have not been out of*

the house for three days. We are now 15 people at Hotel Pax. Every-
body expects the next move to be on the west/southwest parts of
Baghdad, and are telling us we will be on the front line."

By now the number of regular Iraqi soldiers had shrunk so dramatically that, according to an unnamed brigadier-general on
April 7, even Defense Minister Sultan Hashim Ahmad went off
with officers to fight with some troops at the Diyala Bridge.

"We go to our uncle's house," wrote Thuraya al Kaissi on April 8.
"He has a generator so we can watch TV, and they showed the Amer-
ican troops coming into the city. I couldn't eat or drink anything. I was
too nervous."

As it was, that morning Centcom had exacted a price from Al
Jazeera for its balanced reporting of the Anglo-American invasion.
Around 7:45 A.M. local time, a U.S. warplane fired two missiles at
its office as its chief correspondent, Tariq Ayub, a Jordanian of
Palestinian origin, described a pitched battle between the Iraqis
and the Americans for the network's 7 A.M. news bulletin from the
roof of his office in a residential area near the Jumhuriya Bridge.
Ayub was killed, and his Iraqi cameraman, Zuhair, was wounded.
The bombing was recorded by a correspondent of Abu Dhabi TV,
whose office was near Al Jazeera's. Ayub's colleague, Maher
Abdullah, sitting in a room downstairs in front of the monitors,
saw the American plane fire missiles. "On our Al Jazeera screen
there was this battle [between the Iraqis and the Americans], and
we could see bullets flying," said Abdullah. "And then we heard the
aircraft. The plane was flying so low that those of us downstairs
thought it would land on the roof. We actually heard the rocket
being launched. It was a direct hit. The missile actually exploded
against our electrical generator. Tariq died almost at once. Zuhair
was injured." Centcom claimed that its aircraft had responded to
gunfire coming from the Al Jazeera office—a lie—which was just
what it had said about firing a tank shell from the Jumhuriya
Bridge at the fifteenth and sixteenth floors of the Palestine Hotel
that killed two journalists, Taras Protsyuk of Reuters and Jose

Couso of Spanish TV. "The Centcom allegation was categorically and absolutely denied by other reporters and our reporters on the ground," said Hamad bin Thamer, Al Jazeera's chairman.[32] This was the culmination of harassment to which Al Jazeera had been subjected since the start of the invasion, with American hackers attacking its English-language website, http://english.aljazeera.net, on March 24, replacing it with a red-white-and-blue U.S. map and the slogan "Let Freedom Ring!"[33] Two months earlier Al Jazeera—which had one of its journalists embedded with the U.S. Third Infantry Division in Nasiriya—had given the Pentagon the coordinates of its Baghdad office and received assurances that its bureau would not be attacked (as had happened in Kabul in November 2002). A day before the deadly incident, on April 7, an Arab-American spokesman for the U.S. State Department had visited the headquarters of Al Jazeera in Doha and repeated the assurance.

At noon that day, addressing the daily press conference, al Sahhaf said, "I now inform you that you [the world media] are now too far from reality." This would turn out to be al Sahhaf's last press conference.

American A-10 jets sprayed burning phosphorus to mislead heat-seeking Iraqi missiles before turning their cannons on the Planning Ministry, near the Jumhuriya Bridge, and blasting it with depleted-uranium shells designed for heavy tanks, which lit up the sky with a thousand orange and red pinpoints of light.

Elsewhere in the capital, the Second Brigade of the U.S. Third Infantry Division set up its base in Saddam Hussein's official residence just as the U.S. First Marines Expeditionary Force captured Al Rashid military airport in the east, thus completing the encircling of the capital. On the streets, five hundred Iraqi soldiers armed with rocket-propelled grenades counterattacked as U.S. tanks took up positions on the bridges in central Baghdad. As Iraqi regular troops, the Baath militia, and Fedayeen Saddam sniped at the American forces from rooftops, American A-10 attack aircraft strafed them. "I fired my last missile, a Sam-3, from a battery in the Tigris Compound area [in central Baghdad] at a low-flying U.S. aircraft at 8 P.M. on 8 April," said an unnamed brigadier-general. "In my headquarters we stayed at our post in uniform. Then on 9 April morning, we went out in civilian clothes to check on our crews in the city. That's when we saw the looting [which had started the night before]."[34]

THE FALL OF BAGHDAD

"As well as the power being off we have many water shortages," wrote Thuraya al Kaissi on April 9. *"My uncle tells us that on TV there are pictures of people smashing the statue of our president—and of many American troops in the city. But we do not see any [troops] in our [Adhamiya] neighborhood."*

On the late afternoon of that day, U.S. Marine Corps tanks entered eastern Baghdad from the south and took control of the district on the eastern bank of the Tigris encompassing the Palestine and Sheraton hotels. Just behind these multistory hotels in the middle of Al Firdaus (lit., Paradise) Square,[35] next to the striking Al Shuhada (lit. Martyrs) Mosque, stood a twenty-eight-foot (nine-meter) cast-iron statue of Saddam Hussein with his right arm stretched out. (See Map, "Greater Baghdad, April 3–11.")

Soon some Iraqi men equipped with ropes and sledgehammers attempted to topple the statute, with no success for more than an hour. *"Around 6 P.M. we turned on the electricity generator to check the news,"* Salam Pax wrote on his website. *"Lo and behold, holy cow in the sky, what do we see? Iraqis trying to pull down the Saddam statue in Al Firdaus [Square]. That the American troops are so deep in the city is not as surprising as the bunch of people trying to pull that thing down."*

By that time the scene had attracted most of the 150 foreign journalists and television crews staying at the Palestine Hotel. They were soon joined by a U.S. Marines maintenance team, which arrived with an M-80 recovery tank, equipped with a crane, to assist the Iraqis. This assured a swift downfall of the much-detested statue.

"By an astonishing coincidence," noted Kim Sengupta of the *Independent*, just as the statue's legs cracked, "Lieutenant Tim McLaughlin was at hand with the Stars and Stripes flag with which he covered the face of Saddam. This image was shot by the world TV cameras. Later [as the toppling continued], it was replaced by an Iraqi flag."[36] Once the statue fell and the head was severed from the body, the Iraqis pelted the body parts with garbage and shoes, the ultimate Arab ignominy. Others jumped up and down on the metal carcass.

These images were relayed around the world and dramatically captured the Anglo-American triumph—in contrast to what had happened in Kabul on November 12–13, 2001. Because of the strict ban on graven images or even photographs in the Taliban-administered Afghanistan, there were no statues of Mullah Omar or Osama bin Laden to be toppled, or even posters or portraits of them to be torn or defaced.[37] But in Baghdad, with every important city square adorned with Saddam's statue and every shop and office displaying his picture, TV camera crews and photographers had a field day.

Interestingly, the Arab TV channels focused on the lawlessness and looting in Baghdad, with the state-run television stations of Jordan and Egypt playing the event in a low key. Even though firmly pro-American, the Jordanian and Egyptian leaders felt distaste for the manner in which a fellow Arab ruler had been overthrown militarily by the world's sole superpower—without the sanction of the international community—resulting in the loss of sovereignty for a member of the Arab League, a unique event since the establishment of the league in 1945. This subdued feeling informed all the Arab TV channels, both public-service and commercial.

By contrast, when the image of Saddam's toppled image appeared on Fox News Channel, its anchor, Neil Cavuto, went agog with triumphalism, addressing those who opposed "the liberation of Iraq" thus: "You were sickening then, you're sickening now." At least this was less intimidating than the examples that Tim Robbins, a Hollywood actor active in antiwar protests cited in a speech to the National Press Club in Washington. "A friend of the family tells of listening to the radio down south as the talk-show host calls for the murder of a prominent antiwar activist," Robbins said. "Death threats have appeared on other prominent antiwar activists' doorsteps for their views. Susan [Sarandon] and I have been listed as traitors, as supporters of Saddam, and various other epithets. Every day the airwaves are filled with warnings, veiled and unveiled threats, invective and hatred directed at any voice of dissent."[38] Those in the Bush government were less scathing of their opponents, but equally joyous at the downfall of a tyrant—considered a menace to the United States by three successive administrations—conveyed so simply yet powerfully to the world at large.

The Bush White House formally declared the end of the regime of President Saddam Hussein, which had originated in the coup by the Baathist military leaders in July 1968.

Now, although his regime was finished, Saddam was not. Indeed, according to "Abu Tiba," on April 9, he and his two sons were in three separate safe houses in Adhamiya, a Sunni district full of Saddam loyalists, five miles (eight kilometers) northwest of Al Firdaus Square. Among them, Uday saw the toppling of his father's statue on a satellite television channel, according to "Abu Tiba"; this affected him strongly. "[After that] he was so tense," said "Abu Tiba." "It became very hard to talk to him. He used to get very angry at us [bodyguards], shouting at us endlessly."[39]

Saddam, however, remained calm. That day he was sighted north of Al Adhamiya Palace near Imam al Adham Abu Hanifa al Numan Mosque[40] mingling with people in the street. (See Map, "Greater Baghdad, April 3–11.") Abu Dhabi TV would later broadcast a videotape of the potbellied Saddam, in his standard olive uniform and black beret, riding in a limousine surrounded by Qusay, his personal secretary, Abid Hamid Mahmoud, defense minister Sultan Hashim Ahmad, and machine gun–wielding bodyguards—with his right arm raised in acknowledgment of the acclaim of a large adoring crowd in a street in Adhamiya. He stood unsteadily on his car seat to savor the moment just before his bodyguards pushed him down and rushed the limousine off. Abu Dhabi TV would air his message, taped indoors, separately. In it he called on Iraqis not to abandon hope and to prepare to fight back when the time was right—advice he would follow himself by going underground soon afterward. "We are confident that victory will be ours at the end, and that God will help us as much as we can ourselves," he said. "We have the stamina and belief that all our people, men and women, will fight on. If you give up, then corruption will prevail, and you will pay the price due to those with weak souls." He added, "Those among you who declare a voice of weakness, remind them to declare instead a call for steadfastness and calm in the storm not only on this earth [but also hereafter]. And you have to have dignity that would cause you good destiny here and hereafter."[41]

Apparently, that is also the message he conveyed to his immediate family, which included three daughters—Raghad, who trained to be an English translator at Baghdad University, Rana, and Hala. "We heard on the radio that the Americans had entered the city and occupied it, so at noon that day [April 9] we all left," Raghad said in a telephone interview with Christina Lamb of the *Sunday Times* in June from somewhere in Iraq. "After a few days everyone went their own way. We tried to hide in Baghdad. We had not expected it to happen so quickly."[42]

In the larger, national context, those who fought to the end out of patriotic feeling and/or loyalty to the regime found it hard to accept defeat.

"I think it was the psychological war that won over the 'real' war for us," said the unnamed Iraqi brigadier-general to the *Independent*. "Those Americans talking to us over our own radios— that was what succeeded. I would talk to my missile crews and suddenly on the same frequency they would talk in Arabic with Egyptian or Lebanese accents, and they would say, 'We have taken Nasiriya, we have captured Najaf, we are at Baghdad airport.' It was the psychological war that did the worst damage to us. The Americans knew all our frequencies. We had no radio news broadcasts, just the Americans talking to us on our radio network. I could have replied to these voices, but we were ordered not to, and I obeyed for my own security. We could no longer talk to each other on the radios. But we could hear the Americans."[43]

By the end of the third week, Centcom had staged a total of thirty thousand air sorties, dropped twenty thousand bombs, and discharged 750 cruise missiles. Overall, 70 percent of the munitions dropped or fired were precision-guided—by laser or by Global Positioning Satellite (GPS)—seven times the figure for the 1991 Gulf War. The cost of the invasion was running at $1.1 billion a day, with Britain bearing 8 percent of it.

NOTES

1. *Defense News*, May 19, 2003.
2. Cited in *Newsday*, July 25, 2003; *The Times* (London), July 25, 2003.
3. For full details, visit http://slate.msn.com/id/2081098.
4. The documentary was broadcast on BBC Radio 4 on June 19, 2003.
5. *Middle East International*, April 18, 2003, p. 26.
6. Dilip Hiro, *Neighbors, Not Friends: Iran and Iraq After the Gulf Wars*, p. 168.
7. *Observer*, September 29, 2002; *Independent*, April 12, 2003.
8. April 17, 2003. It is noteworthy that Ahmad Chalabi's Petra Bank was closed down by the Jordanian government in August 1989, four months after the closure of Mebco Bank in Switzerland.
9. *Financial Times*, April 14, 2003.
10. "We have actually seen the weapons," said Reuben Brigety of Human Rights Watch in Basra. *Guardian*, May 30, 2003. Later, Ann Trenemann of *The Times* conducted an investigation in the Basra area and published an article entitled "Mapped: The Lethal Legacy of Cluster Bombs" along with part of the UN map "Basra Governorate, Dangerous Areas, August 2003" on September 11, 2003.
11. Cited in *Independent on Sunday*, April 13, 2003.

12. On April 3, 2003, for instance, in the western desert the British Special Forces raided Saddam Hussein's palace on the Tharthar Lake.

13. *Guardian*, April 9, 2003.

14. *Sunday Times*, June 29, 2003.

15. *Independent*, April 7, 2003.

16. July 6, 2003, pp. 34–35.

17. *Sunday Times*, April 20, 2003.

18. Worried about the loss of the Saddam International Airport, Saddam dispatched two senior commanders to the airport to survey the scene and report to him directly. They left, never to return, signalling the start of large state military desertions. Interview with Dr. Mustafa Alani of the Royal United Services Institute, London, August 2003.

19. *Financial Times*, April 25, 2003. The BBC World Service Radio, run as a distinct section with its own mandate and management within the BBC, is more open to dissenting voices in international affairs than its domestic counterpart.

20. *Guardian*, May 28, 2003.

21. *Time*, May 12, 2003, p. 29.

22. See further Dilip Hiro, *Neighbors, Not Friends: Iraq and Iran after the Gulf Wars*, p. 102, p.105.

23. See earlier pp. 196–197.

24. *Independent*, April 17, 2003.

25. *Time*, May 12, 2003, p. 27.

26. Cited in *Independent on Sunday*, April 13, 2003.

27. Later Abu Hatim's aide Ali Atiya claimed, rightly, that Amara was the only city that had liberated itself through its own efforts. *Independent*, June 27, 2003.

28. This was the name of the airport until 1986, when a vastly enlarged facility was inaugurated and given its new name.

29. *Observer Magazine*, July 6, 2003, p. 35.

30. *Sunday Times*, June 29, 2003. See Map, "Greater Baghdad, April 3–11."

31. *Newsday*, July 25, 2003; *The Times*, July 25, 2003.

32. *Independent*, April 9, 2003; *Guardian*, April 9, 2003. On April 14 the Pentagon spokeswoman Victoria Clarke notified the Committee to Protect Journalists in the U.S. that "coalition forces were fired upon and acted in self-defense by returning fire." The committee reported in late May that there was no evidence that U.S. forces were fired upon from the Palestine Hotel. *New York Times*, May 28, 2003.

33. It was no coincidence that Al Jazeera's Basra office at the Sheraton Hotel was also hit.

34. *Independent*, May 27, 2003.

35. The square was named "paradise" because, during the regime of Abdul Karim Qasim (r. 1958–63), the pedestal carried the statue of an unknown soldier who, by virtue of dying for his country, had gone to heaven.

36. The statue, designed in Baghdad and cast in Italy, was erected on Saddam Hussein's sixty-fifth birthday on April 28, 2002.

37. The failure of Afghan women to throw away their head-to-toe shrouds (*burqas*)—much less burn them—after the defeat of the Taliban left scores of Western television and still cameramen pleading with the women to lift the veil just a little to give them a "human interest" visual image of America's triumph in Afghanistan. See further Dilip Hiro, *War Without End*, p. 358.

38. *Observer*, April 20, 2003.

39. *Newsday*, July 25, 2003.

40. Imam al Adham, the Grand Imam, is the honorific of Abu Hanifa al Numan, the founder of the Hanafi code within the Islamic law, which has the largest following among Sunnis.

41. *New York Times*, April 19, 2003; *Guardian*, April 19, 2003.

42. June 15, 2003. The Centcom knew where Raghad and her children were living and had her house under surveillance in the expectation that Saddam would at some point contact her.

43. May 27, 2003.

Chapter 8

WEEK FOUR: ALL OVER, ALMOST

"Who could imagine that Saddam Hussein would fall in this way? My family are pleased that the President is gone—especially my father— but it is hard for us to welcome the Americans."
— Thuraya al Kaissi in her diary, April 10, 2003[1]

"The coalition forces will be led to the weapons of mass destruction as Saddam's regime collapses."
— British prime minister Tony Blair, April 8, 2003[2]

APRIL 10, THE DAY OF LOOTERS

THE PRECIPITATE FALL of Saddam Hussein's regime in Baghdad brought in its train what it had earlier in Nasiriya, Najaf, Karbala, and Basra: arson, looting, and lawlessness. But Baghdad being the national capital, with a population of 5.8 million—a third of them underprivileged Shias—the scale was unprecedented, involving tens of thousands of looters and arsonists.

The ransacking started with government warehouses and other public buildings, and spread to hotels, shops, and the villas of the Sunni elite, including those of Abid Hamid Mahmoud, Barzan Ibrahim al Tikriti, Ali Hassan al Majid, and Saadoun Shakr al Tikriti—the personal secretary, half brother, and first cousins of Saddam, respectively. Using wheelbarrows, donkey carts, pickup trucks, tractor-trailers, and even hijacked red double-decker buses, the looters made off with the "liberation" booty—refrigerators, ceiling fans, television sets, computers, office files, home furnishings, cars—with audacity and verve. By the afternoon they had stripped bare the Central Bank and the ministries of information, education, trade, and finance—as well as the central TV headquarters and several embassies. Those who converged on the villa of Tariq Aziz with pickup trucks and tractor-trailers carted away everything from paintings to plumbing, from cutlery to curtains, sparing only books in English by Richard Nixon and Henry Kissinger and Sicilian Mafia novels by *The Godfather* author Mario Puzo. By now the smoke from the burning ministries and markets filled the air, which had earlier been polluted by the fires raging in the oil-filled trenches around the capital. The Al Araby market went up in flames, as did the Directorate of Identity Documents and Nationalities. All told, 158 government buildings would be ransacked and torched—the glaring exception being the heavily guarded ministry of oil in the Shaikh Omar neighborhood, later to be occupied by U.S. Marines. The wrecked public premises would include ministries and directorates, schools, hospitals, public utilities, police stations, food and medicine warehouses, and public-sector undertakings.

The documents found at the headquarters of the Directorate of General Security (*Muderiye Amn al Aam*) dealing with governmental property and public security by the Lebanese-born Hala Jaber of the *Sunday Times* gave a chilling insight into the workings of the fallen regime's massive security and intelligence apparatus, which vetted even those wishing to change houses or apply for low-grade civil-service jobs. "Hundreds of thousands of charred files lie scattered in the bombed-out headquarters of the *Amn al Aam*," reported Jaber. A study of handwritten notes showed citizens put under surveillance for being "talkative," "trouble-makers," or having "a disreputable wife" or "bad sisters"—or trading with Iran, smuggling, trying to leave Iraq, or visiting the German or Russian embassies—or refusing to participate in Baath Party demonstrations.

Choosing at random, Jaber came across the case of Doreid Farhat Jawal, a Communist Party member who escaped to Czechoslovakia in mid-1979 after being exposed as a party member soon after the party's daily newspaper, *Tareeq al Shaab* (People's Path), was banned in April of that year.[3] As a result, his family was put under surveillance for the next twenty-four years. The handwritten note of March 13, 2003, at the General Security Directorate read: "There was nothing to record against the family which consisted of his sisters—Soudud, living in London as a student, and Ghada living in Australia as a housewife."

Others under suspicion had "secret surveillance" written next to their names. For surveillance, the General Security officers made use of friends, neighbors, and acquaintances. A file marked "Rumors and Public Opinion" noted the following in a neighborhood called New Baghdad in recent days: "The Turkish troops plan to invade and occupy north Iraq once the Americans launch their war." The rumor current in the Zafaraniya district was that "Osama bin Laden has been arrested by the Americans." Each and every document was signed by an officer mentioning his rank.[4] Besides these scattered papers, there were probably stacks of polythene garbage bags filled with documents shredded in a hurry by the security officers in the dying hours of the fallen regime at the back of the damaged building. This had been the case with most of the sixty security and intelligence offices scattered around the capital, as well as the imposing gray-colored headquarters of the General Intelligence Department (*Dariat al Mukhabarat al Ammaa*, commonly called Mukhabarat), which focused on political opposition at home and abroad, in the affluent neighborhood of Mansour that was bombed by Centcom.

A return visit by Muhammad Jassim, a former prisoner—accompanied by Robert Fisk of the *Independent*—to the Kadhimiya neighborhood's security and intelligence station in an upscale villa (once the property of an Iraqi of Iranian origin expelled after the outbreak of the Iran–Iraq War in 1980) under

Hashim al Tikriti, brought home the nefarious activities of Saddam's brutal agencies. Jassim was accused of being a member of the al Daawa al Islamiya (The Islamic Call) faction, which has a following among Shias, and which was as high on the list of Saddam's political targets as the Communist Party. "They put my hands behind my back like this and tied them, and then pulled me in the air by my tied wrists, using the hook in the ceiling [fitted originally to hold an electrical ceiling fan, made redundant later by air conditioning]," said Jassim. "They used a little generator to lift me up, right up to the ceiling. Then they'd release the rope, hoping to break my shoulders when I fell."[5]

Jassim emerged from the torture with all his limbs intact. Others were not so fortunate. "Missing eyes, ears, toenails and tongues mark those who fell into the hands of Saddam's powerful security services," noted Craig Smith of the *New York Times*. "A network of Baath Party informers, intelligence service investigators, secret police and the feared Fedayeen Saddam preyed on the populace to snuff out dissent before it could spread."

Among those who had had their tongues mutilated was Faris Salman Adnan Dulaimi, a twenty-three-year-old Shia merchant in the northern Shia neighborhood of Shaab. His "crime" was that in December 2002 he had brawled with a local intelligence officer (who had arrested Faris's two uncles after the 1991 Shia uprisings) after he and his remaining uncle had gone to the intelligence office for information about the missing uncles. In the heated exchange, Faris was overheard calling Saddam Hussein "the son of a dog" by a member of the Fedayeen Saddam who was in the office within hearing range. To escape instant punishment, Faris and his uncle fled. They returned home after ten days when they received a message that it was safe to do so. It was not. The General Security officers arrested Faris and his uncle. They were in jail for two months and were tortured with electric shock. Then, on March 5, Faris was blindfolded and put into a van. He was now in the hands of the Saffa (lit., elimination) unit of the Fedayeen who, working with the Eieen (lit., eyes) section—charged with finding Saddam's enemies—carried out the punishment: cutting off tongues (for insulting Saddam or Uday), ears (for deserting the military), or hands (for those who stole public property or smuggled).

The van arrived in Shaab in the afternoon with an escort of seven white pickup trucks carrying more than one hundred black-uniformed Fedayeen Saddam. They rounded up the neighbors for a rally outside the café near Faris's house, and asked his mother to bring along a picture of Saddam. One Fedayee kept Faris's arms steady, another held his head in a grip, a third forced open his mouth, and a fourth pointed a gun to his temple. The fifth Fedayee, with a video camera, recorded the scene. "I was standing and they told me to stick my tongue out or they would shoot me, and so I did," said Faris Dulaimi. Then "Ali," a member of the Saffa unit, stepped forward, read aloud the court's verdict, gripped Faris's tongue with a pair of pliers, and sliced it up with a sharp knife without any form of anesthetic, with the severed pieces falling on the ground. Holding up a piece of the tongue to the crowd, "Ali" shouted, "You see this? This will be the fate of anyone who dares insult the president." He then threw the bit on the ground. Another Fedayee scooped it up and said it would be given to Uday "as a present." Others stuffed Faris's mouth with cotton wool and led him back to the van, which took him to a local hospital. There he got five stitches and no painkiller. Then they tossed him back into his cell in the Ziyona Prison.

A fortnight later, when the American bombing started, the prisoners were moved from jail to jail. After the fall of Baghdad, their prison warden decided to release them all—but only after he had each of them sign a statement saying they would return to prison when they were called to do so.[6]

Ticked off by the audacious appearance of Saddam Hussein and his sons in the Adhamiya neighborhood on April 9, Centcom rushed its troops to the district early the next day. They focused on the Imam al Adham Abu Hanifa Mosque, where

Saddam and his close advisers were reported to have taken refuge. The resulting gun battles with Saddam loyalists lasted four hours, during which the dome of the mosque was smashed. But he was not found in the mosque.

Saddam and his sons were, however, very much in the Adhamiya district. Indeed, according to "Abu Tiba," having realized belatedly that his side had lost irretrievably—at least for the time being—Saddam held a closed-door meeting with a handful of top leaders of his regime at a safe house in Adhamiya. They decided to leave Baghdad and mount resistance from the Sunni-majority provinces.[7]

That day, residents of Baghdad had their first taste of living under foreign occupation. Each of the Iraqi men lining up to cross the Tigris by means of one of the twelve bridges was ordered by the American troops to drop his trousers and raise his shirt in full view of others, including women and girls, to demonstrate that he was not a suicide bomber.

In Baghdad the long-oppressed Shias were too busy helping themselves to assorted moveable property to resort to revenge killings, but that was not the case in the south. Such killings were common in Basra, for instance, and had popular support, reported Nicholas Kristof of the *New York Times* from the city. So too was lawlessness, except that it was condemned by the common folk as well as by clerics. "Robbers come at night, 20 to 30 together, and throw grenades, and break into private homes," a middle-aged man told Kristof. "They ask for money, and if they don't get it, they shoot you on the spot."[8]

Najaf witnessed particularly gory murders on April 10. Acting as an intermediary to conciliate different factions among Shias, Abdul Majid Khoei, discreetly armed with a pistol and accompanied by Maad Fayad, a journalist, went to the office of the care-taker of the Imam Ali shrine, Shaikh Haidar al Kalidar, who came out of hiding to meet him. Most Shias in Najaf considered Kalidar to be a stooge of Saddam Hussein and hated him. His appearance drew a crowd of angry Shias outside his office. To disperse the crowd, Khoei reportedly fired pistol shots. This enraged the mob, who considered the use of firearms within the holy shrine sacrilegious. They dragged Kalidar, Khoei, and Fayad out of the shrine and attacked them with knives. Fayad managed to flee, but both Kalidar and Khoei died of stab wounds. The marauders were said to be shouting slogans in favor of Hojatalislam Muqtada al Sadr.[9]

Later, *Newsday* would cite a U.S. source saying Khoei had agreed to use CIA cash to enlist support among prominent Iraqi Shias. "We allocated $13 million to the al Khoei operation," the source said. "It was part of a covert program to strengthen Shiites who are pro-Western, and to recruit new allies. I don't know where the $13 million is. A good chunk of it is missing." This was denied by Abdul Hassan Khafaji, who was in charge of Khoei's finances.[10]

Though he was the only surviving son of the assassinated Grand Ayatollah Muhammad Sadiq al Sadr, the wide-eyed, black-turbaned, richly bearded thirty-year-old Muqtada was only a *hojatalislam* (lit., Proof of Islam) in the Shia religious hierarchy, a rank below ayatollah (lit., Sign of Allah), and based at the Al Kufa Mosque in a run-down neighborhood of Najaf. His religious standing rose sharply when, on April 7, Grand Ayatollah Kadhim Husseini Hairi, based in the Iranian holy city of Qom, appointed him as his deputy in Iraq. Hairi, a native of Iraq, went to Qom in 1973 as a protégé of Ayatollah Muhammad Baqir al Sadr, who was executed by Saddam Hussein's government in 1980 for his opposition to the Baathist rule.[11] Hairi belonged firmly to the interventionist school in Shia Islam, in which clerics play an active role in politics. "Muqtada al Sadr is our deputy and representative in all *fatwa* affairs which need permission from the Faqih [Islamic Jurisprudent], and he is also a deputy who can assign other deputies all over Iraq," said Hairi's declaration. The next day Hairi issued a *fatwa* urging Iraqis to "kill all Saddamists who try to take charge" and "cut short any chance of the return to power of the second-line Baathists." He called on Shia leaders to "seize as many positions as possible to create a fait accompli for any coming government"; to teach the Iraqi people "not to collapse morally before the means used by the Great Satan [the United States] if it stays in Iraq: It will try to spread moral decay, incite lust by allowing easy access to stimulating satellite channels and spread debauchery to weaken the people's faith"; and to abort the Great Satan's plans. Claiming to be acting in the name of the prestigious Hawza al Ilmiya, Muqtada al Sadr started sending signed letters and cash by couriers to Shia clerics in Iraq and deputizing clerics, who in turn appointed officials to run everything from civil-defense militias to post offices, and authorized the seizure of public institutions.[12] Thus the Hawza, until then a virtual monopoly of Grand Ayatollah Sistani, came to contain partisans of both quietist and interventionist schools. While refraining from issuing religious decrees on day-to-day affairs, Sistani sent his representatives to the Shia communities in Iraq and took a public stand on such significant issues as the stance toward the infidel invaders; the relationship with the occupying Anglo-American forces; looting public and private property; and revenge killings. Through his son, Muhammad Rida, the grand ayatollah declared, "I want to see Iraq governed by Iraqis and not by Americans."

Muqtada al Sadr's deputy in Baghdad's Saddam City was Shaikh Muhammad Fartousi. He in turn appointed Sayyid Hashim, who had arrived from Najaf as the messenger of al Sadr, to take charge of the local Qadisiya Hospital. Hashim asked what the hospital's needs were. "We provided the goods from the government warehouses that had been protected from looting," he told Roula Khalaf, the Arabic-speaking Middle East editor of the *Financial Times*. "We are also paying salaries to employees. The office of al Sadr has a lot of money and it is running the affairs of society. Security [in Sadr City] has been restored and guidance from the Hawza al Ilmiya has ended the chaos."[13]

In the north, the Kurdish militia entered Mosul (population 1.8 million), a city that was two-thirds Arab, after a cease-fire agreement with the commander of the Iraqi garrison. The truce was the result of severe bombing, where the Americans made liberal use of cluster bombs and ammunition, a tactic also deployed by the Centcom in the Kirkuk area.[14] "We did not call it an Iraqi surrender, because we took no prisoners and we let them keep their guns," said Mishan Jubbouri, a broadcaster on local Kurdish television, who claimed to be involved in arranging the covert deal.[15] The celebrations that followed turned into looting and arson—which included the torching of the historic market. Soon Iraqi soldiers would abandon their arms and head south in civilian clothes.

The oil fields around Kirkuk, which produce about a third of Iraq's petroleum output of three million barrels per day, had been secured by paratroopers of the U.S. 173rd Airborne Division. The militia of the Patriotic Union of Kurdistan (PUK) entered Kirkuk (population 600,000) after the Iraqi troops abandoned the city following heavy bombardment by the U.S. B-52 bombers. This violated the agreement between Turkey and the United States that the Kurdish forces in Iraqi Kurdistan would not enter either Kirkuk or Mosul—a move that the Turkish government feared would lead to the emergence of an independent Kurdistan in northern Iraq, which would revive the irredentist movement among Turkey's ethnic Kurds. Under pressure from the Pentagon, the PUK agreed to withdraw its troops. In reality, though, its militia merely changed clothes, transforming themselves from fighters to returnees to a city from which they claimed to have been expelled by Saddam's regime. Noting this, the Turkish government continued to protest, threatening to send its troops into northern Iraq to "control the terrorists." There was much nervousness in Ankara.

By contrast, in Paris the French government felt relieved, confident that with Baghdad's fall, the Anglo-American invasion would soon end. President Chirac said, "France, like every [other] democracy, welcomes the fall of Saddam Hussein's dictatorship and hopes there will be a rapid and effective end to the fighting." He called for UN involvement in the rapid restoration of Iraq's economy and "full sovereignty," thus hinting his opposition to any U.S. plans to preserve a long-term political-economic influence over a post-Saddam government. While expressing his delight at the downfall of Saddam Hussein's regime, French foreign minister Dominique de Villepin said, "We must ensure that what is today cherished by the Iraqi people becomes the hope of the entire region toward a settlement of the Israel-Palestinian conflict."[16]

APRIL 11

Though Centcom had not fully secured southern and central Iraq, it shifted the focus of fighting to the north of Baghdad, with the city of Tikrit, near Auja, the native village of Saddam Hussein, as its main target. Tikrit was the northern headquarters of the Republican Guard and the site of Saddam's largest presidential palace complex, spread over 2.5 square miles (6.5 square kilometers). The Centcom bombed it heavily, with its Special Forces on the ground painting the targets.

On April 11, the oil city of Khanaqin, just outside the southernmost tip of Kurdistan, changed hands as the Iraqi troops withdrew and the Kurdish militia moved in.

That day George Bush and Tony Blair appeared on Freedom TV, beamed into Iraqi homes after local Iraqi TV was off the air permanently. Centcom issued playing-card pictures of the fifty-five most-wanted Iraqis (Aces: Spades, Saddam; Clubs, Qusay; Hearts, Uday; Diamonds, Abid Hamid Mahmoud, and so on) to its search parties and others.

Iraqis on the run had three options: Either go underground in the urban sprawl of Greater Baghdad or in the Sunni heartland to its west and northwest, or seek temporary refuge in Syria as a stopover for an onward journey to Belarus or Georgia. Therefore the Iraqi town of Qaim along the Syrian border, protected by the Special Republican Guard, suffered raids by U.S. bombers.

However, the four aces sought by the Centcom were very much in Baghdad. On April 11, Saddam and his two sons attended the Friday noon prayer at the Imam al Adham Abu Hanifa Mosque in the Adhamiya district, according to "Abu Tiba," one of Uday's bodyguards. (See Map, "Greater Baghdad, April 3–11.") Word of their presence circulated rapidly among the congregation, and as they left the mosque, they were mobbed. It was then that, answering an old woman's probing question about his actions, Saddam blamed the treachery of his commanders for the defeat. That was Saddam's last public appearance.

Later that day, according to General Saifuddin Hassan al Rawi, No. 12 in the deck of playing cards, Saddam split from his sons, with Qusay pleading with him in the car for them to stay with him. Saddam replied, "Splitting up gives us a better chance of survival."[17] Later, his sons would discard his counsel and stay together, and pay the ultimate price. Another passenger in the car was Saddam's personal secretary, Abid Mahmoud. Saddam would separate from him soon afterward.

Unlike his sons, who grew up in luxury, Saddam was the son of a landless peasant who died before his birth. He was punished harshly by his stepfather and sent to school at the age of ten by his maternal uncle, in whose house he had taken refuge after running away from home. He was a self-made man who on his way up the political ladder had made many enemies—whom he had so far outwitted. As early as 1959 he became a fugitive when he was a member of the team that tried, unsuccessfully, to assassinate Iraqi prime minister Abdul Karim Qasim. Since then he had learned how to protect himself, and had survived many attempts on his life.[18] A key element of his personal security was that he slept in a different bed every night. He did so by maintaining dozens of safe houses in and around Baghdad, all ready to receive him at a moment's notice. And he always left his choice to the very last minute. This pattern of his became so internalized that even on such monumental issues as accepting or rejecting UN Security Council Resolution 1441, he would decide at the eleventh hour.

A typical safe house of Saddam's discovered by U.S. forces was one in an "upscale neighborhood in central Baghdad"—most probably Mansour. The split-level one-bedroom house had a sunken bar stocked with vintage Italian wines, expensive cognacs, and Scotch whiskeys—the same brands found in his other presidential palaces, where meals were often served on the official china of the Kuwait royal family—carrying the Sabah family seal and decorated in gold and maroon trim—stolen from Kuwait in 1990. The Mansour safe house had a mirrored bedroom with lamps shaped like women and framed prints of such scenes as a topless blonde woman perched on a stone pedestal pointing to a huge snake that had entwined a muscular naked man—also blond—as he tried to decapitate the open-mouthed snake with its tongue protruding; and a dragon with its talons extended swooping on an aroused woman in chains. The high camp paintings on the wall turned out to be the work of Rowena Morrill, a New York artist and the daughter of an Army chaplain—like one of the many now providing spiritual comfort to tens of thousands of American GIs in Iraq.

Just then a few thousand GIs were conducting mopping-up operations in Karbala. In Hilla it was only after heavy combat between 4,500 paratroopers of the U.S. 101st Airborne Division and the Fedayeen that the former finally managed to occupy the town. In Diwaniya, the Iraqis' attacks on U.S. supply lines with mortars and rocket-propelled grenades resulted in an eight-hour firefight. In Najaf, Iraqi snipers continued to target the U.S. forces. As if this were not enough, intra-Shia tensions escalated in the city. Supporters of the radical Muqtada al Sadr demanded that Sistani leave Najaf within forty-eight hours. Sistani's acolytes whisked him away to a safe house.

This incident, however, did not interrupt the process whereby, in the wake of the political-administrative vacuum created by Saddam Hussein's ouster, the Najaf-based Hawza al Ilmiya, the clerical conclave dominated by Sistani, was becoming the nerve center of the Shia network. It was operating through the mosques nationwide to administer to scores of neighborhoods in Iraq's urban centers, which included providing armed vigilantes to maintain law and order.

In the southern border town of Samawa, sniping and attempted suicide bombings were the order of the day as far as the Iraqis were concerned, while protesters in Zubair demanded the withdrawal of the Anglo-American forces.

To show that it was serious about reconstructing Iraq after having decimated it, the Bush administration named Umm Qasr as the base of the U.S. Office for Reconstruction and Humanitarian Assistance (ORHA), to be headed by retired general Jay Garner, a friend of Rumsfeld and a staunch supporter of Israel. Without consulting Colin Powell, Rumsfeld gave Garner an eighteen-month contract. Garner set up his office on April 14, only to see President Bush name L. Paul Bremer as his successor three weeks later.

Umm Qasr itself was a prime candidate for reconstruction. According to a report by a *Wall Street Journal* correspondent, following the ouster of the local Baath Party officials in the town, the police fled, and the fighting and bombing had left the industrial and municipal infrastructure in tatters.

In Ramadi, west of Baghdad, Centcom dropped six bunker-buster bombs on a complex housing-and-intelligence center, acting on a tip that Barzan Ibrahim al Tikriti, a half-brother of Saddam (and a mere five of clubs in the playing-card deck), was inside. He was not. He would be apprehended in Baghdad several days later.

The capital remained unstable, with bitter fighting in the northern neighborhood of Waziriya. In the Mansour district the checkpoints manned by the non-Iraqi Fedayeen Saddam were so well established that Centcom had to bomb them.

Looting continued unabated. "The wanton destruction of St. George's church was unexpected," reported Suzanne Goldenberg of the *Guardian*. "The looters at the church stole the pews, and hacked through the First World War plaque on the wall for a treasure. They also made off with the TV set of the pitifully poor caretaker. Soldiers in a U.S. tank watched it happen."[19] There were numerous such dispatches sent by foreign journalists.

It was once again Thuraya al Kaissi who provided the rare personal touch. *"Oh, my God! All this looting!"* she wrote on April 11. *"Why don't the Americans stop them? The looters are smashing everything. They have stolen everything from the Further Education College where my father works, and then they set it on fire. They even stole the fire engines! Why don't the Americans stop them?"*

This question was uppermost in the minds of all those who witnessed the looters ransacking and torching building after building, and the scandalous failure of the U.S. forces to do anything. "If they [the American troops] had shot a few of the looters at the beginning, the looting would have stopped," said an Iraqi doctor. "Instead, I saw them standing by, taking photographs, cheering the looters." They reflected the view held by senior Bush officials as well as the president himself. To them, large-scale looting was a commendable manifestation of the popular rage against a tyrannical dictatorship that had just been overthrown, an example of mass catharsis. In the words of Rumsfeld, "It's untidy, and freedom is untidy; and free people are free to make mistakes and commit crimes and do bad things." There was actually a much deeper rationale, which Bush, in an interview explaining his Afghanistan policy, articulated: His strategy there was "to create chaos, to create a vacuum" in the belief that out of this vacuum "good would come."[20] But to allow—even encourage—people to pillage on a monumental scale led some commentators to call Bush and Rumsfeld the most boneheaded philistines since Hulagu, a grandson of Genghis Khan who torched Baghdad, the capital of the Islamic empire, in 1258.

While the fall of Baghdad four days earlier than planned had created euphoria in the political and military circles in Washington and London, in occupied Iraq the Anglo-American troops were too jumpy to savor the ousting of Saddam. In Nasiriya, for instance, U.S. Marines, fearing a suicide attack, opened fire on a minibus, killing two children and injuring nine adults.

"At a checkpoint we encountered some extremely nervous U.S. Marines," reported David Willis of the BBC from Baghdad. "Because I was on the phone at the time they made me lie in the road. They forced me from the car at gunpoint because they are nervous about people with cell phones, which they believe are being used to orchestrate attacks on Americans. It gives you some idea of how jittery people are."[21]

Over the coming weeks and months the nervousness would get worse, and a chastened Bush administration would approach the UN Security Council members to share the increasingly onerous burden—political, military, and financial—of occupying Iraq, but with little success. France, Russia, and Germany were not prepared to act as subordinates of the United States. Their common stance was spelled out at the summit of President Chirac, President Vladmir Putin, and Chancellor Gerhard Schroder in St. Petersburg, Russia, on April 11. Expressing a common view, Putin welcomed Saddam Hussein's downfall with a caveat: "We are against changing regimes by use of force. While Che Guevera's attempt to export socialist revolution thankfully failed, now Bush was trying to export capitalist revolution." The three leaders resolved to repair the damage done to the United Nations by the Anglo-Americans by bringing them back into international law and to ensure that the reconstruction of Iraq was done under the UN aegis—aims they would fail to achieve fully, despite the fact that three out of five Americans wanted the United Nations to play "a significant role" in Iraq.

APRIL 12

"Today I hear my school has been looted," wrote Thuraya on 12 April. *"My friend came to the house and said everything was gone. When will we ever have a normal life?"*

Far worse calamity hit Iraq—more like humanity at large—that day. The National Museum, containing Iraq's archaeological collection of 170,000 items, was looted, resulting in the loss of 3,000 items, most of them invaluable ancient artifacts.[22] After having been closed during the run-up to the 1991 Gulf War, the refurbished museum reopened only in 2000. In anticipation of the Anglo-American invasion, the Iraqi troops dug trenches and set up defensive positions around it. There was a two-day gun battle between the Iraqis and the Americans after the latter's entry into Baghdad. The skeleton staff of the museum fled. Toward the end, the desperate Fedayeen broke into a storeroom to set up a machine-gun nest at a window. Once the last of the Fedayeen was put to flight on April 12, the looting began.

"In the city's most important museum, the mob has turned upon its own heritage, stealing and systematically smashing priceless antiquities that once were the glory of Iraq," wrote Robert Fisk in the *Independent on Sunday*. "Our feet crunched on the wreckage of 5,000-year-old marble plinths and stone statuary and pots that had endured every siege of Baghdad, every invasion of Iraq throughout history—only to be destroyed when America came to 'liberate' the city. The Iraqis did it. They did it to their own history, of the Assyrians and the Babylonians, the Sumerians, the Medes, the Persians and the Greeks." In darkness, Fisk tipped over statues and stumbled into broken winged bulls. "When I shone my torch over one far shelf, I drew in my breath. Every pot and jar—'3500 BC' it said on one shelf corner—had been bashed to pieces."

According to Neil McGregor, director of the British Museum in London, "This was without question the greatest disaster for a national collection since the Second World War." Yet, when told of "the vandalizing of relics of the birth of civilization," Rumsfeld said, "It is the same picture of somebody walking out of some building with a vase, and you see it 20 times. And you think, My goodness, were there that many vases? Is it possible that there were that many vases in the whole country?"[23] Such cultural illiteracy left most people in "old Europe" and elsewhere baffled and angry. Despite a worldwide outcry at the loss of archaeological treasures of the era when human civilization as we know it was emerging—with settled agriculture, the alphabet, the numerical system, and time measurement—it would be April 21 before the U.S. Civil Affairs brigade arrived.

In the meantime, the dominant mood in Baghdad was anger, stemming from continued anarchy and lack of electricity and water.[24] "The Americans are calling for people who could restore the water treatment systems, electricity and police," reported Caroline Hawley of the BBC in Baghdad. "There is a major catch [though]: there is no system to pay them."

APRIL 13–14

While the United States allowed Turkey to send its military observers to Iraqi Kurdistan to check whether the two Kurdish parties had withdrawn their fighters from Mosul and Kirkuk, it was unable to compel the KDP and the PUK to do so: It had only 380 Special Forces commandos in the area, aside from the paratroopers guarding the oil fields. By contrast, the KDP and the PUK had deployed ten thousand troops in the two northern cities. In Mosul, the uneasy relationship between the majority Arabs and minority Kurds, now emboldened by the presence of the Kurdish militia, deteriorated into interethnic violence in which more than twenty people were killed. During the mayhem, the rare book and manuscript library of Mosul University was sacked, a forerunner to similar destruction in Baghdad. That day the museum in Kirkuk, controlled by the PUK militia, was looted. A similar fate befell the major sculpture in the ancient cities of Nineveh, Nimrud, and Hatra.

Centcom remained focused on Tikrit. Following massive bombing on April 12, more than three thousand troops of the U.S. First Marine Expeditionary Force entered the city, which appeared deserted. But, once they were inside, they faced a fierce attack by the Iraqi tanks. The resulting combat was also intense. By the next day, the American forces had prevailed, but pockets of resistance remained. That day the Bush administration put a $200,000 bounty on Saddam Hussein's head.

A week after its second "Thunder Run" into Baghdad, Centcom had not established control over all of the sprawling city. By its own account, its writ did not run in ten to fifteen of the capital's fifty-five to sixty zones. It attributed the continuing resistance to "the non-Iraqi foreign volunteers," implying that the local residents were pliant. That was hardly the inference one could draw from Rumsfeld's statement that "there's a transition period [in Iraq], and no one is in control. That's what happens when you go from dictatorship with repressed order to something that is going to be different."[25]

Actually, unknown to him and Centcom, an indigenous institution was taking control, surreptitiously, in many parts of Iraq. It was the Shia mosque as represented by the Hawza al Ilmiya in Najaf. On April 13, the Hawza activated its long-established underground communications system, perfected under Saddam Hussein, which relied exclusively on conveying messages in coded words through trusted messengers, avoiding written notes and the telephone, and distributed photocopied instructions to all Shia mosques in the country through messengers. It instructed clerics to set up local committees to organize the affairs of the neighborhood as well as all civil and religious activities. These clerics collected looted property on the premises of mosques to be returned to the owners, public or private. The activities of Shia clerics became common knowledge in Saddam City, the largest Shia suburb of Baghdad, whose name had been changed instantly to Sadr City, after the assassinated Grand Ayatollah Muhammad Sadiq al Sadr, in the wake of the fall of Baghdad.

While validating old regime documents with his religious ink stamp, Shaikh Amir al Muwamadawi said, "The clergy is taking control over what is happening in the streets, especially here in Sadr City. We are not seeking power or gains. We want security. There is an eagerness to establish an Islamic state in this country." He described relations with the Anglo-American forces as "sensitive," and added, "The British and Americans would not accept invaders. How can we?"[26] At Buratha Mosque in another Shia district of Baghdad, the senior cleric, Shaikh Saad al Safar, claimed that they had secured water plants and electricity substations and hospitals, and that Shia defense committees, with members wearing dark green fatigues and carrying Kalashnikovs, were manning checkpoints.

They were of course nowhere near the National Library and Archives, established in 1920 and containing nearly two million books, documents, and newspapers, or the Awqaf Library, full of Qurans belonging to the Ministry of Religious Affairs, in the downtown area. Both were torched on April 14, with the National Library smoldering for two days. "When I caught sight of the Quranic Library burning, I raced to the offices of the occupying power, the U.S. Marines' Civil Affairs Bureau," reported Robert Fisk. "An officer shouted to a colleague that 'this guy says some biblical [sic] library is on fire.' I gave the map location, the precise name—in Arabic and English. I said that smoke could be seen from miles away and it would take only five minutes to drive there. Half an hour later, there wasn't an American at the scene—and the flames were shooting 200 feet in the air." Between six hundred to seven hundred manuscripts in the library were burned, and more than one thousand, stolen. The tragedy was that many of them were over a thousand years old. "When Baghdad fell to the Mongols in 1258, these books survived," said a Ministry of Religious Affairs official. "If you talk to any intellectual Muslims in the world, they are crying right now."[27] Also ransacked was the Saddam Manuscript Library, with forty thousand manuscripts.

APRIL 15–16

Having captured Qaim, the American troops cut off the Iraqi-Syrian oil pipeline, which had helped Iraq offset to some extent the negative impact of UN sanctions. That day the residents of Mosul had their first taste of freedom of speech. U.S. troops fired on an anti-American political rally in the city and killed ten people.

Centcom conceded that it controlled only the western part of Tikrit, with its eastern part, on the other side of the Tigris, still under pro-Saddam forces. (See Map, "Week ending April 16, 2003.")

By now, Nasiriya and the surrounding area had been sufficiently pacified to enable the U.S. military to assemble eighty Iraqi delegates at Talil air base, in the shadow of the four-thousand-year-old ziggurat of Ur, the birthplace of Abraham, to discuss the political future of Iraq. The meeting was opened by Jay Garner, head of the U.S. ORHA, and chaired by Zalmay Khalilzad, a personal envoy of President Bush. The two Kurdish parties attended in full force, as did other factions recognized by Washington, except the Supreme Council of Islamic Revolution in Iraq (SCIRI). Some tribal leaders turned up as well. While the delegates deliberated at Talil, deciding finally to hold a larger meeting in eleven days in nearby Nasiriya, twenty thousand Shias demonstrated against the United States and called for an Islamic Iraq, shouting "No no to America, no no to Saddam (*La la Amreeka, la la Saddam*)," bracketing the two in the same breath.

Significantly, the protesters in Kut (population 300,000), the capital of Wasit province in the south-central region, also shouted "No no to America, no no to Saddam," and referred not to "liberation" by the United States but to its "aggression." They were followers of Shaikh Said Abbas, a fifty-two-year-old tribal leader and former teacher with a square face and well-trimmed gray beard. A suave and charming man, Abbas came to Kut from his native village when he was twenty-two and became a schoolteacher. For his refusal to join the Baath Party, he was arrested and tortured. When

Kut fell to U.S. forces, he was woken up in his sleep in the middle of the night by his followers and carried to city hall. He declared himself mayor and took up residence there. City officials came to pay him homage, and exiled Iraqi Shias returning from Iran arrived carrying banners reading, "Freedom Yes; Occupation No." His claim to mayoralty was challenged by Colonel Ron Johnson, the U.S. Marine commander of the sector. The U.S. Special Forces men hanging around their headquarters at the main local hotel said they had considered assassinating Abbas.[28] Oblivious to this threat to his life, Abbas addressed a thousand faithful at Friday prayers on April 18. "Iraq cannot be unified until it is governed by its own people," he said. "To this end we will sacrifice ourselves." The stand-off would continue for several days, with the police station manned by "collaborating" policemen being burned down five days later.

The rise of the Shias, forming 60 percent of the Iraqi population and suppressed since 1638, when Mesopotamia was incorporated into the empire of Sunni Ottoman Turks, was to be expected. Indeed this was one of the main reasons why in 1991 President George Bush Sr. had shied away from supporting the Shia uprisings against Saddam Hussein.

Now feelings ran high as hundreds of thousands of Shias marched or drove from all over Iraq to Karbala to commemorate the fortieth anniversary of Imam Hussein's death, a ceremony forbidden by the secular Baathist regime since 1974.

That day, forty U.S. Marines raided the house of Dr. Rihab Taha, the biologist wife of General Amr Muhammad Rashid, former oil minister, but failed to find evidence of Iraq's alleged weapons of mass destruction.

Once U.S. forces had pacified the eastern section of Tikrit on April 16, the latest Gulf war, lasting four weeks, was over for all practical purposes—although it was not until May 1 that President Bush announced a formal end to "major operations" against Iraq.

AFTER APRIL 16

Security continued to elude Baghdadis, *"(Syrian/Lebanese/Iraqi) Fedayeen were somewhere in the area,"* wrote Salam Pax on April 17. *"They go hide in civilian districts to shoot a single useless mortar shell or a couple of Kalashnikov shots which bounce without any effect on the armored vehicles. But the answer is a hell of mortars or whatever on all the houses in the area from where the shot came. This has been happening all over Baghdad. I still can't bring myself to sleep upstairs. I'd rather sleep under as many walls and roofs as possible. Fist-size shrapnel gets through the first wall but might be stopped by the next."*

As a consequence, the toll of civilian deaths in the capital kept rising. The estimate was put at 1,700 to 2,356, with another 2,000 or so missing, and a further 10,000 injured.

What about Suha Abdul Rahman al Azi, an Iraqi Airways ticket agent, and Ammar Khadham al Habibi, an Oil Ministry administrator, and their families?

"I am sad because it was like losing one of our sons when we watched the Americans coming in," said al Azi. "And lots of innocent people were killed, especially children. A missile landed very close to where we were staying with my husband's brother even though there was no military base or soldiers around. We came back home two days after the Americans came into the city so we could protect the house from looting. Everything was fine here but this morning the Americans exploded a bomb in a school across the street and blew out the windows. . . . I am very sad about the airport because it is almost destroyed. I had my friends who were caught there during the fighting and some of them were killed. And I worry about the buildings. They spent 12 years building it and it was the biggest one in the Middle East. There is too much tragedy around. People are still crying about those who died, and the Americans are everywhere. There are no jobs and no money from the government. What happened in Baghdad was a big surprise. We expected the Iraqis to do something, to fight. We believed the minister of information, al Sahhaf. Where did our leaders go? Why did the army disappear? We were so disappointed. We hoped we would win this war. Even without the leaders, we put our hope in the [Iraqi] people. We thought they would fight; instead, they looted. Or maybe the looters came from outside the country. As an Iraqi, it will be very hard [for me] to work with an American government." She neatly summed up the views of those who were loyal Baath Party members.[29]

Ammar Khadham al Habibi was thankful that he and his family survived unharmed. "We expected chemical weapons [from the Americans], we thought we would die, we expected the worst," he said. "But now we think of all those people who died for nothing. What for? Why? Where is our leader?" As an Oil Ministry employee, he was asked to report for work on May 1. But when he arrived at the ministry, nobody was allowed inside. "You know why the [oil] ministry was saved—this is a war for oil," he said. "The Americans want to protect their interests and everything else can be destroyed. When I went to the ministry of oil, I pointed to the ministry of irrigation, which was burning nearby, and asked why they did not protect that too. The [American] soldiers said it was not their job. I told them that the people who [now] love you will start to hate you."[30]

THE FINAL COUNT

During the four-week invasion, Centcom's 1,800 aircraft mounted 37,000 air sorties, involving 20,000 strikes, of which 15,800 were directed at ground forces, 1,400 at air forces, and 800 at suspected hiding places and installations for proscribed weapons, including surface-to-surface missiles. Of the 28,000 bombs and missiles dropped or fired—about half directed at the Republican Guard—23,000 were precision-guided missiles, 750 were cruise missiles, and 725 were Tomahawk missiles. Centcom dropped 1,566 cluster bombs and an unspecified number of cluster munitions. (See Map, "Week ending April 16, 2003.") It used dozens of napalm bombs. The total cost of the invasion was $45 billion.[31]

In human terms, the Pentagon lost 191 soldiers, and Britain lost 31. By contrast, according to Iraqi Body Count, the Anglo-American research group, Iraqi civilian fatalities were between 6,000 and 7,000, and military casualties, dead and injured, were between 10,000 and 45,000.[32]

NOTES

1. *Sunday Mirror*, April 13, 2003.
2. Cited in *Independent*, April 11, 2003.
3. The Iraqi Communist Party, the strongest and best organized in the Middle East, was the first to suffer the jack-boot of Saddam Hussein on his way to supreme power in July 1979. See Dilip Hiro, *The Essential Middle East*, p. 113.
4. For a full description of Iraq's several security and intelligence agencies, see Dilip Hiro, *Neighbors, Not Friends: Iraq and Iran after the Gulf War*, pp. 54–56.
5. April 17, 2003.
6. *New York Times*, April 25, 2003.
7. *Newsday*, July 25, 2003; *The Times*, July 25, 2003.
8. April 12, 2003.
9. In August the local authorities, working with the occupying U.S. forces, arrested twelve suspects in the murder. *New York Times*, August 26, 2003. For an interview with Dr. Haidar Muhammad Hussein al Kalidar regarding Saddam Hussein's religious lineage, see Dilip Hiro, *Iraq: In the Eye of the Storm*, pp. 71–72.
10. *Newsday*, May 2, 2003; *Guardian*, May 3, 2003.
11. See further Dilip Hiro, *The Longest War: The Iran-Iraq Military Conflict*, p. 28 and p. 35. In 1999 the late ayatollah's cousin, Grand Ayatollah Muhammad Sadiq al Sadr, was reportedly assassinated by Saddam's henchmen.
12. *New York Times*, April 26, 2003.
13. April 25, 2003.
14. See Map, "Iraq:Places of Resistance and Oil Fields."
15. *New York Times*, August 10, 2003.
16. *Independent*, April 11, 2003.
17. *Sunday Times*, June 29, 2003.

18. For a biography of Saddam Hussein, see Dilip Hiro, *The Essential Middle East*, pp. 195–99.

19. April 25, 2003.

20. Cited in *International Herald Tribune,* April 7, 2003.

21. Cited in *Independent on Sunday*, April 13, 2003.

22. Chicago University's Oriental Department listed the three thousand missing objects. *Sunday Times*, April 20, 2003. Baghdad's National Museum was the seventh-largest archaeological museum in the world.

23. Cited in *New York Times*, April 22, 2003.

24. By then the British troops in Basra had arranged joint patrols with local police to quell civil disorder and looting.

25. *Financial Times*, April 14, 2003.

26. *Guardian*, April 15, 2003.

27. *New York Times*, April 15, 2003. "These collections offered a representative sample of the intellectual output of Islamic civilization," said Tim Winter, a divinity lecturer at Cambridge University in Britain. "The loss of a thousand years of interpretation will impoverish Islamic thought, and strengthen the extremists indifferent to it anyway."

28. *New York Times*, April 19, 2003.

29. *Guardian*, May 8, 2003.

30. Ibid.

31. *Time*, May 12, 2003, p. 27; *Washington Post*, July 20, 2003.

32. *Guardian*, August 19, 2003. In addition, there were deaths of American and British soldiers for non-combat reasons.

PART III · THE AFTERMATH

CHAPTER 9

IRAQ UNDER OCCUPATION

"We dominate the scene and we will continue to impose our will on this country [Iraq]."
—L. Paul Bremer, U.S. proconsul to Iraq, in BBC-TV interview on
June 29, 2003[1]

"The struggle with the Americans has to be carefully managed, 'the electric shock' method must be applied: relentless shocks that haunt the Americans all the time everywhere, without giving them a break to regain balance or power."
—A militant Islamist website[2]

"No one likes to have their country invaded and their army defeated, even if it was for a good reason. I would prefer to be governed badly by Iraqis than governed well by foreigners."
—A former Iraqi soldier in Ramadi[3]

"If you tell people you are going to war because there is an imminent threat to national security, and then in the aftermath nothing is found, it opens up a credibility gap of a kind that is dangerous in a democracy. It is hard to sustain the thesis that Iraq was weaponized at operational readiness as we were led to believe."
—Dame Pauline Neville-Jones, former head of the Joint Intelligence
Committee of the United Kingdom, on BBC News 24
on July 4, 2003 [4]

THE BUSH TEAM had counted on Iraq's long-suppressed Shia majority to be in the vanguard of those greeting American forces as liberators. They had been expected to cooperate with them in creating the New Iraq as dreamed of by the neocons—a multiparty democracy, with the country's denationalized petroleum industry thrown open to U.S. oil giants and its government signing a peace treaty with Israel to end the war it had declared against the newly established state in 1948.

Now, to Washington's great dismay, Iraqi Shias had taken to demonstrating against the American "occupation," shouting slogans like "No, no to America; no, no to Saddam" and "No, no to America; yes, yes to Islam (*La la Amreeka, Nam nam Islam*)."

The commanders of the U.S. occupation forces were so ignorant about the workings of the Shia mosques in Iraq that it was only on April 18, the second Friday after their capture of Baghdad, that they realized that Shia clerics had taken over the administration of the capital's Sadr City, with its million-strong Shia population. That day hundreds of young Shias in blue uniforms, armed with Kalashnikovs, were out in the streets—as worshipers congregated for their weekly prayers in mosques and heard sermons exhorting them to "unite with one another and send America and Britain out of our country"—to man checkpoints, guard public places, and mingle with the crowds.

In the larger, national context, what conveyed, dramatically, the full force of the religious Shias not only to the American officers in Iraq but also to their political masters in Washington was the gathering of one and a half million Shias—men and women—in Karbala to commemorate the fortieth day of mourning the death of Imam Hussein in 681 A.D., a memorial banned by the Baathists for nearly thirty years.[5] Karbala was now run by a recently elected ten-member council, led by Shaikh Abdul Mahdi al Karbali, and patrolled by the largely unloved Free Iraqi Force of the INC, with the U.S. troops controlling the territory a few miles away. As portrayed in countless color prints, Imam Hussein was a bearded, turbaned warrior with a strong face and large expressive eyes, astride a white stallion. He was the second son of Imam Ali, a cousin and son-in-law of Prophet Muhammad. The main current into this sea of pilgrims flowing toward Karbala from the south was a fifty-mile (eighty-kilometer) convoy of ramshackle taxis, shining Korean mini-buses, over-used Japanese pickup trucks, and plodding donkey carts—interspersed with the rare air-conditioned bus. Many of the faithful carried green flags of Islam reading "Imam Hussein, we are coming for you." The last words of Imam Hussein—"Death with dignity is better than a life of humiliation"—seemed pertinent to most pilgrims. On the outside wall of Imam Hussein's shrine a decree issued by Grand Ayatollah Ali Sistani read, "No one should join a political party without a cleric's permission [because the parties' agendas remain unclear]." Nearby, Sistani's deputy said, "Our celebration will be perfect only when the American occupier is gone and the Iraqi people are able to rule themselves by the principles of Islam."

The Shia ritual is centered around the betrayal of Imam Hussein in his hour of need by those who had invited him to fight for what was right. Believers mortify themselves to expiate the guilt they feel for failing the Martyred Imam. The more pious arrive bearing whips of mortification—such as thick cat-o'-nine-tails made from chains—to flagellate themselves. "For 25 years these whips were hidden in our houses [banned by the Sunni-dominated Baathist regime]," a mourner told the *New York Times*. "The father taught his son how to flagellate." Most Shias, however, limited themselves to beating their chests rhythmically while chanting "Hussein, Hussein"; the few zealots lashed their shoulders and backs with chain whips to draw blood as the chanting rhythm-keeper shouted into a battery-powered loudspeaker, "Yes, yes, Hawza; yes, yes, Iraq." When footage of this ritual was transmitted into millions of American homes and offices, it conveyed dramatically the strength and religious zealotry of Iraqi Shias—much to the discomfiture and embarrassment of prowar U.S. politicians and opinion-makers.

On this fortieth day of commemoration, the sermons from Shia mosques called on Iraqis to take the destiny of their country into their hands and for Shias to take their rightful place in post-Saddam Iraq. A specific call was also issued to avenge the assassination of Grand Ayatollah Muhammad Baqir al Sadr by Saddam's agents. Banners held high read, "Bush = Saddam"; "No, no, to America; yes, yes, to Islam."

The book stalls did a busy trade selling tracts by Iran's Ayatollah Ruhollah Khomeini, who was a close friend of Ayatollah Muhammad Baqir al Sadr, and by other hard-line clerics, such as Grand Ayatollah Kadhim Husseini Hairi, who, based in the Iranian holy city of Qom, had appointed Hojatalislam Muqtada al Sadr his sole deputy in Iraq.

All this was too much for Donald Rumsfeld. In an interview with the Associated Press, he said that the United States would not allow an Iranian-style religious government to rule Iraq[6] So much for the right to self-determination for Iraqis, the purported end purpose of Operation "Iraqi Freedom." But Shia clerics had an answer for Rumsfeld: If the Iraqi people chose to have an Iranian-style Islamic democracy, that was their "inalienable right," and no foreigner had the right to exclude any option for them.

But Rumsfeld was then too immersed in a self-congratulatory mood to take heed of criticism. After all, having devised a highly innovative military plan, he had trounced an army of nearly four hundred thousand—albeit an armed force poorly equipped and lacking air cover—in less than a month, and occupied a country the size of California. He was so intoxicated with his recent triumph that at the cocktail party he threw to celebrate Baghdad's capture, he deliberately excluded Colin Powell from the guest list. By contrast, the list of invitees included the representatives of all the members of the "Coalition of the Willing"—down to the micro-dots of the Marshall Islands in the Pacific Ocean.

As it happened, the Pacific Ocean would be the background to Bush's declaration of a formal end to the war on Iraq aboard the

USS *Abraham Lincoln* aircraft carrier, anchored off San Diego, on May 1. Poised in the copilot's seat in a Navy submarine hunting and refueling jet, a four-seater Viking S-3B, he arrived at the deck of the aircraft carrier dressed as a pilot. He emerged with a flourish, waving, conscious of his "Top Gun" flight suit.[7] Surrounded by eager sailors and fighter pilots, he let it be known he had taken control of the jet in midflight, and referred to his days as an Air National Guard pilot in Texas. With an eye to recycling these images in his reelection campaign, the presidential officials kept the aircraft carrier waiting offshore overnight in order to furnish the best possible angle for Bush's television address to the nation, with the ocean as his backdrop rather than the San Diego shoreline, and with a banner in the background reading "Mission Accomplished." "The battle to topple Saddam Hussein's government was one victory in a war on terror that began on September 11, 2001, and still goes on," Bush declared. Critics called it a gratuitous and expensive stunt—probably the most expensive photo op in history—that cost taxpayers $1 million to $3 million: delaying the warship, keeping the crew at sea, and paying for air patrols and presidential security.

This manipulation, of course, was nothing compared to the monumental confidence trick played on the American public by the Bush administration during the run-up to the invasion of Iraq. Central to the argument for attacking Iraq was the assertion, repeated endlessly, that Saddam possessed weapons of mass destruction, and that the only way to get rid of his WMD was to overthrow his regime. Now that Saddam was ousted and the Anglo-Americans had occupied Iraq, it was incumbent on Bush—and Blair—to unearth the WMD they alleged Saddam had concealed.

The primacy of the WMD was underscored by none other than Paul Wolfowitz, the prime mover behind the invasion of Iraq. In a July 2003 *Vanity Fair* interview, he said that, of the three main motives for invading Iraq—"Saddam's possession of weapons of mass destruction, alleged link with Al Qaida and oppression of the

Iraqi people"—there was only one issue, WMD, which "everyone could agree on" as "the core reason." On the Al Qaida link, he admitted that "the subject was of the utmost disagreement within the [U.S.] bureaucracy." Ending Saddam's oppression was "a reason to help the Iraqis, but it's not a reason to put American kids' lives at risk, certainly not the scale we did."

As mentioned earlier (in Chapter 4, p. 151), Task Force 20—consisting of the CIA, the army's Delta Force and the Navy's SEALs—was charged with investigating the sites suspected of being storage depots of long-range Scud missiles or chemical and biological weapons, and had infiltrated Iraq before the invasion. Within Task Force 20 was the two-hundred-strong Mobile Exploitation Team (MET) Alpha, looking specifically for WMD. Both these contingents were part of the thousand-member Iraq Survey Group (ISG), whose mission was to collect all possible information about Saddam's regime. Consisting of some 880 Americans—most of them drawn from the CIA, the Defense Intelligence Agency, and the Pentagon's Defense Threat Reduction Bureau—and 120 Britons, it was under the field command of General Keith Dayton, and directed by an unnamed member of the National Security Council at the White House.[8]

On the eve of the invasion, Centcom had a list of nineteen high-priority suspected sites with WMD, and sixty-nine priority suspected sites with possible clues to the whereabouts of the WMD. Within a month of the fall of Baghdad, seventeen high-priority and forty-five priority sites were checked out. Nothing was found. "There had to have been something to use, and we haven't found it," said Colonel Richard McPhee, leader of the U.S. Army's Seventy-fifth Exploitation Task Force of biologists, chemists, computer experts, and document specialists. "Books will be written on that in the intelligence community for a long time. My unit has not found chemical weapons."[9] By then, according to Stephen Cambone, the Pentagon's undersecretary for intelligence, 110 of the 500 low-priority sites had also been checked, and a suspected bioweapons laboratory trailer was found in late April. As explained on pp.126–127, this trailer turned out to be producing hydrogen.

In an interview with the Berlin-based *Der Tagesspiegel* (The Daily Mirror), Hans Blix cited General Amr al Saadi, special weapons adviser to Saddam, who dealt with UN inspectors: "Nothing else will come out after the end of the war." Saadi surrendered to U.S. forces on April 12, thinking—according to his German wife, Helma—that he would be questioned for about three hours and then released. (He has been held incommunicado since then.) Saadi repeated his assertion that all WMD had been destroyed. "I don't see why he would still be afraid of the regime," said Blix. "Other leading figures have said the same."[10]

Faced with this embarrassing reality, Bush and Blair resorted to saying it would take weeks, even months, to find WMD since Iraq is as large as France (Iraq has 169,235 square miles/438,318 square kilometers compared to France, which has 212,655 square miles/550,776 square kilometers). "The U.S. and Britain did not have patience for prolonged inspections before the war in Iraq," said Blix in a BBC interview. "However, I notice now that when the American inspectors do not find anything, then it is suggested that we should have patience."[11]

Meanwhile, not to be outdone, Rumsfeld came up with his own explanation in a characteristically Rumsfeldian way. "It's hard to find things in a country that's determined not to have you find them," he told the Council on Foreign Relations in New York. "It's also possible that they decided to destroy them prior to the conflict." [12] If the latter was the case, there would be telltale signs of recent destruction, which Task Force 20 should have been able to detect readily.

Rumsfeld also suffered from a bout of amnesia when he declared on June 24 that "I don't know anybody in any government or any intelligence agency who suggested that the Iraqis had nuclear weapons." He had to be reminded by Nicholas Kristof of the *New York Times* that on the eve of the October 10–11, 2002, congressional vote on war, George Tenet released a CIA report that asserted: "Most analysts assess that Iraq is reconstituting its nuclear weapons program," and that in his interview on NBC's *Meet the Press* on March 16, Dick Cheney said, "We believe, he [Saddam] has, in fact, reconstituted nuclear weapons."

Two days later, U.S. forces found parts of centrifuges for uranium enrichment and pertinent documents under a rosebush in the back garden of Mahdi Shakur Ubaidi, the scientist in charge of developing centrifuges for uranium enrichment. The Bush White House hailed this as "a great find," ignoring Ubaidi's statement that he had buried these parts in 1991 on the order of Qusay Saddam Hussein. International Atomic Energy Agency spokesman Mark Gwozdecky said, "The findings and comments of Mr. Ubaidi appear to confirm that there has been no post-1991 nuclear weapons program in Iraq, and are consistent with our reports to the Security Council."[13]

POLITICAL FRONT

Equally dismal was the progress of the U.S. occupation authority regarding co-opting Iraqis to share the task of administering and reconstructing Iraq.

A gathering of about 250 delegates in Baghdad that deliberated for ten hours on April 28 under the inept chairmanship of Jay Garner was a fiasco. This time, SCIRI sent a low-level delegation to discuss "civil matters," not the next government. In consequence, thousands of Shias gathered near the meeting's venue to offer prayer in protest at their underrepresentation.

By then, to the disgust of many, Jay Garner had established his headquarters inside Saddam Hussein's Republican Palace compound, now ringed by rolls of razor wire and concrete blocks and guarded by tanks. And Ahmad Chalabi, the Pentagon's poster boy, had set up the Iraqi National Congress office at the Iraq Hunting Club, the favorite haunt of Uday Saddam Hussein, in the Mansour neighborhood. At his first press conference there, Chalabi said that the United States, not the United Nations, should help form a new Iraqi government. When asked, "What do you think of the fact that the few people in Baghdad who have heard of you think you are a thief?" he replied, "This was an aggression committed against me by the Jordanian military at the behest of Saddam's regime—I will clarify this issue very soon."[14] Breaking his silence on the subject, King Abdullah of Jordan said in an interview on U.S. television, "I would imagine that you'd want somebody who suffered alongside the Iraqi people. This particular gentleman [Chalabi] left Iraq when he was eleven. What contact does he have with the people on the street?"

Foremost among those who did have ongoing contact with the populace were clerics, whether Shia or Sunni. To the dismay of U.S. policy makers, the mosque emerged as the epicenter of political revival in Iraq—rather than the secular forces favored by Washington. On the day Chalabi insisted that the United States be the sole power broker in Iraq, twenty thousand Sunnis marched in Adhamiya, Baghdad, carrying placards in English that read "No, No to American Occupation Forces" and "Go Away from Iraq," and shouting slogans such as "No Bush, no Saddam, yes to Islam"; "No Shias, no Sunnis, yes, yes, for United Islam"; and "We want true freedom, not American puppets." The protesters' starting point was the Imam al Adham Abu Hanifa al Numan Mosque, the site of Saddam Hussein's last public appearance. The march was sponsored by the Iraqi National United Movement (INUM). In its statement, signed by Shaikh Ahmad al Kusaibi, the imam of the Abu Hanifa mosque, the INUM called on Iraqis to oppose a federal Iraq, which the United States wanted to set up. "America attacked Iraq to defend Israel," said Kusaibi. "We don't have weapons of mass destruction." Addressing the American occupation forces, he said, "You are the masters today, but I warn you against thinking of staying. Get out before we force you out."[15] This represented mainstream Sunni opinion.

There was also a marginal current among Sunnis consisting of those who were loyal to the ousted dictator, in the Sunni heartland north and west of Baghdad. They were expected to do "something" on April 28, Saddam's birthday, but they did nothing more than fire celebratory shots in the air in Falluja (population 200,000). Later, at about 9 P.M., some two hundred protesters marched to the local primary school in a residential area, where one hundred paratroopers of the U.S. Eighty-second Airborne Division were stationed, to demand their departure and the reopening of the school. The mob got rowdy. Feeling threatened, U.S. troops fired at it, killing eighteen people. The GIs claimed they acted in self-defense after they had been fired at. The locals said that the American soldiers committed murder, and must pay "blood money" as is the local custom, but the Pentagon had ruled out payment of any compensation for any purpose at the outset. Locals also alleged that the troops were using binoculars and night-vision goggles to ogle the women.

In an interview with the *New York Times,* Falluja's police commander, Omar Isawi, said, "The Iraqi army fled the day Baghdad fell [on April 9]. We have chosen a new mayor [Taha Hamid Badawi]. And the imams in the mosque have helped stop the looting. When U.S. troops came April 20, they said they would stay two or three days. But their number is increasing." The local American commander explained that they were not prepared to move out to the edge of the town: "We want to help them build themselves up and build a [new] police force." The next day, the paratroopers left under cover of darkness. Earlier that day, however, a group of American GIs arrived at a Sunni mosque that had been damaged by U.S. bombing and now displayed anti-American banners protesting the damage. The soldiers tore them down. "We're taking down any sign that's against U.S. forces," said the commanding officer. "We are here for the people."[16]

The next day, at a rally protesting the killings outside the main U.S. post in the main street, the Americans fired again and killed four more. By the weekend of May 3–4, Falluja was festooned with banners in English and Arabic that read: "Sooner or Later U.S. Killers, We'll kick you out"; and "Go Out of Our City. If Refuse We Will Kill You. Because You Are Come Here For Petrol, Not For Freedom." Outside the main hospital flew an Iraqi flag, soaked in blood, along with a sheet reading, "Our Power is Islam."

Islam was also the driving force in the Shia south. Ayatollah Muhammad Baqir al Hakim, a sixty-three-year-old black-turbaned cleric with a kindly face and a straggly white beard, returned here after twenty-three years in Iran. As he traveled twelve miles (twenty kilometers) by car from the Iranian border to Basra on May 11, tens of thousands of flag-waving Shia lined up and threw flowers at his convoy while chanting "Yes to Islam, no to Saddam"—a scene the U.S. hawks had visualized for the "liberating" Anglo-American troops without the Islamic cry. Actually, al Hakim was accompanied by several hundred members of the military wing of his SCIRI, called the Badr Brigade, but they traveled in civilian clothes and without arms, having been banned by the occupation forces. (Earlier, many more of the armed personnel of the Badr Brigade—estimated to be ten thousand to fifteen thousand strong—had slipped into Iraq from Iran, with most of them ending up in Najaf, Karbala, Amara, and Kut.) "We want an Islam of independence, justice, and freedom," al Hakim told a rally of thirty thousand in Basra. "We will not accept a government that is imposed on us." He demanded that "a government be formed by Iraqis which should work toward ending the occupation by peaceful means."

BREMER TAKES OVER

This went down badly with sixty-one-year-old L. Paul Bremer, the new U.S. proconsul to Iraq. Responding to the fast-moving situation, Bremer arrived in Baghdad on May 12, eleven days ahead of the official start of his assignment. He inherited Garner's staff of six hundred, of which only seventeen were Arabic-speakers, at the Republican Palace complex, soon to be surrounded by a fifteen-foot high wall of pre-fabricated, blast-proof concrete blocks. A career diplomat, he had served the state department from 1966 to 1989, and had the approval of Powell. After several postings in Asia and Africa, he became the executive aide to secretaries of state Henry Kissinger and George Shultz, then ambassador to the Netherlands, and finally President Reagan's counter-terrorism envoy at large. He left public service to become managing director of Kissinger Associates, a consultancy firm. In 2000 he quit consulting to become chairman of the congressionally appointed National Commission on Terrorism. He recommended that CIA guidelines restricting recruitment of those with human-rights violations—imposed by the Clinton administration in 1995—be dropped.

Bremer took formal charge of occupied Iraq in the wake of the twenty-seven-clause UN Security Council Resolution 1483 adopted by fourteen votes to nil, with Syria abstaining, on May 22, which confirmed the status of the Anglo-American alliance as the occupying Authority and provided a legal framework for Iraqi oil exports to resume.

Diplomatic bargaining at the council had started a fortnight earlier, when the Bush administration returned to the United Nations—which it had arrogantly declared "irrelevant to the problems of the twenty-first century" on the eve of invading Iraq— barely a month after capturing Baghdad with a draft resolution. It realized that without UN authority, it could not sell Iraqi oil. Moreover, only the United Nations had the authority to end economic sanctions on Iraq and certify the representative nature of its future government. Blair reportedly told Bush that on March 26, Britain's attorney general, Lord Goldsmith, had told his cabinet that military action in Iraq must be limited to achieving Iraqi disarmament, and that after the war, any activity beyond the essential maintenance of security would be unlawful without a further Security Council resolution.[17] Finally, even the most pliant members of

Bush's "Coalition of the Willing" wanted a UN resolution as a prerequisite to joining Washington in the occupation of Iraq.

This time, the French-Russian-Chinese-German quartet, which had opposed the unilateral war on Iraq, was receptive to examining the American draft because it wanted to alleviate the suffering of Iraqis, which could be done only by resuming oil exports. Horse trading followed. Russia wanted the UN inspectors to declare Iraq free of WMD before sanctions were lifted. But it went along with a promise to review the roles of Unmovic and the IAEA. The early American draft proposed that the U.S.–U.K. occupation—called the Authority—be "subject to automatic renewal after 12 months." France wanted to limit the life of the resolution itself to one year. As a compromise, Washington agreed to have the council review the resolution in a year's time. There were provisions for legal immunity to oil sales until December 31, 2007, and an advisory board to monitor the Authority-controlled Development Fund of Iraq, with one of the board members to be named by the United Nations.

The original American draft proposed that the UN secretary-general appoint a "coordinator" to liaise with the Authority. Under pressure, the final draft mentioned a "special representative" of the United Nations whose "independent responsibilities" included "working intensively with the Authority, the people of Iraq and others concerned to advance efforts to restore and establish national and local institutions for representative governance, including by working together to facilitate a process leading to an internationally recognized, representative government of Iraq." Kofi Annan would give the job to Sergio Vieira de Mello, a gray-haired, lean-faced Brazilian of fifty-five, with a doctorate from the Sorbonne in Paris and a record of thirty years of service with the United Nations that involved human-rights protection and peacekeeping in Lebanon, Bosnia, Cambodia, Kosovo, and East Timor.[18]

Gunter Pleuger, the German ambassador to the United

Nations, reflected the view of many in the Security Council chamber when he said, "The war we did not want and the majority of the Council did not want has taken place. [But] we cannot undo history. We are now in a situation where we have to take action for the sake of the Iraqi people."

As the supremo of the newly named Coalition Provisional Authority (CPA), Bremer's first act was to fire all Iraqi military personnel and civil servants and abolish the ministries of defense and information, as well as all military and security courts. He also dissolved the INC's 700-strong Free Iraqi Force, alienating Chalabi, who, being a staunch advocate of wiping out the institutions of Saddam's regime, had influenced the Pentagon's decision to that effect. Since Centcom had earlier ordered the disbanding and disarming of SCIRI's Badr Brigade, Bremer had no option but to treat the Free Iraqi Force in the same way. He also disbanded the Baath Party, with its membership of nearly 450,000, and banned about 30,000 of them from working in the public sector.[20] This controversial decision would leave many schools, colleges, and hospitals short of senior staff. When, for instance, Baghdad University reopened after summer vacation, two thousand teaching and administrative staff members were told to stay home.

Bremer scuttled Garner's plan to call an assembly of three hundred delegates to elect an "Iraqi Authority/Government." Instead, he gave the seven-member Leadership Council of the U.S.-recognized opposition groups until June 6 to give him names of those who should be on the advisory "Political Council" he had in mind. This angered the Iraqi leaders, who demanded to know what powers the Political Council would have. They complained to UN Special Representative de Mello as soon as he arrived in Baghdad on June 1 about the lack of authority being offered to them. A consummate diplomat, de Mello reportedly listened to them sympathetically, and set out to consult a wide body of opinion in the country against the backdrop of quickly deteriorating security.

His rapid-fire decisions on important matters were designed to establish Bremer—a man with sharp features and a rich thatch of hair—as a quick-thinking, decisive proconsul, a contrast to the dithering Garner. But, in their haste, Bremer and his superiors at the Pentagon did not think through their decisions. To dismiss nearly four hundred thousand military and security personnel from the defense and interior ministries with a one-off payment of $40 was a recipe for disaster. Among those who immediately criticized this step was Ramiro Lopez da Silva, the United Nations' Humanitarian Coordinator in Iraq since 2002. Lack of re-employment possibilities for the dismissed soldiers could lead to "low-intensity conflict" in rural Iraq, he warned. Da Silva's statement proved prescient. A later study by the International Crisis Group, a multinational think tank, said, "The CPA's decision to disband the army and the ministry of interior is said to have greatly strengthened this group [of guerrillas] as it drove many alienated people to joint the clandestine resistance."[21]

In the immediate aftermath, the dismissed soldiers resorted to protesting outside Bremer's CPA headquarters at the Republican Palace. On June 18 the U.S. troops guarding the CPA premises fired on demonstrating former soldiers, killing two and injuring several. "If by Monday [June 23] noon the Americans do not find a suitable solution to our tragic situation, we will take up arms," said Tahseen Ali Hussein, a dismissed soldier. "We will start ambushes, bombings and even suicide bombings."[22] Bremer relented. Just before the deadline, the CPA announced that it would pay the disbanded soldiers "close to their original salaries." The money was to come from the Iraqi assets frozen in the United States after Iraq's invasion of Kuwait in 1990.

The dismissal of hundreds of thousands of Iraqi civil and military personnel coupled with inadequate policing worsened the security situation. Whereas in the police state run by Saddam, murder—except that carried out clandestinely by its security and intelligence services—had been rare, now in Baghdad alone fifteen to twenty-five civilians were shot dead daily. In July the city mortuary reported forty-seven times more gunshot deaths than for the previous July.[23] Baghdadis lodged an average of one thousand complaints daily, from missing ID papers to murder. But in contrast to ten thousand policemen in the capital before the invasion, there were now only four thousand working from police stations, four-fifths of which had been ransacked.[24]

Lack of security outside Baghdad was dramatically illustrated by Thomas Friedman of the *New York Times*. A five-car convoy he was in was robbed in daylight just outside Baghdad on the highway to Amman. The gunmen, who arrived in BMWs, drove off with thousands of dollars in cash. Friedman's convoy drove for another two hours before coming across an American military patrol. "Sorry, we just don't have enough people," explained the unit commander.[25] Doubling of the U.S. military police to four thousand made little difference to Iraqis, as none of the Americans knew Arabic or had any understanding of Islam or Iraq's social mores. Indeed, confident of the Americans' ignorance of Arabic, Iraqi boys would go up to unsuspecting soldiers, smile, and say, "My father is with your sister"—or something to that effect—and sarcastically enjoy the troops smiling back at them, thinking they were being friendly.

Large-scale looting had by now evolved into daylight carjackings, revenge killings, and armed robberies in cities where small arms, AK-47 Kalashnikov assault rifles, hand grenades, and ammunition were for sale openly. "Armed gangs compete for bounty, shooting and stabbing their rivals," reported Phil Reeves of the *Independent* from Baghdad. "Gunfire has become as much a feature . . . as the piles of rotting rubbish that now cover the entire city." The root of the problem lay in what happened immediately after the fall of Baghdad. By allowing looters and arsonists a free rein, the United States had diminished its authority. It now faced an uphill task to make up the lost ground.

Bremer promised to improve security against the background of escalating resistance to the occupiers. The example of Hit, one hundred miles (sixty kilometers) northwest, was illustrative. The town had not been bombed or looted. When the Americans arrived on May 7, many threw their weapons in the Euphrates and welcomed them. Three weeks later, someone fired a rocket-propelled grenade at one of the Third U.S. Infantry convoys. In retaliation, the American GIs kicked down doors and climbed over walls in a neighborhood in a search-and-arrest raid while an assault heli-copter circled above. Word spread fast that soldiers had burst in on Muslim women in their homes, finding them in various states of immodest dress. "We are Muslims, and we don't allow people to trespass on our property and go into our houses and search our women," Abu Ahmad, an enraged local resident, told the *New York Times*.

By mid-June, the U.S. military authorities were describing the area north and west of Baghdad as "semi-permissive," where "sub-versive forces" were active, mounting sniper attacks, ambushes, and bombings. They responded with ground raids, air strikes, and dragnets to isolate and destroy what they called "the remnants of the old regime" and to whittle down their attackers until a new Iraqi authority emerged to maintain order.

The result was a series of campaigns, starting with Operation "Peninsula Strike" on June 11. Four thousand soldiers of the Fourth Infantry Division were equipped with drones, F15 fighters, AC-130 Hercules gun-ships and AH-64 Apache attack helicopters in the thirty-square-mile (seventy-eight-square-kilometer) penin-sular area north of Baghdad. Then the troops moved north to Dujayal and Balad, killing twenty-seven. After cordoning off neighborhoods, troops conducted house-to-house searches for weapons or "any sign of loyalty to Saddam Hussein" in and near Balad. This included the village of Dhuluiya, a stronghold of the Jabburi tribe, which was out of favor with Saddam Hussein because some senior officers from the tribe were involved in two attempted coups against him. Pointing to two bloodstained quilts on which two men of the Jabburi tribe had died when the U.S.

soldiers tried to arrest them in the middle of the night in Dhuluiya, Salah Jabburi told the *Independent on Sunday* with understated sarcasm, "I suppose it was a successful operation from the American point of view." Nonetheless, the guerrillas continued their struggle.

On June 24 came a sudden jolt to the widely held view that the British troops in the Basra-Amara area were better at peacekeeping than their American counterparts, when violence erupted in Majar al Kabir, sixteen miles (twenty-five kilometers) south of Amara.

The trouble began when the British decided to disarm the people in the region around Amara. Over the weekend of June 21–22, the British went into Abu Ala village, near Majar al Kabir, to search for weapons. "Most people objected to the search operation because it was against the tribal principle of owning a gun," said Ali Atiya, a Shia member of the underground militia called Hizbollah (lit., Party of God), led by Abu Hatim (a.k.a. Abdul Karim Mahoud al Hatab), which had fought the Saddam regime for over twenty years. "The guns are used for tribal celebrations, funerals, fighting other tribes, protecting our cows and sheep, and above all, fighting Saddam." He objected vehemently to the British use of dogs—considered filthy in Islam—in their searches. "As Muslims we cannot accept dogs in our homes." His friend Falih Salim said, "A British soldier held the underwear of a woman and stretched it in public. How can we accept this as Muslims and as Shias?" Such actions by the British inflamed the feelings of the local people.

On the morning of June 24 six soldiers of the (British) Royal Military Police arrived at the police station of Majar al Kabir, demanding to see the weapons used by the Hizbollah. Children started throwing stones at them. About three hundred to four hundred people gathered outside the station. The British fired at the demonstrators, killing two. Then Iraqi gunmen stormed the police station, and killed six British troops and injured eight.[26] This event made the Anglo-Americans rethink their drive to disarm every Iraqi.

That day, U.S. forces mounted their second campaign, codenamed Operation "Scorpion," followed on June 29 by the Fourth

Infantry's Silver Lions Battalion's Operation "Sidewinder," whose purpose was to "project an intimidating display of power." In twenty simultaneous predawn raids between Baghdad and Samarra, 75 miles (120 kilometers) to the north, the American message was "Don't mess with us." The commanding officer, Lieutenant-Colonel Aubrey Garner, said, "We have the flexibility to bring firepower anywhere anytime. Our ability is almost magical." At the end of the weeklong counterinsurgency campaign, the battalion had killed 30 Iraqis and arrested 282, and confiscated 96 Kalashnikovs and 217 rocket-propelled grenades, and in the process had 27 of its troops wounded.[27] Bremer kept up the bullish tone. "We are going to fight them [the resistance] and impose our will on them and we will capture or kill them until we have imposed law and order on this country," he said in an interview with the BBC on June 29.

"[For the Americans] to be conducting huge sweeps north and north-west of Baghdad was eerily reminiscent of Vietnam: thousands of troops backed by jets and helicopters swarming into sleepy towns north of Baghdad on the Tigris, churning up the countryside and terrifying the locals; troops pumped up on adrenaline and a dose of Wagner's *Ride of the Valkyries*—used in *Apocalypse Now*—ramming into metal gates and dragging suspects from their homes," reported Jon Swain of the *Sunday Times*, who covered the Vietnam War for the same newspaper. "As in Vietnam, the operation ended with a communiqué—listing hundreds of suspects rounded up and weapons captured or destroyed—with a paragraph about how hearts and minds have been won by providing a football field or repairing a school. The reality, judging by the last week's sudden surge in attacks including the first mortar attack on U.S. forces, is that these operations have done little or nothing to improve security."[28] A mortar attack, aimed at the U.S. military headquarters in Ramadi, destroyed its target.

Also, the frequent after-dark attacks on the U.S. forces at Baghdad

International Airport, combined with an occasional missile fired at incoming military aircraft, led some U.S. air crews to adopt the old Vietnam tactic of corkscrewing tightly down on the runways instead of risking sniper fire during a conventional final approach. In fact, the CPA cancelled its plan to open the airport to civilian flights on July 15.

"There are some [Iraqis] who feel that if they attack us we may decide to leave prematurely," said President Bush in Washington on July 2. "They don't understand what they're talking about if that's the case. My answer is 'Bring them on.' We got the force necessary to deal with the security situation." That day, ten U.S. soldiers were injured in three attacks. On the eve of July Fourth, Lieutenant-General Ricardo Sanchez, commander of U.S. forces in Iraq, revealed that over the past month and a half there had been an average of thirteen attacks daily, killing twenty-five Anglo-American soldiers and injuring 177.[29] Bush's provocative language provoked outrage from Democrats, who accused him of endangering American lives. "I am shaking my head in disbelief," said Senator Frank Lautenberg. "I never heard any military commander invite enemies to attack U.S. troops."[30]

That day, Washington raised the bounty on Saddam's head from $200,000 to $25 million, in the mistaken belief that resistance was organized solely by "the remnants of the old regime," and that many Iraqis were not cooperating with the American authorities because they feared the return of Saddam and his two sons. To bring about the sons' capture or death, the United States raised the bounty on their heads to $15 million each. By now, thirty-two of the fifty-five most-wanted Iraqis, publicized in a pack of fifty-five playing cards, had surrendered or been captured.[31] These included the surrender of Tariq Aziz (No. 43 in the pack) and the arrest of Mrs. Huda Salih Mahdi Ammash (No. 53 in the pack)—a biologist nicknamed "Mrs. Anthrax" by the United States who was the sole woman on the Baath Party regional command and the only woman on the wanted list. Despite her detention, and the earlier surrender by General Amr al Saadi, the Americans still had no clue where to find the

WMD Iraq was supposed to have. Nor did the arrest of Abid Hamid Mahmoud, Saddam's personal secretary, on June 20, and his revelation that he and Uday and Qusay Saddam Hussein had fled to Syria after the war but were expelled by the Syrian government, bring the U.S. authorities any closer to finding the two brothers.

Meanwhile, the guerrillas extended their attacks to the Iraqi collaborators. On July 4, a remote-control bomb killed seven Iraqi policemen and hurt forty others—all of them newly recruited and trained by the U.S. military—as they began marching in the street near the police station after their graduation.

These attacks occurred against the backdrop of rampant lawlessness, electricity and gasoline shortages, wrecked telephone exchanges, a nightly curfew, and 60 percent unemployment. Iraqis felt bewildered and frustrated at the chaos and mayhem. A survey in Baghdad on July 8–10 showed that 80 percent of its residents were "most affected" by power cuts; 67 percent by street attacks; 50 percent by attacks at home or workplace; and 49 percent by lack of clean drinking water. Three out of four Baghdadis felt that Iraq was now a more dangerous place than before the Anglo-American invasion.[32] This state of affairs had made Iraqis so resentful, they came to believe the worst of the Americans. When, for instance, a room next door to a mosque in Falluja blew up (caused by a bomb explosion during a class in guerrilla warfare), killing the preacher and seven others, the locals insisted that a U.S. warplane had fired a missile at the building.

POWER SHORTAGES

Iraqis could not help comparing the speed with which Saddam Hussein's government had restored electricity after the devastating 1991 Gulf War with the U.S. failure to do so. They were not impressed by the official explanation that power supplies were in trouble due to sabotage and looting. Nor were they impressed by the later claim made by Bremer that "with few exceptions" Baghdad was now receiving twenty hours of electricity a day. After hearing this statement from Bremer at his press conference on June 21, Patrick Cockburn of the *Independent* walked over to Al Rashid Street, about half a mile from Bremer's office, and talked at random to Shamsuddin Mansour, a petty shopkeeper in an alleyway off the main street. "We have had no electricity for six days," said Mansour. "Many of our people are suffering from heart problems because of the heat. We live with as many as 42 people in a house and do not have the money to buy even a small generator. Without lights at night it is easy for gangs of thieves to take over the streets, and the shooting keeps us awake. If we try to protect ourselves with guns, the Americans arrest us." This was a telling example of how Bremer and his staff members had insulated themselves into the self-contained, air-conditioned "bubble" of the Republican Presidential Palace, complete with its own hospital and cinema, from which they emerged only in armored air-conditioned vehicles with military escort.

Lack of electricity meant no clean drinking water. It also meant that pumps could not extract petroleum from oil wells. Iraqi saboteurs were at work in the oil and gas industry. In June they badly damaged the oil pipeline linking the Kirkuk oil fields to Turkey and set ablaze the gas pipeline near Hit supplying fuel to power stations all over Iraq. Toward the end of that month, Al Jazeera showed an explosion at an oil pipeline near Ishaqi, forty-five miles (seventy kilometers) northwest of Baghdad. Little wonder that Iraq's oil output, at 750,000 barrels per day, was a quarter of its pre-invasion figure.

Mass media communication between the occupiers and the occupied was poor. The official TV channel, unveiled in May by the Iraq Media Network (IMN) and run by the Pentagon's contractor, SAIC, was on for only a few hours each night, and mainly showed reruns of entertainment programs. Its news and comment presentation lacked credibility. "Our news program is crap," said one IMN official. "It is completely unprofessional," with "intentionally faking interviews and production stories that turn out to be based on patently false rumors."[33] By contrast, Al Alam (The Flag), the Iranian TV network—which Iraqis could receive with a large antenna, and which provided much news and analysis, often with an anti-Anglo-American tilt—was popular. Those with satellite dishes turned either to Al Jazeera or Dubai-based Al Arabiya, both of which were critical of the Anglo-American troops and reported Iraqi resistance assiduously and swiftly, but accurately. As before, the Americans continued to harass Al Jazeera. Its bureau chief, Wadah Khanfar, complained that Al Jazeera offices and staff had been subjected to "strafing by gunfire, death threats, confiscation of news material, and multiple detentions and arrests" by U.S. soldiers.[34]

On the positive side, the print media was thriving. Iraqis, deprived of anything but official propaganda for a generation under Saddam's despotism—when more than five hundred Iraqi journalists, writers, and intellectuals were executed or disappeared after imprisonment—were eager to exercise freedom of speech and expression. In Baghdad alone, there were sixty publications covering the whole political, religious, and ethnic spectrum, as well as sports and entertainment, with some magazines splashing Britney Spears and Madonna on their covers. Most of the U.S.-recognized Iraqi political groups had started newspapers, with the INC daily *Al Sabah* (The Morning)—funded by the U.S. occupation authority—reporting copiously on CPA activities.[35] The Iraqi National Accord's *Baghdad* daily had a better reputation, but very limited circulation. The most widely read was *Al Zaman* (The Time), owned and edited by Saad al Bazzaz, an INC member who started the paper in London in 1997 and brought some of his British-trained staff to team up with the former journalists of *Al Jumhuriya* (The Republic), the Iraqi government's newspaper—which he used to edit, until his defection in 1992. Reflecting popular anger and frustration, most newspapers berated the U.S.

occupation force's failure to restore security, public utilities, and government. Sectarian publications such as *Sada al Sadr* (Echo of Sadr) weekly, published by Hojatalislam Muqtada al Sadr, made a point of printing lists of Baath Party "tyrants who are wanted by the people." *Sada al Sadr*, as well as other Shia publications, such as *Al Haqiqa* (The Truth) and *Al Daawa* (The Call), described every Iraqi killed by the Americans as "a martyr." Writing in *Al Saah* (The Hour), a mouthpiece of Sunni clerics, Shaikh Ahmad al Kusaibi of the Imam al Adham Abu Hanifa Mosque praised "the martyrs of Falluja and Ramadi" for attacking U.S. forces. This was too much for Bremer, who issued a decree prohibiting the press from publishing material that "incites violence against any individual or group, including coalition personnel."[36]

POLITICAL STALEMATE

What made matters worse for Iraqis was that the continued disrepair of Iraq's economic infrastructure went hand in hand with political stalemate. Angered by Masud Barzani's vocal denunciation of the dismissal of Garner[37]—who had planned on handing over significant authority to the Leadership Council of the exile groups and Kurds—Bremer ordered searches of his Kurdistan Democratic Party offices in Baghdad and elsewhere. In a provocative act that deeply offended most Shias, the U.S. troops ransacked the offices of the much-revered Hawza al Ilmiya.[38] When Ayatollah Muhammad Baqir al Hakim, now settled in Najaf, his native city, refused to meet any U.S. or U.K. officials, Bremer ordered searches of SCIRI's offices with the purported aim of finding evidence of its links with Iran. He found nothing tangible.

Apprehensive that SCIRI would do well in the elections for mayor in Najaf and elsewhere in the south, Bremer canceled the elections in mid-June. Bremer's fear was not shared by U.S. officers in Najaf, who attributed whatever little influence SCIRI had to its funds. "They [SCIRI] came into town with some money which they spread around," Major David Toth told David Rohde of the *New York Times*. "But we do, too."[39] Bremer's decision fueled anger at the occupation forces, especially in Najaf, where the American-appointed mayor, Abu Haidar Abdul Munim, a Sunni and former military officer in the ousted regime, was so unpopular that there were repeated demonstrations against him, a few of which escalated into riots. Finally, on June 30, the local commander removed Abu Haidar Abdul Munim from office after a standoff with his private security guards and arrested him for stealing public funds. His job went to Haidar al Mayyali, a Shia. This reduced tensions in Najaf, where the Friday prayer sermon at the Imam Ali Mosque was often delivered by Ayatollah Muhammad Baqir al Hakim.

In these sermons, he often referred to the martyrdom of fifty-two members of his extended family, who were executed by Saddam Hussein's regime between 1980, when he escaped to Iran, and 2002: five brothers, seven nephews, and other relatives. In his house in Tehran he had their pictures, adorned by red roses, in a tableau in a black-and-white "hall of martyrdom," which often provided the background to his media interviews. Saddam had resorted to this butchery with a message: He would stop only if al Hakim returned to Iraq. This tale of tyranny carried out by Saddam resonated with his Shia audience, who lost an estimated thirty thousand kinsmen in the wake of the failed uprisings after the 1991 Gulf War.[40]

With the collapse of the Saddam regime, mass graves were being unearthed in the south. The dead were mainly those killed by the government during the 1991 Shia uprisings. At a site at the village of Mahawil, near Hilla, a mass grave the size of a football field contained up to three thousand corpses. Saddam's systematic slaughter of political opponents started in 1978, when he was vice president, with some 1,900 Communists "disappearing" in less than a year,[41] and ended roughly a decade later with the mass murder of an estimated 100,000 Kurds in Operation Anfal for their alliance with the Iranians during the Iran–Iraq War (1980–88). Attacks on the dissident Shias and army deserters hiding in the marshes in the south, however, continued well into the early twenty-first century. The estimated aggregate toll of Saddam's massacres was put at 250,000 to 300,000—far higher than the estimated 160,000 to 240,000 Iraqi fatalities during the Iran–Iraq War.[42] Al Hakim's SCIRI had helped set up the Freed Prisoners Association, with an office in an elegant villa on the Tigris belonging to Saddam's personal secretary, Abid Hamid Mahmoud. There, volunteers sifted through the files carted off from the intelligence buildings and published lists of the dead, thus laying them to rest after their disappearance into prisons.

While refusing to cooperate with Bremer's CPA, al Hakim agreed to meet UN Special Representative Sergio Vieira de Mello, who had lost no time in exercising his right to contact any Iraqi he wished. He held meetings not only with political and religious leaders but also with numerous groups of lawyers, teachers, journalists, engineers, doctors, artists, and women activists. What he heard from these assorted groups and individuals seemed to be in line with the findings of the *Spectator*/Channel 4 TV survey of Baghdadis in July. Two-fifths wanted political power to be transferred to Iraqis immediately, with another one-third saying "within one year or less." While 13 percent opted for the Anglo-American troops departing immediately, another 45 percent wanted them to do so "within a year or less." Such views dovetailed with those prevalent among Americans. When asked to speculate on how long U.S. troops would stay in Iraq, 57 percent opted for a period up to twelve months.[43]

The *Spectator*/Channel 4 TV survey showed that half of the interviewees were neither hostile nor friendly toward the occupying forces. Of the rest, 18 percent were hostile and 26 percent were friendly. That is, among those who had an opinion, more than a third were against the Anglo-American forces. It was therefore not surprising to see guerrilla attacks rising.

The signs were unmistakable. The Iraqi resistance, learning from experience, was getting better organized and putting the occupation force more and more on the defensive as reports of low morale among American GIs began filtering out. "We were told the fastest way home was through Baghdad, and that is what we did," said Sergeant Filipe Vega on ABC News' *Good Morning America* on July 16, 2003. "Now [four months after that] we are still here." Many of his comrades had the same question on the tips of their tongues: "Why are we still here?" The soldiers' e-mails and website texts reflected sagging morale. "It's hot, we've been here for a long time, it's dangerous, we haven't had any real downtime in months, and we don't know when we're going home," wrote Private Isaac Kindblade, of the 671st Engineers Company. The morale was low because "the rules of engagement are crippling. We are outnumbered. We are exhausted. We are in over our heads. The president says, 'Bring 'em on.' The generals say we don't need more troops. Well, they [president and generals] are not over here." Kindblade added, "Somewhere down the line we became an occupation force in [Iraqi] eyes. We don't feel like heroes anymore." Summarizing the working and living conditions of the GIs, an officer said, "Soldiers get literally hundreds of flea or mosquito bites, and they can't [use] cream or Benadryl to keep the damn things from itching. Soldiers are living in the dirt, with no mail, no phone, no contact with home, and no break from the daily monotony at all."[44]

While concrete walls were erected around all U.S. bases to protect them from car bombs, sandbags went up high in front of all police stations. The American GIs peered discreetly through the loopholes. Like the Israeli occupation force in the Palestinian Territories, U.S. military convoys resorted to patrolling the streets of the capital with one vehicle in front—with a heavy machine gun trained on the road—and one vehicle at the rear, with a heavy machine gun pointing straight ahead to prevent anyone from ramming the convoy at speed.

Bremer and his superiors were losing the initial confidence they had displayed about imposing their will on Iraq and on Iraqis. Bremer now became more receptive to the findings of the UN Special Representative, de Mello. He set aside his idea of having an Advisory Council of Iraqis. Instead, he agreed to appoint an Interim Iraqi Governing Council, with powers to hire and fire ministers for the interim government and establish a constitutional committee to chart the country's future. Bremer wanted to move away from the exile opposition and induct many Iraq-based technocrats into the council, but he did not get very far. Clearly his decision to enhance the powers of the subsequent council was dictated by the rising guerrilla activity—a fact that neither council members nor Bremer nor the Pentagon dared acknowledge in public, for fear of appearing to "reward terrorism."

THE INTERIM IRAQI GOVERNING COUNCIL

U.S. soldiers cordoned off a large section of central Baghdad on July 13 as the Paul Bremer–appointed Interim Iraqi Governing Council of twenty-two men and three women presented itself to the world media at the Convention Center. It was a landmark in the post-invasion history of Iraq. The council consisted of thirteen Shias, eleven Sunnis, and one Christian (Yonnadam Yusuf Kanna of the Assyrian Democratic Party).[45] Among the Sunnis were five ethnic Kurds and one ethnic Turkoman (Ms. Shangul Shapuk, an engineer and writer). Leaving aside the six technocrats—lawyers, businessmen, senior civil servants, and engineers, all but one being Sunni—the remaining members represented a broad political spectrum. Among the ethnic groups, Kurds, who formed one-sixth of the national population, were fully represented, with the leaders of two nationalist parties (KDP and PUK), one Islamic party, and one socialist party participating. As for ethnic Arabs, representation varied widely between Sunnis and Shias. The Sunni Arabs were technocrats, the two exceptions being Adnan Pachachi, eighty-year-old former foreign minister in the pre-Baathist period and a favorite of the U.S. State Department who had set up the Association of Independent Democrats, a paper organization committed to secularism; and Muhsin Abdul Hamid, leader of the Islamic Party, which was banned by the Baathist regime. At the popular level, the proportion of Islamic Sunnis to secularists was probably two to one. The corresponding figure for Shia Arabs was widely put at nine to one. Yet the six Shia leaders belonging to religious parties were balanced by three secularists—Chalabi, Iyad Alawi of the Iraqi National Accord, and Hamid Majid Mousa of the Communist Party—who most likely represented about 10 percent of the Arab Shia population. Of the religious leaders, only Ayatollah Abdul Aziz al Hakim's SCIRI had popular backing. But his rivals, Grand Ayatollah Ali Sistani and Hojatalislam Muqtada al Sadr, who refused to work with the occupation authorities, commanded at least three times as much of a following as did SCIRI.

Now, all of these CPA-appointed members sat in a semicircle on the platform against the background of a large map of Iraq inscribed with "Majlis al Hukum" (The Governing Council). The oldest member, Ayatollah Muhammad Bahr al Uloom, eighty-one, opened the press conference with the Islamic incantation "In the Name of Allah, the Compassionate, the Merciful *(B'ism Allah al Rahman al Rahim)*"—to the obvious embarrassment of Bremer and his sidekick, John Sawers of Britain, both of them seated in the front row among the audience. "The establishment of this council is an expression of the national will in the wake of the collapse of the former oppressive regime," declared al Uloom, leader of an insignificant London-based Shia group called Ahl Ul Bayt (People of Faith).

None of the council members who spoke or answered journalists' questions referred to the United States or the United Kingdom—except Ahmad Chalabi. "While I salute the resistance of the Iraqi people to Saddam and his regime, I would like to take this opportunity to express my gratitude and the gratitude of the Iraqi people to President Bush, the U.S. Congress and the people of the United States for helping the Iraqi people to liberate themselves from the scourge of Saddam," he said.[46]

Toward the end of the press conference, Chalabi moved to the edge of the podium and took a bow in front of Bremer, a public recognition of his subordination to the United States. "This was a bit strange as they [council members] were dodging questions about what powers they actually had in their hands and whether Bremer would have the right to veto their decisions," noted Salam Pax, who attended the press conference for the *Guardian*. However, it was obvious that as the proconsul of the primary occupying power, Bremer retained ultimate authority, including a monopoly on defense and security. The immediate task of the council, to be housed initially in the old Military Industrialization Establishment, was to elect or select its president.

Among the female council members was Aqila al Hashemi, a Shia who had been a director-general in the office of Deputy Prime Minister Tariq Aziz, responsible for dealing with the humanitarian aspects of the United Nations, conducted in the main by the UN headquarters in Baghdad. Her appointment annoyed the neocons in Washington. Their mouthpiece, the *Weekly Standard,* referred to a speech she gave at the 114-member Non-Aligned Movement meeting in Kuala Lumpur in February 2003. According to the Associated Press, she said, "The defense of Iraq is now the defense of the civilized world. The war is just like a machine, and if it is not stopped with Iraq, the American war machine will continue rolling over Third World countries."

However, al Hashemi was not one of the "Big Seven" on the council who really mattered. Besides the two Kurdish leaders, Masud Barzani and Jalal Talabani, they were Ahmad Chalabi, Iyad Alawi, Ayatollah Abdul Aziz al Hakim, Adnan Pachachi, and Ibrahim Jaafari (of al Daawa al Islamiya, Shia). Nor was she in the nine-member Presidential Council that the Governing Council would name after eighteen days of very heated deliberations.

Besides the "Big Seven," it contained Ayatollah Muhammad Bahr al Uloom and Muhsin Abdul Hamid. All told, there were five Shias and four Sunnis.[47]

The Governing Council had no say whatsoever in Operation "Soda Mountain" in the north of Baghdad, which resulted in 611 arrests and the confiscation of 1,346 rocket-propelled grenades and 4,300 mortar rounds. "American soldiers break into our homes and take money," Umm Tahsin (Mother of Tahsin) told the *Guardian* correspondent in Tikrit. "They bring sniffer dogs into our homes, and we consider dogs impure. My husband was made to stand outside [while they searched]. Every family is allowed to have one Kalashnikov for self-defense. They took ours."[48] The alienation created by such heavy-handed actions gave succor to the resistance movement, whose attacks showed greater sophistication. The ten "security incidents"—as recorded by the U.S. military over two days in mid-July in Baghdad—included Improved Explosive Devices (IEDs), which are mortar shells tied together, on roads near Baghdad airport, and attacks on the GIs in the neighborhoods of Hurriya, Iqtissadiyeen, and Shabab. And the incidents recorded by the United Nations—but *not* by the United States—in one twenty-four-hour period included rocket-propelled grenades fired at an American base near Mosul, a heavy machine-gun attack in Karbala, a ground-to-air missile fired at a U.S. C130 cargo plane at the Baghdad airport, and three attempts to shoot down an American helicopter in Karbala.

While the Pentagon had no option but to acknowledge the death of a serving soldier whether in combat or otherwise, it felt no need to be honest and open about the numbers of wounded. In an interview with National Public Radio on August 3, Colonel Allen De Lane, in charge of the airlift from Iraq into Andrews military air base near Washington, said, "Since the war started, I can't give you an exact number [of the injured], because that is classified information. But I can say to you over 4,000 have stayed here at the Andrews clinic. And that number doubles when you count the people that come here to Andrews and then we send them to other places like Walter Reed and Bethesda [Veterans' Hospital]. When the Andrews clinic started absorbing the people coming from the theater [in April], those numbers went up to over 1,200. That number even went up higher in May, to about 1,500, and continues to rise." By contrast, the total injured since May 1 were: 827 (according to the Pentagon); 926 (Centcom).

Iraqi resistance grew from several seeds: the humiliation that people under military occupation feel; revenge killings by families whose close relatives had been killed by U.S. forces; outraged Iraqi nationalism; Islamic militancy; and retaliation by those who had lost power. Predictably, a plethora of guerrilla groups cropped up. In late July a masked member of the Salafiya Jihad Group appeared on Al Arabiya TV, vowing that they would bring "God's vengeance on the Occupation forces."[49] While independent Sunni Islamists had set up Jaish Muhammad (Army of Muhammad), former Iraqi soldiers had established Jaish Muatasim (Army of Sheikh Muatasim). Among Shias were Jaish Hizbollah (Army of the Party of God), inspired and trained by the Hizbollah of Lebanon, whose activists had arrived in the Basra area; and Jaish al Mahdi (Army of the Mahdi)—sponsored by Muqtada al Sadr—which had not yet resorted to guerrilla attacks.

Summing up the overall scene, Jihad Abid Hussein al Alwani, imam of Salih Mosque in Ramadi, said, "Resistance is concentrated in mosques." He was questioned by the American commander for eight hours on the incendiary content of his sermon. "I asked them whether they would not resist if Germans or Fidel Castro occupied Washington, and of course they said Yes."[50]

Yet Bremer's CPA kept attributing the guerrilla activity exclusively to "the remnants of the old regime." As it happened, while his Interim Governing Council was giving a press conference on July 13, a bomb went off at a police station in a Baghdad suburb, killing at least one person. The subsequent audiotape aired on Al Arabiya said, "No one from Saddam's followers carried out any jihad operations that Saddam claims. The attacks are a result of our brothers in jihad." The speaker was referring to a claim made by Saddam in his most recent audiotape.

SADDAM, DEAD OR ALIVE

Between April 28, his birthday, and July 4, American Independence Day, Saddam Hussein's companions had managed to fax statements and/or deliver audiotapes of his messages addressed either to "Iraqis, Arabs and the Islamic world" or to Iraqis alone, with each statement beginning with an appropriate verse from the Quran. The letters were faxed to the London-based *Al Quds al Arabi* (The Arab Jerusalem); the audiotapes were delivered to one of the Arab TV channels, often Al Jazeera.

In his first message, Saddam blamed Iraq's defeat on "the treason by the army generals." He added, "Rise up against the occupier. Don't trust those who speak about Sunnis and Shias because the only issue now for your great country is the occupation. There is no priority but to drive out the infidel, the criminal and cowardly occupier."

In his second message, delivered on May 5, Saddam exhorted Arab and Kurd, Shia and Sunni and Muslim and Christian "to kick the enemy out of our country." Calling for a guerrilla war, he advised Iraqis to make mosques centers of resistance. "The Iraqi people must keep up their civilization in which they are one country, one people as they are now [and not opt for federalism]," he added. "We have to go back to the secret style of struggle that we [in the Baath Party] began our life with."[51]

His next message, on June 12, warned that if "the infidel thief and criminal Bush" and "shameless Blair . . . are still here after the first stage of our resistance, we will transfer our defense to other countries." He called for attacks on the forces of any country that had sent troops to Iraq, including Denmark and Poland.

Saddam's fourth message, recorded on June 14, was played to Al Jazeera in Doha over the telephone on July 3, and aired the next day.[52] After declaring that he was "in Iraq with a group of leaders" and relaying "the good news that jihad cells and brigades of male and female mujahedin have been formed throughout Iraq," Saddam showed that he was monitoring the situation closely. "Not a day passes without them [the infidel occupiers] suffering losses in our great land thanks to our great mujahedin," he said. "The coming days will be days of hardship and trouble for the infidel invaders. They aim to destroy Iraq, and what they called the weapons of mass destruction was nothing but a cover for their plans. We sacrificed what we did except the great [Islamic] faith and honor. We sacrificed power but did not renege on our pledge to God and did not stab the nation in the back by surrendering. We thank God for everything. We fulfilled our obligations to you, and sacrificed what we had [meaning power]—except our values, which are based upon deep faith and honor." He urged Iraqis "not to give infidel invaders or their aides any information or help," and to continue "resisting the American and British infidels" and protecting "heroic resistance fighters."[53]

The figures released by the Pentagon on July 9 indicated the score so far of Iraq's "heroic resistance fighters," to use Saddam's phrase. Of the 212 U.S. military personnel killed so far in Iraq, 74 had died since May 1 through hostility or other causes. General John Abizaid, a Lebanese-American Christian once known as the Pentagon's "mad Arab," who succeeded General Tommy Franks on July 1, 2003, said plainly that U.S. troops were now facing "a classical guerrilla-type campaign"—a phrase the Bush team had assiduously avoided because of its association with the messy and protracted American involvement in the Vietnam War.

In this murky situation, made worse by daunting reconstruction needs and a crippling shortage of money, there was a flash of dramatic achievement for the Bush administration on July 22.

UDAY AND QUSAY KILLED

That day, following a tip-off, U.S. troops killed Uday Saddam Hussein, Qusay Saddam Hussein and his fourteen-year-old son Mustafa, and their bodyguard, Abdul Samad, in the Falah neighborhood of north Mosul. Between the two, Qusay was the more important, being general supervisor of the Republican Guard, chief of the Special Security Organization, and deputy chairman of the Baath Party's Military Bureau.[54]

Uday and Qusay had arrived in Mosul on June 30 to stay in the newly built, porticoed, four-story villa of Nawaf al Zaidan, a tribal leader and a wealthy building contractor who often claimed blood ties with Saddam to gain government contracts. Since this was false, both he and his brother Salah—who made a similar statement—were jailed by Saddam. After his release, he had made his peace with the regime. On the eve of the invasion, he had turned his villa into a virtual Baath Party ward office. But after its end, ever the opportunist, he flew the yellow flag of the Kurdistan Democratic Party to save his villa from looting. That made Zaidan's house, which was fairly isolated, attractive to Uday and Qusay as a hideout, as did the city of Mosul itself, which was far removed from the Sunni Triangle and not closely associated with their father or their clan.

What worked against the brothers was their failure to stay on the move every few days, as their father apparently continued to do. But it must have been the huge bounty placed on their heads that proved irresistible to Zaidan. After much thought, equivocation, and consultation with his son, Shahlan, Nawaf al Zaidan informed the local U.S. commander about his Most Wanted Guests on the evening of July 21.

The next morning, Nawaf left home early to buy breakfast for his guests. Around 8 A.M., a force of two hundred—consisting of paratroopers of the 101st Airborne Division and commandos of Task Force 20—mounted a "cordon and knock" operation. After cordoning off a large area around the villa, Task Force 20 commandos used a megaphone to order everybody in the house to step outside. When Nawaf returned around 9 A.M., they arrested him and led him away. They knocked outside the house around 9 A.M., and were distracted when Nawaf's son, Shahlan, arrived in a BMW. They arrested him too and whisked him away. Then they returned to the house and were about to break in when firing started from an area on the first floor encased in thick walls and bulletproof glass. Four soldiers were injured. Then, according to Lieutenant General Ricardo Sanchez, the commander of U.S. forces in Iraq, the army continued to "prep the objective," with an onslaught on the first floor that included grenades, rockets, and fifty-caliber heavy machine-gun bullets. When that failed, the local commander called in a Kiowa CH helicopter to hit the room with rockets. At noon, the Americans made a second attempt to storm the building. They reached the ground floor but came under fire as they tried to move up the stairs. They withdrew. At about 1 P.M., the U.S. assault team fired twelve TOW antitank missiles at the strong room on the first floor. Finally, at 2 P.M., the soldiers went in again. All was quiet.

During the onslaught, Nawaf and Shahlan al Zaidan sat in an American military vehicle and smoked while the people in the neighborhood were either paralyzed with fear or unbearably nervous. "We ran from room to room trying to find the best place to shelter, and calling out 'Allahu Akbar,' " said Leila Muhammad, a neighbor. "Why did they not opt for a slow siege and allow the neighbors to escape to safety before the onslaught began?" The windows of many houses were shattered, and shrapnel and metal from the rockets and missiles scattered all over the area. The Americans could have cleared the area and turned on arc lights and loud music, as they had done to Panama's president, General Manuel Noriega, after he took refuge in the Vatican embassy in Panama City in 1989.

Who decided to blast the place? Lieutenant General Sanchez

said that it was "an operational decision" taken by the commander on the ground. Later, when questioned on the subject, Paul Wolfowitz replied that it was a matter of "speed and secrecy." In other words, the decision to kill Uday and Qusay Saddam Hussein was made at the highest level, either by Rumsfeld alone, or by him, Dick Cheney, and George W. Bush jointly. It would have been better to give them the "General Noriega treatment," capture them alive, and put them on public trial. After all, since Saddam Hussein had put Qusay in charge of concealing the WMD and concomitant facilities after the 1991 Gulf War, he would have been a singularly valuable source of information on Iraq's WMD.[55]

In retrospect, Zaidan's neighbors put two and two together. "There was something wrong when Nawaf [al Zaidan] decided to transfer all his valuable furniture out of the building, saying he was moving to a new house," said "Salwan," the neighborhood grocer. "They say Nawaf took his millions to Kuwait or the [United Arab] Emirates. But he still owed me 40,000 dinars [$40]." On the other hand, he paid another, upscale grocer, Thaier Dabbagh, cash on the spot. "For about three weeks Nawaf would buy expensive foodstuff and pay for them up front, which was very unusual for him, so I figured he had important guests," said Dabbagh. Significantly, no one actually saw the brothers; they doggedly remained inside the house for twenty-three days.[56]

After a twenty-four hour delay, the Pentagon released pictures of the slain brothers. "Iraqis are [still] frightened of Saddam Hussein and his regime," explained Rumsfeld. "To get closure, to have two vicious members confirmed dead, I believe, will contribute to more Iraqis coming forward [with information about Saddam]." The first Iraqis to see these images were the members of the Interim Governing Council. The photographs showed the bodies of Uday and Qusay, laid out on body bags, from the chest upward. Uday's face had a diagonal purple gash across it, and his shaven head had small patches of dried blood on it. Both brothers had bushy black beards—either a result of their thirteen weeks on the run or a deliberate attempt at disguise. Uday had in the past worn a beard, so there was no doubt about him being dead. But Qusay had sported only a mustache. So, to convince the skeptical, the military barber gave him the closest shave possible—to make him look like the Qusay Iraqis were accustomed to seeing.

When a group of mostly Arab journalists looked at the bodies brought to the Baghdad International Airport, they found that the faces were waxy and heavily made up. Between them they had received twenty bullets, and a hole in the top of Uday's head was visible. Lieutenant-General Sanchez's claim that Uday had died due to "a blow to the head" by "a blunt object" was a pathetic attempt at lying. What a military mortician had done was to wash the blood off Uday's face and stitch up his nose and mouth—which had been penetrated by a bullet. Qusay had two bullet wounds to his head, in and just behind his right ear.

The Iraqi Red Crescent were allowed to collect the corpses of Uday and Qusay Saddam Hussein, along with that of Mustafa, eleven days after their death. They were buried at a cemetery near the village of Auja, where Saddam's mother, Subha al Talfa, was already interred in an azure-domed mausoleum draped with Iraqi flags. More than one hundred members of Saddam Hussein's extended family gathered. One of them intoned, "Oh, God, welcome Uday and Qusay as martyrs on the Day of Judgment, as heroes killed in a glorious battle against a foreign invader."[57]

By contrast, Bush lost no time in welcoming the news of the deaths of Uday and Qusay. Appearing in the White House Rose Garden along with Rumsfeld and Bremer, he said that the death of "two of the regime's chief henchmen" was proof that the former regime was gone and "will not be coming back." With this, his administration could now focus on the sole remaining target: Saddam Hussein.

Tony Blair, the most important of Bush's foreign allies, was in the midst of a tour of the Far East when he got the news. "It is a great day for New Iraq," he declared.

BLAIR IN TROUBLE

On July 17, Tony Blair was awarded a Gold Medal by the U.S. Congress, thus making him the second Briton to be so acclaimed, the first being Conservative British prime minister Sir Winston Churchill. While Blair was basking in the afterglow of this honor, he received the news that Dr. David Kelly—a leading chemical and biological weapons expert of his government who had served as a UN inspector for seven years and visited Iraq thirty-seven times[58]—had committed suicide. He did so out of the dejection and distress he felt after being named, on July 9, as the source whose briefing to BBC Radio defense correspondent Andrew Gilligan had resulted in the journalist saying that the September 24, 2002, dossier on Iraq's WMD had been "sexed up" by Blair's director of communications, Alastair Campbell—which was contested by Campbell. Kelly admitted to his managers that he had met Gilligan, but denied making the accusation. To discredit the BBC story, the defense ministry made Kelly's name public. This led the House of Commons Foreign Affairs Committee (FAC) to invite Kelly—a shy, soft-spoken man of fifty-nine—in for further testimony on July 16, which was televised. This, and the threat of losing his job and pension, drove him to suicide.

Blair ordered an independent inquiry to be led by Lord Hutton, a senior judge, with a mandate to find out whether the government's treatment of Kelly had contributed to his death. But the hearings, starting August 11, widened their scope to examine critically the British government's campaign during the run-up to the invasion of Iraq.

Actually, Blair's postinvasion troubles had started with the resignation of Clare Short, secretary for international development, on May 12, in protest at his betrayal of a promise to work for UN involvement in postwar Iraq, and at his earlier cooperation with Bush. "I had to depart because the government has breached international law and proper support for the UN, and misled people about the possibility of getting a second resolution [at the Security Council]," she said.

Later, in her interview with the BBC and testimony to the House of Commons FAC, Short made a comprehensive case. First, Blair had misled the cabinet by spinning the claim of forty-five-minute deployment—all weaponized, ready to go, immediately dangerous—likely to get into the hands of Al Qaida, thus creating a false sense of urgency. Second, she claimed, Blair had entered into "a secret pact" with Bush in early September 2002 to go to war in the following spring, and then told the cabinet that he would try to "constrain the U.S." Third, none of the raw intelligence repeated in face-to-face briefings to cabinet ministers by MI6 and the Defense Intelligence Staff backed up Blair's claim that WMD could be deployed "within forty-five minutes." Fourth, the cabinet had held no discussion of the available options in the run-up to the war: No option papers were prepared for the cabinet. Fifth, the cabinet's Defense and Overseas Policy Committee had never met to discuss the Iraq crisis. Finally, the Foreign Office was "sucked out" of the decision to go to war.

Soon after, a poll showed that 63 percent believed Blair had misled the country over Iraq's biological and chemical weapons. Another poll showed that 66 percent thought the Blair government was "not trustworthy or honest"; this figure had been 30 percent at the time of the June 2001 general election. At 35 percent, Labour's popularity was two points behind the Tories for the first time in eleven years.[59]

In a language uncannily similar to that used by the Bush administration's domestic critics, Robin Cook told the BBC, "They [the government] were not looking at intelligence to try to get a balanced judgment, a guide to policy out of it—they were looking to intelligence to support a conclusion they had already drawn, which is that they were going to go to war." In his testimony to the House of Commons FAC, comparing "raw intelligence" to "alphabet soup," he said, "On this occasion, those bits of the alphabet which supported the case were selected." Second, he revealed that the majority of the September 2002 dossier was derivative. He spoke with an insider's knowledge: As foreign secretary from 1997 to 2001, he was the boss of MI6. Third, MI6 briefings to cabinet ministers indicated that Iraq's biological and chemical weapons program did not represent a high risk. Finally, the February 2003 dossier, "a glorious and spectacular own goal," had not been discussed in cabinet.[60]

The arguments advanced by Short and Cook were so powerful that they affected popular opinion. Those who thought Britain was right in attacking Iraq fell from 64 percent in early April to 47 percent three months later.

A worse fate awaited Blair as he and the leading figures of his administration had their testimonies to the Hutton Inquiry contradicted by their close aides and official e-mails and other documents. This damaged Blair's standing to the extent that, at 43 percent, more Britons wanted him to resign over the Kelly controversy than stay on the job.[61]

The governmental side was led by Blair, his secretary of defense Geoff Hoon, Joint Intelligence Committee (JIC) chairman John Scarlett, and Alastair Campbell, who acted as the day-to-day intermediary between Blair and Scarlett in the course of the drafting of the September 24, 2002, dossier.

Blair said that Scarlett's JIC, and not his office at 10 Downing Street, had the "ownership" of the dossier. He took responsibility for the government's decision before the outing of Kelly, and admitted to chairing several meetings at which the Kelly issue was discussed—thus contradicting statements he made in the wake of Kelly's suicide, when he said "categorically" and "emphatically" that he had played no role in the naming of the scientist.[62] His claim that the JIC owned the dossier clashed with evidence from Dr. Brian Jones, head of the scientific and technical section of the Defense Intelligence Staff (which interpreted raw intelligence on WMD), who said that there were two further drafts after the JIC meeting, and that the full JIC did not meet to sign off on the final version, which was produced by a special group that included Alastair Campbell. Furthermore, the minutes of the September 18 meeting of the JIC, chaired by Scarlett, explicitly stated that ownership of the dossier lay with 10 Downing Street.

This undermined the very foundation of Blair's case that the dossier was the work of the JIC, and not of his own office.

Hoon denied any involvement in the naming of Kelly. But his special adviser, Richard Taylor, said that the naming strategy was discussed at a meeting in Hoon's office on July 9, the day Kelly's name was made public.

Echoing Blair, his political boss, Scarlett maintained that the JIC retained "ownership" of the dossier and that there had been no interference from Campbell in its preparation. He said he was unaware of any unhappiness in the intelligence services other than concern over the precedent of putting intelligence into the public domain. Also, he let slip that the forty-five-minute claim referred to battlefield munitions (namely, mortars and artillery shells) and not Scud missiles with a range of 410 miles (650 kilometers), thus inadvertently undermining the dossier's dramatic claim that Iraq could launch WMD within forty-five minutes toward British bases in Cyprus.

In stark contrast, Dr. Brian Jones—describing himself as "probably the most senior and experienced intelligence official working on WMD"—said he and his colleagues were skeptical of the forty-five-minute claim because (a) there was no evidence of significant chemical or biological weapons production activity in Iraq; (b) the claim was based on a single, secondary source; (c) the source appeared not to know about the subject; and (d) the claim was "nebulous" and secondhand, possibly from a source aiming "to influence rather than inform [British intelligence]." His former colleague "Mr. A"—a serving chemical weapons expert at the Ministry of Defense—giving evidence over an audio link, said the forty-five-minute claim raised more questions than it answered.

"Are you [the informant] referring to a technical process?" he asked. "Are you referring to command and control process?" Jones added that if biological or chemical agents were not loaded into Scud missile warheads, they could not be called "weapons of *mass* destruction." He referred to "deep disquiet among my [intelligence] colleagues about the way significant evidence they had supplied for the dossier had been altered." He gave an example of "over-egging": Instead of saying Iraq had "possibly" or "probably" produced chemical agents, it made an unqualified claim that Iraq had produced chemical agents and continues to do so. He said that he wrote to his superiors, setting out his concerns, before publication, and gave repeated warnings about the wording of the dossier, but his objections were ignored. (Dr. Jones retired in early 2003.)

Campbell stated that he had not "hardened up" the dossier, and had had "no input, output, influence upon them [JIC] whatsoever at any stage" in its drafting or in the inclusion of the forty-five-minute claim. In reality, his and other memos showed that he was heavily involved in making recommendations to Scarlett, many of which were accepted. He pressed for a starker description of the nuclear threat, and got it. The final version hinted that Iraq could have a nuclear capacity "within two years."[63]

Compared to the exhaustive and grilling hearings conducted by the House of Commons FAC and the Hutton Inquiry in Britain, the U.S. Senate hearings on the subject of intelligence on Iraq were a mild affair.

LACK OF INQUEST IN THE UNITED STATES

Aside from Gregory Thielmann, a freshly retired director of the State Department's Intelligence and Research Bureau, no serving or retired government bureaucrat came forward to spill the beans. When Joseph Wilson went public on his CIA assignment to check the claim of Iraq trying to buy uranium oxide from

Niger by publishing an op-ed piece in the *New York Times* on July 6, 2003, somebody in the Bush team leaked that his wife, Valerie Plame, an energy-industry analyst, was an undercover CIA agent, thus committing a federal criminal offense. Conservative columnist Robert Novak, citing "senior administration officials," said in his syndicated column that Wilson got the assignment because of his wife's link to the CIA. At a press conference, Wilson explained that he published the article because, at that time, senior administration officials maintained that his findings had been shared with "only low-ranking intelligence officials," which was untrue. Why leak confidential information on his wife, he asked. "It wasn't to intimidate me, because I had already said my piece," he said. "Clearly this was to keep others from stepping forward."[64]

When asked about Iraq's Niger connection on July 14 at an Oval Office press conference, Bush said, "The larger point is, and the fundamental question is, did Saddam Hussein have a weapons program? And the answer is, Absolutely. And we gave him a chance to allow the inspectors in, and he wouldn't let them in. And, therefore, after a reasonable request, we decided to remove him from power, along with other nations, so as to make sure he was not a threat to the United States and our friends and allies in the region."[65]

What about the seven hundred and thirteen inspections at four hundred and eleven sites that Unmovic and the IAEA carried out in Iraq between November 27, 2002, and March 18, 2003? What about the desperate efforts Bush, backed by Blair, made to get the second resolution passed at the UN Security Council? What about the trip he made to the Portuguese island of Terceira in the Azores on March 14 to meet Blair and Spanish leader Jose Maria Aznar? One is left wondering why none of the journalists present pointed out any of these bare facts.

It is instances like this that leave alert, skeptical columnists, such as Paul Krugman of the *New York Times,* gnashing their teeth and feeling frustrated that "nobody is being held accountable for misleading the U.S. into a war [on Iraq]."[66]

One is also left wondering why a call by Senator Bob Graham to impeach Bush for lying to the American people on the vital issue of war and peace did not get off the ground.

But it might—if Iraq turns out to be a giant incubator for Islamist and secular terrorists, instead of a cradle of democracy, as Bush and his team are hoping and praying it will.

NOTES

1. Cited in *Guardian*, July 1, 2003.

2. Cited in *New York Times*, August 13, 2003.

3. Cited in *Observer*, July 6, 2003.

4. Cited in *Independent on Sunday*, July 6, 2003.

5. Islam enjoins a forty-day mourning period for the dead. See further entries on "Ashura" and "Shias" in Dilip Hiro, *The Essential Middle East*, pp. 53–54 and pp. 485–86.

6. April 25, 2003.

7. A U.S. toy manufacturer would soon start making a Bush doll dressed in a flight suit.

8. The Iraq Survey Group would later be expanded by a further three hundred to four hundred members with fresh intakes from the United States, Britain, and Australia, raising the strength of the Mobile Exploitation Team to three hundred.

9. This Task Force had arrived in Iraq, believing that Saddam Hussein had given "release authority" to those in charge of a chemical arsenal. *Washington Post*, May 11, 2003.

10. May 23, 2003.

11. Cited in *Independent on Sunday*, June 8, 2003.

12. *Guardian*, May 29, 2003.

13. *Financial Times*, June 27, 2003.

14. *Independent*, April 19, 2003. "Very soon" has yet to happen.

15. *Guardian*, April 19, 2003; *International Herald Tribune*, April 19–20, 2003.

16. *Wall Street Journal*, April 30, 2003.

17. In a memorandum to the leading cabinet ministers, Lord Goldsmith wrote, "My view is that a further Security Council resolution is needed to authorize imposing reform and restructuring of Iraq and its government." *Guardian*, May 22, 2003.

18. He was currently serving as the UN High Commissioner for human rights, and took a four months' leave of absence to take up his temporary job in Iraq.

19. *New York Times*, May 23, 2003.

20. According to the Coalition Provisional Authority, some thirty thousand Baath members forming 5 to 10 percent of the total, were disqualified from public-sector jobs. Others put the number of disqualified Baathists at eighty thousand.

21. *Guardian*, August 25, 2003.

22. *New York Times*, June 20.

23. *Guardian*, August 16, 2003.

24. Under the old regime there were fifty thousand policemen nationwide.

25. August 13, 2003.

26. *Independent*, June 26, 2003.

27. *New York Times*, July 7, 2003.

28. July 6, 2003.

29. Eighty percent of the attacks were in the Sunni triangle of Ramadi-Tikrit-Baghdad. *Guardian*, July 18, 2003.

30. *The Times* (London), July 4, 2003.

31. The latest one to surrender was Muhammad Said al Sahhaf. True to his flamboyant style, he did so after giving an interview on Abu Dhabi TV. *New York Times*, June 27, 2003.

32. *Spectator*, July 19, 2003. p. 13.

33. *Newsweek*, August 11, p. 23.

34. *Independent*, July 30, 2003. Wadah Khanfar added that in many cases Al Jazeera did not broadcast the unsolicited videos, hand-delivered by unidentified Iraqis, showing ambushes of U.S. convoys.

35. *Newsweek*, August 11, p. 23.

36. Paul Bremer closed down *Al Mustaqila* (The Independent) when it printed an article in which the author called for "death to all spies and those who cooperate with the U.S.," adding that "killing them is a religious duty."

37. Masud Barzani had first worked with General Jay Garner when he was appointed by the Pentagon to oversee the "safe haven" for Kurds in northern Iraq after the 1991 Gulf War.

38. *The Times*, May 30, 2003.

39. June 19, 2003.

40. See further Dilip Hiro, *Neighbors, not Friends*, pp. 37–38.

41. See further Dilip Hiro, *The Essential Middle East*, p. 113.

42. See Dilip Hiro, op. cit., p. 157.

43. The breakdown of 57 percent was: 3–6 months, 14 percent, and 6–12 months, 33 percent. For the rest: 12–24 months, 28 percent; more than 24 months, 21 percent. *Observer*, April 13, 2003.

44. Cited in *Observer*, August 10, 2003.

45. Of the twenty-five members, twelve were insiders living in Arab Iraq, four were based in Iraqi Kurdistan, and the rest were exiles.

46. He applauded Paul Bremer's order to outlaw the Baath Party, which was his idea anyway. *New York Times*, July 14, 2003.

47. Chairmanship was to rotate monthly according to the members' first name in Arabic.

48. July 21, 2003.

49. This group had evolved from the Muslim Brotherhood, suppressed by Saddam Hussein. For Salafiya movement, see Dilip Hiro, *The Essential Middle East*, p. 462.

50. Cited in *Guardian*, July 18, 2003.

51. On May 5, two Iraqi men with Tikriti accents wanted to deliver a tape to Al Jazeera in Baghdad. But when they asked a journalist from the *Sydney Morning Herald*, accompanied by his Iraqi translator, in the street, where the Al Jazeera office was, they were told to go to the nearby Palestine Hotel, heavily guarded by U.S. soldiers. So they quickly handed over the tape to the Australian journalist's translator and vanished. *Independent*, May 8, 2003.

52. We don't know the source [of the tape]," said Ibrahim Hilal, editor in chief of Al Jazeera. "We have no reason to doubt its authenticity." Saddam's voice and language are so unique that it is easy to authenticate his tapes. "Saddam's voice is unmistakable," said a producer at the BBC World Service's Arabic section. "No double would be able to imitate it. His language is so archaic, and he uses lots of historical facts—mentioning fighters from the past struggles—as well as religious terms." *Sunday Times*, April 6, 2003.

53. *New York Times*, July 5, 2003; *Daily Telegraph*, July 5, 2003; *Guardian*, July 5, 2003; *Independent*, July 5, 2003.

54. See further Dilip Hiro, *The Essential Middle East*, pp. 194–95.

55. See further Dilip Hiro, *Neighbors, not Friends*, pp. 55–56, 63. Among those who viewed the rocketing of the hiding place of Uday and Qusay Saddam Hussein as "overkill" was Sergio Vieira de Mello. *Guardian*, August 21, 2003.

56. *Independent on Sunday*, August 10, 2003. In early August the U.S. troops demolished Nawaf al Zaidan's villa to ensure it did not turn into a shrine.

57. The U.S. troops removed the Iraqi flags from the tombs of Uday and Qusay Saddam Hussein, but left untouched the one over the tomb of Mustafa Qusay Hussein.

58. During this period David Kelly reportedly passed on information to Britain's Secret Intelligence Service, known as MI6, thus behaving like many of his American colleagues working for the United Nations. See further Dilip Hiro, *Iraq: In the Eye of the Storm*, pp. 101-2, 105-9, and 112-13.

59. *New York Times,* June 28, 2003.

60. *Independent,* June 18, 2003.

61. *New York Times*, September 8, 2003.

62. Yet Lord Hutton did *not* recall Tony Blair for cross-examination, thus tarnishing his impartiality.

63. *Independent*, September 4 and 6, 2003; *Guardian*, September 5 and 6, 2003; *Independent on Sunday*, September 7, 2003.

64. *New York Times*, August 8, 2003. The tactic seemed to have worked.

65. *Washington Post*, July 15, 2003.

66. June 11, 2003. A fortnight later Paul Krugman wrote, "We have a moral obligation to demand accountability—in the face not only of a powerful, ruthless political machine but also of a country not yet ready to believe that its leaders have exploited 9/11 for political gain."

Chapter 10

"NEW IRAQ": CRADLE OF DEMOCRACY OR INCUBATOR FOR TERRORISTS?

"The [Iraq] war has widened the rift between Americans and West Europeans, further inflamed the Muslim world, softened support for the war on terrorism, and significantly weakened the global public support for the pillars of the post–World War II era—the UN and the North Atlantic Alliance."

—Andrew Kohut, director of Pew Research Center for the People and the Press, summarizing a survey of fifteen thousand people in twenty-one North American, Middle Eastern, and European countries[1]

"People say to me, 'You are not Vietnamese. You have no jungles and swamps to hide in.' I reply, 'Let our cities be our swamps and our buildings be our jungles.' "[2]

—Iraq's Deputy Prime Minister Tariq Aziz

"In Islam, the infidel has no right to relieve the oppression of believers. If we want to change the regime, we'll do it ourselves."

—Abdul Majid Nouri, sign writer in Falluja, sitting in his shop festooned with a banner in English reading, "Our aim is not to kill you but our independence is more precious than your blood." [3]

REPORT ON 100 DAYS IN IRAQ

THE CONTENT OF the Bush administration's "100 Days in Iraq" report on August 11 clashed with the reality on the ground, and its timing could not have been worse, from the White House's viewpoint. There was no mention in it of either Lieutenant-General Ricardo Sanchez's statement on July 31—"We are fighting a low-intensity conflict against a multifaceted enemy. The sophistication of the attacks is increasing"—or of the fifty-six American soldiers killed in hostile action since May 1.

The report was released four days after a huge car bomb exploded outside the Jordanian embassy in the Ghazaliya neighborhood of Baghdad, killing nineteen people and injuring fifty. The C4 military plastic explosive was detonated by remote control, and the blast badly damaged the embassy building. No group claimed responsibility. Speculation centered on those wishing to punish Jordan for allowing the Anglo-American Special Forces to operate from its soil before and during the invasion of Iraq; and on those, conversely, who strongly disapproved of the Jordanian government giving refuge to Saddam Hussein's widowed daughters, Raghad and Rana, and their nine children, on July 31. Still others pointed to the Iraqi National Congress's journal, *Al Muatamar* (The Congress), which had attacked Jordan for "hosting pillars of the deposed regime," a charge vehemently denied by the Jordanian government.

"Most of Iraq is calm, and progress on the road to democracy and freedom not experienced in decades continues," concluded the 100-day report serenely. "Only in isolated areas are there still attacks."

Such isolated areas seemed to include the whole metropolitan area of Baghdad, which, with nearly six million inhabitants, accounted for a quarter of the national population. On August 19, at 1:30 P.M. local time, a far more lethal bomb exploded outside the United Nations headquarters at the old Canal Hotel in the capital's eastern district of seventh Nisan, killing twenty-three, including the UN's

Special Representative to Iraq, Sergio Vieira de Mello, and injuring a third of the three hundred people inside the building—about half of the UN's foreign staff.

According to U.S. officials, the bombing was a suicide attack directly targeting de Mello in his office on the third floor. In order to provide maximum shrapnel, the bomb makers had mixed 10,600 pounds (4,800 kilograms) of C4 military plastic explosive with old shells and munitions before loading the lethal weapon onto the flat bed of a Soviet-made Kamaz truck, which was then parked below de Mello's office.[4] Commenting on the worst attack on the United Nations in its fifty-eight-year history, Secretary-general Kofi Annan said, "Nothing can excuse this act of unprovoked and murderous violence." In President Bush's words, "By their tactics and targets, these murderers reveal themselves once more as enemies of the civilized world."

On August 21, in their two-page statement broadcast by Al Arabiya TV, a group calling itself "The Armed Vanguard of the Second Muhammad Army" claimed responsibility, saying it did not regret killing "the Crusaders"—the term invariably used by Al Qaida and its associate organizations. "We will continue to fight every foreigner in Iraq." Four days earlier, the same television channel had aired a tape by Abu Abdul Rahman al Najdi, a spokesman of Al Qaida based in Afghanistan, who claimed that the recent attacks in Iraq were the work of *jihadis* (i.e., those who conduct jihad) and urged them to continue their struggle.[5]

The attack on the United Nations was almost unanimously condemned abroad, and rightly described as an atrocity. In Iraq, however, feelings were mixed. Many Iraqis considered the United Nations to be working—knowingly or inadvertently—for American intelligence, a perception rooted in fact.[6] Thirteen devastating years of sanctions, which had impoverished most Iraqis by 90 percent, were imposed by the United Nations. "The U.S. consistently maintained that UN resolutions authorized the attacks," noted the Doha-based *Gulf Times*, apparently referring to the six times since the end of the 1991 Gulf War that the Pentagon had mounted air strikes against Iraq (August 1992, January 1993, June 1993, September 1996, December 1998, and February 2001) before its March 2003 invasion.

De Mello was probably targeted because he was seen to be attempting to legitimize the American occupation through such means as the U.S.-appointed Interim Iraqi Governing Council. While Bremer deliberately shunned the limelight at the council's inauguration on July 13, de Mello said on Iraqi TV, "Your convening marks the first major development toward the restoration of Iraq's rightful status as a fully sovereign state." He also lobbied the UN security council to pass a resolution "welcoming" the Iraqi Governing Council, a move initiated by Washington. In that sense, de Mello was out of tune with popular Arab opinion, as expressed by the Arab League, whose members spurned the U.S. invitation to recognize the Interim Governing Council and/or send peacekeeping forces to Iraq.

By their action, the truck bombers were saying to the non-Arab nations being courted by Washington to send troops to Iraq: You will be treated in the same way as the occupying Americans and Britons. As a result, Japan, which had been considering sending one thousand soldiers to Iraq, had second thoughts.

The adverse impact of the bombing extended beyond diplomacy and politics to economic and humanitarian sectors. The International Monetary Fund and the World Bank withdrew their staff. Many nongovernmental organizations pulled out. And the UN Humanitarian Coordinator's Office reduced its staff by a third. This was an enormous setback to the plans for economic reconstruction, which were predicated on political stability and reconstruction.

After two weeks of deliberation, all that the Iraqi Presidential Council had to show for itself was the appointment of a committee of twenty-five to discuss a "mechanism for drawing up a new constitution." The council members had yet to realize something that de Mello had: The primary issue for the Iraqi people was *sovereignty*.

Only if and when Iraqis were convinced that the Anglo-American occupation was coming to a swift end would their sense of humiliation end. De Mello had argued that guerrilla resistance was draining sustenance from a growing feeling of humiliation. However, the end of occupation was nowhere in sight, and neither the members of the Presidential Council nor the Governing Council seemed to be pressing for it.

Meanwhile, the claim of "10 signs of better infrastructure" made by the White House's "100 Days in Iraq" report lay in shreds as the pipeline carrying oil to Turkey was bombed near Baiji, 125 miles (200 kilometers) north of Baghdad, on the third day of the resumption of oil exports on August 13. The saboteurs detonated a roadside bomb, made up of four 155-millimeter artillery shells, with rocket-propelled grenades and automatic weapons. Then, to severely disrupt the repairs, they mounted another successful attack on the pipeline near the previous site. Around the same time, water mains in Baghdad were blown up too. As it was, thanks to sabotage and power cuts, oil output at one million barrels per day was roughly a third of the prewar level.

At 3,300 megawatts, the electric output was about two-fifths of the pre-invasion figure. Though water-purification capacity had been restored in Baghdad to near pre-invasion levels, actual production was much less, due to frequent electricity cuts. This was the case elsewhere as well. "The root problem is electric power," said Major Charles Mayo in British-occupied Basra. "People have been pulling down power lines to steal the copper. So no power is going to the power station or oil refinery where petrol and diesel are made. Also the infrastructure is 1970s technology which had little maintenance. So there is no quick fix."[7]

Most Iraqis were not impressed by such explanations. They remembered the speed with which Saddam's regime had restored essential public utilities—electricity, telephones, and water—after the relentless bombing during the 1991 Gulf War, and were now baffled by the slowness of the world's most technologically advanced nation.

Lacking reliable intelligence in a country still reeling from the almost total destruction of its administrative and security infrastructure, the Bush administration was equally at a loss as to who was behind these dastardly bombings. Yet to reassure the agitated Iraqi public, Bremer's CPA let it be known that it had recruited more than one hundred former senior agents of Saddam's feared General Intelligence Department, popularly called *Mukhabarat*. Such recruitment had started within weeks of the fall of Baghdad on April 9. Among those who were hired was Muhammad Abdullah, a colonel with ten years' experience in *Mukhabarat* and eight in military intelligence. "We were under strict instructions not to publicize our work with the Americans, but dozens of former *Mukhabarat* officers have already been recruited," he told Mark Franchetti of the *Sunday Times*. "They need us." And "they" were paying him $700 a month, a princely salary.[8]

At the same time, Bremer's CPA kept repeating the mantra that "the remnants of the old regime" were solely responsible for the insurgency. This was not so. The residue of the ousted regime was just one element in the guerrilla struggle, which was dominated by Iraqi nationalists of Sunni persuasion who were inspired and guided by militant Sunni clerics. They functioned as members of cells within traditional clan and tribal networks or operated under the command of former security and intelligence officers. These resistance groups, with an estimated total strength of five thousand to seven thousand—bearing such names as Jaish Muhammad, Jaish Muatasim, Muslim Fighters of the Victorious Sects, and General Command of the Iraqi Armed Resistance and Liberation Forces—mostly used mosques after Friday prayers as places to gain recruits, who were then interviewed individually by the cell commander. If found satisfactory, the recruit was advised to cut filial ties and not to communicate with family members as a prelude to being sent to one of the local training camps that had been set up in the area along the Syrian border.

There was also the Ansar al Islam, whose surviving militia had escaped from Iraqi Kurdistan into adjoining Iran during the invasion. Some two hundred of them had reportedly slipped back into Iraq. But their size was dwarfed by the non-Iraqi Arab Islamist militants who had infiltrated Iraq—a country that shares long, porous borders with Saudi Arabia, Jordan, and Syria—now in the midst of near-chaos. In mid-September, Colin Powell put this figure at two thousand.

These volunteers came from the Muslim world, where anti-American feelings had risen sharply in the wake of the invasion of Iraq. This was quantified in mid-May 2003 by the U.S.-based Pew Research Center in its survey of fifteen thousand people in twenty-one countries. Its latest figures for those who had unfavorable views of America, juxtaposed with the figures of summer 2002, were: Jordan, 99 percent (75 percent), Palestinian Territories, 98 percent (not available), Indonesia, 83 percent (36 percent), Turkey, 83 percent (55 percent), and Pakistan, 81 percent (69 percent).[9]

What aided these militant volunteers was the fact that Iraq was now awash not only with small arms and ammunition but also rocket-propelled grenades, mortars, artillery and anti-tank shells, and ground-to-air missiles that Iraqis had looted from the unguarded arms dumps that the advancing American troops, in their rush to reach Baghdad, had failed to destroy immediately. Also, since all Iraqi adult males had served in the military, they knew how to handle small arms and explosives.

Those arriving from abroad were mostly Sunni. "We are seeing a developing marriage of convenience between the ex-Baathists who have the money, the contacts, and the ground knowledge, and [new] jihadist volunteers who have the specialist skills and are coming to Iraq to fight Americans on Arab soil," said a security official in Baghdad. "The U.S. has dangerously underestimated how important Iraq has become to them. They are drawn not only because U.S. and British troops are in [Iraq] but [also] because Iraq represents an ancient and powerful idea of Arab culture and history."[10] The

Americans' ignorance of Iraqi history and culture—even at the highest level—was compounded by their lack of knowledge of either Arabic or the terrain of the country. In contrast, Iraq loomed large in the minds of Islamists everywhere. After all, Baghdad had been the capital of the Islamic empire under the Abbasids for five centuries—from 750 A.D. to 1258—with a brief interruption when the emperor moved the capital northward to Samarra (836–92 A.D.) on the Tigris. Baghdad also holds the tomb of Abu Hanifa al Numan (699–767 A.D.), the founder of the Hanafi Code of Islamic law, the largest subsect among Sunnis.

The motive and ideology that had driven the Sunnis among the Iraqi insurgents were aptly summarized by Mullah Mustafa Kreikar, the founder of Ansar al Islam, now living in Oslo as a political refugee. "There is no difference between this [American] occupation [of Iraq] and the Soviet occupation of Afghanistan in 1979," he said in an interview with the Lebanese Broadcasting Corporation on August 10. "The resistance is not only a reaction to the American invasion, it is [also] part of the continuous Islamic struggle since the collapse of the Caliphate [in 1924]. All Islamic struggles since then are part of one struggle to bring back the Caliphate."[11] Islamists like Kreikar believe that only when the Caliphate is restored will Islam regain its past glory. But they are not clear on how this is to be achieved, or how the Caliph is to be chosen.

On the Shia side, there were activists from Lebanese Hizbollah, a militant Shia organization well versed in guerrilla activities maintained against the Israeli occupiers of South Lebanon for nearly two decades. They made a beeline for Shia-dominated southern Iraq. Their fingerprints could be seen in the killing of a British officer by a remote-control bomb and the slaying of three British soldiers in an ambush in the Basra area in mid-August—replications of Hizbollah operations against occupying Israeli troops.

Among Shias worldwide, Twelver Shias are the largest subsect, the others being Fivers and Seveners; all Iraqi Shias are Twelvers. They are so called because they believe in twelve imams, an imam being the supreme leader of Muslims after Prophet Muhammad, who died in 632 A.D. They are waiting for the return of the last imam, Muhammad al Qasim, who went into spiritual occultation as an infant in Samarra in 873 A.D. They consider him as their *mahdi* (lit., the guided one), who will reappear to institute the rule of justice on earth before the Day of Judgment.[12] Until such time, Shias are enjoined to select one of the living grand ayatollahs as their guide and follow his interpretations of Islam.

It was this concept of *mahdi* that inspired Hojatalislam Muqtada al Sadr in Najaf to urge his followers to join his Jaish al Mahdi (Army of the Mahdi). This alarmed the U.S. occupation authorities, even though al Sadr had stressed this "army" did not need to be armed at present. Nonetheless, al Sadr's call also raised concerns in the competing camp of SCIRI's leader, Ayatollah Muhammad Baqir al Hakim, who had seen his Badr Brigade outlawed by the Americans.

It was against this background that a bomb exploded on August 24 outside the SCIRI office near Imam Ali's shrine, killing three security guards and injuring ten others. The apparent target was sixty-six-year-old Grand Ayatollah Muhammad Said al Hakim, uncle of SCIRI's leader. Suspicion fell on Saddam loyalists and al Sadr partisans.

To cool the rising tension in Najaf, in his Friday sermon on August 29, Ayatollah Muhammad Baqir al Hakim called on all Iraqis to unite to fight the old regime, thereby pointing his finger at Saddam's followers for the attempted attack on his uncle. "The men of the ousted regime are those who are now targeting the grand ayatollah [*marja*]," he said. "The occupation forces have not fulfilled their legal obligations [to provide security], and we condemn this attitude and we hold the occupation forces responsible for the lack of security in the country. From the start we declared publicly that they should let Iraqis take responsibility for security, and we said that an Iraqi force of the faithful should be established to take charge of protecting the holy places of Iraq because the occupying forces cannot approach them. Until this situation changes there will be no security in Iraq."[13]

As al Hakim, accompanied by his bodyguards, left the mosque from the Kubla Gate to go to his car, 1,650 pounds (750 kilograms) of C4 plastic explosives, hidden in two vehicles, exploded, tearing a four-foot-wide crater in the tarmac road, turning the surrounding cars into flaming torches, and demolishing several shops across the street. The ornate facade of the shrine collapsed above the side gates, and tiles were ripped off or scorched as vehicles blew up against the thirty-foot-high (ten meters) wall. In the aftermath of the explosion, armed police and shrine guards, brandishing their weapons, kept the furious crowd at bay as relatives swarmed over ruined shops. The bomb, which killed ninety-five people, was so powerful that all that would later be identified of al Hakim's body was one hand—thanks to a distinctive ring he wore on one of his fingers. This hand would be enclosed in a casket and taken to the Imam Hussein Mosque in Baghdad.

Starting on Sunday, the three-hundred-thousand-strong funeral procession for the corpse of al Hakim crawled from Baghdad to Najaf via Karbala for three days. Before the start of the journey, an unnamed cleric at the Imam Hussein Mosque said over the loud-speaker, "Yesterday we faced the tanks of Saddam, today the tanks of the Americans. We are not afraid of the Americans."[14] The mourners picked up the cue and chanted slogans that equated America with Saddam. "We will humiliate Saddam! We will humiliate Bush!" they shouted.

Saddam was quick to disavow responsibility in a message recorded on an audiotape and aired on September 1. As usual, he began with an appropriate verse from the Quran. "O believers, if a corrupt person brought you news, check it well before accusing arbitrarily; otherwise you will regret your decision," it said. "Many of you may have heard the snakes hissing, the servants of the invaders, occupiers, infidels, and how they have managed to accuse the followers of Saddam Hussein of responsibility for the attack on al Hakim without any evidence," said the former president of Iraq, stressing that he was "the leader of the great Iraqi people, Arabs,

Kurds, Muslims, and non-Muslims," not "the leader of a minority or a group within a group," meaning respectively Sunnis or the Tikriti clan. "They rushed to accuse before investigating. They did that to divert attention from the real culprits. The true answers can only be found through an honest investigation by a national government in the future. That can only happen once the invaders and occupiers are kicked out of Iraq, which will happen soon, God willing." He ended with a call: "Oh, great heroes, intensify your brave blows against the foreign aggressors from wherever they come and whatever their nationalities."[15]

A rumor that spread quickly in Najaf in the wake of the bomb named the Wahhabis, a puritanical subsect within Sunni Islam originating in Saudi Arabia, as probable culprits. It gained credence with reports (later withdrawn) of the local police arresting several foreigners, including four Saudis and two Kuwaitis, as suspects.[16] This speculation had to do with events of the early nineteenth century. Between 1802 and 1810, Wahhabi militants from Arabia attacked Najaf and Karbala and stripped the tombs of Imam Hussein and Imam Ali of all embellishments and furnishings: They regarded embellishing graves as un-Islamic.[17] Also, in theological terms, Wahhabis hold Shias in low esteem. In recent times, Wahhabis have been in the forefront of Al Qaida; in fact, its leader, Osama bin Laden, is one. That said, Imam Ali, a cousin and son-in-law of Prophet Muhammad, is also sacrosanct to Sunnis, who call him Caliph Ali and regard him as a legitimate successor to Prophet Muhammad.

So Al Qaida leaders, hiding in the mountains along the Afghanistan-Pakistan border, felt the need to state their position. The organization's spokesman, Abu Abdul Rahman al Najdi, taped a statement on September 3 that would be broadcast by Al Arabiya four days later. "We strongly deny that Al Qaida had any hand in this bombing which killed Muhammad Baqir al Hakim, violated the sanctity of one of God's houses, and killed innocent people," said al Najdi. "Our highest aim is to fight the Americans and kill them everywhere on earth, and drive them out of Palestine, the Arabian Peninsula and Iraq." He added, "We have no [other] motives. Those who killed Baqir al Hakim are the Americans and Jews. They wanted to get rid of him because they know that his loyalty is to Iran." Another motive, he concluded, was to incite trouble between Shias and Sunnis, and turn Shias against Al Qaida.[18]

Those who attributed the bombing to intra-Shia rivalry between the Muqtada al Sadr and al Hakim camps seemed wide off the mark: No Shia would entertain the thought of placing a massive bomb outside the holiest shrine of his sect.

Oddly enough, the theme of the funeral address given by the assassinated cleric's brother, Ayatollah Abdul Aziz al Hakim, was the same as stated earlier by Saddam and later by al Najdi— removal of the Americans from Iraq. "This [occupation] force is primarily responsible for all this blood and the blood that is shed all over Iraq every day," said al Hakim. "Iraq must not remain occupied and the occupation must end so that we can build Iraq as God wants us to do." [19]

Bremer's Coalition Provisional Authority and their civilian superiors in Washington were too shaken by the Najaf massacre and the subsequent outpouring of grief by the Shia masses in public—and their equating of the Bush administration with the vile dictatorship of Saddam—to respond coherently. They were still in a daze on September 2 when the news reached them that a car bomb had exploded at the (supposedly) secure headquarters of the Baghdad police. It was intended to kill Police Chief Hassan Ali al Ubaidi. He was unhurt, but the detonation killed one police officer and injured ten more. In between, Ayatollah Muhammad Bahr al Uloom, one of the two Shia clerics on the Interim Governing Council, "suspended" his membership in the council in protest at the lack of security provided by the CPA.

The inference was clear and chilling: Those behind the bombings selected their targets carefully, to convey different messages.

The assault on the UN headquarters was meant to frighten Western or Western-dominated institutions—business corporations (particularly oil companies), nongovernmental organizations, and international financial institutions—and it worked. The massacre at Najaf seemed to have more than one objective: to highlight that Shias, though three-fifths of the national population, were not a monolithic force, and to sow the seeds of a possible civil war along the Shia–Sunni divide, thus bringing into focus the scenario most feared by the U.S. policy makers: Iraq, possessing the world's second-largest oil reserves, consumed by a civil strife that would suck in all its six immediate neighbors, three of them oil-rich, and have a devastating impact on oil prices. The last major civil war in the region was in Lebanon, which does not have oil; it lasted more than fifteen years, from April 1975 to October 1990, and consumed 150,000 lives. At different times it sucked in not only neighboring Israel and Syria but also Egypt, Iraq, Libya, France, the United States, Britain, and Italy.[20] The Bush White House could ill afford to indulge its tendency of crediting what it wanted to believe—such as Iraq possessing WMD and having links with Al Qaida—rather than more plausible scenarios taking into consideration the potential for anarchy and the Iraqis' growing reluctance to accept military occupation, along with severe disruption to public utilities for the immediate future.

U-TURNS AT THE WHITE HOUSE AND THE CPA

Attention now turned to the twenty-five-member cabinet that the Interim Governing Council appointed on September 1. Its religious composition was the same as the council's: thirteen Shias, eleven Sunni, and one Christian (Bahnam Polis, in charge of transport). The foreign ministry went to Hoshyar al Zebari of the Kurdistan Democratic Party, and the oil ministry to Ibrahim Muhammad al Uloom, son of Ayatollah Muhammad Bahr al

Uloom. The absence of a defense minister was understandable. But what was incomprehensible was the absence of a ministry of religious affairs, which made Iraq the only Arab country without such a ministry.

It had taken the Governing Council, which met every other day, seven weeks to name the cabinet. Naseer Chadirji, one of its Iraq-based members, admitted publicly that "the Governing Council has given nothing to the people." Heavily guarded at all times and rarely seen in public, the council members were as remote from the Iraqi people as Bremer and John Sawer. Another council member, Mahmoud Uthman, a Kurdish leader, said, "The CPA have all the executive powers in this country. The budget belongs to them, security belongs to them. Then they ask us to deliver."

But the shock waves resulting from four major bomb explosions in three weeks made Bremer reconsider his insistence on maintaining exclusive control of security. He agreed to compromise. Under his guidance, the council and the CPA set up a six-man joint security committee, with three members from each side. "We should find ways quickly to give Iraqis more responsibility for security," he now declared. "The U.S. advisers from the coalition will not only yield authority, they will thrust authority [on Iraqi ministers]."[21]

Bremer reflected the nervousness that had gripped the top decision makers in Washington in the wake of the devastating bomb detonations, which brought to the fore the multifaceted flaws in their post-Saddam planning. "The Pentagon simply did not understand or give enough priority to the transition from their military mission to the political mission," said Timothy Carney, who until recently had been overseeing the Iraqi industry ministry, in a BBC interview. "There was a great gap in our knowledge of what Iraq was like."[22]

By then it seemed that the Bush White House was beginning to comprehend the unrealistic nature of the neocon scenario—based on the rosy predictions of Chalabi and company—it had adopted: The switch-over of the Iraqi military and police to the American side would obviate the need for extra U.S. troops for peacekeeping, and the income from oil output, pushed up to its maximum capacity under efficient American management, along with the spurt in the economy caused by the lifting of UN sanctions, would pay for the reconstruction of the war-torn country. In this script there was no role for the guerrilla or insurgent. In real life, however, this character would come to determine the direction and speed of the story of "New Iraq."

In the economic field, by August 2003, oil output had inched up to 1.2 million barrels per day, about two-fifths of the pre-invasion level. The figure of six million barrels per day for Iraq's oil output in three years after Saddam's overthrow was now seen for what it was— part of the hype disseminated by the neocons to sell the idea of invading Iraq to the American public. And the bill for reconstructing Iraq after four weeks of relentless bombing and thirteen years of economic sanctions? In an interview with the *Washington Post*, Bremer put the cost of renovating the old electricity grid in Iraq at $13 billion over five years, and repairing and upgrading the water-supply system at $16 billion over four years. His aggregate estimate for putting right the country's economic infrastructure over the next decade was "tens of billions of dollars."[23]

The solution, the Bush White House concluded wearily, was more troops and more money. With the Pentagon spending $1 billion *a week* on maintaining its soldiers in Iraq, and the federal budget deficit spiraling to $500 billion, Bush had much to worry about when he realized that his administration would have to spend $71 billion on Iraq during fiscal year 2003–04, with $51 billion on the U.S. troops and the rest on rebuilding Iraq's economic infrastructure and military and judicial systems.

It was this consideration that would lead him to address the nation on September 7 in a televised speech on the subject. Aware of the impending second anniversary of 9/11, he linked his invasion of Iraq to the ongoing war on terrorism. "We will do whatever is necessary, we will spend what is necessary, to achieve this essential victory in the war on terror, to promote freedom, and to make our nation more secure," he said. "Our strategy in Iraq has three objectives: destroying the terrorists; [two] enlisting support of other nations for a free Iraq; and [three] helping Iraqis assume responsibility for their own defense and their own future."

In pursuit of the second objective, his administration had earlier sent out appeals for help to seventy countries. Only twenty responded positively, yet meagerly—none of them Muslim or Arab. All but one were European. Altogether, they would contribute 11,000 soldiers. Leaving aside Poland's 2,500 and Australia's earlier 2,000 troops, the average for the remaining eighteen came to a derisory 117. Most of them would receive U.S. funds for joining this "Broad Coalition of the Willing." Compared to the 140,000 American GIs in Iraq—a third of them in Baghdad—and another 35,000 in neighboring Kuwait, the joint contribution of the Broad Coalition was pitiful.

The size of the U.S. military presence in Iraq loomed large in the minds of the American people. Equally important to them was the purpose of the exercise. A Gallup poll in late August showed that 54 percent thought that the Bush White House did not have "a clear plan for handling the situation in Iraq."[24] Howard Dean, the leading contender for the Democratic nomination for presidency, went a step further. "It was a terrible blunder for the president to have sent troops to Iraq without having any idea what was going to happen," he said. "A fifteen-minute speech does not make up for fifteen months of misleading the American public on why we should go to war against Iraq." Referring to Vietnam, he added, "The government is *again* feeding misinformation to the American people in order to justify an enormous commitment of U.S. troops."[25]

With nothing to say about the WMD Saddam was supposed to possess, which were the casus belli for his invasion of Iraq, Bush in his September 7 speech played up the significance of the bombing of the UN headquarters in Baghdad. "Terrorists in Iraq have attacked representatives of the civilized world, and opposing them must be the cause of the civilized world. Members of the United Nations now have an opportunity—and the responsibility—to assume a broader role in assuring that Iraq becomes a free and democratic nation." He seemed oblivious of the fact that the Security Council had never passed a resolution saying Iraq should become "a free and democratic nation."

Earlier, instructed by Bush, Colin Powell had turned to the UN Security Council—which he and Bush had dismissed as "irrelevant" and "a talking shop" barely five months earlier—to propose a multinational force under U.S. command, with the CPA maintaining full military and political control of Iraq.

This was unacceptable to France. In an interview with *Le Monde* on August 22, French foreign minister Dominique de Villepin said that the allies must switch from "a logic of occupation" to "a logic of sovereignty." A week later he elaborated the concept in an address to the annual gathering of French ambassadors. "It is time to move resolutely into a logic of sovereignty for Iraq," he said. "A true change of approach is needed. We must end the ambiguity, transfer responsibilities and allow the Iraqis to play the role they deserve as soon as possible." He proposed that the U.S.-appointed Iraqi Governing Council should be replaced by "a real provisional government whose legitimacy would be reinforced by the UN," and called on the Security Council to pass a resolution scheduling elections for a constitutional assembly by the end of 2003. He warned that the alternatives Iraq faced were "terrorism and also looming anarchy." Endorsing his foreign minister's stance, President Jacques Chirac stressed that the transfer must happen soon, with UN involvement, because only the United Nations can give legitimacy with "the support of regional countries." Once this framework was in place, then the United Nations should get involved in reconstruction "in a manner to be worked out with Iraqis."[26]

Preeminent among the regional countries was Saudi Arabia. In an interview with the *Independent* in mid-August, Prince Turki al

Faisal, the Saudi ambassador to Britain, said, "A UN umbrella must be established for Iraq, then all can cooperate. The Security Council Resolution 1483 is not sufficient nor in its present form is the Interim Iraqi Governing Council. The UN should have the leading role. A new, legal Iraqi government should resolve all these problems [of security and reconstruction] if it is a government all can recognize as representative of the Iraqi people."[27]

At the Security Council, the French position had the backing of Germany and Russia. Among the politicians and media of these countries, there was little, if any, sympathy at the sight of the Bush administration's policy—an amalgam of unilateralist ideology and imperial arrogance—dissolving in the shifting sands of Iraq.

On the other hand, there was much sympathy for the Iraqi people, who deserved better than being delivered from Saddam's tyranny only to find themselves at the front lines in the violent struggle between the America and Islamist militants—from whom Saddam's despotism, for its own selfish reasons, had insulated them.

NOTES

1. *International Herald Tribune,* June 4, 2003.

2. Cited in *Time,* April 7, 2003, p. 23.

3. *New York Times,* July 27, 2003.

4. The new twelve-foot-high (four meters) perimeter wall was built so near the main building that it offered little protection from a powerful bomb, and the machine-gun nest placed on the roof was irrelevant to truck bombing.

5. Abu Abdul Rahman al Najdi also confirmed that Osama bin Laden and [Taliban leader] Mullah Omar were alive and well. *Guardian,* August 20, 2003.

6. See Dilip Hiro, *Iraq: In the Eye of the Storm,* pp. 101–2, 105–9, 112–13.

7. *Guardian,* August 11, 2003.

8. September 21, 2003.

9. *International Herald Tribune,* June 4, 2003.

10. *Observer,* August 31, 2003.

11. *New York Times,* August 13, 2003.

12. See further Dilip Hiro, *The Essential Middle East*, entries on "mahdi," p. 310, and "Twelver Shias," p. 533.

13. Agence France Presse, August 29, 2003; *The Times*, August 30, 2003.

14. *New York Times*, September 1, 2003.

15. This tape was aired by two Arabic channels, Al Jazeera and the Lebanese Broadcasting Corporation. *Independent*, September 2, 2003.

16. Later the police said it had arrested four suspects, all of them Iraqi nationals, whose sectarian affiliations were not disclosed.

17. See further entry on "Wahhabism and Wahhabis" in Dilip Hiro, *The Essential Middle East*, pp. 564–65.

18. *Guardian*, September 8, 2003.

19. Earlier, in an interview with an Egyptian newspaper, Abdul Aziz al Hakim said, "We told the Americans that their policy in Iraq was wrong and their dealing with the situation illogical."

20. See further Dilip Hiro, *The Essential Middle East*, pp. 297–300.

21. *Guardian*, September 3, 2003.

22. June 26, 2003.

23. August 27, 2003.

24. *Sunday Times*, August 31, 2003.

25. *Guardian*, September 9, 2003.

26. *New York Times*, August 29 and 30, 2003. For once, Ahmad Chalabi found himself on the same side as the French leaders. "The [Iraqi] people need to see an accelerated timetable for the restoration of sovereignty to reinforce the national pride and self-respect that stem from self-government," he wrote in an op-ed piece in the *Washington Post* on August 31, 2003.

27. August 11, 2003.

CHAPTER 11

SUMMARY AND CONCLUSIONS

"This was a war made in Washington, pushed by a handful of neoconservatives and pursued for reasons of U.S. foreign strategy and domestic politics. What made this war inevitable was not increased threat from Iraq, but a regime change in the U.S. And WMD were never the primary concern of the Bush administration in the way they had to appear in Britain to persuade Parliament of the urgent need for war."

—Robin Cook, former British foreign secretary, on July 11, 2003[1]

"Robust debate in a democracy will almost always involve occasional rhetorical excesses and leaps of faith. But there is a big difference between that and a systematic effort to manipulate facts in service to a totalitarian ideology felt to be more important than basic honesty. Unfortunately, it is no longer possible to avoid the conclusion that what this country is dealing with in the Bush presidency is the latter."

—Al Gore, the Democratic candidate who won the popular vote in the 2000 Presidential election, on August 7, 2003[2]

"We didn't know the Vietnamese enough to empathize with them; we did not study their history or culture. We didn't see that they saw us as just replacing the French as the colonial power. We were fighting the Cold War, but to them it was a civil war. That was our mistake."

—Robert McNamara, U.S. defense secretary (1961–69), on May 23, 2003[3]

367

"America may be able to inflict damages to the region in the short term, but resistance of the regional nations will finally inflict the biggest blow to America, and will culminate in the fall of America's superpower image."
—Ayatollah Ali Husseini Khamanei, leader of Iran, to Syrian president Bashar Assad on March 16, 2003[4]

GIVEN CARTE BLANCHE by UN Security Council Resolution 1368, in the immediate aftermath of 9/11, which claimed over 3,050 lives, U.S. president George Walker Bush prepared to attack the Taliban regime in Afghanistan. Of the many countries that offered to participate in this war, he accepted only the offer of Britain, led by Prime Minister Tony Blair.

To the surprise of many, including the Americans, the Taliban unraveled with astonishing speed, fleeing Kabul after five weeks of relentless bombing by Centcom. Washington's swift victory stemmed primarily from its success in marrying high-tech weaponry with conventional ways of gathering intelligence—while avoiding the deployment of ground troops on a large scale, which the Soviets in the 1980s and the British in the nineteenth century had done, thus exposing themselves to deadly ambushes. Instead, Centcom successfully coordinated its long-range airpower, reliable tactical intelligence from the ground, and several hundred highly mobile Special Forces troops (some of them riding horses like nineteenth-century warriors), operating with much firepower and covered by electronic support—such as Predator drones armed with missiles—to safeguard them from ambushes. While implementing this complex, multifaceted strategy, the top U.S. policy makers proved flexible enough to alter the strategy quickly if it failed to deliver the expected result, as happened during the Special Forces' large-scale night raid on October 19–20, 2001, in Kandahar. No such nimbleness was shown by the Taliban strategists. Never having been exposed to the kind of heavy, almost nonstop air raids Centcom inflicted on them, the Taliban behaved like classic Afghan fighters: bluster one day and melt away the next. Those who survived went home and threw away their distinguishing black turbans, or changed sides for money. In any case, once Pakistan, having cut its umbilical cord with the Taliban—its own creation in the first place—turned against them, they were doomed: Their collapse was only a matter of time.

The quick collapse of the Taliban brought much relief and satisfaction in Washington and London. The scenario of Muslims worldwide venting their rage against the Anglo-American alliance for pummeling a poor, underdeveloped Afghanistan with high-tech weaponry did not materialize. The active involvement of anti-Taliban Afghans in the U.S.-led war, followed by the spontaneous jubilation of Kabulis at the flight of the Taliban, indicated to many, Muslims and non-Muslims alike, that the oppressive Taliban regime was widely unpopular. But then again, only three of the fifty-seven members of the Islamic Conference Organization had recognized the Taliban regime;[5] and, at the United Nations, the country's seat rested with the anti-Taliban regime of the Northern Alliance.

While Bush could claim that he had delivered on his declaration that those who harbored terrorists would share in their fate, a closer examination of his war aims showed that they had not been accomplished fully. He had been completely successful in preventing Afghanistan from harboring and sustaining international terrorism in the future, since the infrastructure of the training camps was totally destroyed and the country's leadership replaced. He had had a great deal of success in preventing the much-weakened Al Qaida from posing a continued threat to the West. But his success in bringing Osama bin Laden and other Al Qaida leaders to justice was partial. Both bin Laden and his ideological mentor, Dr. Ayman Zawahiri, remained at large. Over the coming months, they would publicly taunt Bush and Blair in audio- and videotapes broadcast periodically by Al Jazeera and other Arabic television channels.

In other words, Bush and Blair had not completely drained the swamp that bred Islamist terrorists. Instead of focusing on finishing the onerous task of decimating Al Qaida and its associates—in which they had the ongoing backing of the international community—they planned to invade Iraq, an illegal adventure disapproved of by the majority of UN Security Council members that would result in creating a bigger, more menacing swamp conducive to breeding Islamist extremists. Until then, the authoritarian but secular regime of Saddam Hussein had ensured that there were no Islamist extremist groups functioning inside Iraq. (This is currently the case in Syria, which is run by an authoritarian but secular Baathist regime that suppressed Islamist militants mercilessly in the early 1980s.) So, by overthrowing Saddam's regime despite opposition from Muslims worldwide and most of the international community, Bush and Blair ended up abetting Islamist terrorism, not combating it, at a time when Al Qaida and associated groups were active enough to mount a dozen major terrorist attacks—in the Arab and Muslim world, from Morocco to Indonesia, where a bomb claimed 202 lives; and elsewhere, in Kenya, Russia, and India.[6]

Part I of this book provides an analytical chronicle of how and why Bush, actively assisted by Blair, attacked Iraq. Given their different publics and political systems, the two leaders pursued different strategies, or rather stressed different aspects of an overarching strategy. The difference between the two publics is aptly summed up by the fact that opposition to war in Britain before and after March 20, 2003, remained steady at around 40 percent (later rising to 53 percent), whereas the corresponding figure in the United States was half as much. And the jibe that Ian Duncan Smith, leader of the Conservative Party, which voted for war, directed at Blair in Parliament—"You are rapidly becoming a stranger to the truth. . . . You have duped us into going into war. You have created a culture of deceit and spin at the heart of the government"—on the eve of Blair's departure for Washington to receive a U.S. congressional Gold Medal on July 17, neatly encapsulated the difference between the political systems of Britain and America.[7] In Britain the prime minister is held accountable and questioned routinely by the opposition leader and the media, which is not the case with the present American president.

The accusations of Bush and Blair against Saddam Hussein rested on the triad of Tyranny, Weapons of Mass Destruction, and Terrorism.

The fact that Saddam Hussein was a brutal ruler had begun to emerge soon after he became vice president of Iraq in 1975. Following his forced resignation of President Ahmad Hassan Bakr in July 1979 and assumption of supreme power, he arrested sixty-eight top Baathist civilian and military leaders, charging them with a major "anti-state conspiracy." All were tried summarily and twenty-two were executed, with Saddam getting his colleagues in the Baathist leadership to do the shooting.[8] He then carried out a massive purge of trade unions, the Baath Party militia, student unions, and local and provincial governments, weeding out all those who were less than totally loyal to him. His invasion of Iran in 1980, resulting in an eight-year conflict, provided him with an overarching pretext to suppress brutally any sign of dissent or opposition in the name of Iraqi nationalism, which provided the ideological underpinning for his war. As for bankrolling the conflict, the Western powers, including the United States, were generous with their loans and grants.

Saddam committed the worst of his atrocities during and soon after the 1980–88 war, with the persecution of ethnic Kurds reaching its peak under Operation "Anfal" in the spring of 1988. Operation "Anfal" was implemented by his first cousin, General Ali Hassan al Majid, who won the odious sobriquet of "Chemical Ali" due to the extensive use of poison gases against Kurds. Following the gruesome bombing of the Kurdish town of Halabja with chemical bombs, which killed 3,200 to 6,800 people, mainly civilians,[9] the United States doubled its financial aid to Iraq, and the British government's Exports Guarantees scheme authorized a further loan of £450 million to Baghdad.

Six weeks after Saddam had used chemical weapons for the first time against Iranian forces in October 1983, he had a ninety-minute meeting with Donald Rumsfeld, then President Ronald Reagan's roving ambassador to the Middle East. The declassified documents show that Rumsfeld made no mention of poison gases. Instead, he discussed Iraq erecting an oil pipeline through Jordan to the Gulf of Aqaba, with the contract going almost certainly to Bechtel Corporation. To assist Baghdad financially, Washington's Eximbank provisionally guaranteed $485 million of the estimated $570 million cost of the project.[10]

So the description of the "torture chambers" and "mass graves" in Iraq with which Paul Wolfowitz peppered his testimony to Congress after his visit to Iraq in July 2003 was both naïve and hypocritical. If there was a time to condemn Saddam for his atrocities against political dissidents (such as Communists and Islamist al Daawa activists) and ethnic minorities (such as Kurds)—and penalize him—it was when he was actually committing them, not fifteen to twenty years later.

IRAQ'S WEAPONS OF MASS DESTRUCTION

The issue of Iraq's WMD, which came up at the UN Security Council in the wake of the 1991 Gulf War, was covered comprehensively in the council's Resolution 687 (April 1991), and was linked to the lifting of economic sanctions against Iraq, imposed in August 1990, once UN inspectors had certified that the regime had been disarmed of its nonconventional weapons.

When Richard Butler withdrew Unscom inspectors to enable the Pentagon to start its Operation "Desert Fox" in December 1998—during which it fired ninety more cruise and Tomahawk missiles than it had during the 1991 Gulf War—he did Saddam a favor. The Iraqi dictator was now rid of them, and he never had to lift a finger. Moreover, Washington's unilateral decision, backed as before by London, split the five Permanent Members of the Security

Council, which pleased Saddam. Having concluded, rightly, that sanctions would never be lifted so long as he was in power—as the Clinton administrations had made abundantly clear—Saddam tried to erode them, an enterprise for which he received the tacit backing of most Arab countries.

On the other hand, by not letting in UN inspectors for nearly three years under a different regime of Unmovic, set up in early 2000, Saddam inadvertently provided an opportunity for the American and British leaders to exploit the absence of international inspectors for their agenda. Following 9/11, that meant attacking Iraq under the guise of disarming it by attributing all sorts of activities to the regime allegedly bent on acquiring an arsenal of WMD and equipping itself with medium-range missiles to deliver them.

Once the Taliban had been overthrown and the initial accusations of Saddam being in cahoots with bin Laden had failed to stick in the absence of credible evidence, both Bush and Blair focused on WMD. As Paul Wolfowitz put it in his July 2003 *Vanity Fair* interview, the one issue on which the State and Defense departments, the National Security Council, the vice president's office, and the White House agreed was that Saddam had acquired WMD.

In that context, Britain's September 24, 2002, dossier became a prime document on both sides of the Atlantic. That is why both Bush and Blair ignored Iraq's acceptance of the unconditional return of UN inspectors on September 16. In a rational world, the Blair government would have explained publicly that, with Iraq agreeing to let in UN inspectors, the purpose of the dossier was served, and that it was passing on its intelligence to the United Nations. Instead, it continued "hardening up" the document by tinkering with words *without* receiving any fresh intelligence. Blair was all set to break new ground by making available to the world at large some of the nuggets of secret intelligence, normally the prerogative of senior cabinet ministers, and nothing was going to stop him from making history.

Actually, he was trying to compensate for the disastrous attempt he and his defense secretary, George Robertson—emulating President Bill Clinton and his defense secretary, William Cohen—had made in early 1998 to "educate" Britons on the menace posed by Saddam as a precursor to striking Iraq. To its credit, the Clinton administration was mature enough to acknowledge its failure later. "The serious threat Mr. Saddam poses was overblown [by the Clinton administration] in the effort to sell the possible [American] attack, some senior U.S. officials now say," Steven Erlanger reported in the *New York Times* on November 8, 1998. "Defense secretary William Cohen appeared on television brandishing a bag of sugar in an effort to describe how small a dose of biological and chemical weapons it would take to threaten Americans." Robertson did the same in London, referring to real sugar as "theoretical anthrax," capable of killing "tens of thousands."

This time Blair was determined to do a thorough job. This meant taking an old, dry, and equivocal report of the MI6, produced by intelligence analysts, and "sexing" it up to the extent of producing an almost entirely different document, with the political motive of swinging the electorate to back military action against Baghdad. In this he had the active cooperation of his director of communications, Alastair Campbell, a skilled spinmeister with a background as a tabloid journalist.

Contrary to the popular notion that spinning amounts to lying, it does not. To spin is to choose one fact out of several, or one facet of a multifaceted fact, and highlight it to serve a predetermined purpose. So spun information still remains in the realm of "fact."

Overall, between telling "the truth, the whole truth," and lying, there exist several options: spinning, deliberate misinterpretation, inadvertent misinterpretation, misinforming or misleading, and disinforming. Many facts are open to different interpretations. For instance, the aluminum tubing that Iraq bought could be used for rocket engineering or for centrifuges to enrich uranium. What senior officials in Washington and London did was to give always the most dire interpretation of a fact supplied by an agent or gathered through technological means. As for misinforming or misleading, if an American or British official says Iraq has violated twenty-two of the twenty-seven Security Council resolutions, he/she is misinforming, because there have been sixty-five resolutions on Iraq. The Oxford English Dictionary defines "disinformation" as "the dissemination of deliberately false information, especially when supplied by a government or its agent to a foreign power or to the media, with the intention of influencing the policies or opinions of those who receive it." In the wake of Senator Frank Church's damning report on the CIA, the *New Republic* of June 30, 1975, revealed that the CIA had a special section for disinformation, with "expensive facilities for producing fake documents and other means for misleading foreigners." Lastly, there is the lie, concoction, fabrication, or invention. For example, "Tariq Aziz has defected" or "Saddam has paid Colonel Qadhafi $3.5 billion to give him and his family refuge in Libya."

Though the Bush White House's shenanigans on Iraq have received most of the attention of critics, it must be noted that it has deployed similar tactics elsewhere as well. According to a report—"Politics and Science in the Bush Administration"—prepared for the House Committee of Government Reform's Minority Staff Special Investigation Division, the Bush administration pursues its political agenda by manipulating scientific advisory committees, distorting and suppressing scientific information, and interfering with scientific research and analysis. For instance, it dropped three experts on lead poisoning from the Advisory Committee on Childhood Lead Poisoning Prevention and appointed replacements with ties to the lead industry. The White House edited the report of the Environmental Protection Agency (EPA) on global warming to the extent that its scientists said it no longer "represents scientific consensus on climate change." And it refused to let the EPA conduct analyses on air-quality proposals that differed from its Clear Skies initiative.[11]

During the run-up to the invasion of Iraq, Bush, Blair, and their senior aides resorted to an armory of spins, deliberate misinterpretations, misinformation, disinformation, and outright lies. How Bush and Blair—known to be avid readers and followers of the Bible—managed to square this behavior with their Christian morality is a question that has yet to be asked in public. Meanwhile, the American public is belatedly waking up to the fact that it was conned by Bush. A poll for Democracy Corps showed that 46 percent agreed with the statement, "President Bush misled about the dangers and threats Iraq posed before the war," and 53 percent agreed with the statement, "I cannot trust what President Bush is saying about weapons of mass destruction in Iraq."[12] Before the war, Bush and Blair had had to coax their respective intelligence apparatuses to come up with "facts" they could marshal to advance their agenda by winning the approval of their politicians and voters for war on Iraq.

As revealed by the Lord Hutton Inquiry in Britain in August and September 2003, Blair had an easy time with his intelligence chiefs. The heads of the MI6, Defense Intelligence Staff (DIS), and Joint Intelligence Committee (JIC) dutifully lined up behind him. The DIS chief did not forward the letters of his subordinates who protested against the misuse of their intelligence analysis in the drafting of the dossier to JIC head John Scarlett, who in his testimony to the Hutton Inquiry acted as an unabashed crony of Blair.

The case with Bush, however, was quite different. The number and size of the U.S. intelligence agencies—the CIA, the DIA, the National Security Agency, the Bureau of Intelligence and Research, and nine others[13]—implied that enormous effort and concentration would be needed to make them all sing from the same score. But 9/11 provided a unique opportunity to circumvent this bureaucratic maze. Rumsfeld grabbed it and set up his own Office of Special Projects (OSP) under William Luti, an acolyte of Leo Strauss and thus in the same league as the leading neocons—Paul Wolfowitz, Stephen Cambone

(Rumsfeld's undersecretary for intelligence), and Richard Perle. Taking his cue from Rumsfeld, Israeli prime minister Ariel Sharon set up a special intelligence unit in his office outside of the established intelligence apparatus.

9/11 was a godsend for the neocons, who thrive on fear and paranoia. Even at the best of times they do not like to see the United States feel safe and secure. Though the environment for the acceptance of their views on national security improved after 9/11, it was still hard for them to sell the eschatological idea of eliminating Islamist terrorism by re-creating the Arab world in the American mold. So they devised the concept of finding Saddam guilty of a crime he *might* commit, later—like providing WMD to bin Laden to unleash mayhem on the United States.

While the neocons were busy disseminating their theses through the media, Rumsfeld leaned heavily on CIA director George Tenet—who was also pressured by Dick Cheney and his chief of staff, Lewis Libby—to come up with the link between Saddam and Al Qaida and evidence of the Iraqi dictator reconstituting WMD. Tenet obliged. "The politicization of intelligence is pandemic, and deliberate disinformation is being promoted," said Vince Cannistraro, former CIA chief of counterterrorism. "They choose the worst-case scenarios on everything, and so much of the information is fallacious. . . . The serving officers are blaming the Pentagon for playing up fraudulent intelligence, a lot of it sourced from the INC [Iraqi National Congress]."[14]

Rumsfeld's OSP went on to link up with the special intelligence unit that Sharon set up in his office and establish a back channel to Blair's office, thus circumventing the Joint Intelligence Committee structure. The OSP expanded tenfold, yet its representative never attended the joint sessions of the various intelligence agencies. It had resorted to examining already existing intelligence and reaching startling new conclusions. This would enable Rumsfeld to tell a Senate Committee after the invasion that the United States had not gone to war against Iraq because of "fresh evidence of

WMD," but because we saw "what evidence there was [prior to 9/11] in a dramatic new light" after 9/11.[15]

By saying this, Rumsfeld contradicted what Blair's office had told British journalists in its briefings during the summer of 2002: The prime minister has been alarmed by "new, disturbing intelligence appearing on his desk," much of it originating in Rumsfeld's Office of Special Projects![16]

In his dealings with British politicians and the public, Blair had an uphill task in convincing them of the imperative need to attack Iraq. With a two-century history of empire and empire-building, there is more interest in the Third World among Britons than there is among Americans. The membership of the fifty-one-nation British Commonwealth is predominantly Afro-Asian. And broadcasters like the BBC and Channel 4 produce a stream of well-informed TV documentaries on the Third World. Being better informed on the subject than its American counterpart, the British public judges events in such countries as Iraq and Afghanistan with greater understanding than the American public does. The last foreign demon it got worked up about was Egyptian president Gamal Abdul Nasser, in the mid-1950s. The rise of Ayatollah Ruhollah Khomeini in Iran in 1979 did not disturb the British public unduly.

Generally speaking, Britons are also keen on following legal procedures, at home and abroad. Therefore it was paramount for them to see there was UN Security Council authorization for military action against Baghdad. Polls showed that only 15 percent of Britons would support attacking Iraq without a Security Council mandate.

That is why Blair pulled out all the stops to harden the September 2002 dossier. He combined the single-source, uncorroborated information from an MI6 agent—claiming another single, uncorroborated source—about the mere forty-five minutes required for the deployment of Iraq's chemical or biological weapons with earlier, unverified MI6 intelligence that Iraq possessed some twenty surface-to-surface missiles with a 410-mile

(650-kilometer) range, to concoct the frightening scenario of Saddam's military hitting two British military bases in Cyprus within three-quarters of an hour. Thus Iraq posed an imminent threat to Britain. Q.E.D.

By this logic, Iraq's WMD threatened thousands of U.S. troops stationed in adjoining Kuwait. Yet, in its propaganda blitz against Saddam, the Bush administration never mentioned this menacing threat. There seemed to be no need for it. Bush had an easy time convincing the U.S. politicians and public of the malevolent intent of the brutal Butcher of Baghdad.

Recent history shows that by and large in the United States the only Third World leaders who gain a high profile are those who are inimical to the United States, or shown to be so. In the 1960s it was Fidel Castro, until the Vietnam War filled all the space there was for Third World affairs. After the oil price hikes in 1973–74, the greedy potbellied oil shaikhs became figures of hate, to be replaced by Khomeini in the 1980s, with Qadhafi joining him in the mid-1980s. Then Saddam took over as the demonic figure after he invaded Kuwait in 1990. He remained the arch-villain throughout the decade. During the run-up to the first anniversary of 9/11, Bush found it politically expedient to morph the elusive bin Laden into the long-established ogreish Saddam, and then followed it up with a reference to "Al Qaida becoming an extension of Saddam's madness," and adding, "You can't distinguish between Al Qaida and Saddam when you talk about the war on terror."[17] This strategy worked so well that on the eve of the war, 55 percent of Americans believed it likely that Saddam was directly linked to 9/11. This percentage would rise to 69 in September. "Americans don't like Al Qaida, they are horrified by 9/11, and they know Saddam Hussein is a bad guy in the Middle East," explained Andrew Kohut, director of Pew Research Center for the People and the Press. "The notion was reinforced by those hints [by Bush and his senior advisers], the discussions that they had about possible links with Al Qaida terrorists."[18]

Having decided in principle in February 2002 to oust Saddam, Bush gave the go-ahead to Rumsfeld to prepare a "conceptual" war plan. By leaking a version of this plan in early July to the *New York Times*, Bush set the parameters of the subsequent debate: It was to be primarily about "how" to overthrow Saddam, and not why. This was a prelude to Bush seeking war powers from the current Congress instead of waiting for the next one to be installed in January. In the subsequent public discourse, both the pro- and antiwar camps were agreed that the United States would prevail in Iraq; the only debate was how long it would take, and whether Iraqis would come out in the streets with flowers or Kalashnikovs.

Bolstered by Blair's fifty-page dossier of September 24, 2002, the release soon after of the CIA's claim that Saddam was reconstituting nuclear weapons, and Bush's own statement in his October 7 speech in Cincinnati in which he attributed allegations made by an Iraqi defector to the IAEA regarding Iraq's nuclear program,[19] the president prepared the ground for convincing a congressional majority to give him war powers on October 11, 2002.

It came out later that, six weeks before the congressional authorization, Bush had approved the overall war strategy at a meeting with Rumsfeld at his Crawford ranch.[20] Immediately, Rumsfeld ordered Operation "Southern Focus," thus starting an air campaign against Iraq to be capped by a ground invasion seven months later. In between came the implementation of the six phases of the "unseen" war—from psychological warfare against the Iraqi regime; to infiltration by the Special Forces to hide communications equipment inside Iraq; to lies about Saddam's plans to flee to Libya, Russia, or Belarus; to Saddam transferring his WMD to Syria; to sending a barrage of e-mails and telephone messages to Iraqi generals encouraging them to defect and explaining how to contact UN headquarters to do so; and so on.

The third major element in the charge sheet against Saddam was terrorism. There the intelligence agencies of Britain—as well as those of France and Germany—repeatedly said there was no ongoing formal high-level link between the Iraqi government and Al Qaida. Yes, there had been low-level exploratory meetings between the two sides because of their common hatred of the United States and the Saudi rulers, but these talks had not moved forward or upward. "As members of the National Security Council staff from 1994–99, we closely examined nearly a decade's worth of intelligence and became convinced that religious radicals of Al Qaida and the secularists of the Baathist Iraq did not trust one another or share sufficiently compelling interests to work together," wrote Daniel Benjamin and Steven Simon, authors of *The Age of Sacred Terror*.[21]

Regarding Saddam's freelance sponsorship of terrorism, all that Blair would say is that the Iraqi government gave $25,000 to the families of those Palestinians who carried out suicide attacks on Israelis. After the outbreak of the Second Palestinian Intifada (uprising) against the Israeli occupation in September 2000, the Palestinian Authority gave a $2,000 check to the family of each Palestinian killed in the uprising to compensate it for the loss. Following this, the Palestine Liberation Front (PFL), a pro-Iraq Palestinian faction, started giving a $10,000 check to the family of the latest Palestinian "martyr." Later, when Palestinian militants resorted to suicide bombings, the Front raised the compensation first to $15,000, and then to $25,000. Of some 1,500 Palestinians killed during the first two years of the intifada, only seventy were suicide bombers. In other words, Saddam's surrogate, PFL, did not go around offering $25,000 to any Palestinian who would carry out a suicide bombing.[22]

When it came to pinning the terrorist label on the Saddam government, all the Bush administration had to do was point a finger at the Mujahedin-e Khalq Organization (MKO, People's Mujahedin). An anticlerical Iranian group opposed to the regime in Tehran, the MKO, placed on the State Department's list of terrorist organizations in 1997, had located its headquarters in Baghdad since 1986. Its National Liberation Army was trained and

armed by the Iraqi military, and it engaged in self-confessed terrorist activities against the Iranian government. Moreover, while
MKO representatives around the world publicly condemned 9/11,
inside Iraq the MKO rejoiced. "There were celebrations at all the
Mujahedin camps [in Iraq] on September 11," Ardeshir Parkizkari,
thirty-nine, a former member of MKO's central council and now
a political refugee in Europe, told the *New York Times*. "I was in
one of their prisons then. And we were never treated so well as we
were that day—given juices and sweets. They called the events of
September 11 God's revenge on America." [23] Yet the MKO's political wing, the National Resistance Council of Iran, even though
listed as a terrorist organization after 9/11, continued to function
openly in the United States, with its head office in Washington.

According to the single page headlined "Support for International Terrorism" in the White House's twenty-page document, "A
Decade of Deception and Defiance," released on September 12,
2002, the last terrorist act attributed to Iraq was a failed attempt
to assassinate former U.S. president George Herbert Walker Bush
in April 1993, during his visit to Kuwait.[24]

So it was not surprising that during an informal meeting with
a group in the Oval Office, Bush Jr. reportedly referred angrily to
Saddam as "that guy [who] tried to kill my dad." There is no
record of him saying so in public. It would be foolhardy to do so.

When all is said and done, the ultimate responsibility for
invading Iraq lies with President Bush. So it is essential to examine
his motives and agenda, as well as his leadership qualities and style.

BUSH'S AGENDA AND LEADERSHIP

By Bush's own account, there is a spiritual aspect to his leadership.
This goes back to his addiction to alcohol during the early 1980s,
and his successful—albeit dogged and painful—switch from Jack
Daniel's to Jesus Christ, assisted and inspired by the evangelical

preacher Billy Graham, to the extent that he took to starting his day with readings from encapsulated evangelical sermons, a habit that persisted even after he became president. "Right now, I should be in a bar in Texas, not the Oval Office," he told a five religious leaders at the White House in September 2002. "There is only one reason I am in the Oval Office and not in a bar: I found faith. I found God. I am here because of the power of prayer."[25]

Apparently it is during prayer that God guides Bush. That is an inference one can draw from his statement to Palestinian prime minister Mahmoud Abbas in June 2003: "God told me to strike at Al Qaida and I struck them, and then he instructed me to strike at Saddam, which I did," adding that "now I am determined to solve the problem in the Middle East."[26] Since Bush was ready to act against Al Qaida by early afternoon on September 12, 2001, God must have moved pretty fast to instruct him.

More seriously, if Bush is taking his instructions from God, then all this temporal debate about how he should be administering the United States is quite meaningless.

Though Bush remains a member of the United Methodist Church, a respectable denomination—a political necessity, one assumes—he is heavily influenced by such evangelicals as John Ashcroft and Franklin Graham. Evangelical Christians believe that the Second Coming of Jesus Christ will be facilitated with the return of all Jews to the land of Israel, and that in turn will be accelerated if Iraq—the most anti-Zionist Arab state—has a government friendly with Israel. In these evangelical quarters, Bush's faith is seen as subjective, with stress on doing "the right thing." Out of this belief and practice have emanated the self-confidence he shows once he has settled on a course of action.

In his day-to-day dealings with the media, however, this confidence often comes through as self-righteous propaganda that percolates down. At press briefings, from Bush on down, the United States is always "on plan," whether waging war or consolidating peace; the economy is always on the up; the tax cuts are beneficial to the poor; and the Washington-led coalitions are always the largest in history. The absence of nuance or qualification is truly staggering. At a joint press conference with Blair at Camp David on March 27—the second week of war—while Blair conceded that there were differences in the international community on Iraq, Bush declared baldly, "We have a broad coalition with us."

What appears as serene self-confidence to his admirers is seen as blinkered vision by his critics, made worse by his short attention span and inability to grasp the complexities of an issue, especially in foreign affairs, and retain its varied aspects in his brain while expressing his opinion or explaining his decision—reluctantly.[27]

Bush's confidence tends to transmute into swagger when he expresses simple thoughts in slogans: "Bin Laden, dead or alive!" His admirers see this as a plus. "The notion that the president is a cowboy . . . is not necessarily a bad idea," said Cheney in his NBC television interview on the eve of the invasion of Iraq. "He cuts to the chase." When guerrilla actions started in Iraq, Bush threw down the gauntlet: "Bring them on." But when, apparently taking him on his word, they escalated their attacks, Bush appealed to the "civilized world" to bolster the Pentagon's presence in occupied Iraq.

When this behavior is combined with his inarticulateness (his bald statement to Bob Woodward, "I don't have to explain anything," boils down to "I have great difficulty explaining myself"), and tendency to speak in broad generalizations—"I want to bring about world peace"; "I want to end human misery"; "I want to usher in democracy"—one can well understand why former South African president Nelson Mandela was moved to refer to him as a U.S. president "who has no foresight and who cannot think properly."[28] All leaders want to work for peace and prosperity. That was why the five major victors of World War II established the United Nations in 1945, with U.S. president Harry Truman insisting that the headquarters be on American soil.

Among Bush's close advisers, the ideologue Paul Wolfowitz has been particularly clever in engaging with him on Iraq by playing up his simplistic thoughts on human suffering, peace, and democracy, arguing that Saddam's overthrow would lead to the oil-rich Arab Middle East turning democratic and making genuine and lasting peace with democratic Israel, with abundant oil flowing freely to the United States.

Bush, of course, has a view of himself, which he expressed in a long interview with Bob Woodward in August 2002. He described himself as "fiery," "impatient," "a gut player," "one who liked to provoke people around him," and "someone who likes to talk—perhaps too much—in meetings."[29] His impatience was well captured at a joint press conference with Blair during the early days of the war on Iraq. When asked whether the war would "last months, not weeks," he could hardly wait for the journalist to finish his question. "However long it takes to win," he declared hastily.

Being a self-confessed "impatient, gut player" implies a failure to give proper weight to history, experience, and rational thought, and to think through a complex problem. It also implies hasty action. In his impatience to overthrow Saddam—a decision born more out of emotion than cool, rational thinking based on hard evidence and a realistic assessment of the consequences of such a gigantic act—Bush concluded that the Iraqi leader was insane. In an interview with *Time*, a senior presidential adviser quoted Bush as saying, "If there is one thing standing between those who want WMD and those who have them, it is this madman. Depending on the sanity of Saddam is not an option."[30] His impatience proved infectious, so it was not surprising when Rumsfeld refused to give the Pentagon planners enough time to prepare for the post-Saddam era—which would prove disastrous.

Bush combines his impatience with an all-out campaign to achieve his immediate goal by hook or by crook. He and his team have shown no compunction about bending or breaking the rules, or distorting or mishandling the evidence, to get what they want. This approach brought them success in the Florida recount battle, the passage of the 2001 tax cut, the Afghanistan campaign, and the

2002 election. But they tend to shy away from the unglamorous task of a steady, consistent follow-up. Afghanistan is a good example. Instead of remaining focused on the postwar issues of that benighted country and keeping up the pressure on the remnants of Al Qaida in Afghanistan and Pakistan, they turned immediately to Iraq. The clue to Bush's aversion to tackling an onerous task with slow, dogged determination lies in his upbringing. He was raised in wealth and privilege, and his success in business as well as politics came through family connections in corporate and political circles.

The constant itch to move on to something new means that Bush and his team seldom look back to examine what they have done and draw lessons from it—much less to concede that, being human, they made mistakes. Iraq provides a telling example. At first it was the weapons of mass destruction. When weeks and months passed after the Anglo-American occupation of Iraq with no trace of WMD, the comments of Hans Blix grew caustic. "Personally, I found it peculiar that those who wanted to take military action could—with 100 percent certainty—know that the weapons existed, and at the same time turn out to have zero percent knowledge of where they were," he told Swedish Radio.[31]

There was no riposte from the Bush White House, which was now busily declaring that overthrowing the Butcher of Baghdad was a noble achievement, and that Iraq needed to be reconstructed economically and politically as a beacon of hope to the rest of the Middle East. No major nation was impressed enough to dip into its pocket. The cost of the economic reconstruction of Iraq in the U.S. fiscal year 2003–04 came to $20 billion, with another $51 billion to maintain the military occupation of the country. That was when the American taxpayer finally woke up to protest. If the Bush team were to publish the estimated damage to Iraq's economic and administrative infrastructure caused by the Anglo-American invasion, it would provide a proper perspective to Americans and others to assess the $20 billion being discussed.

That is unlikely to happen. Meanwhile, it is worth noting that the estimated damage to Iraq's infrastructure in the 1991 Gulf War was $200 billion.[32]

Faced with protests at home, the Bush White House argued that "Iraq is now central to terrorism"—overlooking the fact that it was the Pentagon's invasion of the country that produced ideal conditions for local and foreign Islamist extremists to thrive there. The neocon apologists of the administration have now come up with their "flypaper" thesis: As Iraq attracts more and more Islamist terrorists, we will swat them. This reasoning assumes that there is a finite number of such terrorists to be killed or captured, and ignores the fact that all Al Qaida and its associated groups do is provide coordination and money, and that the supply of the key element—recruits—is limitless: Even 0.1 percent of the 1.3 billion Muslims worldwide comes to 1.3 million.

Behind his genial demeanor, the conservative Bush is an inflexible and intolerant man. Such is the conclusion of Jack Glaser, Arie Kruglanski, and two other psychologists in their article, "Political Conservatism as Motivated Social Cognition," in *Psychological Bulletin* (September 2003). Their study showed that "political conservatism can be explained as a set of neutrons rooted in fear and aggression, dogmatism and intolerance of ambiguity." The common points between Adolf Hitler, Benito Mussolini, Ronald Reagan, and Rush Limbaugh, the American right-wing talk show host, were that they all "preached a return to an idealized past and condoned inequality." Referring to George W. Bush, the authors wrote, "The telltale signs are his preference for moral certainty and frequently expressed dislike to nuance," and that "this intolerance of ambiguity can lead people to cling to the familiar, to arrive at premature conclusions, and to impose simplistic clichés and stereotypes." Separately, Glaser said that "aversion to shades of gray, and the need for closure" could explain why the Bush administration ignored intelligence that contradicted its belief about Iraq's WMD.[33]

Little wonder that Bush runs the White House like an army garrison where absolutism and smiting enemies and cast-iron certainty are the watchwords, and nuance and ambivalence are taboo. Along with this rigidity has come secrecy of Nixonian proportions. Anybody who expresses dissent in public or leaks anything of substance is called "disloyal" and cast out.

The same treatment is meted out to long-term allies and partners. Unlike all previous post–World War II American presidents, Bush has shown himself unable and/or unwilling to engage with allies as equals with legitimate interests and viewpoints of their own to be respected. Even in the case of Britain, Bush exploited Blair's backing to garner legitimacy for an invasion that was strictly his own administration's obsession. The role that Bush is prepared to give his allies is that of spear carriers in a historical movie made in Hollywood. This is what he means when he says other nations will have to "adjust" to the will of the United States. Thus there is no question of Washington's partners and allies having any input in the policy-making process. This is often justified under the doctrine of exceptionalism, the United States being the Exceptional Nation. Historian Margaret Macmillan, in her *Peacemakers*, writes, "Faith in their exceptionalism has sometimes led to a certain obtuseness on the part of Americans, a tendency to preach at other nations rather than listen to them, a tendency that American motives are pure where those of others are not."[34]

As a firm believer in America's exceptionalism, Bush wants to be the sole determinant of the policy on "the war on terror." It is noteworthy that soon after 9/11 he dropped the distinction he had initially made between terrorism with "a global reach" and local movements "fighting in pursuit of geographically specific objectives." Actually, what he wants is unrestrained latitude to continue using terrorism as a platform to raise the bogeyman of external threat to further his political agenda, which in practice is conceived and formulated by the hawks in his administration, led by Cheney, and articulated by the likes of Richard Perle. "This new century now challenges the hopes for a new world order in new ways," Perle wrote in the (London) *Spectator* on the eve of the war. "We will not defeat or even contain fanatical terror unless we can carry the war to the territory from which it is launched. This will sometimes require that we use force against [the] states that harbor terrorists, as we did in destroying the Taliban regime in Afghanistan." The "we" in that case had a clear mandate from the UN Security Council (Resolution 1368 of September 12, 2001), which was followed by NATO activating Article 5 of its charter—"An attack on one member is an attack on all." Most important, the United States was responding to an attack it had actually suffered. None of these conditions applied in the case of Iraq.

What Bush did in Iraq was to initiate not a preemptive war but a preventive one. Preemption is a response to an imminent, demonstrable threat, such as the assembling of troops along an international border or pointing missiles in a particular direction. Prevention, on the other hand, is a response to a threat that is not overt and can at best only be surmised. By a sleight of hand, *The National Security Strategy of the United States of America*, issued in September, 2002, obliterated the distinction between preemptive and preventive war. "We must adapt the concept of imminent threat to the capabilities and objectives of today's adversaries," it said. "Rogue states and terrorists do not seek to attack using conventional means. They rely on acts of terror and the use of weapons of mass destruction—weapons that can be easily concealed, delivered covertly and used without warning."[35] By widening the right of "preemptive self-defense" to include "preventive defense" against a possible enemy who *might* be developing a weapons *potential* that it *might* deploy in the future, the Bush administration struck at the very foundation of international law, built up since the Treaty of Westphalia in 1648 between the Catholic and Protestant countries of Europe.

Yet it took UN secretary-general Kofi Annan a year to challenge the Bush Doctrine. Referring to Washington's argument that nations had "the right and obligation to use force preemptively" against nonconventional weapons systems even while they were still being developed by a state, he told the UN General Assembly on September 23, 2003, "If it [this doctrine] were to be adopted, it could set precedents that resulted in a proliferation of the unilateral and lawless use of force, with or without credible justification. This logic represents a fundamental challenge to the principles on which, however imperfectly, world peace and stability have rested for the last 58 years."[36]

In the case of either preemptive or preventive war, 100 percent reliable intelligence is a sine qua non. As is crystal-clear by now, such intelligence was not available in Washington or London. What is more, it is unlikely to be in place in the near future, according to Gregory Treverton, deputy chair of the CIA's National Intelligence Council from 1993 to 1997. "The Bush doctrine is bedeviled at its core by the capabilities of U.S. intelligence," he wrote in the *New York Times* on August 24, 2003. "It places stresses on intelligence it cannot bear. Though U.S. ISR—intelligence, surveillance and reconnaissance—is unparalleled, it is not good at detecting objects hidden under foliage, buried underground or concealed in other ways, nor is it good at precisely locating objects by intercepting their signals. . . . Prewar U.S. intelligence on Iraq was far from good enough to identify, let alone target, specific biological, chemical or nuclear weapons." Given this, the U.S. failure at the United Nations was inevitable. "The problem arose not from any fecklessness of the UN but rather from asking nations to take hard, potentially dangerous decisions about dealing with threats that have not materialized, and whose imminence is a matter of judgment."[37]

While Bush had armed himself with a doctrine contained in *The National Security Strategy of the United States of America*, a document every incoming president is required to produce afresh, Blair had nothing more than intelligence dished out in two dossiers, one on September 24, 2002, and the other on February

3, 2003. This would lead Sir John Stanley, a former Conservative minister and a member of the House of Commons Foreign Affairs Committee, to muse: "Never before has Britain gone to war specifically on the strength of intelligence assessments." Intelligence assessments? More like a compendium of deliberate misinterpretations, misinformation, disinformation, and outright lies—to invade the sovereign Republic of Iraq, which posed no imminent threat to the United States, Britain, or any of Iraq's neighbors.

In Baghdad, in tactical terms, Saddam wanted to drag the inspections out into summer, knowing that it would be too hot for the Anglo-Americans to invade and that the following autumn would get close to the early stage of the presidential primaries in the United States, which would inhibit Bush from taking a precipitate action against Iraq. Strategically, Saddam wanted Bush and Blair to think he possessed WMD that he would use if attacked, hoping that this would deter them from invading Iraq. Explaining Saddam's evasive behavior, Hans Blix would tell the Berlin-based *Der Tagesspiegel* (The Daily Mirror) after the war that it was due to Saddam's desire to dictate the conditions under which outsiders could enter Iraq for inspections. "For that reason he said 'no' in many situations and gave the impression he was hiding something." However, added Blix, a " 'Beware of the dog' sign does not mean there is a dog inside the house."[38]

In London and Washington, how intoxicated the policy makers had become on the heady "intelligence" concoction of their own can be judged now in the sober light of the morning after. "We will in fact be greeted as liberators," declared Cheney in his NBC television interview on March 16.[39] Addressing the U.S. Veterans of Foreign Wars five days earlier, Wolfowitz had said, "Like the people of France in the 1940s, they view us as their hoped-for liberators. They know America will not come as a conqueror." This transformed Ahmad Chalabi—a convicted embezzler who escaped from Amman in the trunk of a friend's car—into the Iraqi Charles de Gaulle. To compare Iraq under the dictatorship of Saddam to a

France occupied by German troops required a leap of stunning illogic. Like their president, Bush, the supposedly hard-nosed neocons came to trust their "gut instincts" more than their actual knowledge of Iraq, battlefields, or military psychology. In their overheated imagination they visualized Saddam's regime collapsing like a sand castle at the blast of the Pentagon's gunpowder.

Their imagined scenario had percolated down the civil and military bureaucracy not only of the United States but also of the United Kingdom. Note the words of Group Captain Al Lockwood, spokesman for the British forces in the Gulf, at 1 P.M. on March 21: "If I was a betting man, hopefully, we'll be in Baghdad in the next three or four days."

This was the first of the Pentagon's four scenarios—Instant Triumph, within a few days, with the regime collapsing. The next-best scenario was Immediate Victory—in seven to ten days, with the Iraqi army defecting and the Shias in the south welcoming the Anglo-American forces. A briefing given by Colonel Steven Boltz, a U.S. Fifth Corps intelligence officer, to Bernard Weinraub of the *New York Times* on March 17 (but published on March 31) summarized this rosy version: Iraqis will welcome the American troops in crushing Saddam's regime, and the war will intensify as the Americans and the British surge toward Baghdad while Iraqi soldiers surrender in large numbers in the south.

The next scenario was Quick Success—in ten to twenty days. By capturing Baghdad on April 9, the twenty-first day of the invasion, the Anglo-Americans managed—just—to get into this slot, which was in the realm of reality, not myth. Every single day after Week Three would have raised the political temperature in the Arab and Muslim world sharply. A clear indication of this could be discerned in the tone and content of the statements that Egyptian president Hosni Mubarak and Jordanian king Abdullah made. Mubarak's warning on April 1 of the war creating one hundred bin Ladens was followed by Abdullah's strong condemnation of Washington's plan for regime change in Iraq a week later. These leaders felt an acute need to reflect the rising popular discontent at the Anglo-American invasion to preserve their fast-dwindling legitimacy. Iran condemned the invasion with its leader, Ayatollah Ali Khamanei, forecasting a doomed scenario for the United States in the medium to long term. Turkey, ruled by the Justice and Development Party, with its roots in moderate political Islam, maintained silence on the war—having earlier denied the Pentagon the use of its bases for ferrying troops into northern Iraq—and focused on the developments in Iraqi Kurdistan. While posting forty thousand troops along the Iraqi border ready to enter Kurdistan to control Kurdish "terrorists" (read: Iraqi Kurdish militiamen), it held its hand because of warnings not only from the United States but also from NATO and—more crucially—Germany, with whom it has lucrative economic ties due to the more than two million Turkish workers settled there. Within Iraq itself, by not ordering the torching of oil wells, Saddam demonstrated that he did not want to go down in history as having damaged Iraq's precious natural resource. By not fleeing or surrendering formally, he showed Iraqis and other Arabs that he was a true Iraqi nationalist who preferred banishment, resistance, or death to surrendering the sovereignty of his nation.

The final scenario on the Pentagon list was Delayed Success, three weeks to three months. No matter how things shaped up on the battlefield, any major fighting beyond four weeks was too fraught—diplomatically and politically—to contemplate. So Bush's curt reply to a journalist's question on March 27, "However long it takes . . ." was more rhetorical than realistic.

INVASION AND THE AFTERMATH

Overall, if there was one bright spot in the Iraq saga for the Bush team, it was the actual conduct of the war. True, the Anglo-American invaders encountered more resistance, offered more resolutely, than they had expected. But the highly original element the Pentagon's planners came up with—"Let us do things that Saddam does *not* expect us to do"—worked. Central to that strategy was the plan to get Iraqi generals to stop doing their job—undeclared noncooperation, which was to be won primarily with bribes, and which was to be fostered within the context of a total communications breakdown between the Iraqi central command and the regional commands. This was to be achieved with the Pentagon's high-tech weaponry, combined with relentless propagandistic and psychological pressure on active military officers.

Saddam had planned on countering the communications breakdown by using a messenger service, as he had done during the 1991 Gulf War. But what he had not envisaged was an undeclared strike by many of his generals, which came about only after they, their troops, and Iraqi civilians had been exposed daily to the unparalleled ferocity of the world's most powerful and technologically advanced military machine, and which brought home to them the hopelessness of trying to defend Baghdad without any air support.

The reason Saddam had not visualized the "betrayal" scenario was plain. The first and foremost requirement for promotion in the military was total loyalty to him. Before any Iraqi was considered for a commission in the military, he was vetted by the Baath Party's security bureau—chaired by Saddam, with his son Qusay as his deputy—for his loyalty to the leader and the party. (Baath Party documents seized after the invasion showed many instances where Saddam promoted an officer on the grounds of unquestioning loyalty to him rather than leadership qualities.) To ensure that officers remained loyal, he set up Military Security in 1992 with a mandate to maintain internal security within the armed forces. It did so by posting at least one unquestionably loyal officer in every military unit. This system served him well—it aborted half a dozen military coup attempts against his regime over the next decade.

The collapse of Saddam's regime—founded on domestic terror, political cunning, and gargantuan personality cult—brought immense relief to most Iraqis. But the fact that this release from the iron grip of Saddam and his security-intelligence apparatus was effected by America left them confused. They were suspicious of Washington. After all, the United States was primarily responsible for the UN sanctions that had pauperized them and brought them incalculable suffering; it was irrevocably linked with Israel, which had taken away Palestinian land and occupied Palestine for thirty-six years; and it was a country fast running out of its oil deposits, which Iraq had in abundance.

It was this ambivalence, prevalent among Iraqis, at being "liberated" and occupied simultaneously by a superpower they distrusted deeply—encapsulated in slogans such as "No, no to Saddam; no, no to America"—that would shape the course of events in the coming weeks and months, with the future of Iraq, either as a vibrant, stable democracy or as an incubator of Islamist extremists, in the balance.

For the things that went wrong in postwar Iraq—and they were many—the U.S. policy makers had only to examine their prewar actions and list their commissions and omissions.

Even the hard-nosed realists among them had apparently not studied *On War* (1832), a classic by Karl von Clausewitz, the preeminent Prussian general and expert on military affairs. "Philanthropists may easily imagine that there is a skillful method of disarming and overcoming an army without causing great bloodshed," he wrote. "[But this] is an error, which must be extirpated; for in such dangerous things as war, the errors which proceed from a spirit of benevolence are the worst."[40] Anybody accepting the wisdom of these words would have seen the Dick Cheney–Iraqi National Congress scenario of Iraqi soldiers defecting en masse and civilians showering the Anglo-American troops with flowers as a chimera, and would have prepared plans to bolster the Anglo-American military presence to four hundred thousand to five hundred thousand soldiers, as recommended by General Eric Shineski, chief of army staff, who was summarily silenced by Rumsfeld.

A more recent book they should have read carefully was *Storm*

Command, by General Sir Peter de La Billiere. As commander of forty five thousand British troops in the 1991 Gulf War, the second-largest deployment after the Pentagon's, he does not fall in the category of "Western liberal pessimists" or "Nervous Nellies of Old Europe." Explaining the decision not to march to Baghdad in 1991, he wrote, "We did not *have* a [UN] mandate to invade Iraq or take the country over, and if we had tried to do that, our Arab allies would certainly not have taken a favorable view. . . . The Arabs themselves had no intention of invading another Arab country. The Islamic forces [i.e., forces of the thirteen Muslim members of the coalition] were happy to enter Kuwait for the purpose of restoring the legal government, but that was the limit of their ambition." La Billiere had no doubt that the Western troops would have reached Baghdad in another day and a half. "But . . . we would have split the Coalition physically, since the Islamic forces would not have come with us, and risked splitting it morally and psychologically as well. . . . The American, British and French would have been presented as the foreign invaders of Iraq and we would have undermined the prestige which we had earned around the world for helping the Arabs resolve a major threat to the Middle East. The whole Desert Storm [operation] would have been seen purely as an operation to further Western interests in the Middle East." Finally, what would have been achieved by such a move? "Saddam Hussein . . . would have slipped away into the desert and organized a guerrilla movement. . . . We would then have found ourselves with the task of trying to run a country shattered by war, which at the best of times is deeply split into factions. . . . Either we would have to set up a puppet government or withdraw ignominiously without a proper regime in power, leaving the way open for Saddam to return. In other words, to have gone on to Baghdad would have achieved nothing except to create even wider problems." [41]

Bush and his team had failed to register a salient fact of recent history: It was the foreign occupation of Afghanistan, a Muslim country, that had led to the rise of Islamist extremism and terrorism, which culminated in 9/11; and, that it was the continued presence of American troops on Saudi soil *after* the Iraqis had been expelled from Kuwait that alienated Osama bin Laden, until then part of the Saudi establishment, from the House of Saud.

While obsessed about Iraq since September 11, 2001, they failed to study its history and culture, a blunder made by their antecedents in the 1960s in the case of Vietnam and the Vietnamese. They therefore missed the immense importance of Iraq as a leading player in the history of Islam—Baghdad was the capital of the Islamic Empire from 750 A.D. to 1258, with one interruption, and the site of the ninth-century classic *The Thousand and One Nights*—with more shrines holy to Sunni and Shia Muslims than any other country.[42] The occupation of Iraq by the infidel troops of the United States and Britain was bound to inflame feelings in the Arab and Muslim world and turn the occupied Iraq into a latter-day Afghanistan. They seemed oblivious of the analysis offered by bin Laden and Dr. Ayman Zawahiri. The Al Qaida leaders argued that the United States intended to occupy Iraq no matter what the Iraqi government did or did not do, and that most Arab leaders would side with Washington on this issue, and that Baathism and Arab nationalism were not the means to restore the independence and dignity of Arabs, something only Islam and jihad would deliver.

What has actually happened is something deadlier than the worst scenario sketched by "liberal pessimists." The Anglo-American invasion of Iraq has led to an alliance of Arab nationalism with Islamist militancy, a most powerful compound with serious implications for the rest of the Arab Middle East. It is a development that has yet to be registered by the Bush or Blair teams in Washington or London.

Reality continues to elude the American occupiers in Baghdad, with their superiors ensconced in the air-conditioned luxury of the former Republican Presidential Palace of Saddam, surrounded by razor wire, an absurdly high wall of concrete blocks, and tanks. For several weeks Paul Bremer, the U.S. proconsul to Iraq, refused to acknowledge the existence of a guerrilla movement that got going within weeks of Bush declaring "Mission Accomplished" on May 1. After the commander of the Centcom forward base in Qatar, General John Abizaid, a Lebanese-American, did so in early July, Bremer's office continued to attribute all attacks on American troops to "the remnants of the old regime." They were only part of the story.

The objectives of the guerrillas were to hurt the occupying power and to elicit overreaction, which, they reckoned, would further alienate Iraqis from the occupiers. This was the strategy that militant Irish nationalists in Northern Ireland adopted in the early 1970s—to great effect. And this is what happened in Iraq. The series of large-scale raids that the American troops carried out, in a style reminiscent of Vietnam, north and west of Baghdad in June made hundreds of thousands of Iraqi feel humiliated. This swelled the ranks of insurgents. As the brother of an Iraqi who works for Bremer's CPA in Baghdad put it, *"The American behavior makes us feel inferior."* [43]

Iraqis are a proud people with a strong sense of identity whose country achieved a literacy rate of 90 percent in the early 1980s. Iraq has a highly skilled population with tens of thousands of trained technocrats. As patriotic Iraqis, with no love for Saddam, they resent the military presence of Anglo-Americans—untutored in their language, religion, or culture—which they find humiliating. On top of that, they find themselves deprived of basic security and reliable public utilities, which, for all its sins, the ousted regime did provide.

Iraqis are highly skeptical of the Bush administration's claim that it came to liberate them. A survey of Baghdadis by the *Spectator* in July quantified this feeling. When asked the reason for the Anglo-American attack on Iraq, only 23 percent said, "To liberate us from dictatorship." Twice as many said, "To get oil"; and a little less than that, "To help Israel." Those who said "To find and destroy WMD" made up a puny 6 percent.[44] "Those with education know why the Americans are here," said thirty-five-year-old Mustafa Touma, an immunologist. "They came for oil. Americans want to occupy our land and our people [for that purpose]."[45]

However, there are several barriers to U.S. oil companies acquiring rights to Iraq's oil deposits, which, at nearly 12 percent of the world total, are the second largest in the world. The Geneva Conventions on War do not allow an occupying power to tinker with the occupied country's resources. Also, Saddam's regime had signed nearly thirty major oil-development contracts with companies based not only in Russia, France, Spain, and Italy, but also Canada, India, China, and Vietnam. It would be unrealistic to expect that these companies, as well as their governments, would simply roll over and let U.S. oil giants grab Iraqi oil. Finally, given the rampant anti-Americanism that exists in oil-rich southern Iraq, it would be hazardous for American corporations to develop the industry there.

POLITICAL PACE-SETTING BY GUERRILLAS

Whether by chance or design, the guerrilla movement came to set the pace of political reconstruction. Its rising activity made Bremer drop his plan of appointing an "Iraqi Political Council" as an advisory body, and opt for an "Interim Governing Council" with powers to draft a constitution and appoint a cabinet. He was also influenced by the advice of Sergio Vieira de Mello, the special representative of the United Nations, appointed in accordance with Security Council Resolution 1483, after the Bush administration had returned to the council it had earlier scorned.

While functioning in separate groups, the insurgents seemed to share certain common aims. This could be deduced from the high-profile major targets they chose in five successive weeks in August and September: the Jordanian embassy, the UN headquarters in Baghdad, Ayatollah Muhammad Baqir al Hakim in Najaf, the police headquarters in the capital, and a U.S. intelligence center in Irbil. The diverse messages implicit in these attacks all had one thing in common: "Iraqis, don't cooperate with the infidel occupiers." The attack on the United Nations was the most telling. It discouraged such countries as India, Pakistan, and Bangladesh from sending their troops to help the Pentagon with peacekeeping.

The unknown group that targeted Ayatollah al Hakim apparently did so because his party, SCIRI, cooperated with the Americans, and his brother Abdul Aziz was a member of the Interim Governing Council. Of the three major sectarian-ethnic communities, Shias, constituting three-fifths of Iraq's population, faced the most acute dilemma. As a group that had been held down since 1638, when Iraq (then Mesopotamia) was incorporated into the Sunni Ottoman Turkish Empire, they had sought solace in religion. The collapse of the Ottoman Empire in 1918 brought no relief, as it was succeeded by an Arab monarchy that was Sunni— and so too was the Baathist leadership that seized power in 1968.

During the Saddam regime, Shia clerics developed an underground system of communications that avoided the written word and the telephone and relied exclusively on messengers carrying coded messages. With the fall of Saddam, this system came to the fore and, as described earlier (on p. 300), enabled the clerical establishment to take over civilian functions among Shia communities throughout Iraq—much to the chagrin of the Americans.

Ideologically, SCIRI, fostered by the Islamic Republic of Iran during the 1980–88 Iran-Iraq War, had no love for Washington. Yet it did not want to be left out in the post-Saddam era that the Pentagon's military machine was set to usher in. It therefore followed a schizophrenic policy encapsulated by the slogan "No, no to America; no, no to Saddam." Later the mourners of Ayatollah al Hakim went on to shout, "America is the enemy of Islam" *(Amreeka adou Islam)*.

By contrast with SCIRI, the other factions among Shias, led respectively by Grand Ayatollah Ali Sistani and Hojatalislam Muqtada al Sadr—with far greater followings than SCIRI—kept clear of the occupying powers.

At the other extreme were 4.5 million Kurds, two-thirds of whom lived in Kurdistan, where they had enjoyed autonomy under the air umbrella of the United States and Britain since 1991.[46] They openly and enthusiastically cooperated with the Americans. They have pinned their hopes on a federal Iraq under a new constitution, a prospect that makes Turkey nervous. Turkey fears that its own Kurdish minority will then demand a similar status.

Federalism is going to be a contentious issue for the drafters of the constitution. Equally contentious will be the relationship between state and mosque. The absence of a minister for religious affairs in the cabinet appointed by the Interim Governing Council does not augur well for those who want Iraq to be an Islamic state, albeit a moderate one. A vast majority of Shias seems to support this idea, as does a very substantial minority of Sunnis.

But such a scenario runs counter to the plans that U.S. neocons have for "New Iraq." They see any such development as a plus for Iran, which, for them, is the next country to be put through a "regime change"—by force, if need be.

The neocon scenario visualized the overthrow of Saddam sending an unmistakable signal to Palestinians that, with the collapse of one of the last radical, anti-Zionist Arab states, they have no choice but to make peace with Israel on the latter's terms. Under Israeli prime minister Ariel Sharon, that means "peace for peace," not "peace for land." Much to their disappointment, this has not happened. There is no slackening of the Palestinian resistance to the Israeli military occupation. And this in turn is inspiring the Iraqi guerrillas in their struggle against the Anglo-American occupation. What the neocons failed to realize is that the Palestinian rage, fueled by the daily stealing of their land by Jewish settlers operating in cahoots with Israeli soldiers, has nothing to do with the events in Iraq, Syria, or Iran. "Far from bringing stability to the region, and creating conditions in which a permanent settlement of the Palestine-Israel conflict can be achieved, the ill-starred Anglo-American invasion of Iraq has made peace in the Middle East an even remoter prospect than it was before," noted the *Independent* on September 18, 2003.

Seeing the quagmire into which the Bush administration has landed itself in Iraq, all those plans of the U.S. hawks of radically reordering the Arab Middle East—whereby Iraq becomes a client state of Washington with a pro-American government installed in Baghdad that acts as a pressure point against Iran and Syria; the clerical regime in Iran is destabilized, if not overthrown, thus making Israel secure far beyond its borders; and the power of the Organization of Petroleum Exporting Countries (OPEC) and Saudi Arabia is broken—will have to be put on hold.

As for "New Iraq," at the planning stage the Bush team was confident of creating it as a friendly, stable, and democratic state within two years. "Achieve two of those adjectives and consider yourself lucky," wrote Roy Olivier, a French expert on the Middle East and Islam, after the end of the war. Crucially, there can be no democracy without nationalism, and Iraqis will sooner or later challenge the American presence, he predicted.[47]

This is already happening, with the Bremer-appointed Interim Governing Council (IGC) trying to carve out an independent position for itself at the expense of Bremer's Coalition Provisional Authority (CPA). The contentious issue between them is security, with the IGC demanding that it take over this function and the CPA refusing to part with it, arguing that the IGC has neither the adequate force nor the expertise nor the funds to do the job properly.

Beyond this specific issue lies a weightier one: sovereignty. The IGC wants to be invested with sovereignty as quickly as possible. On this subject, at the UN Security Council it has the backing of France, the bête noire of America, the godparent of the IGC. Iraq has a history in which puppets created by foreigners turn into fervent Iraqi nationalists, a fact that seems to have escaped the American neocons.

AMERICA'S DOMESTIC POLITICS

Though Bush has burned his fingers by invading Iraq when it posed no threat to the United States, he has not yet drawn the right lesson from this unlawful war, much less admitted publicly that he made a mistake. Given his character and modus operandi, it is not surprising that he has tried to shift his focus from Iraq as the hotbed of WMD to Iraq as a nest of terrorists, both secular (followers of Saddam) and Islamist (followers of bin Laden).

However, Bush's emphasis on using military as the primary— almost sole—means to wage an ongoing war on terrorism has not diminished. In the case of Iraq, Bush has gone beyond countering terrorism. He has used the Pentagon for the sociopolitical engineering of a complex country. The trend began with his father's presidency, as Dana Priest, a *New York Times* journalist, points out in her remarkable book, *The Mission: Waging War and Keeping Peace with America's Military* (2003). It was Bush Sr. who, while declaring war on drugs, named the Pentagon as "the single lead agency." Then William Perry, defense secretary in the first Clinton administration, publicly expressed the view that the U.S. armed forces could be used to "shape" the world in the way the White House wanted. Clinton's National Security Council gave the commanders-in-chiefs of the five regional commands broad powers, which led to close contacts with foreign governments and militaries at several levels. "The shift was incremental, little noticed, de facto," notes Priest. "The military simply filled a vacuum left by an indecisive White House, an atrophied State Department, and a distracted Congress." [48]

Following 9/11, this dependence on the military drove the

Bush Jr. administration. And after the adoption of the new National Security Strategy a year later, which included the doctrine of preemptive and preventive wars, the Pentagon became paramount, playing as it did a central role in foreign policy and intelligence. "The Pentagon has banded together to dominate the government's foreign policy, and they've pulled it off," W. Patrick Lang, the former chief of Middle East intelligence at the Defense Intelligence Agency, told Seymour Hersh of the *New Yorker* in May 2003. "They're running Chalabi. The DIA has been intimidated and beaten to a pulp. And there's no guts at all in the CIA." What is more, in the Middle East, the Bush White House has coupled military intervention with a total disregard for public opinion in the region, offset by periodic patronizing attempts to disseminate an amateurishly crafted American message—which results in alienating the very constituency whose backing it needs to succeed.

What is worrisome is that the primacy of the Pentagon has occurred against the background of Americans' rising love for the military. In their *The Generation of Trust: How the U.S. Military Has Regained the Public's Confidence Since Vietnam*, published by American Enterprise Institute for Public Policy Research, David King and his co-author cite Gallup surveys on confidence in church, Congress, and the military from 1975 to 2002. They showed that "a great deal" or "quite a lot" of confidence in church declined from 68 to 45 percent, and in Congress from 40 to 29 percent, but rose in military from 58 to 79 percent. In 1975, when the United States quit Vietnam in disgrace, a Harris survey found that only 20 percent of eighteen- to twenty-nine-year-olds had "a great deal of confidence" in those who ran the military. By contrast, a recent poll of 1,200 undergraduates at Harvard University showed that 75 percent trusted the military to do the right thing "all the time" or "most of the time."

Yet, the examples of Iraq and Afghanistan have demonstrated beyond doubt that the world is too complicated to be shaped by the sheer military might of Washington. In any case, such power is limited. Of the thirty-three combat brigades that the Pentagon has, sixteen are in Iraq, and five more are elsewhere—South Korea, Germany, Kosovo—leaving only twelve brigades to defend the continental United States. The Defense Department simply does not have enough manpower to deal effectively with any major crisis abroad.

Despite this, Washington shows little sign of easing off on Islamic Iran and the Baathist-ruled Syria. They are important neighbors of Iraq, with whom they share long, porous borders. Despite its differences with Iraqi Baathists led by Saddam, the ruling party in Damascus remains wedded to Arab nationalism. It also has a long-established strategic alliance with Tehran. The fifty-six million Shias in Iran feel affinity with their fifteen million fellow Shias in Iraq. Neither this fact nor the length of the Iranian-Iraqi border—730 miles (1,170 kilometers)—can be altered by the threat or use of "overwhelming force" against Iran by the United States. On the contrary, faced with such threats, both Iran and Syria should be expected to undermine Washington's plans for Iraq—if only for their self-preservation. The more the United States finds itself bogged down in Iraq, the less will be its ability to threaten the Iranian and Syrian regimes. So the American claims that Islamist militants are entering Iraq from Syria and Iran are not surprising. Nor should anyone be astonished to discover that the Syrian and Iranian governments are intent on creating conditions in Iraq that would help bring about the defeat of Bush in the November 2004 presidential election.

As it is, in the course of flexing its military muscle and dazzling friend and foe with its high-tech weaponry, the Bush administration has alienated not just the Muslim and Arab world but also Europe, both "old" and "new." Daily the gap grows wider between how Americans see themselves ("compassionate, and generous champions of democracy and freedom") and how the rest of the world sees them ("arrogant, and driven by narrow self-interest regardless of international law and commitments").

This widening gulf worries such unquestioning America-lovers as Blair. He has warned of the dangers of the United States turning isolationist. This is alarmist talk. For several reasons—political, economic, telecommunications, and others—the first decade of the twenty-first century is vastly different from the 1920s and 1930s, when the United States distanced itself from Europe (although not from Latin America, its historic backyard). Today, for starters, the United States is so indebted to foreigners that isolationism is not a viable option. Its economy is increasingly dependent on imported oil. At the current rate of extraction, its own petroleum reserves would be exhausted in a decade. By that time there would be only five countries in the world with large quantities of oil available for export. Saudi Arabia would be one of them; so would Iraq.

NOTES

1. *Independent*, July 11, 2003.
2. *New York Times*, August 8, 2003.
3. *Guardian,* May 23, 2003.
4. Associated Press, March 16, 2003.
5. They were Pakistan, Saudi Arabia, and the United Arab Emirates.
6. *Independent on Sunday*, September 7, 2003.
7. *New York Times*, July 17, 2003.
8. See Dilip Hiro, *Inside the Middle East*, McGraw Hill, New York, and Routledge & Kegan Paul, London, 1982, p. 146.
9. See further Dilip Hiro, *The Essential Middle East*, p. 176.
10. See Dilip Hiro, *The Longest War: The Iran-Iraq Military Conflict*, p. 159.
11. *International Herald Tribune*, August 20, 2003. For details of the Bush administration's manipulation of the Environmental Protection Agency's report on global warming, see "Bush covers up climate research" by Paul Harris, *Observer*, September 21, 2003.
12. *New York Times*, September 22, 2003.
13. They are the U.S. Army Intelligence Center, Office of Naval Intelligence, Marine Corps Intelligence Activity, and Air Intelligence Agency (Defense Department); Non-Proliferation and National Security (Energy Department); National Reconnaissance Office and National Imagery and Mapping Agency

(Executive Office of the President); Federal Bureau of Investigation (Justice Department); and Office of Intelligence Support (Treasury Department).

14. *Observer*, May 11, 2003; *Sunday Times*, June 1, 2003.

15. *Guardian*, July 10, 2003.

16. Following Donald Rumsfeld's admission, all Tony Blair did was come down from "Iraq's weapons" to "Iraq's programs for. . . ." Ibid., July 19, 2003.

17. *Washington Post*, September 27, 2003.

18. Ibid., September 6, 2003.

19. Ibid., October 21, 2002.

20. *Washington Times*, September 3, 2003.

21. *International Herald Tribune*, July 21, 2003.

22. See Dilip Hiro, *Iraq*, pp. 190–91.

23. July 1, 2003.

24. See further Dilip Hiro, *Iraq*, pp. 63–64.

25. David Frum, *The Right Man: An Inside Account of the Surprise Presidency of George W. Bush*, Doubleday, New York/Weidenfeld & Nicolson, London, 2003, p. 203. Of five religious leaders, three were Christian, one Jewish, and one Muslim.

26. *Ha'aretz* (Tel Aviv), June 24, 2003.

27. An early example of this came in February 2001, after the Pentagon had struck Iraqi defense facilities in the south, some of them above the thirty-third Parallel. "Saddam Hussein has got to understand that we expect him to conform to the agreement he signed after Desert Storm," said Bush. "We will enforce the no-fly zone, both south and north." The UN Security Council Resolution 687 on the Gulf War ceasefire that Saddam accepted had nothing to do with no-fly zones. Dilip Hiro, *Neighbors, Not Friends: Iraq and Iran after the Gulf Wars*, p. 303.

28. Cited in *Observer*, March 16, 2003.

29. *Washington Post*, November 20, 2002.

30. March 31, 2003, p. 172.

31. *International Herald Tribune*, August 7, 2003. Earlier, one of the UN inspectors, Bernd Birkicht, said, "We received information [from America or Britain] about a site, giving the exact geographical coordinates, and when we got there we found nothing. Nothing on the ground. Nothing under the ground. Just desert." *Independent on Sunday*, June 8, 2003.

32. Dilip Hiro, *The Essential Middle East*, p. 161.

33. Arie Kruglanski said, "The variables we talk about are general human dimensions. These are the [conservative] dimensions that contribute to loyalty and commitment to the group. Liberals might be less intolerant of ambiguity but they may also be less decisive, less committed, less loyal." *Guardian*, August 13, 2003.

34. Cited in *Observer*, March 23, 2003.

35. Page 17.

36. *New York Times*, September 24, 2003; *Guardian*, September 24, 2003.

37. For a fuller version of this article, visit www.armscontrol.org.

38. *Der Tagesspiegel*, May 23, 2003; *Guardian*, September 18, 2003.

39. Dick Cheney's interview with Tim Russert, host of *Meet the Press* on March 16, 2003.

40. Cited in *International Herald Tribune*, April 7, 2003.

41. General Sir Peter de La Billiere, *Storm Command: A Personal Account of the Gulf War*, HarperCollins, London, 1992, pp. 304–5.

42. Iraq has shrines of five of the twelve Imams of Shia Islam and shrines of two leading figures of Sunni Islam.

43. *Sunday Times*, June 22, 2003.

44. July 19, 2003, p. 13.

45. *Guardian*, April 16, 2003.

46. France was part of the air umbrella until September 1996, when one of the two Kurdish parties invited Saddam Hussein to help it eject the other party from the regional capital of Irbil. Saddam obliged.

47. *International Herald Tribune*, May 14, 2003. A cynic might ask, "How well has the United States succeeded in installing democracy in Haiti after the death of Francois Duvalier in 1971, an enterprise backed by the UN Security Council?"

48. Cited in *New York Review of Books*, March 27, 2003, p. 19.

EPILOGUE

BETWEEN PRESIDENT GEORGE W. Bush's television address to the nation on September 7, 2003—when he put the annual cost of occupying Iraq and rebuilding some of its economic infrastructure at $71 billion—and his weekly radio talk seven weeks later, much happened in Iraq, America, and Britain, as well as at the United Nations.

While Coalition Provisional Authority (CPA) chief Paul Bremer claimed progress in normalizing the situation in Iraq, the U.S. ground forces commander in the country, Lt.-Gen. Ricardo Sanchez conceded that the enemy had become "a little bit more lethal," and that daily attacks on the U.S. GIs had risen to fifteen to twenty from a dozen before. The speeches delivered to the UN General Assembly showed that there were wide differences on pre-emptive wars not only between Bush and French President Jacques Chirac but also between Bush and UN Secretary General Kofi Annan, who owed his second term in office largely to Washington's active backing. The French-German-Russian trio voted half-heartedly for UN Security Council Resolution 1511 on Iraq's political future on October 16, saying up front that no member of the triad would contribute soldiers to the multinational force.

IRAQI RESISTANCE

When Lt. Gen. Sanchez said that "The enemy has evolved—a little bit more lethal, a little more complex, a little more sophisticated, and in some cases a little bit more tenacious"[1]—what he meant was that the Iraqis opposed to the U.S. military occupation had gone beyond violent demonstrations and sniper fire directed at the GIs. They had resorted to sophisticated roadside bombings, firing missiles at American planes, well-planned attacks not only on convoys but also military bases, and bombings of politically sensitive targets.

The latest example of violent protest occurred in Baiji, 140 miles (220 kilometers) north of Baghdad on October 4. When some people mounted a pro-Saddam demonstration in the town square, the U.S.-trained policemen recruited from outside the city and commanded by unpopular Gen. Abdullah Jassim, fired on the crowd, injuring four. This enraged the locals who had gathered in their thousands. Carrying Saddam's portraits and shouting "Our spirit, our blood, we sacrifice for you, Oh Saddam!" (*Beruh, beldam nafideq, O Saddam!*), they burned the mayor's office, and put to flight Jassim and 300 policemen who sought refuge at the nearby U.S. base. It was only after the U.S. commander had sacked Jassim and reinstated the earlier police chief did the protest subside.[2]

Iraqi guerrillas became proficient in putting improvised explosive devices (IEDs)—meaning mortars—in soda cans, plastic bags, or dead animals, and leaving them along railroad tracks or roadsides, or dropping them from overpasses and detonating them remotely or with timers. As a result, the number of injured GIs shot up. The statistics given by the spokeswoman at the U.S. military hospital in Landstuhl, Germany, where the more serious cases were flown from for treatment, showed that whereas this infirmary had received an average of 220 patients a week during the war, the weekly figure had risen to 320 since the end of "major operations" on May 1. "We see a lot of shrapnel wounds, some amputations, some burns—mostly from individual explosive devices," she said.[3]

In a daring broad-daylight attack on an American military convoy in Khalidiya 100 miles (160 kilometers) northwest of Baghdad, twenty Iraqi guerrillas killed three (according to Centcom) to eight (according to the locals) U.S. troops on September 18.[4] That day an ambush on another U.S. convoy in Auja, Saddam's home village, led to an all-night battle when the guerrillas also attacked two American bases along the Tigris in a coordinated fashion, using rocket-propelled grenades and small and heavy machine gun fire, killing three. After the fight, the GIs arrested fifty-six adults in a village of 600 people. But that had no effect on the nightly mortar attacks on the U.S. military headquarters at Saddam's old palace complex in nearby Tikrit.

What continued to draw the most media attention were the bombings of high-profile targets. Between September 10 and October 12, there were four such explosions. In the first instance, a suicide car-bomber attacked a U.S. intelligence service base—part of a highly secretive operation run by the Defense Intelligence Agency (DIA)—in Irbil, killing three and wounding fifty, four of them DIA operatives. In a second attack on the UN headquarters in Baghdad on September 22, a suicide bomber killed himself and a police officer about to search him in the parking lot. As a result UN Secretary General Kofi Annan withdrew all foreign UN employees from Baghdad, except a skeleton staff of forty-two.[5]

On October 9, two suicide bombers attacked a police station, manned by U.S.-trained officers, in the Shia neighborhood of Sadr City, killing eight Iraqis. Earlier in the same district the U.S. troops had closed in on the office of a radical Shia cleric and killed two Iraqis.[6] Three days later, in an audacious move, two suicide bombers targeted Baghdad Hotel in the city center, which housed not only U.S. officials, building contractors, and members of the Interim Governing Council

(IGC) but also the operatives of the CIA and the Israeli foreign intelligence agency Mossad. Because of the protection provided by 12-foot-high (4 meters) concrete wall and sandbags placed 100 yards/meters in front of the hotel, the main building escaped major damage. But eight people died and thirty-two were injured, including Muwafaq al Rubaie, an Interim Governing Council member. Another bomb exploded outside the Turkish Embassy five days later.

By now it was clear that the Iraqi resistance consisted of three major strands: nationalists, vehemently opposed to foreign occupation (the leading group in Ramadi and Khalidiya); Islamists, largely former members of the Muslim Brotherhood which had been suppressed by Saddam, who want to establish an Islamic state (now active in Falluja, Samarra and Mosul); and die-hard Baathists incensed by their loss of power (based in the Tikrit-Baiji area). Despite their divergent agendas and motivations, at present they are united in their hostility to the Anglo-American forces, and will remain so as long as the occupation continues. In Mosul, Samarra, and Falluja, for example, Islamist and Baathist guerrillas report to the local committee of Sunni Islamic leaders.

In addition, there was passive resistance from those following either Grand Ayatollah Ali Sistani or Hojatalislam Muqtada al Sadr, who together constitute a large majority of the Shia community. Increasingly, there were violent clashes between the followers of al Sadr and the American forces. On October 9, militant Shias ambushed GIs in Sadr City, killing two. A week later in a firefight between al Sadr partisans, the GIs, and Iraqi policemen in Karbala, the former lost six men and the latter five, including three Americans. If Shias—who have largely been quiescent in the expectation of achieving power through elections in the near future—resort to violence to the extent Sunnis have, then Washington will find it exceedingly hard to restore law and order.

What is swelling guerrilla ranks is the behavior of the GIs—a carbon copy of what the Israeli soldiers have been doing in the occupied Palestinian territories for thirty-six years. "Its [the American military's] 'recon-by-fire,' its lethal raids in civilian homes, its shooting of demonstrators and children during fire fights, its destruction of houses, its imprisonment of thousands of Iraqis without trial or contact with their families, its refusal to investigate killings, its harassment—and killing—of journalists, its constant refrain that it has 'no information' about bloody incidents which it must know all too much about, are sounding like an echo-chamber of the Israeli army," noted Robert Fisk.[7]

An instance of collective punishment meted out by the American GIs to a rural community in Dhuluiya, fifty miles (eighty kilometers) north of Baghdad, in the second half of September took a few weeks to reach foreign journalists in the capital. They found that, for not informing on the resistance, thirty-two farmers had their groves of date palms and orchards of orange and lemon trees uprooted by the U.S. troops with bulldozers as they played jazz music on loudspeakers. "What Israelis had done by way of collective punishment of Palestinians was now happening in Iraq," said Shaikh Hussein Ali Salih al Jabburi.[8]

The failure so far to capture or kill Saddam Hussein added to the frustration and aggressiveness of the occupying forces—especially when he continued to taunt them with his periodic taped messages which were aired by Al Jazeera or Al Arabiya television channel. In his audiotape broadcast on September 17—as the total American military fatalities since the start of the invasion neared 300—Saddam offered 'the pleasant news' about the attacks on the Americans: "The losses have begun to eat away at the enemy like wildfire . . . you should show your anger by attacks, demonstrations, graffiti, and financial contributions to the resistance." He urged Iraqis to "tighten the noose" around the Americans and "conduct jihad" by every possible means. He called on the occupation powers "to withdraw your armies as soon as possible and without any conditions because there is no reason for further losses that will be disastrous for America if your officials continue their aggression."[9]

As it was, an example of the American aggression in Falluja on September 12 was quite fresh in the minds of Iraqis. The U.S. Third Infantry Division soldiers fired heavy machine guns on Iraqi police officers that they themselves had trained, who were in clearly marked police cars, and who shouted they were police in Arabic and English. Eight police officers and one Jordanian guard were killed. Of the thousands of 40 millimeter grenade cartridges fired, hundreds hit the hospital adjoining the police station, setting many rooms on fire. The U.S. military claimed that their troops responded to an attack with a rocket-propelled-grenade and small arms fire. The locals knew better, and protested by holding a one-day strike.

The lightning rod for all this was the continued lack of security and 60–75 percent unemployment. The payment of a single stipend of $40 to 320,000 former Iraqi soldiers (out of 440,000) by early October had no ameliorative impact on the dire circumstances of millions of Iraqi families. With 24 million guns in civilian hands, the country is awash in small arms.[10] In Baghdad, the death toll by gunfire in September was 518 versus six under the ousted regime. The newly U.S.-hired and trained policemen continued the brutal practices of their predecessors. The only difference was that whereas under the old regime corruption was institutionalized, now it's a free for all. So an ordinary citizen is worse off than before. The fear of girls and women being abducted was so widespread that when schools reopened on October 4, classrooms were half-empty, with girls being kept at home by parents forced to choose between education and safety. Working women had taken to leaving home wearing a headscarf and traveling with a male relative.

Foreign businessmen intent on staying in Baghdad found that round-the-clock security cost up to $10,000 a day, requiring a dozen armed guards and two armored vehicles with blackened windows. Nearly 100 former British SAS (Special Air Services) officers worked for foreign security companies. "It's the Wild West out there," said John Geddes, an SAS veteran. "It's not a war zone:

It's worse. During the war there was a frontline, but now it's every man for himself. Iraq today is a very, very dangerous place. The opposition are opposed to reconstruction and anyone involved with it is a target."[11]

The Bush Administration's upbeat prewar estimates of Iraqi petroleum exports generating $20–30 billion annually to finance most of the reconstruction proved elusive. At 70,000 barrels per day, the oil exports in October were a measly 4 percent of the preinvasion figure. With the oil pipeline in the north averaging one act of sabotage a week, no oil exports through Turkey were envisaged for six to twelve months. This compelled Washington to scale down Iraq's oil income to a mere $2–$3 billion during the second half of 2003.[12]

As such, the $20 billion that Bush requested from Congress for Iraqi reconstruction acquired greater significance than before. Even then this sum is only one-fifth of the total cost of reconstruction over the next few years.

BUSH'S DUAL PROBLEM

In his September 7 television address to the nation, President Bush came up with the grand sum of $87 billion, of which $11 billion was earmarked for Afghanistan and $51 billion for maintaining the U.S. occupation of Iraq. That would push the budget deficit for financial year 2003–04 to more than $500 billion, compared to the surplus of $230 billion that the last year of the Clinton Administration produced. Bush's figure came as a shock to the public as well as politicians.[13]

They hardly had time to recover when the *Washington Post* reported that two Bush Administration officials had telephoned at least six journalists, including ones at NBC TV and *Time,* telling them that Valerie Plame, the wife of Joseph Wilson, was a CIA agent. The Intelligence Protection Act of 1982 specifies ten years in jail and $10,000 in fines for unauthorized disclosure by government employees with access to classified information. This story caught the imagination of U.S. news hounds who had until then been treating the President and his Administration with kid gloves. The stink became so malodorous that Attorney General John Ashcroft, a Bush loyalist, announced on September 29 that the Justice Department had opened an investigation in the matter. It had taken his department *eleven weeks* to do so after Robert Novak had published the classified information about Valerie Plame, a nominal energy analyst with Brewster-Jennings and Associates, a CIA front company, who was really a highly prized WMD specialist.[14]

The time lapse in Ashcroft's case, however, was puny compared to the 105 weeks President Bush took to set the record straight on the alleged linkage of Saddam Hussein with 9/11. That happened only because of Cheney's comments on the NBC's *Meet the Press* on September 14. When questioned about the poll showing 69 percent of Americans believing that Saddam was involved in 9/11, he replied: "It is not surprising the people make the connection." Asked if he thought the connection existed, he replied, "We don't know." Three days later, in response to a question about Cheney's remark, Bush said: "No, we've had no evidence that Saddam Hussein was involved with Sept 11."[15]

This was a welcome, though admittedly brief, reversal from the stance Bush had adopted, as the *Washington Post* duly noted: In the previous six weeks he had invoked 9/11 not only for the Iraq policy and oil drilling in the Arctic, but also in response to questions about tax cuts, unemployment, budget deficits and even campaign finance. "Bush's advisers were greedy," wrote Paul Krugman in the *New York Times* on the second anniversary of 9/11. "They saw 9/11 as an opportunity to get everything they wanted, from another round of tax cuts to major weakening of the Clean Air Act to the invasion of Iraq, and they wrapped up as much as they could in the flag."[16]

But, like all else in life, the law of diminishing returns applied to Bush's policy. Further damage came from the failure of Saddam's much-vaunted WMD to materialize, the continuing military casualties in Iraq, which made nine out of 10 Americans believe the war was still continuing, the absence of achievable U.S. goals or a plausible exit strategy in Iraq, and the rapid deterioration in already fraught Israeli-Palestinian relations.

Bush's popularity dropped accordingly. In a *USA Today*/CNN poll, three out of five Americans thought that the Bush Administration lacked a clear plan to handle the situation in Iraq. A *Washington Post*/ABC News survey showed that 46 percent disapproved of Bush's policy on Iraq. And going by the CBS/*New York Times* poll, an unprecedented 53 percent believed the war was not worth it. Worst of all, just as Ashcroft announced an investigation in the Plame scandal on September 29, a *Wall Street Journal*/NBC poll recorded Bush's approval rating at 49 percent, the lowest yet.

Bush's drop was due partly to revelations about the unreliability of the intelligence fed to his Administration during the run-up to the war by the Iraqi National Congress's American representative, who had weekly meetings with William Luti of the Pentagon's Office of Special Plans. They met despite the review by the Defense Intelligence Agency in *early 2003* that concluded that no more than a third of the information provided by the INC was potentially useful, and even in those cases a follow-up had yielded little of value. "All this is coming out now because they didn't have the political spine to do it before," said Vince Cannistraro, former CIA counterintelligence chief. "Now the tide has turned internally in terms of the use of intelligence before the war."[17]

A four-month study of nineteen volumes of classified material by the House Intelligence Committee led its Republican chairman Peter Goss and his ranking Democrat colleague Jane Harman to complain to George Tenet that because there was no fresh information on Iraq after the UN inspectors were withdrawn in December 1998, it relied on old information and some "new piecemeal intelligence"[18]—both of which were not challenged "as a routine matter," and found their way to analysts. "The absence of proof that chemical and biological weapons and their related development programs had been destroyed was considered proof that they continued to exist." Regarding the Iraq-Al Qaida links, they wrote, the intelligence community had a "low threshold" or "no threshold" on using information it gathered. "As a result, intelligence reports that might have been screened out by a more rigorous vetting process made their way to the analysts' desks, providing ample room for vagary to intrude. The agencies did not specify which of their reports were from sources that were credible and that were from sources which would otherwise be dismissed in the absence of any other corroborating intelligence." Finally, Goss and Harman revealed that the Bush Administration had not withheld any pertinent information on Iraq's nuclear capabilities while giving the impression that it had classified intelligence it could not reveal.[19]

Such strictures by the legislative and executive branches of the government were rare. So they should have shaken even the most complacent President. But no, Bush continued to inhabit the cocoon he had spun for himself.

He remarked casually that he learned all he needed to know from morning briefings by Condi Rice and Andrew Card. "I glance at the headlines but rarely read the stories," he added. "It is worrisome when one of the most incurious men ever to occupy the White House takes pains to insist that he gets his information on what the world is saying only in pre-digested bits from his appointees," wrote the *New York Times* on September 30. "It is in Bush's interest as well the nation's for him to burst the bubble he has been inhabiting, and take a hard look at the real world."

Nonetheless, Bush realized that the occupation was in trouble, and something ought to be done about it. The solution according to him—and Condi Rice—was to set up an Iraqi Stabilization Group under Rice, thus ending the near-monopoly that Rumsfeld had enjoyed on Iraq. On October 2, she sent a "confidential memo" (which she leaked to the *New York Times*) to the heads of the departments of Defense, State, and Treasury, and to the CIA, saying that the proposed Iraqi Stabilization Group will have four working committees each under one of her deputies: counterterrorism efforts;

economic development in Iraq, political affairs in Iraq, and the media. Each group will have undersecretaries from the departments of State, Defense, and Treasury, and senior representatives from the CIA.

An angry Rumsfeld said he was not consulted about the new arrangement and that these 'little committees' were irrelevant. He publicly berated Rice for "briefing" the *New York Times,* which was clearly her "pre-emptive" move against him. By so doing, he violated his own dictum enshrined in the rule book he prepared as President Gerald Ford's chief of staff in 1974: "Avoid public spats. When a department argues with another government agencies in the press, it reduces the president's options."[20] Leaving aside the tensions among the President's senior aides, turning the National Security Council into an overtly operational organ is unprecedented, and carries its own risks. The shifting of accountability for postwar Iraq closer to the Oval Office meant that in case of continued failure, Bush would have no else to blame.

The vehemence of Rumsfeld's attack on Rice left Bush nonplussed. According to a senior Administration official Bush asked, "This [infighting] isn't as bad as [George] Shultz and [Caspar] Weinberger, is it?," referring respectively to the secretaries of State and Defense during the Ronald Reagan Administration, to which a senior official replied, "Way worse."[21]

Rumsfeld's spat with Rice came at a time when he had run afoul of the neoconservatives, who now began advocating an enlarged military for America to meet the demands of policing the increasingly restive Iraq. That clashed with Rumsfeld's determination to reinvent the U.S. military as a modern, mobile, downsized force, and his point-blank refusal to send more GIs to Iraq. "Rumsfeld . . . underestimates the importance of nation-building, public-opinion-molding and Middle-East-reforming," said William Kristol, editor of the *Weekly Standard.*[22] Trapped in their blinkered ideology, neocons were immune to the fact that the majority of Americans had by now concluded that war in Iraq was not justified, that in the five months since the official end of the conflict the number of GIs killed due to hostile action had surpassed 100 (with the grand total since the war reaching 330), and that according to the survey by the U.S. military newspaper *Stars and Stripes,* a third of those posted in Iraq felt that morale was low, and that half said they would not re-enlist when their tour of duty ended.[23]

The disquiet about spending $20 billion on Iraq's reconstruction became so intense that nine Republican senators said they would vote for a Democratic amendment which converted half of the sum into a loan. Bush summoned them to the Oval Office and warned them against backing the amendment. The senators were unmoved. This led the president to bang the table and refuse to answer any questions. Bush's behavior led Robert Dallek, a veteran presidential historian, to note that "there is an emerging quality to the tension Bush faces and his reactions to the criticism that is reminiscent of [President Lyndon] Johnson in Vietnam." And, as with Johnson in similar circumstances, Bush's tantrum proved ineffective. On October 16, eight Republican senators joined the vast majority of Democrats to carry the amendment by 51 votes to 47.

Commenting on the state of the Bush presidency William Kristol wrote in the *Weekly Standard* that the Plame-Wilson leak scandal "illustrated the disarray within the Bush administration," and that "the civil war has become crippling." He added, "The CIA is in open revolt against the White House. The state and defense departments are not working together at all. We are way beyond 'fruitful tension.'"[24]

As if Bush's rising troubles at home were not enough, there were clear signs of tension between Washington and the Interim Governing Council (IGC) in Iraq, its own creature.

THE IGC COMES TO LIFE

With Ahmad Chalabi, well versed in handling the Western media, becoming the IGC's rotating president in September, the IGC acquired a higher profile than before. He also knew how the legislative and executive organs of the United States functioned. With Bush's request for $87 billion being scrutinized by the Congress, he flew to Washington ostensibly to lobby lawmakers for the transfer of sovereignty, funds, and security to the IGC, after briefing the foreign journalists in Baghdad on how the CPA was squandering money by sending laundry to Kuwait for cleaning and so on. Other IGC members said repeatedly that they did not want any more foreign soldiers, thus contradicting Washington's entreaties to other countries to dispatch their troops to "stabilize" Iraq.[25]

Chalabi's statements went down badly with Bush's senior advisers. In their meetings with him, they admonished him, telling him to cool it. Given his background as Washington's puppet, he readily fell in line. His testimony to the U.S. Congress on October 2 was a mild affair, and he went out of his way to assure the lawmakers that the IGC would make "no claims" on any of the $20 billion in reconstruction funds requested by the White House.[26] As the last speaker in the "general debate" at the UN General Assembly, Chalabi waxed eloquent about America liberating Iraq.

None of this eased the tensions between the IGC and Paul Bremer, whom many council members publicly criticized for being abrupt, patronizing, and prone to issuing decrees unilaterally without even a symbolic nod at the IGC. "The Council does not have much power, and if you don't have real power you lack credibility," said Mahmoud Uthman, a Kurdish member of the IGC. "We will be seen by Iraqis as puppets." To illustrate the impotence of the IGC, Uthman referred to the CPA's $1.3 billion contract to Jordan for training 30,000 Iraqi police. "We could train them for one-third of the money. But the U.S. wants to do Jordan a favor at our expense."[27] Uthman's views corresponded with the findings of a Gallup poll of 1,178 people in Baghdad in late August–early September showing that three-quarters believed that IGC decisions were "mostly determined" by the CPA. When, after receiving a promise of an $8.5 billion loan by Washington, the Turkish government and parliament agreed to send 10,000 troops to Iraq, the IGC unanimously opposed the move, stating that it did not want soldiers from any of Iraq's neighbors. The Bush Administration ignored the IGC vote.

The kind of IGC work the CPA did encourage was legislation concerning foreign investment, which suddenly became international news on September 21 when Iraqi Finance Minister Kamil al Kilani—attending a meeting of the International Monetary Fund and the World Bank in Dubai in the United Arab Emirates—revealed that the IGC had opened up all the non-petroleum sectors of Iraq's economy to foreign investors, who could own up to 100 percent of any enterprise. Many Iraqis and others wondered why the unelected IGC had rushed to put up Iraq for sale. Such a sweeping measure should have been left to a legitimately elected government.

This did not unduly worry those Iraqis intent on enriching themselves at the expense of their country's welfare. Among them was Ahmad Chalabi's nephew, Salem, or "Sam," a U.S.-trained attorney who liaised with the Pentagon on legal matters, who joined Marc Zell, a right-wing Zionist lawyer to set up Iraqi International Law Group (IILG) in July 2003 to "provide foreign enterprise with information and tools to enter the emerging Iraq and to succeed." Zell was a partner in the Jerusalem-based legal firm Zell Goldberg & Co., which assisted Israeli companies doing business abroad.[28] The IILG claimed to employ three Iraqi lawyers and four "international business attorneys." Until September 25, 2003, Zell was the owner of the IILG website, but the following day this changed when the London-based Guardian Unlimited revealed that Zell had transferred ownership to Chalabi. Yet the content on the website, written by Zell's Jerusalem office staff, remained the same. In it, the IILG claimed to be acting as a counselor to the Iraq-Baghdad Chamber of Commerce as well as the Federation of Iraqi Industries.[29]

Given the parlous state of security in Iraq, and the country's increasingly uncertain future, it was unlikely that any reputable Western company would invest in Iraq in the near future, no matter how lucrative the terms. But that would not preclude their "consulting" such Iraqi-Israeli organizations as the IILG.

IRAQI SECURITY AND CONSTITUTION

The IGC was keen to take up responsibility for security, with Iyad Alawi, its president in October, proposing that the U.S. troops return slowly to their bases and leave day-to-day policing to the IGC's interior minister, Nouri al Badran, a Shia.

This was unacceptable to Washington. In his meeting with *New York Times* editors on September 24, Colin Powell argued that merely handing over power quickly to the IGC would be fraught with security problems. "The *militants* who strike against the U.S. military more than a dozen times a day now would be just as likely to target an unelected government," he said. "These are ex-Baathists. They would go after an illegitimate government that does not enjoy the will of the people just as easily as they would go after us."

In the eyes of Powell and other Bush senior advisers, the IGC's demand for quick handover of power echoed Chalabi's INC plan of late 1998 to overthrow the Saddam regime: It visualized its Pentagon-trained militia initiating guerrilla actions in Iraq and escalating their insurgency, thus precluding the need for the deployment of U.S. ground forces.[30] Nor did the Bush team take seriously the proposal by Ayatollah Abdul Aziz al Hakim, an IGC member, that the militias of the political parties in the IGC be allowed to take over security in cities. Such an arrangement set a dangerous precedent with serious consequences for the future, the Bush Administration said. Overall, it felt that the IGC lacked the legitimacy as well as adequate manpower and equipment to make Iraq secure by ending the activities of the increasingly lethal guerrilla movement.

The assassination of IGC member Aqila al Hashemi was a case in point. Along with other IGC members, the CPA offered troops and armored personnel carriers to protect her. She refused, as did others, saying they did not want to be seen as "creatures of the Americans." They used guards from among relatives and tribesmen, to be trained by the CPA, but the progress was later described as "not totally satisfactory." On September 20, as Hashemi, accompanied by her bodyguards and driver, prepared to leave home for work, nine gunmen fired Kalashnikovs and threw a hand grenade at her party. Her wounds were so serious that she died five days later, and this resulted in Shias losing their majority in the IGC. The remaining IGC members were given increased protection, which isolated them further from ordinary Iraqis whom they were supposed to represent.[31] Thus the guerrillas succeeded in widening the gulf between IGC members and the public.

Nothing illustrated the gap more than a description Chris Woolford—a British technocrat attached to the Ministry of Transport and Telecommunications—gave of the workings of Iraqi ministries in the Republican Presidential Palace Complex in the internal newsletter of the U.K. Regulatory Office of Telecommunications, his normal employer. "The place [Presidential Palace] is awash with vast marble ballrooms, conference rooms (now used as a dining room), a chapel (with murals of Scud missiles), and hundreds of function rooms with ornate chandeliers which were probably great for entertaining but which function less well as offices and dormitories," he wrote. "Within this [ministerial] wing of the Palace, each door along the corridor represents a separate ministry . . . Behind each door military and civilian coalition members (mainly Americans with the odd Briton dotted about) are beavering away trying to sort out the economic, social and political issues currently facing Iraq. . . . It cannot but feel strange as our contact with the outside world—the real Iraq—is so limited." Woolford described how meetings with Iraqi counterparts were difficult, and in any case, "key decisions are still very much taken behind the closed doors of the CPA, or for the most significant decisions, back in Washington DC."[32]

While Powell was diplomatic in the midst of *New York Times* editors in New York, Lt. Gen. Sanchez in Baghdad was brutally frank. In early October, he declared that it would take "years before Iraqis could maintain security," allowing U.S. forces to withdraw. At least 100,000 American troops were likely to be needed for "quite some time," he added. Then Gen. Thomas Metz made specific the phrase "quite some time": 2006.[33]

The question of proper transfer of power to Iraqis would arise only after a constitution has been drafted and a government has been elected, U.S. officials maintained. Progress on that front has been very slow. The twenty-five-strong committee (thirteen Shias and twelve Sunnis), chaired by Fuad Massoum, that the IGC appointed in late July to recommend the procedure for drafting the constitution, voted unanimously on September 8 that a national census be held followed by an election for a constitutional assembly. Three days later during their meeting with Grand Ayatollah Ali Sistani in Najaf, they heard him explain that his religious decree in June specifying an elected assembly to draft the constitution was done to "insure that the constitution would protect the rights of all ethnic and religious groups and prevent radicals on either side to the Sunni-Shia divide from hijacking the process." After the meeting, Kanan Makiya, the Iraqi National Congress's representative on the committee and a secular Shia, said, "Whatever steps are taken on the constitution, if Sistani does not like it, then it is a major crisis."[34]

Sistani's stance was publicly backed by Ayatollah al Hakim. On October 8, delivering a sermon on the fortieth day after the death of his brother Muhammad Baqir, he stressed that the constitution "must be drafted by a panel elected by Iraqis." The key question is: How are these Iraqis to be "elected?" The Shia members of the IGC wanted popular elections for the constitutional assembly. The Sunni members objected to this on practical grounds: The electoral rolls had to be updated, which would take time, and the security and political environment was not right for a general election.

Underlying this argument was the Kurdish (Sunnis) fear that they would not get the federation they want if Shias won a majority on the constitutional assembly. There was also apprehension among Kurds and the groups led by exiles that a popular poll would favor the home-based factions in general and the radical Shia group of Muqtada al Sadr in particular. So they suggested that delegates to the "constitutional convention" be selected by tribal leaders, clerics and through "town hall" meetings convened by U.S. commanders to create local councils.

This vital and deeply contentious subject remains unresolved.

When it comes to writing the constitution, there are three major issues that will test the abilities of the drafters to the limit. Should Iraq be a parliamentary or presidential democracy? Should it be a centralized state or a unified, federal state, as Kurds are demanding? What should be the relations between the state and mosque, if any? Present signs are that most Shias want an Islamic state, albeit a moderate one. As a community that suffered oppression or repression for a three and a half centuries, Shias sought solace in religion just as African slaves and their descendants in America did. So Iraqi Shias today are more religious than Sunnis or Kurds.

Since no other Arab country has the ethnic and religious complexity of Iraq, there is very little that either the Arab League or the United Nations can do to assist in resolving these seemingly intractable problems of occupied Iraq. On the other hand, there is little doubt that Washington will try to steer the constitution toward secularism, but its intervention, even if disguised, will prove self-defeating.

Even though America, backed by Britain, violated the UN charter by invading Iraq, which posed no imminent threat to either of the two countries, or to any of Iraq's neighbors, France and Russia have been willing to assist Washington in avoiding a quagmire in Iraq—but only if the Bush Administration accepts certain minimum conditions. This became obvious in the speeches that Bush, Annan and Chirac delivered to the UN General Assembly in late September.

UNITED NATIONS

Kofi Annan, being the UN Secretary General, was the first to address the annual UN General Assembly session on September 23, 2003.

While criticizing the doctrine of pre-emptive wars (as practiced by the U.S. and the U.K. in Iraq), he called on the United Nations to "consider how it will deal with the possibility that individual states may use force 'pre-emptively' against perceived threats." This was a subtle indictment of the vast number of nations that had spoken against the U.S.-U.K. action but had failed to submit a resolution at the Security Council or the General Assembly condemning the violators of the UN Charter.

For a politician still inhabiting his bubble, Bush said what was expected of him, blatantly ignoring basic facts. "The regime of Saddam Hussein cultivated ties to terror while it built weapons of mass destruction," he said. "It used those weapons in acts of mass murder, and refused to account for them when confronted by the world . . . Because there were consequences, because a coalition acted to defend the peace and the credibility of the United Nations, Iraq is free." (In a single sentence, Bush erased from history more than 710 UN inspections over four months.) Dealing with the present, he said, "This process [of Iraqi self-government] must unfold according to the needs of Iraqis, neither hurried nor delayed by the wishes of other parties." (Apparently, Bush's senior aides had not read the statements of IGC members, including Chalabi, who asked that the U.S.-led occupation troops should leave and be replaced by an international force.) As a sign of his magnanimity, he offered to let the UN "assist in developing a constitution, in training a civil service, and conducting elections."[35]

French President Jacques Chirac's speech, stressing multilateralism, was a contrast. "The United Nations has just weathered one of its most serious trials in its history," he said. "The [Iraq] war, which was started without the authorization of the Security Council, shook the multilateral system . . . No one should be able to accord himself the right to use force unilaterally and preventatively. In an open world, no one can isolate themselves, no one can act alone in the name of all, and no one can accept the anarchy of a society without rules. . . . Multilateralism is guarantee of legitimacy and democracy, especially in matters regarding the use of force or laying down universal norms . . . [I]t ensures the participation by all in managing the affairs of the world."[36]

Earlier, in an interview with the *New York Times,* Chirac called the administration of Iraq by "a governor who is Christian and foreign" dangerous, and "a very difficult situation for any people to accept in the twenty-first century." He referred to his own experience as a military officer in France's colonial war in Algeria in the 1950s. It proved to him that "a vast and powerful army could be defeated by a small group of determined adversaries convinced of the right to run their own country: We know from experience that imposing a law on people from the outside has not worked for a long time."

Whereas Chirac felt that continued governance of Iraq by America would produce more violence and require a longer presence of foreign troops—a view shared by Annan—the Bush Administration believed that relinquishing any authority now would create more chaos.

Given such divergence of views, it was unsurprising to find that the draft resolution on Iraq that Washington submitted at the Security Council—specifying a multilateral security force while the U.S. retained full political-military control of Iraq, with no mention of transferring sovereign to Iraq's IGC—was rejected not only by France, Russia, and Germany, but also by Annan.

The French-Russian-German trio wanted a time-table for a constitution, elections, and independence, demanded that power be transferred within months, and that Annan and the Security Council be given a greater role along with America and the IGC in setting a time to transfer power. This would have required Washington to switch from the logic of occupation to that of Iraqi sovereignty. It refused to do so. The most it agreed to do was to say that the CPA would return governance of Iraq to "the people of Iraq as soon as practicable," and report to the Security Council at least every six months. According to a French official involved in behind-the-scenes deliberations, this left the leaders of France, Germany, and Russia with two options: "Thanks, but not enough," meaning abstentions at the Security Council, or "Good that you are trying; this is one step, there will be more," meaning backing the resolution.

Taking into account the fast-deteriorating situation in the Middle East—the recent Israeli attack on a Syrian target followed by the killing of three American diplomats in Gaza by Palestinian terrorists on October 15—the leaders of France, Russia, and Germany, as well as those of Pakistan and Syria, chose the second option on October 16. So Resolution 1511 on the future of Iraq received a unanimous backing. The resolution approved continued exclusive American control over Iraq's political affairs and a multinational peacekeeping force under U.S. command. At the same time it determined that "the Governing Council and its ministers are the principal bodies of the Iraqi interim administration, which . . . embodies the sovereignty of the State of Iraq during the transitional period."

The backing of the major European powers, however, came with a rider. "As a result of proposals and amendments by us, the Security Council draft resolution was improved," said the statement issued by Chirac, Gerhard Schröder, and Vladimir Putin. "This allowed us, in a spirit of unity, to support it as a step in the right direction of the restoration of Iraq with the participation of the UN. At the same time we believe the resolution should have gone further on two major issues: the role of the UN, particularly in the political process; and the pace of the transfer of responsibilities to the Iraqi people. In that context conditions are not created for us to envisage any military commitment and no further financial contributions beyond present engagement." Pakistan joined the European trio by stating that it would not contribute troops to the occupation force.

So the bulk of the military and financial burden of "stabilizing" Iraq will continue to be borne by the Bush Administration at a time when the growing resistance in Iraq is putting long-term strain on U.S. troops and there is rising reluctance in America to foot the huge cost of Iraq's reconstruction.

In any case, the December 15 deadline to establish the timetable for writing a new constitution and holding elections in Iraq is, as of writing, only weeks away. And a return of the U.S. to the Security Council is most likely, and with it more concessions from it. The pressure on Washington to shorten the transitional period will escalate as resistance in Iraq spreads and intensifies, and as the anger in the Arab and Muslim world rises.

On the other hand, if power is transferred to politicians who have not established a solid base among Iraqis or learnt to accommodate one another in a spirit of mutual tolerance, there will be a breakdown in Iraq that will be exceedingly hard to repair.

Currently the presence of an alien occupation force and the desire to get rid of it is providing Iraqis of diverse political hues with a common objective. Once that state ends, the deep-seated ethnic and sectarian differences and rivalries are likely to come to the fore, paving the way for a likely civil war, which will suck in all six of Iraq's neighbors. Such a conflict in a country with the second-largest petroleum reserves in the world will play havoc with oil prices. It is this frightening scenario that has persuaded the major powers in Europe and elsewhere, who opposed the invasion of Iraq, to work with the Bush Administration and help resolve the enormous challenge of stabilizing postwar Iraq and to insure that it does not turn either into another Lebanon or an Arab version of the Taliban-run Afghanistan.

They all agree that the stakes are uncommonly high—and not just for America, although the American neocons are obsessed with their own country. "Either the United States does what it takes in Iraq, or we lose in Iraq," said William Kristol. "And if we lose, we will leave behind us not blue helmets but radicalism and chaos, a haven for terrorists and a perception of American weakness, lack of resolve in the Middle East and blundering, around the world."[37] Reflecting a similar thought from a different angle, a Palestinian official in a Palestinian camp in Beirut said, "If Israel's superpower ally can be humbled by Arabs, why should we give up our struggle against the Israelis who cannot be as effective soldiers as the Americans?"[38]

But no matter what happens in the international arena, Bush can always count on British Prime Minister Tony Blair, except that he has lost most of his star quality among his fellow citizens, and suffered a further loss to his credibility with the publication in the *Sunday Times* of Robin Cook's diaries on October 5, 2003.

BLAIR'S STAR WANES

Five days after the massive antiwar demonstration in London on February 15, 2003, Robin Cook, then a Cabinet minister, received a presentation on Iraq by Joint Intelligence Committee chairman John Scarlett. "The presentation was impressive in its integrity and shorn of the political slant with which No 10 [Downing Street] encumbers any intelligence assessment," Cook noted in his diary. "My conclusion at the end of an hour is that Saddam Hussein probably does not have weapons of mass destruction in the sense of weapons being used against large scale civilian targets."

Following his meeting with Blair on March 5, when Washington and London were trying to get the second resolution on Iraq passed at the UN Security Council, Cook wrote: "The most revealing exchange came when we talked about Saddam's arsenal. I told him, 'It's clear from the private briefing I have had that S[addam] has no weapons of mass destruction in a sense of weapons that could strike strategic cities. But he probably does have several thousand chemical munitions. Do you never worry that he might use them against British troops?' [Blair replied] 'Yes, but all the effort he has had to put into concealment makes it difficult for him to assemble them for use.' . . . There were two distinct elements to this exchange that sent me away deeply troubled. The time table to war was plainly not driven by the progress of the UN weapons inspections. Tony made no pretence that what Hans Blix might report would make any difference to the count down to invasion. The second troubling element to our conversation was that Tony did not try to argue me out of the view that Saddam did not have real WMD that were designed for strategic use against city populations and capable of being delivered with reliability over long distances. I had now expressed that view to both the chairman of the JIC and to the Prime Minister and both of them had assented in it."

A few weeks earlier, in his book *Blair's Wars,* John Kampfner, the political editor of the *New Statesman,* revealed that on the day Blair held a summit with Bush and Spanish Prime Minister Mario Aznar in the Azores, Foreign Secretary Jack Straw wrote a personal memo to Blair suggesting that Britain should only give "political and moral support" to Bush—something which Aznar did by refusing a dispatch Spanish soldiers to fight alongside the Americans.[39] It revealed a depth of division in the Blair camp not previously known.

With no sign of the alleged WMD of Iraq turning up, public opinion shifted decidedly against Blair and the invasion of Iraq. Six months after the start of the war, 53 per cent considered it unjustified whereas only 38 percent regarded it as justified—back to the numbers before the conflict. What is more, 59 percent said that Blair lied about the Iraqi threat, twice the size of those who thought otherwise. More broadly, at 30 percent, Labour's popularity was the lowest in eleven years.

Given this, Bush, Blair, and Straw set much store by the forthcoming report on the Iraqi WMD by the U.S.-appointed Iraq Survey Group, comprising 1,400 personnel from America, Britain, and Australia. This report would not have mattered much if the occupation had gone smoothly, but it did not.

THE IRAQ SURVEY GROUP REPORT

On October 2, the thirteen-page report of the Iraq Survey Group (ISG) led by Dr. David Kay said starkly, "We have not yet found stocks of [non-conventional] weapons." This was as true of the chemical warfare agents as of the biological ones. The ISG also drew a blank on nuclear arms. The ISG had spent $300 million—five times the annual budget of the Unmovic—to reach this conclusion after the earlier Pentagon's 75th Exploitation Task Force—code-named XTF—had discovered nothing.

Kay wrapped this solid and devastating conclusion in vague testimonies of the Iraqi detainees, numerous secondary documents and—as a sign of desperation—repeated assertions of Saddam's "commitment" to acquiring "one day" the WMD that the Bush-Blair camp had confidently told the world the Iraqi dictator already possessed.

Kay's background gave an inkling of his bias. Until October 2002 he was a vice president of San Diego–based Science Applications International Corp. (SAIC), which had the contract for producing a mobile bioweapons lab. As the SIAC executive for Homeland Security and counterterrorism initiatives, he declared that Iraq could launch terrorist attacks on mainland America. As the leader of the International Atomic Energy Agency (then under Hans Blix) inspectors in Iraq in 1991, he had behaved aggressively, and made headlines.[40]

To support its evaluation of Saddam's intentions, the ISG report referred to "a clandestine network of laboratories and safe houses within the Iraqi intelligence service that contained equipment subject to UN monitoring and suitable for chemical and biological weapons research." The key word here is "suitable." That is, these labs were *capable* of conducting such research. This is true of any modern lab anywhere. The ISG's statement does *not* say that these labs actually engaged in such research. Regarding Saddam's future plans after UN sanctions had been lifted, the key step would remain (and remains) turning lab research into mass production. That would mean building factories, which in turn would require large supplies of electricity and manpower. With Iraq continuing to be the most monitored country in the world even after the lifting of UN sanctions, any such development would have been quickly detected by Washington's satellites.

The one subject on which the ISG report provided substantial evidence was that after 2000 Iraq had developed plans for producing missiles with 400–1,000 kilometers (250–625 miles) range, far above the 150 kilometer range allowed under UN sanctions. But having such plans for the future would not have violated any UN Security Council resolution, because the pertinent Resolution 687 (April 1991) merely prohibited Iraq from actually possessing medium- and long-range missiles, not from research into them, which was the case with WMD.[41]

After reading the ISG report, Hans Blix said that none of this constituted "the serious and imminent threat" used by the U.S.-U.K. governments to attack Iraq.

As expected, Bush drew conclusions which were either ill-advised or false. "The [ISG] report states Saddam Hussein's regime had a clandestine network of biological labs," he said. "They had a live strain of deadly agent called botulinum; that he had sophisticated concealment efforts—in other words, he is hiding his programs; that he had advanced design work done on prohibited longer range missiles."[42]

That "live strain of deadly agent called botulinum" also got British Foreign Secretary Straw excited. The ISG found one vial of C. Botulinum Okra B along with a batch of other (nontoxic) biological samples. Had Straw taken on board Blix's comment on the British September 2002 dossier—"There were exclamation marks where questions marks would have been more appropriate"—he would have asked Kay: "Where and how did the ISG find this vial of botulinim?" But he did not. Ironically, it was a Fox News interviewer who put that question to Kay on October 5. "The Iraqi scientist said that he was asked to hide the botulinum in his refrigerator at home in 1993," replied Kay. "He had been entrusted with many more strains of bioweapons, including anthrax but had returned them saying 'They are too dangerous; I have small children in the house.'"

How would an Iraqi scientist store "a deadly agent" in his domestic refrigerator with young children around? The fact is that it was *not* a deadly agent. What the scientist stored was Botulinum Strain B, which has limited potency and is used for vaccinating live stock or for removing wrinkles, in the form of Botox, in cosmetic surgery. As it could also be used as an antidote to common botulinum poisoning, many labs in the west store it as part of their seed banks.[43]

None of this stopped Straw from declaring that live C Botulinum agent was "15,000 times more toxic than the nerve agent VX." He was clearly, and embarrassingly, referring to Strain A, not Strain B.

However, the behavior of the senior officials of the Bush-Blair camp fitted well the earlier pattern of secrets and lies, which continued, the latest examples being:

- In his television address to the nation on September 7, President Bush said "I recognize that not all of our friends agreed with our decision to enforce the Security Council resolutions *and remove Saddam Hussein from power* . . . No terrorist network will ever gain weapons of mass destruction from Saddam Hussein [which he did not have]." A UN Security Council resolution calling for the removal of Saddam Hussein does not exist.

- When the poll of Iraqis conducted by the State Department's Intelligence and Research Bureau showed "significant levels of hostility to U.S. presence," it was stamped "Classified."[44]

- The number of wounded GIs during and since the invasion of Iraq remains classified.

- So is the estimate of the damage caused by the Pentagon's Operation "Iraqi Freedom" to Iraq's infrastructure.

The net result of this unending series of secrets and lies has been to diminish the trust that people in America and Britain have in their political leaders, thus doing enormous damage to democracy in both countries. This is all the more ironic because these politicians mounted the most audacious confidence trick on their publics with the avowed objective of installing democracy in Iraq. Now they wrongly believe that if they continue blocking reality, popular opinion will fizzle out. But with the occupation costing more in lives and money, this is not happening now, and will not happen in the near future.

Meanwhile, what is the judgment on the source of it all, the invasion of Iraq? "Asked [at a meeting with *New York Times* editors] if

Americans would have supported this war if weapons of mass destruction had not been the issue, Colin Powell said the question was too hypothetical to answer," noted the *New York Times* editorially on September 27, 2003. "Asked if he, personally, would have supported it, he smiled, thrust his hand out and said, 'It was good to meet you.'"

NOTES

1. Associated Press, October 2, 2003.
2. *The ndependent,* October 6, 2003; *Middle East International,* October 10, 2003, p. 14, *Independent on Sunday,* October 19, 2003.
3. Associated Press, October 2, 2003. These figures exclude the patients treated at the military hospitals in Iraq and at Andrews Air Base Clinic and Walter Reed and Bethesda Veterans Hospital in Metropolitan Washington, DC, figures which remain classified.
4. Some residents of Khalidiya told visiting foreign journalists (wrongly) that a mortar attack by the guerrillas on the Iraqi airbase at Habaniya had resulted in sixty American casualties.
5. The UN's locally hired staff numbered 4,230.
6. In a Friday sermon on October 10, Shaikh Abdul Hadi al Daraji, the preacher at the main mosque in Sadr City, said, "America claims to the pioneer of freedom and democracy but it resembles or indeed is a terror organization." *New York Times,* October 11, 2003.
7. *The Independent on Sunday,* September 14, 2003.
8. Ibid., October 12, 2003.
9. *The New York Times,* September 18, 2003; *The Independent,* September 18, 2003.
10. This was in addition to the 650,000 tons of ammunition at thousands of sites in Iraq, which is being destroyed by the U.S. military at the rate of 100 tons a day. It will take 216 months or eighteen years to finish the job. *The New York Times,* October 1, 2003.
11. *Sunday Telegraph,* October 12, 2003.
12. *New York Times,* October 6, 2003.
13. Pew Research poll showed that 59 percent were opposed to the Bush request for $87 billion while 36 percent were for it. Whereas 32 percent wanted to pull out U.S. troops as soon as possible, 64 percent want to keep them "until stable government is formed." *The International Herald Tribune,* September 26, 2003.
14. *The Washington Post,* October 4, 2003.
15. *The New York Times,* September 18, 2003. However, he added, "There's no question that Saddam Hussein had Al Qaida ties." Convincing evidence for this has yet to be produced.

16. September 12, 2003.

17. In characteristically Rumsfeldian way, Donald Rumsfeld said, "If it [intelligence] is off by a lot, that will be unfortunate, and then we'll know that.' *The New York Times,* September 30, 2003; *The Guardian,* September 30, 2003.

18. The reason was that intelligence gathered by many U.S. nationals working undercover for Unscom as inspectors and their support staff dried up.

19. *The Washington Post,* September 28, 2003.

20. *The New York Times,* October 9, 2003; *The Guardian,* October 9, 2003.

21. Cited in *The Guardian,* October 18, 2003.

22. Cited in *The Sunday Times,* September 14, 2003. Of the 200,000 U.S. troops in the region—140,000 in Iraq, 35,000 in Kuwait, and 25,000 in the rest of the Gulf—20,000 were National Guard personnel and reservists who will have their tour of duty extended to 12 months.

23. Associated Press, October 16, 2003.

24. The situation got worse when the State Department leaked its report "The Future of Iraq," prepared by seventeen working groups over the course of one year, which had anticipated the grave postwar problems, to the *New York Times* on October 19, 2003, with its officials claiming that the Defense Department had ignored its findings, and the Defense Department challenging the allegation.

25. *The New York Times,* September 21; *The International Herald Tribune,* September 24, 2003. In an interview with the London-based Al Hayat, published on September 27, Chalabi said that the U.S.-led occupation troops should leave and be replaced by an international force "to protect Iraq from any external dangers," and that a UN Security Council resolution to send peace keepers to Iraq would signal an end to Iraq's occupation.

26. U.S. legislators were undoubtedly aware that American taxpayers would be livid if they found out that their money was being handled by the likes of Ahmad Chalabi, a convicted fraudster.

27. Cited in *The Independent,* October 8, 2003.

28. From 1986 to 2001, Marc Zell was a partner in the law firm of Feith & Zell, in Washington, DC—where Douglas Feith was the managing attorney—with a branch in Jerusalem, which specialized in helping Israeli companies to do business in America.

29. *The Guardian,* October 7, 2003.

30. See further Dilip Hiro, *Neighbors, Not Friends: Iraq and Iran After the Gulf Wars,* p. 154.

31. On September 28, unknown gunmen fired shots at Jalaluddin al Sagher, a SCIRI nominee on the constitutional committee, but he was unhurt.

32. Cited in *The Independent on Sunday,* September 14, 2003.

33. *The New York Times,* October 6, 2003; *The Guardian,* October 18, 2003.

34. *The New York Times,* October 1, 2003.

35. *The Guardian,* September 24, 2003; *Middle East International,* October 10, 2003, p. 28.

36. *The Guardian,* September 24, 2003. Little wonder that a Gallup poll of Baghdadis in September found Chirac to be the most popular foreign leader (forty-two points), followed by Bush (twenty-three points).

37. Cited in *The Sunday Times,* September 14, 2003.

38. *the Independent on Sunday,* September 14, 2003.

39. *The Guardian,* September 15, 2003.

40. See further Dilip Hiro, *Neighbors, Not Friends: Iraq and Iran After the Gulf Wars,* pp. 47-49, 63.

41. For the text of UN Security Council Resolution 687, visit www.un.org/docs/sc/.

42. *The New York Times,* October 3, 2003.

43. It was unclear whether the vial contained bacteria from which toxin was to be extracted or the toxin itself.

44. *The New York Times,* September 18, 2003.

CHRONOLOGY

THE BAATHIST ERA, JULY 1968–APRIL 2003

1968

July 17–31 · Military officers belonging to the Arab Baath Socialist Party, led by Gen. Ahmad Hassan Bakr, mount a successful coup against President Abdul Rahman Arif. The Revolutionary Command Council (RCC) becomes the supreme ruling body.

1969

November · Saddam Hussein is appointed to the RCC.

1972

June · Iraq nationalizes Western-owned Iraq Petroleum Company (IPC), which becomes part of the state-owned Iraq National Oil Company (INOC).

1973

July · The ruling Baathists ally with four other parties, including Communists, to form the National Progressive and Patriotic Front.

October · In the Arab-Israeli war, Iraq sends troops to Syria to fight Israel but does not join the Arab oil boycott of the West.

1974

January · Oil prices have risen 450 percent since October 1973, benefiting Iraq.

February · The Baathist regime bans the commemoration by Shias of the fortieth day of the death of Imam Hussein in 681 CE in Karbala.
Insurgency by the Kurdish minority, aided by the Shah of Iran, escalates.

1975

March · Vice President Saddam Hussein signs a treaty with the Shah of Iran to demarcate their borders along the Shatt al-Arab and "end all infiltrations of subversive nature," which results in the collapse of the Kurdish insurgency.

1978

April · Saddam begins persecuting Communists after they demand general elections and parity with Baathists in power-sharing.

1979

January · About 1,900 Communists have "disappeared."

February · The victory of Islamic revolution in Shia-majority Iran emboldens Iraqi Shias. Saddam reacts by suppressing Al Daawa Al Islamiya (Islamic Call), a militant Shia organization.

July · Saddam compels Bakr to resign on "health grounds" and succeeds him.

1980

June · The Baathist regime holds its first parliamentary poll.

September · Saddam invades Iran. Instead of condemning Iraq as the aggressor and demanding its withdrawal from Iran, the UN Security Council calls on both parties to stop fighting.

1981

While professing neutrality in the Iran-Iraq War, the U.S. supplies intelligence to Iraq through Saudi Arabia and Jordan.

1982

June · Having evicted the Iraqis from its territory, Iran captures some Iraqi land.

November · Ayatollah Muhammad Baqir al-Hakim establishes the Supreme Council of Islamic Revolution in Iraq (Sicri) in Tehran.

1983

October · Iraq uses chemical weapons against Iranian soldiers.

December · As the Middle East envoy of U.S. President Ronald Reagan, Donald Rumsfeld has a ninety-minute meeting with Saddam in Baghdad. He makes no mention of Iraq's deployment of poison gases whose use was outlawed in 1925. He and Saddam discuss an Iraqi oil pipeline to the Jordanian port of Aqaba, with the contract going almost certainly to Betchel Corporation.

November · Soon after Reagan's re-election, the United States resumes diplomatic relations with Iraq broken off by Baghdad during the June 1967 Arab-Israeli War.

1984

February · To assist Iraq financially to build the Aqaba oil pipeline, the U.S. Ex-Im Bank provisionally guarantees $485 million of the estimated $570 million cost of the project. Nothing comes of it since Israel refuses to give a guarantee not to strike the pipeline during a regional crisis or war.

1986

U.S. begins to intervene openly in the Iran-Iraq War, on the Iraqi side.

1987

July · UN Security Council adopts the ten-point cease-fire Resolution 598. Iraq accepts it on the condition that Iran does, which does not happen.

Autumn · Iraq mounts Operation "Anfal" to recover about a third of the Kurdistan region that had declared itself "liberated" with the help of the Iranians. It uses chemical weapons against the Kurds.

1988

March · Iraqi Air Force drops chemical bombs on the Kurdish town of Halabja, killing 3,200–6,800 people, most of them civilians. The United States holds Iran "partly responsible" for the outrage. As a result of Operation "Anfal," at least 100,000 Kurds have died.

Washington's aid to Iraq doubles. Britain's exports guarantees scheme authorizes a further loan of £450 million ($720 million) to Iraq.

August · The Iran-Iraq War ends in a draw after Iraq recovers its lost territory by using chemical weapons on a large scale. Iraq's estimated human losses are 160,000–240,000, and the cost of the war, $154 billion. Iran's human losses are between 195,000 (official figure) and 300,000 (unofficial estimate).

1990

July · Iraq complains to the Arab League that the oil glut caused by Kuwait's overproduction has lowered prices to $11 a barrel, and that a drop of $1 a barrel reduces its annual income by $1 billion. Kuwait continues to produce far above its OPEC quota.

August 2 · Saddam invades and occupies Kuwait. UN Security Council demands Iraq's withdrawal and imposes economic sanctions.

November 29 · UN Security Council adopts Resolution 678 authorizing "all necessary means" to bring about the implementation of eleven earlier resolutions on Iraq if it does not withdraw from Kuwait by January 15.

1991

January 16–February 28 · The Gulf War, started by the U.S.-led coalition of twenty-eight countries, including thirteen Arab and Muslim states, ends with the expulsion of Iraq from Kuwait. Estimated Iraqi death toll is 100,000. The damage to Iraq's economic infrastructure is put at $200 billion.

March · Saddam's government crushes Shia uprisings in the south, resulting in an estimated 30,000 deaths. When it turns its attention to suppressing the rebellion in the Kurdish north, it causes an exodus of 1.5 million Kurds into Iran and Turkey. Later a cease-fire is agreed between the central government and Kurdish militias.

April 4 · UN Security Council adopts the Gulf War cease-fire Resolution

687, which links lifting of sanctions with disarming Iraq of its WMD and destroying the related facilities.

October · America, Britain, and France impose a no-fly zone for Iraq in the north above the thirty-sixth parallel to prevent Saddam's government from resuming control of the three Kurdish provinces forming the Kurdish Autonomous Region.

1992

August · America, Britain, and France impose a no-fly zone for Iraq in the south below the thirty-second parallel.

1993

June · The Clinton Administration fires twenty-three Tomahawk missiles at the headquarters of Iraq's General Intelligence (Mukhabarat) in Baghdad on the grounds that it had plotted the assassination of George Bush Sr., former American President, during his visit to Kuwait in April, even though the trial of the accused Iraqis and Kuwaitis is yet to start in Kuwait City.

1994

Autumn · Saddam's claim that Iraq had been disarmed as required by the UN is not accepted by UN Special Commission (Unscom).

1995

August · Defection of Gen. Hessein Kamil Hassan, a son-in-law of Saddam and former minister of military industrialization, to Jordan sets back any chance of the UN sanctions being lifted.

October · The Iraqi government claims 99.96 percent vote for Saddam in a referendum on his presidency.

1996

March · Iraq holds parliamentary elections after seven years.

September · Invited by Masoud Barzani of the Kurdistan Democratic Party to help him evict the rival Patriotic Union of Kurdistan from the regional capital of Irbil, Saddam does so. He then pulls out his forces from Kurdistan. France withdraws from the allied air surveillance of the north.

1998

February · UN Secretary General Kofi Annan defuses the weapons-inspection crisis between Iraq and the UN.

December · The U.S. launches the 100-hour nonstop bombing of Iraq under Operation "Desert Fox" once Unscom chief recalls all UN inspectors. France withdraws from the air surveillance of southern Iraq.

2000

January · The UN Security Council sets up UN Monitoring, Verification, and Inspection Commission (Unmovic) under Hans Blix, in accord with Resolution 1284 (December 1999), which Iraq has not accepted.

2001

February · Within weeks of taking office, U.S. President George Walker Bush orders strikes against Iraq's air-defense facilities.

September 11 · Three of four planes hijacked by Islamist extremists belonging to Al Qaida crash against targets in New York and Washington, killing 3,066 people, and destroying the twin towers of the World Trade Center and part of the Pentagon. Iraq is one of the three countries at the UN which do not fly their flags half-mast in sympathy with the United States, others being China and Libya.

November · In Rome a West African diplomat sells documents to the Italian intelligence agency showing that Saddam had tried to buy 551 tons of uranium oxide from Niger in July 2000. The Italians pass on the papers to the British intelligence agency MI6.

December · U.S. Defense Secretary Donald Rumsfeld sets up Office of Special Plans to re-examine available intelligence to establish linkage between Iraq and Al Qaida.

2002

Early · Hired by the CIA, Joseph Wilson, a former U.S. ambassador to Gabon, visits Niger to investigate the allegations of Iraq's attempt to obtain uranium oxide from that country in mid-2000.

Early February · Instructed by President Bush, Defense Secretary Donald Rumsfeld orders a "conceptual" war plan against Iraq.

Mid-February · Bush tells three U.S. senators visiting the White House, "We are taking him [Saddam Hussein] out."

March · Following his investigation on the CIA's behalf, Joseph Wilson reports that the alleged sale of uranium oxide by Niger to Iraq could not have occurred, and briefs the CIA and State Department accordingly. Later the CIA's operations and counter-terrorism departments as well as the State Department's Bureau of Intelligence and Research conduct their own investigations and concur that the documents originating in Rome were forged.

May · The Pentagon starts a series of exercises—code-named Operation "Prominent Hammer"—to judge whether its combat troops in Iraq can win while it maintains a deterrent force in other areas.

July · A draft of a conceptual war plan is leaked to the *New York Times*.

August 25 · During a telephone conversation Bush and British Prime Minister Tony Blair decide to produce dossiers to highlight the danger that Iraq poses if its reconstituted WMD are passed on to Islamist terrorists.

August 26 · In a speech U.S. Vice President Dick Cheney says war with Iraq is "inevitable."

August 29 · Bush approves "the goals, objectives and strategy" of the war on Iraq. Rumsfeld orders Operation "Southern Focus" which authorizes the Pentagon to hit Iraqi targets that are not involved in attacking U.S.-U.K. warplanes enforcing the no-fly zone in the south. This in effect means that the Pentagon is starting an air campaign as a preamble to the ground invasion to follow.

September · Fresh U.S. troops start arriving in Kuwait.

September 6–7 · In his talks with Bush at Camp David, Blair reportedly agrees to participate in a war against Iraq provided Bush seeks endorsement for military action from the UN Security Council without giving up his option to act unilaterally if that fails.

September 10 · The newest version of the British dossier, titled *Iraq's Program of Weapons of Mass Destruction: The Assessment of the British Government,* reads: "Iraq continues to have the capability to produce chemical and biological weapons and has probably already done so." A copy is forwarded to Director of Central Intelligence George Tenet in Washington.

September 11 · During the commemoration ceremonies on the first anniversary of 9/11, Bush is always accompanied by Rumsfeld.

September 12 · In Washington the White House releases a twenty-four-page dossier on Iraq, *A Decade of Deception and Defiance.* The document recycles dated and circumstantial evidence. Addressing the UN General

Assembly, President Bush says, "We will work with the UN Security Council for the necessary resolutions" regarding Iraq's disarmament.

September 13 · Tenet expresses reservations about the nuclear issue in the British dossier: "Iraq continues to work on developing nuclear weapons . . . Uranium to be used in the production of fissile material has been purchased from Africa [later narrowed to Niger]." As a result, the final version states that "recent intelligence . . . indicates" that "Iraq has purchased large quantities of uranium ore, despite having no civil nuclear program that would require it."

September 16 · Iraq says UN inspectors can return to Iraq "without any conditions."

September 17 · Blair's chief of staff, Jonathan Powell, points out that the draft British dossier "does not demonstrate he [Saddam] has the motive to attack his neighbors let alone the west." This leads to last-minute "sexing up" of the dossier by tinkering with words without any fresh intelligence input. The sentence "The Iraqi military may be able to deploy chemical or biological weapons within 45 minutes of an order to do so" was altered to "Military planning allows for some of the WMD to be ready within 45 minutes of an order to use them."

September 20 · Bush White House publishes a thirty-three page document, The National Security Strategy of the United States. It says that the United States will exercise its right to strike pre-emptively any hostile country it believes may be developing WMD. This becomes known as the Bush Doctrine.

September 22 · Bush says, "You can't distinguish between Al Qaida and Saddam when it comes to war on terror."

September 24 · The British government publishes a fifty-page dossier, titled *Iraq's Weapons of Mass Destruction The Assessment of the British Government.*

September 30 · The Iraqi Foreign Ministry publishes a twenty-nine-page dossier rebutting the charges made in the U.S. and U.K. documents on Iraq's WMD. The text becomes available at www.uruklink.net/iraqnews/enews20.htm.

October · Fresh British troops start arriving in Kuwait. U.S. troops are conducting war exercises on the Kuwaiti offshore island of Failaka.

October 1 · Following a request by Senator Bob Graham (Democrat, Florida), Tenet passes on the revised National Intelligence Estimate to the

Senate Committee on Intelligence. In it the CIA says that though Iraq's efforts to acquire WMD are "a serious threat" that could encourage "Iraqi blackmail," Baghdad will refrain from "the extreme step" of assisting terrorists in attacking the United States with WMD if Washington does not invade Iraq, and that the Iraqi government has "little reason to provoke Washington." Some days later, however, Tenet says in his testimony to Congress that Iraq is "reconstituting a nuclear weapons program."

October 4 · When John Kelly, U.S. assistant secretary for East Asia, confronts North Korean officials in Pyongyang regarding their nuclear weapons program, they admit they were trying to enrich uranium to be used as fuel for an atom bomb. The Bush White House withholds the information.

October 7 · In a speech in Cincinnati, Ohio, Bush says that it would require Saddam's ouster to end the threat of WMD that could lead to another attack on the United States like 9/11. He asserts that Iraq might seek "to strike targets on U.S. territory with the help of terrorist groups or by moving drones filled with germs or chemical weapons close to the U.S."—or give biological or chemical weapons to a terrorist group or individuals.

October 10–11 · U.S. Congress gives Bush war powers by a comfortable majority.

October 15 · In a referendum for the presidency in Iraq, Saddam Hussein wins a 100 percent vote.

October 16 · Bush White House releases the information about North Korea resuming its nuclear arms program.

November 5 · In the midterm elections the Republicans do well, and regain majority in the Senate.

November 8 · UN Security Council unanimously passes Resolution 1441 specifying a very strict new inspections regime.

November 22 · Centcom establishes a forward base at Salilaya Camp near Al Udaid air base in Qatar.

December · The commandos of the Pentagon's Intelligence Support Activity (ISA) units make periodic forays into Iraq to leave communications equipment at certain locations to be activated later.

2003

January 28 · In his State of the Union speech, President Bush says, "The British government has learned that Saddam Hussein recently sought significant quantities of uranium in Africa."

February 3 · The British government publishes its second dossier on Iraq which turns out to be 90 percent plagiarized from material available on the Internet.

February 5 · The presentation of U.S. Secretary of State Colin Powell at the Security Council, to show Iraq is reconstituting WMD and is involved in international terrorism, fails to convince most Council members.

February 9 · A barrage of e-mails to military and party leaders and thousands of others crashes Iraq's Internet.

Mid-February · The Pentagon briefs key Israeli leaders on its Iraq war plans.

February 15 · Antiwar demonstrations in 600 towns and cities (including 150 in the United States) in fifty-five countries, draw an estimated 15–20 million protesters.

February 24 · The United States and the United Kingdom introduce a draft resolution at the Security Council seeking authorization for military action against Iraq for failing to cooperate fully. It gains the support of only two other members, Bulgaria and Spain.

March 16 · At their meeting on the Portuguese island of Terceira in the Azores, Bush, Blair and Spanish Prime Minister Jose Maria Aznar decide to abandon their draft resolution at the Security Council since it is bound to be defeated if put to a vote.

March 17 · Bush gives Saddam Hussein and his two sons forty-eight hours to leave Iraq. Saddam rejects the ultimatum.

March 18 · The British House of Commons authorizes the government to use "all means" to disarm Iraq of WMD. After having carried out 600 inspections at 400 sites in Iraq and having found no WMD, UN inspectors start leaving.

March 20 · The Anglo-American forces invade Iraq from Kuwait.

March 21 · U.S. Marines use napalm at Safwan near the Kuwaiti border.

March 23 · Facing stiff resistance near Basra, the Anglo-Americans use cluster munitions, and keep on doing so for the next fortnight. The Americans encounter spirited resistance in Nasiriya.

March 24 · Arab League foreign ministers call for an end to the attack on Iraq and withdrawal of foreign troops from the country. The Anglo-American alliance ignores the call.

March 25 · Grand Ayatollah Ali Husseini Sistani issues a religious decree requiring all Muslims to resist the invading infidel troops.

March 26 · Fall of Umm al-Qasr five days after the first Centcom claim to that effect.

March 27 · With the promised instant victory accompanied by jubilant Iraqi civilians cheering the 'liberating' American soldiers, failing to materialize, there is mounting criticism of Rumsfeld in the United States.

March 30–31 · Iraq sets up two defense arcs, manned by the Republican Guard, to protect Baghdad.

March 31 · Fall of Nasiriya. Communications between the Iraqi Central Command and regional commanders are breaking down rapidly.

April 1 · Egyptian President Hosni Mubarak warns of the war creating "a hundred bin Ladens." U.S. Marines use napalm in central Iraq.

April 2 · The tide turns in favor of the Anglo-American forces against the background of their rising use of cluster bombs and munitions and napalm, and communication breakdowns between the Iraqi Central Command and regional commanders, which allows many generals to play truant with impunity and advise the ranks to do the same. The Fedayeen Saddam paramilitary force is unaffected by this, and becomes the major source of resistance.

April 3 · The American troops reach Furat near the Saddam International Airport on the outskirts of Baghdad.

April 4 · The fall of Saddam International Airport. Saddam Hussein's appearance on the streets of the Mansour neighborhood in Baghdad is televised.

April 6 · The fall of Basra to the British troops after fourteen days of fighting. Looting starts.

April 7 · The fall of central Baghdad. The bombing of Saddam's suspected hideout in the Mansour neighborhood fails to kill him.

April 9 · The toppling of Saddam Hussein's statue in Firdaus Square, now controlled by U.S. Marines, is televised worldwide. Four miles to the northwest, Saddam is sighted in the Adhamiya neighborhood near the Abu Hanifa al-Numan Mosque.

April 10 · The Bush White House announces the end of President Saddam Hussein's regime. Large scale looting and arson in Baghdad

IRAQ UNDER OCCUPATION, APRIL 11, 2003–PRESENT

April 11–12 · The fall of Mosul and Kirkuk. Looting and arson in Baghdad leave 156 government buildings in ruin.

April 16 · With the fall of Tikrit, the invasion is almost over. As eighty Iraqi delegates gather near Nasiriya under U.S. sponsorship to discuss the country's political future, 20,000 Shias protest, shouting, "No to America, No to Saddam."

Four weeks of fighting · Centcom's 1,800 aircraft mounted 37,000 air sorties, involving 20,000 strikes, of which 15,800 were directed at ground forces, 1,400 at air forces, and 800 at suspected hiding places and installations for proscribed weapons, including surface-to-surface missiles. Of the 28,000 bombs and missiles dropped or fired—about half directed at the Republican Guard—23,000 were precision-guided missiles, 750 were cruise missiles, and 725 were Tomahawk missiles. Centcom dropped 1,566 cluster bombs, and an unspecified number of cluster munitions. It used dozens of napalm bombs. The total cost of the invasion was $45 billion. In human terms, the Pentagon lost 141 soldiers, and Britain twenty-four. By contrast, according to Iraqi Body Count, the Anglo-American research group, Iraqi civilian fatalities were 6,000 to 7,000, and military casualties, dead, and injured, were 10,000 to 45,000.

April 23 · Almost 1.5 million Shias gather in Karbala to commemorate the fortieth day of mourning of the death of Imam Hussein, a ritual banned by the Baathist regime in 1974. They shout "No no to America, Yes, yes to Islam."

May 1 · Bush announces a formal end to "major operations" in Iraq.

May 12 · The Bush Administration's new proconsul to Iraq, Paul Bremer, a former U.S. diplomat, arrives in Baghdad to take over from (retired) Gen. Jay Garner.

May 22 · UN Security Council passes Resolution 1483 by 14 to 0, with Syria abstaining. It recognizes America and Britain as the occupation powers, called the Authority, which is authorized to sell Iraqi oil. It also lifts sanctions against Iraq.

May 23 · Bremer succeeds Garner and calls himself senior administrator of the Coalition Provisional Authority (CPA), in the midst of rampant lawlessness, frequent power outages and water shortages.

June 1 · Sergio Vieira de Mello arrives in Baghdad as the UN Special Representative to Iraq, and begins consulting various Iraqi groups on the country's future.

June 4 · Bush tells Palestinian Prime Minister Mahmoud Abbas that "God told me to strike at Al Qaida and I struck them, and then He instructed me to strike at Saddam, which I did."

Mid-June · Guerrilla attacks on the U.S. troops are on the rise.

Late June · Rumsfeld disbands the Office of Special Plans.

July 4 · On the American Independence Day, Al Jazeera TV broadcasts a taped statement by Saddam Hussein, in which he applauds the resistance being offered to "the infidel foreign invaders." This is his fifth tape to be aired in the series starting with his message recorded on April 28, his sixty-sixth birthday.

July 6 · In his op-ed in the *New York Times,* Joseph Wilson says that the Bush Administration exaggerated the nuclear threat from Iraq.

July 9 · Gen. John Abizaid, the newly appointed Centcom commander in chief, says that U.S. troops in Iraq are now facing "a classical guerrilla-type campaign."

July 13 · Bremer appoints a twenty-five-member Iraqi Interim Governing Council, consisting of thirteen Shias, eleven Sunnis, and one Christian. Aside from the five Sunni Kurds, the Sunni members are predominantly nonpolitical. It includes leaders of Sciri, Al Daawa Al Islamiya, and the Communist Party.

July 14 · In his nationally syndicated column, Robert Novak discloses that, according to "two senior Bush administration officials," Valerie Plame, the wife of Joseph Wilson, is a CIA agent, and that is why the CIA hired Wilson to investigate the claim of Iraq seeking to buy uranium oxide from Niger.

July 22 · Uday Saddam Hussein and Qusay are killed at a hideout in Mosul by American forces.

August · Guerrilla attacks on the occupation forces are now running at 500 a month, with 97 percent targeted at the American forces.

August 7 · A remote-control car bomb explodes outside the Jordanian embassy in Baghdad, killing nineteen.

August 11 · Lord Hutton, a senior British judge, opens an inquiry into the suicide of Dr. David Kelly, a government scientist specializing in biological and chemical weapons, who, as a UN inspector for seven years, had visited Iraq thirty-seven times.

August 19 · A suicide truck bomb explodes outside UN headquarters in Baghdad, killing twenty-three, including Sergio Vieira de Mello. The Armed Vanguard of the Second Muhammad Army claims responsibility.

August 29 · Two car bombs outside the shrine of Imam Ali in Najaf kill Ayatollah Mohammed Baqir al-Hakim, leader of Sicri, and ninety-four others. In a taped message, Al Qaida's spokesman, Abu Abdul Rahman al-Najdi, denies responsibility for the attack.

September 1 · In an audiotape broadcast by two Arab television channels, Saddam disavows responsibility for the Najaf bombing.

September 2 · A bomb at the police headquarters in Baghdad kills one police officer.

September 7 · In his television address President Bush says that of the $87 billion needed, $11 billion will be spent in Afghanistan, $51 billion on the military occupation of Iraq, and $20 billion on Iraq's reconstruction.

September 10 · A suicide attack at a secret DIA station in Irbil kills three.

September · 12 U.S. troops in Falluja eight Iraqi policemen.

September 17 Bush says there is no evidence that Saddam Hussein was involved with 9/11.

September 18 · A daylight attack on a UN convoy in Khalidiya kills three to eight GIs.

September 21 · Iraqi finance minister Kamil al Kilani says the non-oil sector of Iraq is open to foreign companies which can 100 per cent of an enterprise.

September 29 · U.S. attorney-general says he has opened an FBI investigation in the disclosure of Valerie Plame-Wilson as an undercover CIA agent. Bush's approval rating falls to record 49 per cent.

October 4–5 · Pro-Saddam demonstrators in Baiji burn down the mayor's office and expel the U.S.-trained police force of 300.

October 6 · Condi Rice forms the Iraqi Stabilization Group.

October 9 · Two bombs at a police station in Sadr City, Baghdad, kill eight.

October 12 · Two suicide bombers aiming for Baghdad Hotel, Baghdad, kill eight.

October 16 · UN Security Council unanimously passes Resolution 1511, which approves continued exclusive American control over Iraq's political affairs and a multinational peacekeeping force under U.S. command. The total of the GIs killed in hostile action since May 1 reaches 102.

Appendix II

IRAQ'S WEAPONS OF MASS DESTRUCTION AND MEANS OF DELIVERY: ALLEGED AND FOUND

Precursor Chemicals, 3,307 tons   Found: None

Tabun, a nerve agent   Found: None

Mustard agent   Found: None

Sarin, a nerve agent   Found: None

VX nerve agent, 1.6 tons   Found: None

Anthrax spores raw material, 25,500 liters   Found: None

Botulinum toxin   Found: One vial of Strain B, 10 years old, in an Iraqi scientist's domestic refrigerator

Aflotoxins	Found: None
Ricin	Found: None
Mobile bioweapons laboratories, up to eighteen	Two suspected mobile labs found to be harmless
Bombs, rockets, and shells for poison agents, 30,000	Found: None
L-29 unmanned aerial vehicles for delivering biological and chemical weapons	Found: None
Nuclear weapons material	Found: None
Al Hussein surface-to-surface missile with 410 miles/650 kilometers range, up to twenty	Found: None

Source: *Guardian* (London), September 25, October 3 and 7, 2003

INDEX

About the Author

Born in the Indian subcontinent, **DILIP HIRO** was educated in India, Britain, and the United States, where he received his Master's degree at Virginia Polytechnic Institute and State University. He then settled in London in the mid-1960s, and became a full-time writer, journalist and commentator. His articles have appeared in the *New York Times, Washington Post, Los Angeles Times, Wall Street Journal, Boston Globe, Toronto Star, The Nation, the Sunday Times, Observer, Guardian, Independent, International Herald Tribune, Times Literary Supplement, Economist, New Statesman, Spectator* and *Middle East International.* He is a frequent commentator on Middle Eastern, Central Asian, and Islamic Affairs, and during the build-up to Operation "Iraqi Freedom" appeared as a guest on CNN, MSNBC, Fox News, NBC's *The Today Show,* National Public Radio, Pacifica Radio's *Democracy Now,* BBC Radio and Television, and CBC (Canada).